Communication Development and Disorders in African American Children

Research, Assessment, and Intervention

Edited by

Alan G. Kamhi, Ph.D.

Karen E. Pollock, Ph.D.

Joyce L. Harris, Ph.D.

University of Memphis
Memphis, Tennessee

·P A U L ·H·
BROOKES
PUBLISHING CO.

Baltimore • London • Toronto • Sydney

Paul H. Brookes Publishing Co.
Post Office Box 10624
Baltimore, Maryland 21285-0624

Typeset by Zeko Graphics, Kansas City, Missouri.
Manufactured in the United States of America by
The Maple Press Company, York, Pennsylvania.

Library of Congress Cataloging-in-Publication Data
Communication development and disorders in African American children :
   research, assessment, and intervention / edited by Alan G. Kamhi,
   Karen E. Pollock, Joyce L. Harris.
      p.   cm.
   Includes bibliographical references and index.
   ISBN 1-55766-253-3
   1. Communicative disorders in children.   2. Afro-American
children—Language.   3. Communicative competence in children.
4. Black English—Social aspects.   I. Kamhi, Alan G., 1950–   .
II. Pollock, Karen E.   III. Harris, Joyce L.
RJ496.C67C664   1996
618.92'855'008996073–dc20   96-13473
                                         CIP

British Library Cataloguing-in-Publication data are available from the
British Library.

Communication Development and Disorders
in African American Children

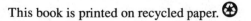

Contents

v

Contributors

Lynda R. Campbell, Ph.D.
Department of Communication Disorders
St. Louis University
3750 Lindell Boulevard
St. Louis, MO 63108-3412

Holly K. Craig, Ph.D.
Communicative Disorders Clinic
University of Michigan
1111 East Catherine Street
Ann Arbor, MI 48109-2054

Joyce L. Harris, Ph.D.
School of Audiology and
  Speech-Language Pathology
University of Memphis
807 Jefferson Avenue
Memphis, TN 38105

Eva Jackson Hester, M.A.
Department of Communication
  Sciences and Disorders
Towson State University
Towson, MD 21204

Yvette D. Hyter, Ph.D.
Department of Communicative
  Disorders and Sciences
Wichita State University
1845 Fairmount
Wichita, KS 67260-0075

Alan G. Kamhi, Ph.D.
School of Audiology and
  Speech-Language Pathology
University of Memphis
807 Jefferson Avenue
Memphis, TN 38105

April Massey, Ph.D.
Department of Communication Arts
  and Sciences
University of the District of Columbia
4200 Connecticut Avenue, N.W., MD
  1004
Washington, DC 20008

Wanda K. Mitchener-Colston, Ph.D.
Norfolk State University
492 Stuart Circle
Norfolk, VA 23502-4457

Julia Mount-Weitz, Ph.D.
Bloomsburg University
400 E. Second Street
Bloomsburg, PA 17815

Karen E. Pollock, Ph.D.
School of Audiology and
  Speech-Language Pathology
University of Memphis
807 Jefferson Avenue
Memphis, TN 38105

Lisa M. Rogers, M.A.
Detroit Board of Education
5057 Woodward Avenue
Detroit, MI 48202

Marlene B. Salas-Provance, Ph.D.
St. Louis University
221 North Grand Boulevard
St. Louis, MO 63103

Cheryl M. Scott, Ph.D.
Department of Communication
  Sciences and Disorders
Oklahoma State University
120 Hanner
Stillwater, OK 74078

Ida J. Stockman, Ph.D.
Department of Audiology
  and Speech Sciences
Michigan State University
378 Communication Arts and
  Sciences Building
East Lansing, MI 48824

Francis Terrell, Ph.D.
Department of Psychology
University of North Texas
Denton, TX 76203-0446

Sandra L. Terrell, Ph.D.
Department of Speech and Hearing Sciences
  and Toulouse School of Graduate Studies
University of North Texas
P.O. Box 5446
Denton, TX 76203-0446

Julie A. Washington, Ph.D.
Communicative Disorders Clinic
University of Michigan
1111 East Catherine Street
Ann Arbor, MI 48109-2054

Carol E. Westby, Ph.D.
Department of Communicative
  Disorders and Sciences
Wichita State University
1845 Fairmount
Wichita, KS 67260-0075

Toya A. Wyatt, Ph.D.
Department of Speech Communication
California State University at Fullerton
800 North State College Boulevard
Fullerton, CA 92634

Foreword

As recently as the late 1960s, the language spoken by many African Americans was considered by a large segment of the general public—as well as by many communication disorders professionals—to be deficient in form and substance. This view, which has persisted in one form or another since the introduction of Africans to the New World as slaves, was generally grounded in the absurd notion that persons of African descent are intellectually, biologically, or socially unable to acquire the language systems used by members of the larger society.

Remarkably, these views persisted despite the publication of research in numerous articles and books since at least the late 1930s that demonstrated otherwise. For example, Lorenzo Turner, the noted African American language scholar of the 1930s, carefully documented in his classic volume, *Africanisms in the Gullah Dialect*, that the English spoken by African Americans reflected legitimate survivals of phonological, grammatical, and semantic forms from the African languages that had been spoken by their slave ancestors (Turner, 1949).

In 1940, Melville Herskovits, the renowned anthropologist, published his landmark volume, *The Myth of the Negro Past*. In this work, he not only reaffirmed the validity and significance of Turner's work, but also cited numerous other African cultural survivals among modern-day African Americans (Herskovits, 1958).

In the 1960s and 1970s, the then–newly established field of sociolinguistics began to gain prominence among scholars and practitioners. Led by the writings of such individuals as William Labov, William Stewart, Joe Dillard, Roger Shuy, Orlando L. Taylor, and Walt Wolfram, among others, the logic and the legitimacy of the language forms spoken by African Americans were documented as rule-governed systems that conformed to language universals.

In the field of communication disorders, the topic of African American language systems—and what, if anything, to do about them—came to the forefront in the late 1960s. At that time, a small group of African American members of the American Speech-Language-Hearing Association (ASHA) challenged the then-prevailing view that the language patterns of a significant number of African Americans were deficient and in need of treatment. Citing the emerging literature in the fields of sociolinguistics and ethnography, these pioneers withstood often hostile and skeptical attitudes from colleagues to successfully advocate the establishment of new norms, clinical instruments, intervention procedures, attitudes, and policies toward language diversity in general and the language of African Americans in particular.

The 1990s present a substantially different environment. Considerable research on African American speech is conducted from the vantage point that it is legitimate, not pathological and in need of treatment. Moreover, intervention paradigms have been advanced that take linguistic and cultural diversity into account. The topic of communication and communication disorders in African American populations is now a part of the intellectual mainstream in the communication sciences field. Articles on the subject are beginning to appear in the most prestigious journals, papers are read at virtually all national and regional professional meetings, and book chapters abound.

When the pioneering studies of language acquisition and disorders in African American children from a cultural perspective began to emerge in significant numbers in the 1960s and 1970s, most focused almost exclusively on linguistic structure. During the 1980s, studies on African American children's language acquisition began to appear that concentrated on the meaning and the use of language, in addition to its form. The 1990s have witnessed heightened interest in the language discourse of African American children. Yet the growing amount of information on communication development and disorders in African American children has been embedded largely within more general books on multicultural populations.

Surprisingly, until now a scholarly book has not been published from the framework of communication sciences and disorders that has focused totally on African Americans or African American children. Therein lies the significance of this historic volume, which is based on the proceedings of an important 1994 conference at the University of Memphis on this same topic.

While Taylor (1985) and Battle (1993), for example, have written important books on communication development and disorders in multicultural populations in general, this present book is the first to focus exclusively on African American children in a systematic and comprehensive manner that emphasizes normative and applied issues. The authors have marshaled an impressive array of information on both theoretical and clinical considerations.

Some might question the need for an entire volume on communication development and disorders in African American children. There are several reasons why such a volume is needed. First and foremost, African Americans comprise the largest percentage of people of color in the United States. According to the 1990 U.S. census, which acknowledges a significant undercount of people of color, 25% of the American population is represented by people of color: 12% African American; 9% Hispanic/Latino; 3% Asian/Pacific American; and 1% Native American/Eskimo/Aleut (Bureau of the Census, 1990). Although 1% of the U.S. population has a communication disorder, results from the National Health Interview Survey (Schoenborn & Marano, 1988) indicate that there is a greater prevalence of speech impairment among people of color than among whites.

Second, more research has been completed on communication development and disorders in the African American population than on any other group in the United States, with the exception of white Americans. No single book, however, with the exception of this one, has seriously addressed clinical and research issues pertaining to African American children exclusively. Information on communication development and disorders in African American children has been synthesized in this volume, thus providing an invaluable reference for both clinicians and researchers, as well as exposure to an intellectually rigorous treatment and critical analysis of this rich information.

Third, African American children—especially those from low socioeconomic status families—are among the most victimized groups in the United States because they use language systems that often differ from the white and middle-class mainstreams. Nowhere is this situation more evident than in the area of education. For example, while the preferred narrative style in the classroom is often topic-centered narratives that are presented in analytic, sequential, and linear manner, many African American children prefer a topic-associational narrative style that does not necessarily match teacher expectations. Topic-associating stories frequently are viewed by teachers and communication disorders professionals as incoherent, inconsistent, disconnected, and rambling. The use of this non-preferred narrative style can result in discrimination by teachers and clinicians. Because of these and many other incongruencies between home and school communication, African American children are frequently the object of negative attitudes and low expectations, leading to low self-esteem.

African American children have historically faced a disproportionate representation in special education classes and placement in speech-language therapy. For example, although they comprise 16% of the students in public schools, African American students are only 8% of those in programs for the gifted. In contrast, African American children represent 35% of the "educable mentally retarded," 27% of those labeled "trainable mentally retarded," and 27% of the "severely emotionally disturbed" (Harry, 1992). A large proportion of African American children are placed in special education classes by the time they enter secondary school (Harry, 1992) or tracked into vocational, rather than college preparatory, programs (Oakes, 1985). The lack of sensitivity toward the cultural and linguistic attributes of many African American children has contributed to culturally biased, invalid assessments and inappropriate educational placements. Furthermore, negative attitudes and reactions toward these children who speak what is commonly referred to as African American English (AAE) have resulted in discriminatory educational and professional practices. AAE speakers may be denied access to educational opportunities and stigmatized, not only in school, but in future employment situations.

Implications of the scholarship represented in this volume are far reaching. Future initiatives that focus on conducting research, assessing linguistic skills, and treating communication disorders in African American children would be well informed by the discussions provided in this book. While considerable additional research is needed on language and communication behaviors of African American children, especially among those from middle-class environments, the chapters in this volume indicate that we know far more now than we ever have known before.

Orlando L. Taylor, Ph.D.
Debra M. Garrett, M.C.D.
Howard University
Washington, D.C.

REFERENCES

Battle, D.E. (1993). *Communication disorders in multicultural populations.* Boston: Andover Medical Publishers.

Bureau of the Census. (1990). *Statistical Abstract of the United States: 1990* (110th ed.). Washington, DC: Author.

Harry, B. (1992) *Cultural diversity, families, and the special education system.* New York: Teachers College Press.

Heath, S.B. (1983). *Ways with words.* Cambridge: Cambridge University Press.

Herskovits, M.J. (1958) Reprint. *The myth of the Negro past.* Boston: Beacon Press.

Oakes, J. (1985). *Keeping track.* Princeton, NJ: Yale University Press.

Schoenborn, C.A., & Marano, A. (1988). *Current estimates from the National Health Interview Survey* (United States, Vital and Health Statistics, Series 10, No. 173, DHHS Publication No. 89–1501). Washington, DC: National Center for Health Statistics.

Shade (1990). *Engaging the battle for African American minds.* Washington, DC: National Alliance of Black School Educators, Inc.

Taylor, O. (1985). *Nature of communication disorders in culturally and linguistically diverse populations.* San Diego, CA: College-Hill Press, Inc.

Taylor, O. (1986). *Treatment of communication disorders in culturally and linguistically diverse populations.* San Diego, CA: College-Hill Press, Inc.

Turner, L. (1949) Reprint. *Africanisms in the Gullah dialect.* Chicago: University of Chicago Press.

For the Reader

It is sometimes difficult to please everyone with regard to terminology. For example, some authors prefer "Black" over "African American" and "Black English" over "African American English." We think it is important to be consistent throughout the book and so have chosen to use the term "African American." In some cases, authors may refer to African Americans as Black or use Black English or Black English Vernacular as they are citing research that used these terms or are making distinctions that require these terms. Because not all African American children speak African American English (AAE) and not all mainstream children speak Standard American English (SAE), authors were encouraged to use the phrases "AAE-speaking children" and "SAE-speaking children."

Finally, the majority of the volume's authors and editors preferred the adjective "white" to the alternate terms "Caucasian" and "European American." Therefore, while acknowledging that "white" is not parallel to "African American," we decided to use "white" throughout this book.

Acknowledgments

This volume is based on papers presented at the 1994 Memphis Research Symposium on Communication Disorders in African American Children and Youth. Karen E. Pollock was the Conference Chair and Judy Fellows was responsible for local arrangements. The other members of the conference committee were Terry Douglas, Joyce L. Harris, Alan G. Kamhi, Maurice Mendel, and Merlin Taylor. The conference was sponsored by the School of Audiology and Speech-Language Pathology at the University of Memphis and the Office of Special Education and Rehabilitative Services (OSERS) in the U.S. Department of Education. Since the early 1990s, our program has received funding from OSERS to prepare scholars to conduct research on minority children and youth with communication disorders.

In memory of our good friend and colleague
Sallie Starr Hillard
whose optimism and joy of learning
enriched all of us who knew her

Introduction

This volume is based on papers presented at the 1994 Memphis Research Symposium on Communication Disorders in African American Children and Youth. The purpose of the conference was to provide a forum for scholars from around the country to present and discuss their research on communication development and disorders in African American children and youth. Although there are other forums where research on this topic can be presented, this conference was the first one that focused solely on this topic.

The first five chapters in this volume address issues in research, assessment, and intervention. In the first chapter, Holly K. Craig discusses the challenges of conducting research. After reviewing some of the problems with existing and modified assessment procedures, she provides suggestions for data collection and scoring that are not biased against African American English (AAE)–speaking children. Joyce L. Harris, in Chapter 2, discusses the problems involved in recruiting African American participants for research. She traces the roots of suspicion and uncooperativeness that many African Americans have toward researchers and suggests that one way to reduce this suspicion is to pose socially responsible research questions that are relevant to community issues and concerns.

In Chapter 3, Julie A. Washington examines the current status of assessment with AAE-speaking children. After discussing the problems with standardized assessment instruments, she presents alternatives to norm-referenced assessment, focusing primarily on language sample analysis procedures. In Chapter 4, Sandra L. Terrell and Francis Terrell discuss the influence of sociocultural and psychological factors on the communication behaviors of African Americans. They review studies examining the impact that self-esteem, anger, and mistrust have on speech and language behaviors and show that language samples taken from African American children who mistrust white examiners may not provide an accurate reflection of language ability. In Chapter 5, Lynda R. Campbell discusses service delivery issues, emphasizing the benefits of collaborative models and the importance of involving the family and maintaining the integrity of children's use of AAE.

The nine chapters in the second half of the book address various aspects of communication development and disorders in African American children. In Chapter 6, Toya A. Wyatt discusses the acquisition of the AAE copula. Understanding the variable use of the copula has important implications for the differential diagnosis of language impairment in AAE-speaking children. In Chapter 7, Ida J. Stockman reviews what is known about the phonological characteristics of AAE and its acquisition by African American children. She then presents guidelines to assess and treat AAE-speaking children who have phonological disorders. In Chapter 8, Marlene B. Salas-Provance examines the organic and acoustic characteristics of the speech of AAE-speaking children. Among the disorders discussed are cleft lip and palate, hearing disorders, and sickle cell anemia.

Chapter 9, by Julia Mount-Weitz, focuses on vocabulary development and disorders in African American children. After reviewing the literature on lexical acquisition, she discusses procedures to assess and enhance vocabulary knowledge. The next two chapters focus on the narrative abilities of AAE-speaking children. Eva Jackson Hester in Chapter 10 illustrates the variability in narratives produced by AAE-speaking children and discusses how children develop the flexibility to code-switch and style-shift. Yvette D. Hyter and Carol E. Westby in Chapter 11 show how narratives can be used to explore preadolescent and adolescent attitudes about events in the world. They provide some specific guidelines for clinicians to use oral narratives to foster communication competence.

In Chapter 12, April Massey examines cultural influences on the language input to AAE-speaking children. She finds considerable variability in the communication patterns and preferences within seemingly homogenous cultural-linguistic groups and even within individual family units. This variability leads her to argue strongly against the simplistic lists of cultural behaviors that have proliferated since the 1970s. In Chapter 13, Cheryl M. Scott and Lisa M. Rogers discuss the writing of African American children and youth. Writing is of crucial importance in both the early stages and the long-term development of literacy. Scott and Rogers discuss the specific ways cultural factors affect writing, citing research that shows how children's self-esteem and literacy development may be harmed when teachers focus on the elimination of AAE features rather than on meaning. In the final chapter, Wanda K. Mitchener-Colston addresses the issues involved in working with African American adolescents and youth. She presents an intervention approach that targets the communication skills needed to enhance personal-social interaction and to be successful in the workplace.

In their foreword to the book, Orlando L. Taylor and Debra M. Garrett write that it is surprising that until now a scholarly book has not been published that has focused totally on communication development and disorders in African American children. Why has it taken so long to conduct and publish the kind of research represented in this book? The obstacles and barriers that have had to be overcome to reach this point are discussed in several of the chapters in this book and in Anna F. Vaughn-Cooke's afterword. Although the barriers may be a little less formidable than they were in the 1960s, they still exist for many of the contributors in this volume who have devoted a significant amount of time and energy and, in some cases, entire careers toward the pursuit of knowledge about African American children's language development and disorders. We hope that this book is just the beginning of widespread dissemination of research in this area.

Communication Development and Disorders
in African American Children

The Challenges of Conducting Language Research with African American Children

Holly K. Craig

$\mathbf{M}$any researchers, clinicians, and educators are concerned about the status of African American children, especially as these youngsters enter and participate in formal education. Research addressing the needs of this population is sparse, however, and the generation of new knowledge is appallingly slow. This problematic situation exists within a pressing national context in which the numbers of African American children enrolled in big-city schools are steadily increasing. Unfortunately, many of these children live below the poverty line, putting them at high risk for a variety of educational and health-related problems. In Michigan, for example (University of Michigan Detroit Area Study, 1989), during the 1980s the population segment of the city of Detroit that was African American increased from 58.2% to 75.1%. Approximately one quarter of Detroit's African American adults are unemployed, and approximately 37% live in poverty with annual household incomes of less than $10,000.

African American children who use nonstandard forms of English may be even more disadvantaged because their communication skills are different from the Standard American English (SAE) used in most learn-

1

ing contexts. Nonstandard forms may be more frequent in the discourse of African American children from poor than from middle-class homes (Ratusnik & Koenigsknecht, 1976a). Scott (1994) estimates that, if valid assessment instruments were available, communication disorders in minority populations might occur at two to three times the rate of that for the majority. In the context of these increasing numbers, the need for culturally fair, but diagnostically sensitive, methods for assessing the status of young African American children is urgent. Progress toward these goals, however, has been limited.

The purpose of this chapter is to discuss issues, primarily methodological in nature, that present barriers to conducting language research with this population and to suggest some possible solutions to the problems identified. For speech-language pathologists, the research agenda for African American children has been framed primarily around a single issue: distinguishing language differences from language disorders. Three major types of challenges facing the language researcher attempting to study the language skills of African American children will be discussed: 1) how to prioritize the vast research agenda, 2) how to address this agenda with limited personnel, and 3) how to create appropriate research designs that can yield culturally valid data.

EMERGING PRIORITIES FOR LANGUAGE RESEARCH WITH AFRICAN AMERICAN CHILDREN

Early Priorities

Past research in child language focused on two primary issues. The first addressed the viability and linguistic integrity of the nonstandard forms used by African Americans. A small number of early reports examining the language behaviors of African American children were part of a larger imperative to refute prevailing assumptions that the linguistic system of African Americans was a deficient form of SAE (Bailey, 1965, 1968; Baratz, 1970; Dillard, 1972; Fasold & Wolfram, 1970; Stewart, 1970; Wolfram, 1971; Wolfram & Fasold, 1974). The outcomes of these examinations clearly demonstrated that the differences from SAE were numerous and systematic.

The second research priority has generated the most scholarly comment and empirical effort. It involves a search for ways to accommodate a child's dialectal differences for language analysis and assessment purposes so that children with normal language skills can be differentiated from children with language disorders. The most frequently used language tests were developed for SAE-speaking children and normed on those in the majority culture. As recognition has increased that the nonstandard forms used by some African Americans have distinctive characteristics, recommendations have been made to develop scoring adjustments to accommodate response differences due to dialectal influences and to restandardize established tests applying locally generated norms. Evard and Sabers (1979) observed that the development of local norms would be a very cost-effective approach if the established test could adequately measure the behaviors of interest. The work of Haynes and Moran (1989) offers an example of the efficiency of renorming (the sounds-in-words subtest of the Goldman-Fristoe Test of Articulation [Goldman & Fristoe, 1986]) for accommodating distinctive rule-governed phonological features of the dialect, such as final consonant deletions.

A notable example of the success of scoring adjustments is provided by Cole and Taylor (1990). They modified three well-known articulation tests: the Templin-Darley Tests of Articulation, Second Edition (Templin & Darley, 1969), the Arizona Articulation Proficiency Scale: Revised (AAPS–R; Fudala, 1974), and the Photo Articulation Test (PAT; Pendergast, Dickey, Selmar, & Soder, 1969). Each child's response received two separate scores: one consistent with an SAE rendering of the target and one based on the phonological rules of African American English (AAE) adult speakers. These adjustments improved the face validity of each instrument and yielded substantial improvements in the scores obtained for their 10 typically developing subjects. Cole and Taylor's methods offer a way to significantly reduce the number of false clinical diagnoses in dialect speakers.

Washington and Craig (1992a) pursued the accuracy of the adjusted AAPS–R, this time with a group of subjects judged to have "poor speech skills" by their classroom teachers. The AAPS–R did distinguish the children with reportedly "poor" speech skills from those judged by their teachers to have "good" speech skills, but the scoring adjustments failed to alter the associated clinical interpretations of the children's performances. Considered together with an item analysis of the children's response profiles, these results led Washington and Craig to conclude that a scoring adjustment was unnecessary when administering this test with these subjects. The scoring adjustment developed by Cole and Taylor (1990) seemed to address phonological differences reflecting the operation of the regional Southern Dialect of Mississippi as well as AAE, but was not critical to evaluate the articulation of the northern children in the Washington and Craig report. These studies demonstrate the importance of considering regional, as well as cultural, forces in performance outcomes and underscore the complexity of any adjustment or renorming practices.

Unfortunately, there is little evidence that established tests for language fare as well as those for articulation in the development of scoring adjustments and renormings. Washington and Craig (1992b) found that a generous crediting system failed substantially to improve the performance outcomes of 105 African American preschool and kindergarten children on the Peabody Picture Vocabulary Test–Revised (PPVT–R; Dunn & Dunn, 1981). Most children performed more than one standard deviation below the standard score mean of 100 established for the Dunn and Dunn sample. Crediting 16 different items missed by at least half of the children in the sample failed to make an appreciable difference in the performance distributions for Washington and Craig's subjects. This is particularly disappointing because the PPVT–R is one of the most widely used tests of language and because the 1981 revision was developed in part to include African Americans in the standardization sample, a critical omission in the original version of the test (Dunn, 1959). In other work, Wiener, Lewnau, and Erway (1983) found that the administration of another major language test, the Test of Language Development (TOLD; Newcomer & Hammill, 1977), to 196 African American children resulted in a disproportionate clustering of their subjects below the mean, with little performance spread among subjects. This test included African Americans in the standardization sample as well, but like the PPVT–R is not suitable for renorming with African American children because it does not generate a statistically sufficient performance spread across the population.

A number of criticisms can be directed at these renorming and scoring adjustment approaches. Vaughn-Cooke (1983) noted that renorming may solve only the *technical* problem of administering a test normed on mainstream speakers to minorities. Renorming fails to address other more substantive issues and may create additional problems, such as establishing low normative values on the statistical revision of the test and then making these numbers available publicly for potentially inappropriate comparisons and interpretations. In addition, renormings do not resolve the fundamental problem of poor task validity for the minority population. Just because an instrument has been renormed does not mean that it is *valid* for the new application. Crediting alternative responses may not be equivalent to what eliciting the targeted response represented in SAE. Credits and renormings cannot consider the unknown developmental progression of the system of nonstandard forms, nor their associated linguistic and discourse contextual constraints.

Washington and Craig (1992b) observed that scoring adjustments and renormings are not diagnostically useful. The preponderance of African American subjects scoring at the low end of the distribution of a test, with little performance spread among subjects, does not achieve the statistical requirement for a test of a normal performance curve. The performance of an individual child then cannot be compared statistically with normal expectations for his or her own culture.

Washington and Craig (1994) observed that scoring adjustments typically have been developed from the study of adults and adolescents (especially from Dillard, 1972; Fasold & Wolfram, 1970; Williams & Wolfram, 1977). Adult language has a weak correspondence to child linguistic behavior (Berko, 1958; Brown, 1973). Attempts to generate child-derived data for African Americans are scarce and largely unsuccessful (e.g., Washington & Craig, 1992b) or are preliminary (e.g., Nelson, 1993). In the Nelson study, behaviors were synthesized from small numbers of children residing in diverse geographic locales and involved potentially heterogeneous dialectal variations.

In the critical absence of information about African American children's use of nonstandard forms, there is a tendency to give credit to any language difference even if it is not characteristic of AAE. A child may receive scoring credit for any item on a test that would be spoken differently from the SAE target or that has been observed in adult usage. Vaughn-Cooke (1986) observed that this was a problem with an attempt by Hemingway, Montague, and Bradley (1981) to modify the Carrow Elicited Language Inventory (Carrow, 1974). These researchers used responses of a sample of African American subjects who produced language forms that were different from SAE, but not all of these forms were characteristic of AAE. Conceptually, it seems possible to overinterpret performances using a crediting process. Overinterpretation is as potentially dangerous to the child with a disorder as underestimation is to the child without a disorder. Both errors should be avoided.

It is not clear why these adjustments for language have been so unsuccessful. Their lack of success highlights, however, the importance of improving our understanding of the linguistic characteristics of the nonstandard forms used by African American children and of the developmental course of these distinctive behaviors. Overall, it would be efficient to avoid the creation of whole new assessment instruments if widely used tests could accommodate dialect by renorming or with a system of scoring adjustments. Unfortunately, the former method perpetuates the use of tests with poor validity for African American children, whereas the latter method is successful for phonological but not for language disorders.

New Directions

Research priorities must shift away from adjustments to existing tests toward the development of new and more appropriate assessment instruments for the analysis of language behaviors. In a guest editorial accompanying the American Speech-Language-Hearing Association's (ASHA) position statement on social dialects, Vaughn-Cooke (1983) made this point clearly:

> It is not an overstatement to say that a crisis exists in the area of assessment for non-mainstream speakers. Researchers, clinicians, and test developers must intensify their efforts to overcome this crisis and meet the needs of diagnosticians. Diagnosticians do not need more evaluations of the assessment problem, nor do they need more "interim" solutions. They need valid, reliable assessment tools. (p. 33)

The need for culture-fair tests is a long-standing concern and a primary research priority. Sadly, Vaughn-Cooke's statement continues to be accurate. Since 1983, the limitations of renorming and scoring adjustments have been discussed, but new assessment methods remain unavailable. Why?

The task of developing new assessment protocols appropriate to African American children is a huge and daunting undertaking. The following list is a partial rendering of the many areas that would require investigation in a fresh effort of this type and provides a flavor for the fundamental nature of many of the as yet unanswered questions.

Language Profiles There seems to be no substitute for characterizing the language behaviors of African American children in their own right. The ability to appropriately analyze and clinically assess the communication status of children from this population is precluded without language reference profiles. Once reference profiles are available, criterion measures and norm-referenced statements can be developed.

Research into Language Acquisition The course of language acquisition is unknown and represents a serious limitation in our ability to judge appropriateness of verbal expression by age or grade, important referents for evaluating the development of linguistic skills. Most of what we know about AAE has been derived from the study of adolescents and adults, and many of these studies involved ethnographic descriptions of the language characterizing urban gang interactions. Washington and Craig (1994) provide one of the few published, child-centered descriptions of the distinctive language forms used by young African American children during connected discourse. Seymour and Seymour (1981) and Haynes and Moran (1989) have provided developmental information for phonological processes, but information of this type is unavailable for the morphosyntactic aspects of AAE. The course of acquisition of AAE forms needs intensive investigation.

Regional Influences A better understanding is required about regional influences on expressive language. A boundary must be defined between cultural and regional effects in order to determine the generalizability of new measures. It is as yet unclear which linguistic behaviors warrant the generation of local norms and which may be standardized more nationally.

Poverty More information is needed about the influences of social status variables so that the effects of poverty can be discerned from those of culture. African Americans are impoverished at disproportionate levels in the United States (Bureau of Census, 1990). It would be unfortunate and inaccurate to ascribe characteristics to the population as a whole that more accurately reflect a comingling of diverse influences, only one of which is culture.

Exposure to SAE The impact of exposure to SAE, especially the influences of the school curriculum and SAE-speaking classmates, should be investigated. What impact does explicit and systematic exposure to SAE have on the acquisition of SAE, AAE, and the continued use of nonstandard forms?

This research agenda is difficult to pursue in the absence of clear theoretical guidance. To say that AAE is not a deficient form of SAE, although a necessary first statement, is to declare what it is not, rather than what it is. Nonstandard forms used by African Americans most frequently are refered to as "dialect"; however, some argue that these characteristics are better conceptualized as a vernacular (Houston, 1970; Labov, 1970) or a language in its own right that is diverging from the parent language (i.e., SAE) (Bailey & Maynor, 1989; Taylor, 1988; Wolfram, 1987). Lack of theoretical consensus means that priorities within the research agenda for language are essentially unranked, so that all issues seem equally important to pursue. Even when trying simply to characterize the language behaviors of African American children, in the absence of theory it is unclear whether syntactic skills should be prioritized over semantic and pragmatic ones, whether it is more critical to understand dialogue compared to narrative discourse types, and so on.

Theory would improve the researcher's ability to rank-order the many research questions and to select the most revealing methodologies. For example, the creation of a data collection tool would be significantly affected by the theoretical assumption that nonstandard forms are an English vernacular used by African American speakers primarily during informal as opposed to more formal interactions. Methodologically, the researcher would create informal data collection contexts, for example at home with a sibling rather than at school with a teacher. It is not yet clear, however, whether the development of these distinctive forms reflects the acquisition of two languages, a variation on a primary language, or the rules for code switching between linguistic styles. Overall, the magnitude of this research agenda and the lack of consensus on priorities are barriers in their own right.

A PAUCITY OF AVAILABLE RESEARCHERS

An unfortunately small number of scholars are studying the language behaviors of African American children. The need to address minority language issues is so critical that the African American scholar, unlike the majority researcher, faces pressure to develop a research program around the single issue of minority language and may be less able to determine individually the scope of his or her own research program. This pressure is unusual and differs from that of the majority scholar who is more free to develop and pursue a unique line of research. Even if all minority scholars direct their research programs toward this single issue, there are not enough African American scholars to answer all of the questions entailed by this research agenda in a timely fashion. Only 4% of the members of ASHA are minorities of any type, and fewer than 1% of Ph.D.s are minorities (Harris, Logemann, & Scott, 1994). Of course, not all minorities holding doctorates conduct research as a primary activity.

A small number of majority investigators are actively pursuing research programs with African American children, as well. There are some limits, however, on the kinds of answers these researchers can determine. Most obviously, access to the population and interpretation of the data obtained outside of the context of cultural membership are two of the aspects that are profoundly affected. The former can be addressed through collaborations. Ways to address the latter are less clear.

Perhaps the majority researcher can contribute most usefully to the language research agenda by focusing on the identification and description of regularities in the discourse of African American children. Underlying explanations for the rules governing these patterns then may best be made by African American scholars. All researchers of child language, regardless of culture, are sensitive to the distinction between description and interpretation. As adults, for example, we are inherently restricted in our ability to ascribe intent to the patterns we see operating in children's discourse. As a result, we tend to be conservative when interpreting behavioral regularities. The majority researcher must be similarly cautious in interpreting the behavior of children from another culture. The identification and description of linguistic regularities is a huge task. If this task is pursued by majority as well as minority scholars, it can be accomplished.

CREATING INFORMATIVE RESEARCH DESIGNS

Any new investigation operating within an established theoretical framework benefits from consensus on both a prioritized set of research questions and the methodologies suitable for pursuing pertinent answers. The shortage of valid information about the language of African American children and of undergirding theory means that there is little guidance available for the researcher. Current methods still reflect those developed for the study of children who are speakers of SAE. Which of these methods need to be reframed, and how?

The following issues address a set of decision areas for the investigator approaching the study of the language of African American children. For discussion purposes, these issues are broadly grouped in terms of subject selection and of data collection and reduction decisions.

Subject Issues

Subject selection procedures could be improved in a number of ways, such as ensuring that the subject sample is representative of the population as a whole and assessing the effects of socioeconomic status and of cognition.

Representativeness For appropriate generalizations to be made, subject samples must be representative of the larger population as a whole. It is not clear how to ensure representativeness when studying the language behaviors of African American children. Researchers addressing minority language issues must, like other child language researchers, determine who constitute representative subjects. Are there two subsets, one comprising African American children, or are there only those who are known dialect users? Similarly, who constitute the most informative control groups? Washington and Craig (1994) found that percentages of utterances coding at least one nonstandard form varied widely, from 0% to 39%, in a sample of 45 typically developing preschoolers from low-income urban homes. Because the variables governing this heterogeneity remain unknown, it is unclear how variations in dialect use should be managed in designing research strategies. Should empirical designs hold constant levels of dialect use between subject and control groups? Alternatively, other variables may be just as critical and unique to interpreting the performance outcomes of this population.

In addition to reporting subject selection criteria, language studies usually provide some standard descriptive information. Most child language studies have a developmental reference point such as chronological age or grade. When more information is available concerning the developmental milestones associated with the acquisition of AAE, the size of this unit of analysis should become obvious (e.g., a 6-month age span or a grade level).

Socioeconomic Status   Socioeconomic status (SES) is another likely candidate for required inclusion in subject description protocols, as well as a subject selection variable. There is a rich body of literature showing that the language performances of children from lower SES homes are quantitatively different from those of children from middle-class homes (Howard, Hoops, & McKinnon, 1970; McCarthy, 1954; Shriner & Miner, 1968; Templin, 1957). Interestingly, however, not all reported performance differences have been in the direction of poorer outcomes. Entwisle (1968) found more advanced word association skills, suggestive of larger and richer lexicons, in both African Americans and Anglo-Americans living in slums than in their suburban peers. It is premature and probably incorrect to assume that the system of spoken language of poor African American children is not well developed. Socioeconomic status may affect the numbers of nonstandard forms used by African American children (Ratusnik & Koenigsknecht, 1976a) and also other major aspects of language production, but at this time it is unclear to what extent or in which way.

The effects of impoverished environments are not well understood and present a highly complex set of planning and interpretation issues. Language differences may be affected by lack of exposure to certain types of information and life experiences, as well as a tendency to preserve the linguistic status quo within communities because less affluent families tend to stay and not relocate as many middle-class families do because of job changes and career advancement. As a result, poor communities may not experience natural pressures for change because individuals do not come in contact with the language and cultures of others.

Furthermore, information about the language of middle-class African American children may be limited by observational opportunities. If children from middle-class compared with lower-class homes code-switch to a considerable degree, as suggested by Hall (1976) and Houston (1970), then factors such as the degree of structure inherent in elicitation techniques, the school setting, or the perceived status of the examiner may combine to reduce the likelihood of the middle-SES child using nonstandard forms in structured experimental language contexts.

Cognition   An understanding of the child's cognition, a control variable and subject descriptor in most child language reports, is essential to interpretation of language outcomes. In particular, it is difficult to determine whether a child is presenting a language disorder when poor performance outcomes are obtained, without knowing whether the difficulties are specifically linguistic or are part of a generalized developmental delay. The planning of clinical management is profoundly affected by these interpretations. Unfortunately, there are no culturally valid intelligence tests available for African American children. As

Miller-Jones (1989) discusses, two underlying problems are the controversy over the exact nature of the mental processes examined in most standardized tests and the lack of agreement on a definition of "culture." Contextualist analyses of cognitive performance, especially cultural practice theory, propose that skills are acquired in specific learning activity contexts (Cole, Gay, Glick, & Sharp, 1971; Cole & Scribner, 1973; Scribner & Cole, 1981). Accordingly, culture influences cognition by determining the kinds of activities in which an individual typically engages and, consequently, the kinds of life experiences accumulated over time. When faced with a cognitive task, the individual will interpret the nature of the task and the range of appropriate responses from his or her own history of personal experiences within a particular cultural context. The nature of the task is experienced differently by individuals from different cultures, and the effects on performance may be profound.

Major tests of cognitive abilities were developed and standardized for use with white, SAE-speaking Americans. Unfortunately, these tests are often used to assess the cognitive abilities of children who are not part of that culture. At least two of these widely used tests seem technically adequate for assessment purposes in that African Americans do not cluster disproportionately at the low end of the performance scale. Ratusnik and Koenigsknecht (1976b) examined the performances of 4- and 5-year-old African American children and white children from low- and from middle-SES sections of metropolitan Chicago on the 1972 revision of the Columbia Mental Maturity Scale (CMMS; Burgemeister, Blum, & Lorge, 1972). The 1972 revision included children from different cultural backgrounds, SES, and urban or rural settings. Ratusnik and Koenigsknecht found that the children from middle-SES communities performed better than those from low-SES homes, regardless of race. They found no differences between African American and white children from similar SES backgrounds on the CMMS for other variables of interest, including gender of subjects and race of clinician.

The Kaufman Assessment Battery for Children (K–ABC; Kaufman & Kaufman, 1983) is another test widely used to assess cognition and achievement. Although African Americans score lower than whites (Lampley & Rust, 1986), only specific subtests are problematic (Willson, Nolan, Reynolds, & Kamphaus, 1989). In contrast to subtests such as the Gestalt Closure Subtest, Willson et al. found that the Triangles subtest contained only two statistically biased items, one affecting the performance of African Americans and one that of whites.

The Triangles subtest of the K–ABC and the CMMS may be adequate in a technical sense for evaluating the cognitive skills of African American children. Developed as they were for children from the white, SAE-speaking segment of American culture, their validity for evaluating children raised in other cultural contexts remains questionable.

Summary and Potential Directions　Considerable research is necessary to determine the most appropriate subject selection criteria to study the language behaviors of African American children. Gender and birth order are other variables that can have a potential impact on the language behaviors of any young child, but no information is currently available about their effects on the nonstandard forms used by African American children. As yet there is no consensus on basic subject selection criteria or their descriptors when designing language research or when disseminating outcomes in research reports.

For researchers facing subject selection and description decisions, there are, however, some methodological possibilities worth pursuing. First, it seems important to determine within any subject sample the extent to which subjects are dialect users. Washington and Craig (1994) reported that the percentage of frequencies of utterances containing at least one AAE form varied widely across their subjects. It may be important to characterize subjects in terms of their level of AAE use, especially as Craig and Washington (1994, 1995) have proposed that high-level dialect users are more linguistically advanced than children of comparable SES and gender who use few dialectal forms. Control groups then could be language matched for levels of AAE in addition to other normal developmental characteristics, rather than on the basis of potentially invalid test scores or other devices borrowed from research protocols generated for SAE-speaking children.

In addition, as long as it remains unclear which variables SES affects and how it affects performance outcomes, subjects should be matched for SES and an SES comparison should be included in research designs whenever possible. Over time this literature will help tease apart the effects of poverty from those of culture. Similarly, if researchers routinely include one of the statistically unbiased cognitive measurements, over time these also may provide stronger normative statements in their own right, insights into tasks that are culturally facilitative and those that are not, and directions for the development of new child-centered cognitive measures for African Americans.

Data Collection and Scoring Issues

Like subject selection and description issues, data collection and scoring procedures could be improved in a number of ways. The race of the examiner, the nature of the data elicitation context, and the difficulties involved in studying linguistic structure when the AAE forms remain poorly understood are discussed in the following sections.

Data Collection   Two important decisions face language researchers sampling the spoken language abilities of African American children. The first relates to the race of the examiner. Who should collect the data with African American children? Holding race constant across participants has merit when so many methodological issues have yet to be resolved. Race eventually may be only part of the issue, however, and a shared linguistic system and a shared culture may pose additional constraints on examiner qualifications.

With so few African American clinicians and researchers, ultimately we may need to establish performance expectations for children with examiners of different races and cultures. It may simply be impractical to meet the clinical and educational needs of this increasing segment of the U.S. society if only African American examiners undertake these tasks. It seems important now to characterize the linguistic behaviors of African American children and to establish developmental reference profiles in the context of shared race, but practical requirements may then mandate a next step, which is to define expectations for language behavior in cross-racial interactive contexts. For example, my colleague Julie Washington and I described our preschoolers' dialectal forms during dialogues with African American female examiners. To translate these data into clinical and educational applications, it is important to determine how the frequencies of occurrence and types of forms vary when the examiner is SAE speaking and white. For pre-schoolers, dialect use may vary little with changes in race and culture of examiner. However, dialect use may vary significantly with increases in chronological age and exposure to SAE.

The nature of the language-elicitation task itself is a second data collection issue requiring thoughtful consideration. Structured elicitations constrain the types of responses from children that are judged to be appropriate or inappropriate. Structured elicitations would be inappropriate for the study of African American children's language if the task constraints originated in protocols designed to evaluate SAE-speaking white children—in other words, children of a different culture. Specific task constraints may be different for children from different cultures raised with different life experiences.

Low-structure elicitations, such as language sampling during free play, are more spontaneous and under the child's control, placing fewer externally defined constraints on the child's linguistic behaviors. With so many issues unresolved at this time, language sampling tasks have considerable merit for characterizing the natural language behaviors of young children. In addition, free-play contexts allow the child to determine the pace of the activity. Miller-Jones (1989) observed that, unlike white children, African American children evidence superior perfor-mances on tasks involving multiple changes in format. He hypothesizes that this may relate to the ambient noise and shifting attentional demands that typify urban living, the primary community for African Americans.

Data Coding African American English affects morphosyntax in primary ways. This presents a special challenge to the coding of language samples because most taxonomies are morphological or syntactic or both in nature and would be influenced by the as-yet-unknown effects of the nonstandard (morphosyntactic) forms. Mean length of utterance (MLU), for example, is a measure widely used in language research with young children for matching the expressive skills of subjects. A number of African American forms include and exclude morphemes based on principles that remain poorly understood. For example, an African American child might say either "the teacher she's goin' up here" or "the teacher goin' up here." The first sentence consists of a subject–noun phrase and a pronoun, both referencing the same person, but the second uses only the noun phrase. The appositive pronoun form is an example of including forms in some instances and not in others. Any morpheme count like that involved in MLU would vary depending on the numbers of these additions and deletions in a sample.

Having descriptive reference profiles and normative statements of African American children's use of nonstandard forms would help us distinguish dialect from language disorder. Until this information is available, however, assessment methods that use units of analysis larger than the morpheme are advantageous. The following examples (from Craig & Washington, 1994) reveal how complex some of our preschoolers' sentences were and how this was obvious regardless of whether a nonstandard morphosyntactic form was operating within the utterance: "I like Michael Jordan but he ain't playin on the team no more." "When you done with this you get to play with this one?"

In a different analysis with the same preschoolers, Craig and Washington (1995) coded simple and more complex semantic relationships using a comparable technique. For this purpose, we selected prepositional phrases as a unit of analysis because, again, their complexity is largely unaffected by the morphological nature of the nonstandard forms used by African Americans and they express a relatively large and rich set of meanings. In the following example, it was possible to discern that the first utterance coded a fairly simple locative identification, whereas the second expressed a more complex spatial alignment, even though both utterances involved nonstandard forms: "it won't rain on they head"; "they holdin' onto each other."

The advantage of defining and coding scoring units like clauses and prepositions is important. These units of analysis permit the investigator to isolate the effects of one system on the other so that variables such as syntactic and semantic complexity can be described in the absence of a full knowledge of the ways in which nonstandard forms are expressed and operate. Units of analysis such as these need to be discovered for other linguistic systems so that the expressive language characteristics of African American children can be examined and reference profiles established for various linguistic skills.

Summary and Possible Directions Investigators must be cautious when designing research protocols to select methods for data collection and scoring that are not biased against children raised in the African American culture. This is more complicated than simply avoiding control groups of SAE-speaking white children or interpreting outcomes and making explicit cross-cultural comparisons to a prior literature for SAE-speaking white children. It means that methods used for collecting language data and the ways in which we approach their scoring and analysis should not be rooted in the majority culture. Although more subtle than comparing SAE control groups, it is equally problematic to study the behaviors of African American children with standards derived from the study of SAE-speaking white children. Tasks designed to examine the characteristics of African American children's morphology, syntax, semantics, and dialogue or narrative discourse skills need to probe the ways in which the elicitation techniques constrain AAE or inhibit our ability to determine its unique characteristics.

Data collection techniques that favor low-structure elicitation contexts place fewer majority culture constraints on the language data obtained. When taxonomies derived from the study of SAE-speaking white children are used, they should be considered as only a starting point and their usefulness in yielding culturally valid data should be determined in each instance. Language scoring procedures could be improved by creating taxonomies that are largely unaffected by the morphosyntactic nature of AAE.

SUMMARY

This chapter has discussed barriers to conducting language research with African American children. It has underscored the need to abandon a search for ways to adjust language instruments developed for SAE-speaking children and to refocus research inquiries on the many tasks involved in developing new, culture-fair, and valid language analysis and assessment techniques. Many unanswered questions remain.

Unfortunately, it is difficult to envision a timely response to the problems entailed in this research agenda with the small cohort of scholars involved in these endeavors and with the lack of theoretical consensus on the best ways to create revealing research heuristics. This chapter identifies a small number of critical methodological issues for immediate consideration. These are offered not as definitive recommendations but to stimulate discussion.

REFERENCES

Bailey, B.L. (1965). Toward a new perspective in Negro English dialectology. *American Speech, 40,* 171–177.
Bailey, B.L. (1968). Some aspects of the impact of linguistics on language teaching in disadvantaged communities. *Elementary English, 45,* 570–579.
Bailey, G., & Maynor, N. (1989). The divergence controversy. *American Speech, 64* (1), 12–39.
Baratz, J.C. (1970). Educational considerations for teaching standard English to Negro children. In R.W. Fasold & R.W. Shuy (Eds.), *Teaching standard English in the inner city* (pp. 223–231). Washington, DC: Center for Applied Linguistics.
Berko, J. (1958). The child's learning of English morphology. *Word, 14,* 150–177.
Brown, R. (1973). *A first language.* Cambridge, MA: Harvard University Press.
Bureau of Census. (1990). *Statistical abstract of the United States* (110th ed). Washington, DC: U.S. Department of Commerce.
Burgemeister, B., Blum, L., & Lorge, I. (1972). *Columbia Mental Maturity Scale.* New York: Harcourt Brace Jovanovich.
Carrow, E. (1974). *Carrow Elicited Language Inventory.* Boston: Teaching Resources Corporation.
Cole, M., Gay, J., Glick, J., & Sharp, D.W. (1971). *The cultural context of learning and thinking.* New York: Basic Books.
Cole, M., & Scribner, S. (1973). Cognitive consequences of formal and informal education. *Science, 182,* 553–559.
Cole, P.A., & Taylor, O.L. (1990). Performance of working class African-American chil-

dren on three tests of articulation. *Language, Speech, and Hearing Services in Schools,* *21*(3), 171–176.

Craig, H.K., & Washington, J.A. (1994). The complex syntax skills of poor, urban, African-American preschoolers at school entry. *Language, Speech, and Hearing Services in Schools, 25*(3), 181–190.

Craig, H.K., & Washington, J.A. (1995). African-American English and linguistic complexity in preschool discourse: A second look. *Language, Speech, and Hearing Services in Schools, 26*(1), 87–93.

Dillard, J. (1972). *Black English.* New York: Random House.

Dunn, L. (1959). *The Peabody Picture Vocabulary Test.* Circle Pines, MN: American Guidance Service.

Dunn, L., & Dunn, L. (1981). *Peabody Picture Vocabulary Test–Revised.* Circle Pines, MN: American Guidance Service.

Entwisle, D.R. (1968). Developmental sociolinguistics: Inner-city children. *American Journal of Sociology, 74,* 39–49.

Evard, B.L., & Sabers, D.L. (1979). Speech and language testing with distinct ethnic-racial groups: A survey of procedures for improving validity. *Journal of Speech and Hearing Disorders, 7,* 271–281.

Fasold, R., & Wolfram, W. (1970). Some linguistic features of Negro dialect. In R.W. Fasold & R.W. Shuy (Eds.), *Teaching standard English in the inner city* (pp. 41–86). Washington, DC: Center for Applied Linguistics.

Fudala, J.B. (1974). *Arizona Articulation Proficiency Scale: Revised.* Los Angeles: Western Psychological Services.

Goldman, R., & Fristoe, M. (1986). *Goldman-Fristoe Test of Articulation.* Circle Pines, MN: American Guidance Service.

Hall, W.S. (1976). Black and white children's responses to Black English vernacular and Standard English sentences: Evidence for code-switching. In D.S. Harrison & T. Trabasso (Eds.), *Black English: A seminar.* Hillsdale, NJ: Lawrence Erlbaum Associates.

Harris, J.L., Logemann, J., & Scott, D.M. (1994, November). *Strengthening your research skills: Applying for post-doctoral fellowships through the National Institutes of Health Research Supplements for underrepresented minorities.* Miniseminar presentation at the American Speech-Language-Hearing Association Annual Convention, New Orleans, LA.

Haynes, W.O., & Moran, M.J. (1989). A cross-sectional developmental study of final consonant production in southern black children from preschool through third grade. *Language, Speech, and Hearing Services in Schools, 20*(4), 400–406.

Hemingway, B.L., Montague, J.C., & Bradley, R.H. (1981). Preliminary data on revision of a sentence repetition test for language screening with black first grade children. *Language, Speech, and Hearing Services in the Schools, 12,* 153–159.

Houston, S.H. (1970). A reexamination of some assumptions about the language of the disadvantaged child. *Child Development, 41,* 947–963.

Howard, M.J., Hoops, H.R., & McKinnon, A.J. (1970). Language abilities of children with differing socioeconomic backgrounds. *Journal of Learning Disabilities, 3*(6), 328–335.

Kaufman, A., & Kaufman, N. (1983). *Kaufman Assessment Battery for Children: Interpretive manual.* Circle Pines, MN: American Guidance Service.

Labov, W. (1970). *The study of nonstandard English.* Champaign, IL: National Council of Teachers of English.

Lampley, D.A., & Rust, J.O. (1986). Validation of the Kaufman Assessment Battery for Children with a sample of preschool children. *Psychology in the Schools, 23*(2), 131–137.

McCarthy, D. (1954). Language development in children. In P. Mussen (Ed.), *Carmichael's manual of child psychology.* New York: John Wiley & Sons.

Miller-Jones, D. (1989). Culture and testing. *American Psychologist, 44*(2), 360–366.

Nelson, N.W. (1993). *Childhood language disorders in context: Infancy through adolescence.* New York: Macmillan.

Newcomer, P., & Hammill, D. (1977). *The Test of Language Development.* Austin, TX: PRO-ED.

Pendergast, K., Dickey, S.E., Selmar, J.W., & Soder, A.L. (1969). *Photo Articulation Test.* Danville, IL: Interstate.

Ratusnik, D.L., & Koenigsknecht, R.A. (1976a). Influence of age on black preschoolers' nonstandard performance of certain phonological and grammatical forms. *Perceptual and Motor Skills, 42,* 199–206.

Ratusnik, D.L., & Koenigsknecht, R.A. (1976b). Cross-cultural item analysis of the Columbia Mental Maturity Scale: Potential application by the language clinician. *Language, Speech, and Hearing Services in Schools, 7,* 186–190.

Scott, D.M. (1994, January). Are we ready for the 21st century? *ASHA, 47,* 50.

Scribner, S., & Cole, M. (1981). *The psychology of literacy.* Cambridge, MA: Harvard University Press.

Seymour, H., & Seymour, C. (1981). Black English and Standard American English contrasts in consonantal development of four- and five-year-old children. *Journal of Speech and Hearing Disorders, 46,* 274–280.

Shriner, T.H., & Miner, L. (1968). Morphological structures in the language of disadvantaged and advantaged children. *Journal of Speech and Hearing Research, 11,* 605–610.

Stewart, W. (1970). Toward a history of American Negro dialects. In F. Williams (Ed.), *Language and poverty* (pp. 51–73). Chicago: Markham Publishing.

Taylor, O.L. (1988). Speech and language differences and disorders of multicultural populations. In N. Lass, L. McReynolds, J. Northern, & D. Yoder (Eds.), *Handbook of speech-language pathology and audiology* (pp. 939–958). Philadelphia: B. C. Decker.

Templin, M.C. (1957). *Certain language skills in children.* Institute of Child Welfare Monograph Series, No. 26. Minneapolis: University of Minnesota Press.

Templin, M.C., & Darley, F.L. (1969). *The Templin-Darley Tests of Articulation* (2nd ed.). Iowa City: Bureau of Educational Research and Service, Division of Extension and University Services, University of Iowa.

University of Michigan Detroit Area Study. (1989). *Separate and unequal: The racial divide.* Ann Arbor, MI: Institute for Social Research.

Vaughn-Cooke, F.B. (1983). Improving language assessment in minority children. *Asha, 25*(9), 29–34.

Vaughn-Cooke, F.B. (1986). The challenge of assessing the language of nonmainstream speakers. In O.L. Taylor (Ed.), *Treatment of communication disorders in culturally and linguistically diverse populations* (pp. 23–48). Boston: College-Hill Press.

Washington, J.A., & Craig, H.K. (1992a). Articulation test performance of low-income, African-American preschoolers with communication impairments. *Language, Speech, and Hearing Services in Schools, 23*(3), 203–207.

Washington, J.A., & Craig, H.K. (1992b). Performances of low-income, African-American preschool and kindergarten children on the Peabody Picture Vocabulary Test–Revised. *Language, Speech, and Hearing Services in Schools, 23*(4), 329–333.

Washington, J.A., & Craig, H.K. (1994). Dialectal forms during discourse of poor, urban, African American preschoolers. *Journal of Speech and Hearing Research, 37*(4), 816–823.

Wiener, F.D., Lewnau, L.E., & Erway, E. (1983). Measuring language competency in speakers of Black American English. *Journal of Speech and Hearing Disorders, 48,* 76–84.

Williams, R., & Wolfram, W. (1977). *Social dialects: Differences versus disorders.* Rockville, MD: American Speech-Language-Hearing Association.

Willson, V.F., Nolan, R.F., Reynolds, C.R., & Kamphaus, R.W. (1989). Race and gender effects on item functioning on the Kaufman Assessment Battery for Children. *Journal of School Psychology, 27,* 289–296.

Wolfram, W. (1971). Black and white speech differences revisited. In W. Wolfram & N. Clarke (Eds.), *Black–white speech relationships* (pp. 139–161). Washington, DC: Center for Applied Linguistics.

Wolfram, W. (1987). Are black and white vernaculars diverging? *American Speech, 62*(1), 40–48.

Wolfram, W., & Fasold, R. (1974). *The study of social dialects in American English.* Englewood Cliffs, NJ: Prentice Hall.

2

Issues in Recruiting African American Participants for Research

Joyce L. Harris

. . . science is not the highest value to which all other order of values . . . should be subordinate. (Pope Pius XII, cited in Beecher, 1966)

Until recently, speech-language pathologists, like other behavioral scholars, have operated under the assumption that existing research data represent broadly sampled populations and universally applicable knowledge. In fact, the opposite is true. Almost without exception, existing social and behavioral research inquiries are based on a narrow conceptual frame that samples only one segment of the general population while ignoring others. This long-standing practice, a product of an outmoded view of America as a culturally homogeneous society, becomes increasingly less tenable as the lens of reality rivets attention on the nation's growing racial and cultural diversity. Thus, contemporary social and behavioral scientists are compelled by changing demographic patterns in the United States to rethink long-held beliefs about the validity of existing knowledge bases as behavioral benchmarks or normative references for all segments of the general population. Even a cursory comparison of the most frequently sampled population segment (e.g., white, middle-class, monolingual speakers of Standard American English [SAE]) with nonwhite groups in the general population refutes the notion that the majority population is either an appropriate reference group or a universal template for human behavior. Given this state of the sciences, the extent to which existing data can be generalized and used as a source of normative reference for the broader population is highly questionable.

In much of the scientific community, cultural monocentrism has perpetuated what Stanfield (1993) dubbed the "fallacy of homogeneity" (p. 16) in American society. Cultural monocentrism tacitly, but effectively, negates the social and scientific significance of nonwhites, thereby restricting their inclusion as research subjects. Moreover, the logic of scientific inquiry is shaped by sociopolitical influences, of which the heuristic mind-set of researchers who establish and maintain the scientific distinctions of their respective disciplines is an accurate reflection. For, ultimately, researchers, the brokers of scientific power, will decide which issues and questions are central to the advancement of their self-generated scientific truths. The extent to which scientific inquiry is driven by cultural monocentrism and sociopolitical mores becomes explicit when one considers the paucity of research that is designed to characterize even the most basic developmental and behavioral processes in nonwhites. The sad truth, as Stanfield (1993) observed, is that "It has always been the norm in social science that Eurocentric empirical realities can be generalized to explain the realities of people of color" (p. 28).

Now, opposing voices in the scientific community, as evidenced by the researchers writing in this volume, urge consideration of the influences of cultural and linguistic diversity on human behavior. A culturally informed investigation of behavioral phenomena undoubtedly will recast previous notions of behavioral *deviance* as simply instances of *cultural variation.* Culture influences all aspects of behavior, including language acquisition, development, form, function, and style. Despite the apparent logic of viewing behavior against a cultural backdrop, not everyone has heeded this well-reasoned appeal. Still, far too many social and behavioral scientists remain locked into outmoded, monocentric paradigms, reinforced, perhaps, by the inertia of familiarity and the constraints of social politics. Yet a new generation of social and behavioral scientists has emerged. They are committed to developing enlightened, ecologically valid data sources that acknowledge the centrality of culture to human behavior.

Affiliates of the American Speech-Language-Hearing Association (ASHA) have taken a vanguard position among social and behavioral scientists who promulgate sociocultural awareness in education, clinical intervention, and research (ASHA Committee on the Status of Minorities, 1991). This focus marks the beginning of a paradigm shift (Kuhn, 1970; Taylor, 1993) and the emergence of an opportunity to advance the science of communication and communication disorders. Now, populations previously underrepresented in data sources will be more likely included in population samples or, alternatively, become the reference populations for research inquiry. This likelihood provides a rich untapped vein for current and future researchers.

African Americans, the largest racial-ethnic minority population in the United States, are among those who are disproportionately underrepresented in the literature of communication science and disorders. The trend toward including representative numbers of racial-ethnic minorities in research samples provides the means to augment a knowledge base that heretofore erroneously claimed to represent the full spectrum of human communication.

Generally, African Americans are less likely and less willing than their white, middle-class counterparts to participate in research. Scientists, whether indigenous or alien to the African American community, who choose to conduct research that requires the voluntary participation of African American subjects must have well-planned strategies to counter the challenges inherent to this undertaking. Anderson (1993) speculated that, in our society, people of color have more reason to fear exploitation and injury at the hands of researchers than whites. This, in part, may account for the low participation of African Americans as research subjects.

Fear of exploitation and injury are powerful deterrents to research volunteerism. Kochman (1981) observed that the response of many African Americans to increased social vulnerability is suspicion and uncooperativeness. Perceived vulnerability may cause them defensively to stonewall those who try to elicit personal information from them, believing that self-disclosure is an open invitation to trouble. Feelings of vulnerability are so pervasive that even census taking, for example, is hampered in certain sectors of the African American community. Despite public education and advanced warning that census takers are coming and despite assurance that census information will not be reported individually, many African Americans refuse to participate. This same culturally based closemouthed behavior poses a challenge to researchers seeking to recruit African Americans as research participants. Mainstream researchers, who may be unaware of this group's predilection for non–self-disclosure, often mistake an individual's self-protective behavior for truculence and hostility.

Kochman (1981) observed that the scholarly inquiry needed to challenge these and other negative stereotypes about African Americans has been hampered, to a large extent, by well-intentioned efforts to establish social egalitarianism that ignores the differences between racial-ethnic minorities and the majority population. This noble attempt at establishing a "color-blind society" has had the ironic effect of deflecting scholarly investigation from issues unique to the sociocultural development and behavior of diverse populations, thereby effectively eliminating the discovery of new information.

In the 1990s, there is unprecedented agreement among communication sciences and disorders scholars that more research involving African American children is needed. However, the inclusion of these children in research studies requires not only cultural sensitivity but also unimpeachable research ethics. Cultural sensitivity includes recognition of the issues that underlie African American resistance to scientific scrutiny. Generalized mistrust of mainstream society and its institutions (see Chapter 4) intensifies when African Americans perceive a threat to their children's well-being. Seeing no immediate benefit to their children and viewing research as a meaningless, self-serving exercise, African Americans are reluctant to allow investigators to involve their children in such projects. Moreover, many African American parents fear that research results (e.g., test and IQ scores) will result in punitive diagnostic and educational consequences.

Children are classified among those who most need protection from possible exploitation and injury. Therefore, obtaining legal consent and gaining cooperation from parents or guardians is a necessary prerequisite to all research involving minors. Investigators must ensure the safety and protection of child subjects, as well as assure parents or guardians that adequate, appropriate safeguards are in place. Racial-ethnic minority status adds yet another layer of vulnerability for child participants. For this reason, involvement of African American children as research participants may require considerable effort on the part of recruiters to overcome the reservations that many African American adults have about research. The caveat, then, for those whose research agendas include questions that can only be answered by examining the behavior of African American children is that *potential points of resistance need to be anticipated and dealt with proactively.*

The remainder of this chapter includes a discussion of the issues surrounding the participation by African American children and youth as research participants. General legal, ethical, and sociopolitical provisions that regulate the use of children in human experimentation form the basis for a discussion of issues specifically pertinent to African Americans. The first section briefly exposes the roots of the pervasive aversion of many African Americans to all activities associated with the terms *research* or *experimentation*. Next, the discussion focuses on informed consent, institutional review board (IRB) regulation of research activity, and categories of research exempted from IRB scrutiny. The focus of discussion then shifts to research ethics, especially as ethical practices pertain to vulnerable classes of participants. The chapter concludes with guidelines for practicing social responsibility and cultural sensitivity in designing and conducting research involving African American children.

ROOTS OF RESISTANCE

African Americans unwittingly and unwillingly have been used as human guinea pigs in experiments that were often secretive and deadly (Washington, 1994). These activities were glossed as biomedical research. The reluctance by many African Americans to participate as research participants should be recognized as a deep-seated mistrust of the scientific community that evolved as a protective adaptation to earlier abuses. The proverbial "man on the street" may not be aware of the origin of his mistrust in regard to research participation, but through socialization as an African American he has acquired a sense of the scientific community's history of insensitivity to disempowered individuals and groups. Perhaps feelings of mistrust are only loosely associated with research activities and are more reflective of a generalized mistrust of mainstream institutions and enterprises. It is true that African Americans who are poor, undereducated, or institutionalized have been, and still are, particularly vulnerable to exploitation and injury at the hands of researchers. Despite significant sociopolitical changes and improved lives for most African Americans, stemming from the civil rights movement in the 1960s, vestiges of racism and disempowerment persist and serve to sustain a healthy skepticism of mainstream scientific undertakings. Scientific history verifies the validity of this attitude.

Although most Americans know about the atrocities and war crimes of Nazi Germany, few know about the injury and death inflicted on human participants involved in American biomedical research. Even fewer mainstream Americans know that racial-ethnic minorities and other powerless groups provided the human material for these experiments. Unfortunately, even among those actively and currently engaged in research, this legacy of abuse often is overlooked. The media, especially those targeting African American markets, have not left the retelling of biomedical experimental abuse to chance. Activities that occurred with amazing secrecy, impunity, and regularity in America's research hospitals and laboratories are coming to light. Consequently, relatively more contemporary African Americans than whites know about the prevalence of unethical and often deadly research. Documentaries and feature stories provide chilling reports of inhumanities glossed and perpetrated as legitimate scientific research. For example, the account of secret medical experiments on African Americans was featured in the October 1994 issue of *Emerge: Black America's Newsmagazine* (Washington, 1994).

Although it is beyond the scope of this chapter to provide detailed accounts of the many instances of abuse of human research participants, it may be enlightening to enumerate the kinds of research implicated. African Americans and other vulnerable groups have been subjected to burns (Washington, 1994); testicular exposure to radiation (Hoversten, 1994; Markey, 1994); crippling psychosurgery (Washington, 1994); ingestion of radioactive substances (Markey, 1994); injection of human cancer cells (Washington, 1994); and deadly trials of experimental medicines (Altman, 1993). The most infamous and egregious of the long list of abusive medical experiments is known simply as the Tuskegee Study (Jones, 1981, 1983).

The Tuskegee Study (Jones, 1981, 1983), starting in 1932 and continuing for over 40 years, was a federally funded project undertaken by the U.S. Public Health Service. The investigation's purpose was to study the effects of untreated syphilis on a group of males. Participants in the study were 600 African American men from Macon County, Alabama. The research project came to the American public's attention only in 1972, during an investigation by an ad hoc advisory panel appointed by an official of the Department of Health, Education and Welfare (HEW). Despite intensive investigation by the panel, the federal government never acknowledged any wrongdoing. Refusing to impose harsher sanctions, the panel finally declared the study "ethically unjustified." Not until 1978 when Allan Brandt, a doctoral candidate, found the original research protocol in the National Archives was the investigators' malfeasance established (Katz, 1993). The research protocol revealed that subjects did not voluntarily submit to the experiment, being told only that they were to receive medical treatment from expert government doctors for a serious disease, "bad blood." As an additional enticement, subjects were promised a $50 burial insurance.

Those who find it hard to believe that adults would endure years of life-threatening maltreatment should remember the historical and sociopolitical context in which the Tuskegee Study began. In the early 1930s, the Depression plummeted the nation into unprecedented depths of a social and economic morass. In the depressed economy of 1930s rural Alabama, a $50 burial policy represented a windfall for the poor, uneducated, African American men targeted for the experiments. The offer of a burial policy was culturally apropos and especially attractive, because adequate provision for one's own funeral was (and still is) an important aspect of African American culture. During that time, death was for many African Americans the only predictable life event, and arranging for one's own burial was often the only life event under one's control. The appeal of a "good death" was enhanced by the strongly held belief in a peaceful, trouble-free afterlife. Even the most impoverished managed to eke out pennies, nickels, and dimes over a lifetime, so as "to be put away nicely."

Participation in the Tuskegee Study and compliance with the research protocol was ensured by the social mores of the time and place, which dictated overt servility and submission to whites, even more so if the whites were agents of the federal government. The hundreds of men in the Tuskegee Study epitomized the insignificance of African Americans to white, mainstream America. Their perceived insignificance made them vulnerable to exploitation and use as human guinea pigs by federally funded agents of the scientific community.

The Tuskegee Study's "health care" team, cunningly, included both whites and African Americans. Eunice Rivers, an African American nurse, was employed by the researchers ostensibly to keep track of the subjects over the course of the study, but, by virtue of her race, she was able to gain the trust of local African Americans and to convince them of the program's "benefits" (Jones, 1981, 1983). The research subjects were euphemistically referred to as "Miss Rivers' Lodge," a burial and social club (e.g., Eunice Rivers gave them rides in a government vehicle and provided them with hot lunches) (Jones, 1981, 1983, p. 6). After the development of penicillin, an effective and safe cure for syphilis, nurse Rivers then had the task of tracking down and sometimes removing men from doctors' offices to keep them from seeking medical treatment or leaving the study.

The eventual disclosure of Eunice Rivers's betrayal created a legacy of mistrust of *all* researchers by many African Americans, regardless of the researcher's racial-ethnic identity. Thus, even today, an African American researcher may be seen by other African Americans as a pawn of the white establishment. Moreover, the power imbalance between researchers and their human subjects creates a barrier that can be nearly insurmountable, even when those on either side belong to the same racial-ethnic group. Superior power is accorded to the researcher by virtue of his or her professional status and association with mainstream institutions. More about status-related issues between researchers and subjects will be taken up in a later section of this chapter.

PROCEDURAL SAFEGUARDS

The only redeeming outcome of the flagrant, protracted abuse perpetrated against the men involved in the Tuskegee Study was the establishment of regulatory procedures for conducting federally funded research using human subjects. The National Research Service Award Act of 1974 (PL 93-348) was enacted expressly to protect the well-being and best interests of human subjects in research by ensuring that such projects have an investigative review panel. The primary protection of human subjects is embodied in the principle of "informed consent" (Katz, 1993).

Holder (1985) defined research as a category of activities with the sole aim of discovering or contributing to a body of generalizable knowledge. Researchers in communication sciences and disorders may, at times, find it difficult to differentiate research from customary clinical activities. In contrast to research, customary practice may be generally thought of as a class of activities with the primary purpose of contributing to an individual's well-being. The critical distinction between research and customary practice is whether the data gathered will be disseminated to the scholarly community through books, journal articles, professional presentations, or other such venues. If the answer is yes, even in part, then the activity in question must be classified as research.

The distinction between biomedical and behavioral research is also important. Biomedical research is typically more invasive and potentially life-threatening than behavioral research. Most biomedical research is conducted by, or under the auspices of, physicians who have the expertise and license to prescribe and administer drugs, perform surgical procedures, and provide medical treatment for existing diseases and conditions. Most of the research conducted by speech-language pathologists is clearly in the category of behavioral research and involves activities that are relatively innocuous and noninvasive. Potential research participants and their surrogates must be led to understand the critical distinction between biomedical and behavioral research. Doing so will do much to alleviate fear of physical injury or health risks.

about real

Institutional Review Boards

An IRB is a body established and given authority to approve, disapprove, or modify research protocols involving human subjects. Another IRB function is continuing, periodic review of ongoing research that may result in sanctions of research modification, suspension, or termination. Federal regulations specify that IRBs be composed of at least five members of varied professions and include persons whose concerns are not primarily scientific. In addition to diverse backgrounds, IRBs should include members who are knowledgeable about and experienced with vulnerable participants. Such knowledge should be combined with sensitivity to community attitudes and concerns. When indicated, IRBs should seek ad hoc consultants who possess these special competencies.

Institutional Review Boards employ two mechanisms for review. The first is called an *expedited review*. This category includes "minimal risk" research, meaning that the risk or magnitude of harm foreseen is no greater than that encountered in daily life or during performance of routine physical or psychological tests. Voice recordings, existing data, and archival records are included in this category of risk. Expedited reviews also may be used for minor changes in previously approved research. The IRB chairperson or designee may conduct an expedited review, as long as all the members of the IRB are advised. The second mechanism is a *full review*. A full review must be conducted at a meeting with a majority of the IRB members present. Approval requires a majority vote. The IRB must notify investigators and institutions in writing of its decisions to approve, modify, or disapprove the research.

The main function of the IRB is to ensure that the risk to human subjects is minimal or reasonable in relation to the expected benefit to them and to the advancement of knowledge. The IRB monitors the equability of subject selection. Federally funded research requires that researchers include women and minorities as participants, unless the research objective clearly precludes their participation. The IRB ensures that informed consent is obtained and documented. Furthermore, the IRB monitors provisions for protecting the safety and confidentiality of research participants. Finally, in the case of vulnerable participants, the IRB ensures that additional safeguards are in place to protect the well-being of human subjects.

Informed Consent

Informed consent is both a written document and procedure of disclosure, designed and monitored by IRBs to protect the rights, interests, and well-being of human subjects. Only persons who have reached the age of legal majority (legal age varies by state) may give consent to participate as subjects in research for themselves or someone for whom they are legally, responsible. Informed consent includes the notion that the consenting adult is a person who actively and volitionally chooses involvement in a research study. Furthermore, granting consent implies that participation is undertaken with the full understanding of the decision's implications. The essential components of informed consent are the following:

1. *Disclosure.* This element should clearly state that the study involves research. In addition, the study's purpose, the expected duration of the human subject's participation, the procedures to be employed, and the experimental procedures must be explicit.
2. *Risks.* This element should describe any foreseeable risks of discomfort or injury.
3. *Benefits.* This element should describe potential benefits to the participant or others.
4. *Confidentiality.* This element should clearly state the extent to which the participant's anonymity will be preserved.
5. *Compensation/help.* This element is particularly relevant to risky research. Participants must be told where they may obtain needed treatment or how they will be compensated for their participation in the study.
6. *Responsible party.* This element should include a statement about who to contact for additional information about the study.
7. *Voluntary participation.* This element should include a statement that participation in the study is voluntary and that refusal to participate will not involve penalty or loss of benefits. Equally important, subjects must be informed of their right to withdraw from the experiment once it is under way.
8. *Written document.* This element provides that child participants or legal guardians be given a copy of the informed consent statement.

Assent, a related concept, implies acquiescence, or consent without protest, to the research procedures. Although children cannot grant legal consent to their own participation in research, older children and youth are capable of giving assent on their own behalf. Research ethics dictate that researchers seek assent from human subjects who are capable of expressing their desires. Holder (1985) goes a step further by stating his belief that IRBs should require that investigators respect the "deliberate objections" of a child (p. 157). Lack of assent, even if legal consent has been given, is believed to be reason enough to excuse a minor from participation in a study.

When seeking informed consent from those who may have little or no experience with the concept of behavioral research, researchers must assume nothing. The uninformed may simply not see the point of a research study that has no immediate or apparent practical application. Therefore, the subject solicitation procedure must be carefully planned and fully developed, allowing ample time for a thorough explanation of the project and its procedures. Although informed consent includes a written description of the rights and obligations of research participants, the language of that document may not be clear to some adults. The informed consent document should begin with a clear explanation of the research, using terms that can be understood by a layperson. The noninvasiveness of behavioral research should be emphasized (e.g., no injections, no medications, no physical contact or discomfort). However, the informed consent should specify any expected inconvenience or discomfort. When aversive procedures are used, provisions to alleviate discomfort or stress should be highlighted.

Parents and legal guardians may be expected to have concerns about the handling and dissemination of information about their child. Therefore, measures used to ensure confidentiality must be stressed. Keeping in mind that disclosure of personal information is particularly distasteful to many individuals, especially those who may feel vulnerable in a research situation, all parties who may have access to interview information should be revealed. Likewise, any immediate benefits or compensations for allowing a child to participate in the research should be explained in detail. For example, the researcher might tell parents or guardians that they will be given a videotape of their child engaging in play therapy. A nonmonetary incentive (e.g., educational materials, theater tickets, coupons) may be combined with payment. Participant payment should be carefully specified as a part of the informed consent process, including contingencies for withdrawal before the end of the study. Finally, the rights and protections provided to human subjects and the special protections provided to children must be stressed. It is especially important that potential participants understand that they may refuse to participate without penalty and that they may discontinue participation at any time once the research is under way. Reiteration of the human subject provisions and safeguards, as well as verification that these safeguards and provisions are fully understood, will do much to alleviate feelings of vulnerability and mistrust.

Exempted Research

Investigators whose research requires the use of children as participants should be aware that certain kinds of research involving school-age children are exempted from IRB approval and parental consent. The Department of Health and Human Services provided exemption for research conducted in established educational settings and in which customary educational practices are being carried out. The instructional activities of special education are included among those deemed as "customary educational practices." Data sources for research conducted in educational settings may include educational and psychometric tests, such as achievement, aptitude, and diagnostic tests. The exemption only applies, however, if the data are recorded in such a way that they cannot be directly or indirectly linked to individual children.

Other exempted research for adult subjects (e.g., surveys, interviews) becomes subject to informed consent and IRB approval when the research involves children. Observing the public behavior of adults is usually exempt from informed consent. However, the exemption does not apply to observational research involving children, except when the investigator does not participate in the observed activities. Although it is beyond the scope of this discussion to present an all-inclusive description of IRB policies, suffice it to say that any research protocol designed to take advantage of IRB exemption should be carefully examined to ensure compliance with the spirit and intent of the policy. Educational administrators may attempt to minimize institutional liability by requiring IRB approval for *all* research conducted in their schools. Local policy also should be ascertained before seeking approval of research activity.

ETHICAL CONSIDERATIONS

Ethicists believe that certain individuals have a particular need to have their rights and welfare protected in the conduct of research involving human subjects. Clearly, research that introduces the variables of race and ethnicity is fraught with many potential inequalities between participants and researchers. A number of status-related issues may exist between researchers and participants, including dominant versus nondominant subcultures, professional versus nonprofessional, and standard versus nonstandard English dialect. The legally and socially subordinate position of children to adults is yet another status-related situation, one that frequently combines with others. The following section will discuss the so-called vulnerable class, an umbrella term that describes those who are deemed socially subordinate and most in need of protection.

～ Vulnerable Class ～

Individuals who are especially susceptible to exploitation and injury in research are those with limited freedom or capacity to protect themselves. The subsequent discussion is based on the *International Ethical Guidelines for Biomedical Research Involving Human Subjects* (Council for International Organization of Medical Sciences in collaboration with World Health Organization, 1993). Prisoners, persons with mental or behavioral disorders, institutionalized and frail elderly persons, recipients of welfare or other kinds of social assistance, and children are classified as vulnerable groups. In addition, certain social structures create positions of vulnerability. For example, individuals in a junior or subordinate position within a hierarchically ordered social group (e.g., clinical practicum students) may agree to participate as research subjects only with an expectation of preferential treatment or from fear of disapproval or retaliation if they refuse. Some ethnic and racial minority groups, homeless persons, or refugees also are in need of special protection because of their social vulnerability.

It is clear that many African American children fit in more than one category of vulnerability. First, they are legal minors and are ineligible to grant or withhold consent on their own behalf. Second, they are subordinate to educators and researchers who are empowered by their adult status, education, and authority. Moreover, there is an implicit assumption that these privileged adults know what is best for children. Third, many African American children are among the thousands of American children living in poverty. As such, their parents and guardians are among those who are made vulnerable by their economic dependence on society for sustenance. These individuals may rightly fear that they will lose benefits if they are noncompliant. Such vulnerability is magnified, because most low–socioeconomic status (SES) African Americans lack information about the societal benefits of behavioral research and about their rights as human subjects. African American children and youth are indeed among the most vulnerable members of our society.

According to the International Ethical Guidelines (p. 29), researchers must offer special justification for inviting vulnerable individuals to participate in research studies, and if vulnerable individuals are selected, protecting their rights and welfare must be paramount in all phases of the study. The following summarizes issues that must be addressed appropriately before including African American children in research:

1. *Need.* Research could not be conducted with less vulnerable participants.
2. *Uniqueness.* Research is designed to investigate behaviors that are characteristic or unique to the vulnerable group.
3. *Benefit.* Participants and others in the vulnerable class will be assured reasonable access to diagnostic, preventative, or therapeutic products of the research.
4. *Risk.* Risks are minimal, especially when expected benefit to participants or others in the vulnerable class is limited or nonexistent.

SOCIAL RESPONSIBILITY IN RESEARCH

Social responsibility in research encompasses, but goes beyond, ethical considerations that are designed merely to withstand the scrutiny of IRB review. The socially responsible researcher acknowledges his or her responsibility to the individual participant and to his or her community. Social responsibility also precludes short-sighted, self-aggrandizing research that does little more than initiate or perpetuate negative stereotypes about minority populations. Cole (1986) used the term *victim analysis* to describe a pervasive research design for studies involving African Americans and other minorities. This behavioral research paradigm compares members of vulnerable classes with those whom society holds in higher esteem. Thus, comparisons are made between low-SES African American children and middle-class white children, speakers of SAE and of nonstandard English, poor urban dwellers and more affluent suburbanites, and so forth. The hypothesis always presupposes between-group differences, with variance from the behavior of the majority group being synonymous with "inferior." Cole (1986) acknowledged that most behavioral researchers are not bigoted or malicious in their use of the "victim analysis" research design. Rather, this design, the "gold standard" for multicultural research, is merely reflective of the cultural monocentrism of most mainstream researchers. The real danger in this practice, of course, lies in the potential perpetuation of negative stereotypes as truths cloaked in scientific garb.

Ethnography, spawned from the older discipline of anthropology, offers a model that can be successfully applied to research involving African American subjects. An ethnographic researcher explicitly acknowledges the existence of cultural differences, thereby mitigating cultural mistrust and misunderstanding by meeting these differences head on. Entry into a community may be difficult, however, because members of that community may have had no previous exposure to researchers or even the idea that anyone would be interested in studying them (Facio, 1993). Facio also acknowledged the researcher's inherent struggle to achieve appropriate levels of rapport, trust, and objectivity—a tall order, indeed.

Ethnographers also embrace the emotional aspects of their transcultural research. Facio (1993) remarked that as much care must be taken when leaving a community as when entering. Subjects, once engaged, may feel deserted or even betrayed at the end of their participation in a study. The conscientious researcher acknowledges the potential "interpersonal meaningfulness" the encounter with members of the community may engender. Remembering that self-disclosure is antithetical to the self-protective concerns of many African Americans, researchers should not be surprised that once trust is established, the relationship's strength may be perceived as greater than the typical, situation-specific relationship between a researcher and participant. Therefore, special care must be taken with the ending of the relationship.

A carefully planned postexperimental interview or debriefing procedure should be included in every research protocol. The responsible researcher is obligated to provide an opportunity for comments about the study. Postexperimental debriefing allows the researcher to lift the veil of scientific objectivity enough to share with the participant and surrogate the purpose of the study. During this period, the experimenter can allay the adult's lingering feelings of uncertainty about the child's performance or anxiety about the child's participation in the study. This also is an opportunity for the researcher to probe for and clear up any misconceptions about the experimental activities. Furthermore, experimental debriefings can be used to educate adults about certain aspects of the behavior under investigation. Sometimes printed educational materials are provided and explained during the debriefing. In fact, the educational aspect of the activity is an incentive for many parents. The researcher also can elicit useful feedback about the appropriateness of procedural aspects of the study (e.g., whether the directions to the test site were clear, whether the telephone interviewer was considerate of time constraints for scheduling). Finally, the debriefing procedure allows the researcher to thank the participant for his or her valuable contribution to the advancement of science. A thoroughly debriefed, emotionally satisfied parent or guardian may feel an allegiance to the researcher and the project and may become a referral source for additional research participants from the same community. The postexperimental interview provides closure on the participant–researcher relationship.

Much of the research involving African American children and youth will probably be conducted by white researchers. A 1992 statistic from the Office of Multicultural Affairs of ASHA indicated that less than 200 minorities among its 71,000 members holds a Ph. D. The doctorate is considered the entry-level degree for research careers in communication sciences and disorders (Taylor, 1993). However, it is highly unlikely that all of the small number of minority holders of the doctorate degree are engaged in research in general or in multicultural research in particular. So the supposition is that much of the research involving African American children as research participants will be conducted by researchers who are not African American. Although a discussion of the potential vagaries of cross-racial (researcher–participant) dyads is beyond the scope of this chapter, such racial disparity may be a moot issue. In a sense, all researchers, by virtue of their educational attainment, professional status, and affiliation with mainstream institutions, are in a socially determined elite class that separates them from most of their human subjects. Thus, the potential for miscommunication and misunderstanding between all researchers and members of the target population, regardless of their respective racial-ethnic status, always exists. When possible, researchers should attempt to engage an individual who is a trusted member of the target population as an ally, interpreter, and guide. Working collaboratively with an individual who is a member of the target population may be especially critical when a white researcher wants to solicit African American participants to a research study.

Last, but most important, researchers choosing to employ African American children as participants must pose socially responsible research questions. That is, social responsibility must begin at the conceptual stage of research design, long before concerns about subject recruitment, informed consent, and payment come into play (Cole, 1986). Valid questions seek to address issues that are important to the target population. Facio (1993) implored researchers to consider carefully their obligation to the community. The only way to determine relevance is to know the community and its issues and concerns. Socially responsible researchers avoid paradigms that perpetuate negative stereotypes or that create new ones. When differences between groups are measured, those differences must be interpreted in the context of cultural variance rather than deviance or deficit. Social responsibility in research is a relatively recent focus, one that should be viewed positively, as it marks an end to the authoritarian notion of edict and compliance between the scientific community and human subjects, respectively.

CONCLUSION

This chapter proposed that, although there is a long-unmet need to amass more communication sciences and disorders research that focuses on African Americans, it is imperative that this research be undertaken with sensitivity to the concerns and needs of African Americans. Stating that "research asks so much and gives so little in return," Facio (1993, p. 90) captured the inherent disparity in the relationship between researchers and participants. The scientific community stands to gain by acknowledging and rectifying the imbalance of burden and benefit to human subjects. Generating databases that reflect the sociocultural makeup of the U.S. population requires increased scholarly dialogue on the legal, ethical, and sociopolitical issues surrounding research involving African American children. Such dialogue will undoubtedly reveal the challenges and rewards that await current and future researchers who pursue this line of investigation. The true measure of our success will be the eventual redefining of the logic of inquiry relative to sociocultural diversity in human communication sciences and disorders.

REFERENCES

Altman, L.K. (1993, October 5). Science times: Fatal drug trial raises questions about informed consent. *The New York Times*, p. 3:1.

American Speech-Language-Hearing Association (ASHA) Committee on the Status of Minorities. (1991). Multicultural action agenda 2000. *ASHA, 24,* 321–323.

Anderson, M. (1993). Studying across differences. In J.H. Stanfield & R.M. Dennis (Eds.), *Race and ethnicity in research methods* (pp. 39–52). Beverly Hills: Sage Publications.

Beecher, H.K. (1966). Ethics and clinical research. *New England Journal of Medicine, 274,* 1354–1360.

Cole, L. (1986). The social responsibility of the researcher. In F. Smith, B. Clark, & H. Mitchell (Eds.), *Concerns for minority groups' communication disorders* (ASHA Report No. 16, pp. 93–100). Rockville, MD: American Speech-Language-Hearing Association.

Council for International Organization of Medical Sciences in collaboration with World Health Organization. (1993). *International ethical guidelines for biomedical research involving human subjects.* Geneva: Author.

Facio, E. (1993). Ethnography as personal experience. In J.H. Stanfield & R.M. Dennis (Eds.), *Race and ethnicity in research methods* (pp. 75–91). Beverly Hills: Sage Publications.

Holder, A.R. (1985). *Legal issues in pediatric and adolescent medicine* (2nd ed.). New Haven, CT: Yale University Press.

Hoversten, P. (1994, November 21). Radiation tests used inmates as guinea pigs. *USA Today,* p. A3.

Jones, J.H. (1981, 1983). *Bad blood: The Tuskegee syphilis experiment.* New York: The Free Press.

Katz, (1993). Ethics and clinical research revisited. *Hastings Center Report, 23*(5), 31–39.

Kochman, T. (1981). *Black and white styles in conflict.* Chicago: The University of Chicago Press.

Kuhn, T.S. (1970). *The structure of scientific revolutions* (2nd ed.). Chicago: The University of Chicago Press.

Markey, E.J. (1994, January 13). Compensating America's nuclear guinea pigs. *The Boston Globe,* p. 15:1.

National Research Service Award Act of 1974, PL 93-348, 42 U.S.C. §241 *et seq.*

Stanfield, J.H. (1993). Epistemological considerations. In J.H. Stanfield & R.M. Dennis

(Eds.), *Race and ethnicity in research methods* (pp. 16–36). Beverly Hills: Sage Publications.

Taylor, O.L. (1993). Mentoring people of color: Challenges and opportunities. In N.J. Minghetti, J.A. Cooper, H. Goldstein, L.B. Olswang, & S.F. Warren (Eds.), *Research mentorship and training in communication sciences and disorders* (pp. 99–107). Rockville, MD: American Speech-Language-Hearing Association.

Washington, H.A. (1994, October). Human guinea pigs. *Emerge: Black America's Newsmagazine, 6*(1), 24–35.

3

Issues in Assessing the Language Abilities of African American Children

Julie A. Washington

African Americans reportedly are one of the largest and fastest growing segments of the minority population in this country (Bureau of Census, 1990; Terrell & Terrell, 1993). As the African American population continues to increase nationally, the sense of urgency among speech and language researchers and practitioners to establish language testing instruments that are culturally valid and reliable also increases. Despite this growing concern and a long-standing recognition of the need for culturally fair language tests, there continues to be a critical shortage of valid and reliable assessment instruments for use with African Americans whose primary linguistic system is not Standard American English (SAE).

This chapter examines the status of assessment of children who speak African American English (AAE). The first section provides a brief overview of the language characteristics of AAE. The second section identifies the problems that have been encountered with standardized assessment and provides a review of the research that has attempted to address these problems. The final section presents alternatives to norm-referenced assessment, focusing primarily on language sample analysis procedures.

WHAT IS AFRICAN AMERICAN ENGLISH?

African American English is a systematic, rule-governed linguistic system that is spoken by many, but not all, African American people in the United States. African American English affects the speaker's morphological, syntactical, and phonological systems. This chapter addresses only those features that affect the morphology and syntax of English; the phonology of AAE is beyond the scope of this chapter.

Table 1 presents a list of commonly identified AAE language forms. These features are widely accepted as characteristic of the linguistic productions of African American adults, adolescents, and young children who use AAE. It is notable, however, that these features have been identified primarily from the linguistic productions of adult and adolescent speakers (Dillard, 1972; Fasold & Wolfram, 1970; Stewart, 1970; Wolfram & Fasold, 1974). Investigations of the use and development of AAE forms in very young children are rare and consist almost entirely of unpublished doctoral dissertations that must be considered preliminary in nature (Blake, 1984; Bridgeforth, 1984; Cole, 1980; Kovac, 1980; Reveron, 1978; Steffensen, 1974; Stokes, 1976; Wyatt, 1990).

In the published investigations of the language characteristics of young children, the use of AAE forms in young children has typically been confirmed by comparing children's productions with those forms identified in the literature for adults (Baratz, 1969, 1970). These studies have simply confirmed what practitioners have known all along: that AAE forms are used by some African American children. However, these studies have provided no additional insight into the acquisition, development, or frequency of occurrence of these forms in young children's productions.

The assumption that the linguistic behavior of AAE-speaking children mirrors that of AAE-speaking adults can lead to underestimation and distortion of the children's true abilities. Child language research has established that young children learning language do not function linguistically like adults (Bloom & Lahey, 1978; Brown, 1973; McNeill, 1970; Miller & Ervin-Tripp, 1964). Relying entirely on the adult linguistic model to characterize the productions of African American children therefore may provide an incomplete picture of their abilities. To date, this reliance on the adult model has provided us only with evidence of what the child is doing that is the same as African American adults. It has provided us no insights into the development of AAE forms. Relying on the adult model prevents identification of AAE forms used by African American children that are quantitatively or qualitatively different from those used by AAE-speaking adults and adolescents.

Notable exceptions to this trend are investigations by Ratusnik and Koenigsknecht (1976), Ramer and Rees (1973), and Washington and Craig (1994), in which differences in the use of AAE forms were examined in young children. Ratusnik and Koenigsknecht (1976) and Ramer and Rees (1973) examined the

Table 1. African American English forms identified in 4- and 5-year-old African American children

Definition	Examples
Zero copula or auxiliary "is, "are" and modal auxiliaries "will," "can," and "do"are variably included	"the bridge out" "how you do this"
Subject-verb agreement A subject and verb that differ in either number or person	"what do this mean"
"Fitna"/"sposeta"/"bouta" Abbreviated forms of "fixing to," "supposed to," and "about to," coding imminent action. (Examples of utterances that were not scored for this form were: "they fixin it," "what are we supposed to do to that," "what about they lunch?")	"fitna": "she's fitna backward flip"; "sposeta": "when does it sposeta go"; "bouta": "this one bouta go in the school"
Ain't "ain't" as a negative auxiliary	"why she ain't comin'"
Undifferentiated pronoun case Nominative, objective, and demonstrative cases of pronouns occur interchangeably	"him did and him"
Multiple negation Two or more negative markers in one utterance	"I don't got no brothers"
Zero possessive Possession coded by word order, so that the possessive -s marker is deleted, or the nominative or objective case of pronouns is used rather than the possessive	"he hit the man car" "kids just goin' to walk to they school"
Zero past tense "-ed" is not always used to denote regular past constructions, or the present tense form is used in place of the irregular past form	"and this car crash" "and then them fall"
Zero -"ing" Present progressive morpheme "-ing" is deleted	"and the lady is sleep"
Invariant "be" Infinitival "be" with a variety of subjects coding habitual action ("it's gonna be far away" was an example of when habitual "be" was not scored); or to state a rule	"and this one be flying up in the sky" "if he be drunk I'm taking him to jail"
Zero "to" Infinitive marker "to" is deleted	"now my turn shoot you"
Zero plural Variable inclusion of plural marker -s	"ghost are boys"
Double copula and auxiliary Two forms for a single verb form	"I'm is the last one ridin on"
Regularized reflexive Reflexive pronouns "himself" and "themselves" are expressed using "hisself" and "theyself"	"he stands by hisself"
Indefinite article "a" regardless of vowel context	"Brandon had to play for a hour, didn't he?"
Appositive pronoun Both a pronoun and a noun reference the same person or object	"the teacher she's goin' up here"

From Washington, J., & Craig, H. (1994). Dialectal forms during discourse of urban, African-American preschoolers living in poverty. *Journal of Speech and Hearing Research, 37*, 816–823; reprinted by permission.

use of selected AAE forms in the linguistic productions of low-income African American children. The subjects in these studies were enrolled in preschool and kindergarten and in kindergarten through eighth grade, respectively. Both studies found differences in the performance of the subjects based on age. The frequency of use of AAE forms was higher for the younger children than for the older children. In particular, Ramer and Rees found a steady decrease in the percentage of AAE forms produced from kindergarten through eighth grade.

Washington and Craig (1994) examined the linguistic productions of 45 4- and 5-year-old low-income, African American children who used AAE forms. Using a distributional analysis, they found that many of the features identified in the adult literature indeed characterized the productions of their young subjects, but that the use of these features differed widely across children. Their subjects clustered into three distinct groups of AAE users (the range of AAE forms identified for each group is indicated in parentheses): 1) high AAE-user group (24%–39%), 2) moderate AAE-user group (13%–21%), and 3) low AAE-user group (0%–11%). Washington and Craig found that subject-verb disagreement and deletion of the copula and auxiliary were used by most (75%–100%) of the children and that several other features (double modals, indefinite article, appositive pronoun, and regularized reflexive) were used by only a small percentage (0%–15%) of the children. One adult feature, the remote past "been," was not used by any of the subjects, and another feature, "fitna"/"sposeta"/"bouta" (e.g., "he's fitna break the ice," "she going out with him and you sposeta be gettin' her ready," "she bouta eat the candy") has not been discussed in the adult literature. In a subsequent data set, the remote past "been" was observed in the speech of a 7-year-old African American male child ("I been knowin' how to swim"). The use of this AAE form by an older child suggests that perhaps it is a later developing form. In the absence of normative data, however, it is impossible to know for sure.

Considered collectively, the data from these three studies suggest that the use of AAE forms is probably different for adult and child speakers. Ratusnik and Koenigsknecht (1976) and Ramer and Rees (1973) suggested that younger children use more AAE forms than do their older peers or, by implication, adults. They claimed furthermore that this change in the use of AAE is affected by the children's entry into school, with preschoolers exhibiting more AAE use than school-age children. Washington and Craig (1994) found that even among young children the overall percentage of AAE use varied and that the frequency of use of specific AAE forms also varied.

In addition to age, the frequency of use and the variety of AAE forms identified in a child's repertoire may be influenced by other variables, such as socioeconomic status (SES) and geographic region. African American English is reportedly most prominent in the speech of working-class and low-income African Americans, although it is apparent to a lesser degree in the speech of middle-income African Americans (Craig & Washington, 1986; Dillard, 1972; Labov, 1966; Taylor, 1988; Terrell & Terrell, 1993). Research suggests that middle-income African Americans who do use AAE forms are probably more adept at code switching than their low-income peers (Hall, 1976).

The geographical region in which a speaker lives can also affect the types of AAE forms apparent in the speakers' repertoire. Several of the linguistic patterns identified as AAE forms are shared by regional dialects, such as Southern English (Fasold, 1981; McDavid & McDavid, 1951; Terrell & Terrell, 1993). Consequently, AAE forms used by African Americans residing in the southern United States may not be apparent in the speech of African Americans residing in the northern United States. Accordingly, a distinction should be made between southern and northern AAE forms.

In summary, these studies indicate that the percentage of use of AAE forms can vary widely across individuals and may be influenced by a number of variables. The use of specific AAE forms may be significantly influenced by the region of the country in which a child resides, his or her age, and SES. Future research should focus on identifying and describing patterns of AAE use in children more fully. Until we understand the nature of AAE usage in young African American children, attempts to assess their language skills will be confounded by the presence of both "immature" developmental forms and "nonstandard" AAE forms. Clinicians need to be aware that varied patterns of AAE use will be apparent in their African American child clients, both in the number of different forms used and the percentage of AAE use overall. The forms identified in Table 1, although certainly not exhaustive, should be helpful in determining whether a nonstandard form observed in a child's productions is AAE.

ASSESSMENT ISSUES

The presence or absence of AAE forms in an African American child's repertoire significantly affects assessment choices. Presumably, African American children who do not use AAE forms present no special challenge for the speech-language pathologist in terms of either assessment or intervention. Because SAE forms characterize the language of these children, standardized testing instruments that at least include African Americans in the normative sample should be informative and appropriate. In order to make this assumption, however, a clinician must be confident that the linguistic information obtained is truly representative of a child's linguistic abilities.

In addition to the presence or absence of AAE form use, a distinction should be made between those children who have language problems secondary to a primary medical diagnosis such as Down syndrome, mental retardation, hearing impairment, or cerebral palsy and those who do not. For the former group, there is abundant literature available that describes the nature of the language impairments that accompany these disorders, as well as assessment and intervention alternatives (Chapman, Kay-Raining Bird, & Schwartz, 1990; Chapman, Schwartz, & Kay-Raining Bird, 1991; Ezell & Goldstein, 1989, 1991; Hartley,

1982). In children with Down syndrome, for example, characteristic impairments in comprehension and oral-motor skills, sequencing abilities, and syntax have been identified. The morphosyntactic nature of AAE forms likely precludes selecting syntactic skills as a starting point for assessment and intervention even with an African American child with Down syndrome who uses AAE forms. However, the child's use of AAE forms should not affect the clinician's ability to assess and intervene in other identified areas of impairment. There is no reason to believe that an African American child with Down syndrome should be viewed any differently from other children with Down syndrome who have comparable cognitive skills. Consequently, the clinician can feel relatively confident that the literature provides some useful guidelines for assessment and intervention. Perhaps after becoming more familiar with the child's communication patterns, the clinician will be able to identify and treat syntactic impairments that do not represent AAE but are truly characteristic of the child's medical syndrome.

African American English-speaking children who exhibit language disorders in the absence of hearing, neurological, motor, or cognitive impairments represent the group for whom there is little direction available for assessment and consequently intervention. Assessment instruments that are appropriate and informative with African American children who do not use AAE or those who have a primary medical condition may not be appropriate for AAE-speaking children. Even though many assessment instruments now include African Americans in their standardization samples, the test items are still SAE in form and are normed and scored primarily for use with SAE speakers. Consequently, an African American child who uses AAE forms and is unable to produce the SAE equivalents of given test items would be unfairly penalized with a lower overall score. Thus, rather than accurately assessing the desired language behavior, the final test score would more likely reflect the child's inability to switch from his or her preferred linguistic code to the code used in the testing instrument. By implication, a language impairment identified based on the results of a test of this type would be highly questionable and probably unreliable. The specific issues of identifying language impairments in AAE-speaking children with standardized testing instruments are discussed in the sections that follow.

NORM-REFERENCED ASSESSMENT

Accurate identification of language disorders depends in large part on the assessment procedures used. An assessment instrument is suitable for use when it is appropriate for a child's age, level of linguistic development, cognitive abilities, SES, geographical locale, and cultural background. Several investigations have examined the validity of popular standardized speech and language assessment instruments with culturally or linguistically diverse children in general and African Americans in particular. The findings of these studies follow.

Culturally Biased Assessment Instruments

Stewart (1981) examined the prevalence of test bias using a battery of tests that had been mandated for use by a public school system in a major southern city. The battery included the original Peabody Picture Vocabulary Test (PPVT; Dunn, 1959), the Test for Auditory Comprehension of Language (TACL; Carrow, 1973), the Carrow Elicited Language Inventory (CELI; Carrow, 1974); the Illinois Test of Psycholinguistic Abilities (ITPA; Kirk, McCarthy, & Kirk, 1968), and the Boehm Test of Basic Concepts (Boehm, 1971). Stewart found that these tests consistently led to overidentifying African Americans for intervention services and underidentifying white children. Based on these findings, he argued that many of the test batteries being used by school systems across the United States to determine eligibility for speech and language services are probably unsuitable for African American children. In fact, two of the tests in the battery, the PPVT and the ITPA, have long-standing histories of documented scoring bias when used to test African American children (Arnold & Reed, 1976; Larson & Olson, 1963; Rychman, 1967; Smith & May, 1967; Stephenson & Gay, 1972; Vaughn-Cooke, 1986).

Using the composition of the normative sample as the basis for decision making, Adler and Birdsong (1983) also examined the appropriateness of several popular language tests, language screening instruments, and auditory discrimination tests for poor African American children. Based on the information reported about the normative samples, only one of the seven tests examined, the PPVT–Revised (PPVT–R) (Dunn & Dunn, 1981), was suitable for this population. Unlike the original PPVT (Dunn, 1959), which has been identified as culturally biased by J. Stewart (1981) and others, the PPVT–R was standardized nationally and included poor African American children in the normative sample. The following tests, however, were judged to be unsuitable for use with these children:

- Illinois Test of Psycholinguistic Abilities (revised edition) (ITPA; Kirk, McCarthy, & Kirk, 1968)
- Northwestern Syntax Screening Test (NSST; Lee, 1971)
- Utah Test of Language Development (UTLD; Mecham, Jex, & Jones, 1967)
- Wepman Auditory Discrimination Test (WADT; Wepman, 1973)
- Goldman-Fristoe-Woodcock Test of Auditory Discrimination (G-F-W TAD; Goldman, Fristoe, & Woodcock, 1970)

In theory, one should be able to apply the same standards used by Adler and Birdsong (1983) to determine a test's suitability for African American children. When the standardization sample includes poor African American children, the assessment instrument should be suitable for use with poor African-American clients. In practice, however, this standard cannot be applied as clearly or consistently as one would expect. For example, although the PPVT–R included low-income African American children in the normative sample, when Washington and

Craig (1992) administered it to 105 apparently typically developing, low-income African American preschoolers and kindergartners, they concluded that it was unsuitable for this population. Nearly all of their subjects (91%) scored below the mean of the PPVT–R normative sample.

How could this be, given that this population was included in the normative group? Although they included African American children in the normative sample, Dunn and Dunn (1981) reported no separate norms for their African American subjects. There was no evidence that the children's performance on the test items had been explored separately from the larger standardization group. Any differences in responding based on race and SES would therefore have been overlooked.

In spite of their numerous shortcomings, standardized tests will continue to be the assessment tool of choice for valid reasons. They are time efficient and provide prescribed administration and scoring procedures as well as normative data as a basis for comparison of child behavior. In short, they are quick and easy to administer.

Unfortunately, the findings of Stewart (1981), Adler and Birdsong (1983), and Washington and Craig (1992) are not encouraging for clinicians attempting to locate standardized assessment instruments suitable for African American children. The language data obtained with these instruments have been determined to be culturally biased and unrepresentative of African American children's linguistic abilities. In addition, whereas these instruments result in an overidentification of language impairments in African American children, they also likely result in an underidentification of impairments in white children, thereby presenting an obvious dilemma for the tester.

The development of unbiased assessment instruments that adequately meet the needs of both African American children and their white peers is the most obvious solution to this dilemma. However, the time and cost involved in test development are considerable. Clinicians are faced every day with the need to provide appropriate assessment information for their African American child clients and cannot wait until more tests are developed. Until new instruments become available, the following guidelines are recommended when available standardized tests are used:

1. Examine the normative sample to determine whether African American children were included.
2. Examine the method employed during the instrument's construction with specific attention to whether data indicate that the test developers examined possible differences in performance based on the use of dialect.
3. Examine the data obtained by an instrument once the preceding criteria have been met. Nothing takes the place of real performance data to determine whether an instrument is suitable for a given population. When administering the test to African American clients, if they consistently do not perform as expected, discontinue use of the test.

The time and cost commitments necessary for test development, along with an apparent recognition of the clinicians' immediate need for unbiased test procedures, have prompted several investigators to attempt to adjust or renorm existing tests as an alternative solution. These attempts have met with varying degrees of success and are discussed in the following section.

Language Test Modifications

Washington and Craig (1992) applied a scoring adjustment to the PPVT–R allowing credit for the items missed by more than half of their 105 low-income African American subjects. They discovered that, even when scoring credit was allowed for these 16 items, 86% of the subjects scored below the mean of the PPVT–R norms and 51% scored more than one standard deviation below the mean. They concluded, therefore, that the PPVT–R was inappropriate for either renorming or scoring adjustments and should not be used with this population.

In an effort to extend the norms of another popular assessment instrument to include African American children, Wiener, Lewnau, and Erway (1983) examined the Test of Language Development (TOLD; Newcomer & Hammill, 1977). They administered the TOLD to 198 African American children ages 4–8.5 and found that all of the subjects scored below the mean of the original normative sample. Similarly, when Kercher and Bauman-Waengler (1992) administered the TOLD to their African American subjects, they found that most of the test items (77%–100%) unfairly penalized children who used AAE. The poor performance of the subjects in these investigations suggests that the TOLD is not only unsuitable for use with African American children who use AAE but also inappropriate for either renorming or scoring adjustments because of the lack of performance spread demonstrated by the subjects in these studies.

Nelson and Hyter (1990) established norms for Black English Sentence Scoring (BESS), a procedure developed to supplement the Developmental Sentence Analysis (DSA) and its scoring procedure, Developmental Sentence Scoring (DSS) (Lee, 1974). The BESS was designed to make the DSA, a popular language sample analysis procedure, more appropriate for use with African American children. Using the BESS, utterances that do not contain any AAE forms can be scored with the traditional DSS procedures, and utterances containing AAE forms are scored using the BESS protocol. The BESS procedures give African American children scoring credit for utterances containing appropriate AAE forms that would not typically receive credit with traditional DSS. However, there appear to be at least two issues of concern regarding the use of the BESS as a diagnostic instrument: 1) The AAE forms that are given scoring credit on BESS are largely based on adult linguistic data, and 2) in the absence of normative data that support the use of the DSS with AAE-speaking children, using DSS in conjunction with BESS threatens the content validity of both instruments. The norms developed for the DSS were based on the linguistic productions of 200 children, for whom child language data were well established. Lee (1974) described the DSS as "a method for making a detailed, readily quantified and scored evaluation of a child's use of *Standard English* grammatical rules" (p. xix; emphasis added). Lee maintained furthermore that the DSS is "appropriate only for children who are learning standard American-English grammar" (p. xix) and cautioned that children who are bilingual or use linguistic systems that differ significantly from SAE "should not be evaluated with this technique" (p. xix). Perhaps using the BESS as an instrument scored completely independently of the DSS would handle the latter issue. However, in the absence of developmental and acquisitional data on AAE, resolving the first concern (i.e., scoring based on adult data) appears more difficult.

In a similar vein, Hemingway, Montague, and Bradley (1981) presented preliminary data for modification of the CELI (Carrow, 1974) scoring procedure. The subjects were 57 African American children ages 6–8 years. Following a procedure similar to that used by Nelson and Hyter (1990), Hemingway et al. identified syntactic structures in test items that would be affected by AAE forms. They allowed scoring credit for these items and scored all others using traditional CELI scoring procedures. However, the aforementioned concerns about the BESS also seem applicable to the Hemingway et al. procedures. In addition, the examples of utterances credited by these investigators in their study suggest that several of the linguistic forms given scoring credit may not be AAE forms (Vaughn-Cooke, 1986). These utterances were not mature SAE forms, but it is not entirely clear that they were AAE forms either. Hemingway et al. likely recognized that these forms were not SAE, did not recognize them as developmental forms, and assumed therefore that they were AAE forms. Because few studies have examined AAE forms specific to children, it is unclear what these forms actually represented. Perhaps they *were* AAE forms of which we are currently unaware. Alternatively, perhaps they were surface representations of an as-yet-undiagnosed language deficit. In any case, as clinicians or researchers we cannot assume that all utterances that differ from SAE are AAE forms.

In summary, these investigations highlight the difficulty of modifying existing expressive and receptive language tests. African American language forms are morphosyntactic in nature and can involve form deletions, additions, and word order changes (Craig & Washington, 1994; Vaughn-Cooke, 1986). On an expressive language test, a single grammatical feature affected by AAE (e.g., the copula) may be encountered on many test items. Each time the form appears and the client uses AAE rather than SAE, his or her score on the instrument is adversely affected unless the scoring is modified. However, the more items to which scoring modifications are applied, the more dubious the test's original content validity becomes. When numerous changes are made, it is important to question whether the test still effectively assesses the linguistic behaviors for which it was normed. According to Evard and Sabers (1979), if an existing test closely approximates the linguistic model sought by the investigator and few changes are necessary, then there likely is no validity problem. However, when the changes required are extensive, then restandardization of the instrument is warranted. Evard and Sabers also noted that "the test's norms are not applicable when extensive changes have been made in the test, because the standardization sample was not administered the adapted version of the test" (p. 279). In the attempts to extend the norms of existing instruments to a different linguistic community, researchers who have proposed extensive modifications are likely violating the assumptions of the instruments that they seek to supplement. In short, scoring adjustments and extension of existing norms are not viable solutions for creating unbiased language assessment instruments.

ASSESSMENT ALTERNATIVES

Numerous assessment alternatives exist for clinicians working with children whose primary linguistic system is SAE. As demonstrated in the preceding sections, however, norm-referenced assessment alternatives for children who use AAE forms are virtually nonexistent. In the following sections two major nonstandardized assessment techniques, language sample analysis and criterion-referenced assessment, are presented as potential alternatives to norm-referenced tests. Major language sampling analysis procedures, language-probing techniques, and complex syntax analysis are also discussed. Each of these assessment procedures is evaluated in terms of its appropriateness for use with children who use AAE forms.

Language Sample Analysis

The use of spontaneous language sample analysis as an alternative to standardized testing with children who use AAE forms has been widely recommended (Leonard & Weiss, 1983; Seymour, 1986b; Seymour & Miller-Jones, 1981; Terrell & Terrell, 1993; Vaughn-Cooke, 1986). The goal of language sampling is to collect a representative corpus of a child's utterances for analysis purposes. The sample is then transcribed and analyzed for characteristics of the child's expressive language.

Several variables have been identified in the extant literature that can potentially influence collection of a representative language sample with African American clients. These variables include the cultural relevance of materials used and topics discussed (Leonard & Weiss, 1983; Terrell & Terrell, 1993; Wolfram, 1976), the cultural relevance of tasks selected for elicitation purposes (Holland & Forbes, 1986; Vaughn-Cooke, 1986; Wolfram, 1976), and the effects of the elicitor on the child's linguistic choices (Olswang & Carpenter, 1978; Terrell & Terrell, 1993; Wolfram, 1976). The literature addressing these variables and others is abundant and therefore is not discussed here in detail. These studies emphasize the potential for collection of a biased and unrepresentative language sample if the aforementioned variables are not controlled in the language sampling context.

Leonard and Weiss (1983) recommended language sample analysis as a desirable method for identifying and characterizing the AAE forms evident in a child's repertoire. They suggested that the language clinician identify utterances that differ from SAE productions, compare the utterances with a list of commonly identified AAE forms, and attempt to characterize the child's expressive language abilities. At the very least, these procedures should help the clinician determine whether the child is a speaker of AAE, as well as which AAE forms characterize the child's productions.

As indicated, the features to which the child's productions would be compared derive from data obtained primarily from adult and adolescent speakers of AAE forms. Subsequent investigations have confirmed that many of these forms are evident in the productions of African American children to varying degrees (Baratz, 1970; Ramer & Rees, 1973; Ratusnik & Koenigsknecht, 1976; Washington & Craig, 1994). However, without specific information about the development of AAE, it would likely be difficult to characterize those forms that differ from SAE, but do not appear on the adult list of AAE forms. The clinician would be faced with trying to decide whether these utterances should be characterized as "immature" developmental forms, child-based AAE forms that have not been discussed in the literature, or whether they represent disordered linguistic productions. It is unfortunate that since 1983 when Leonard and Weiss made their recommendations these shortcomings in our ability to characterize AAE still exist.

In addition, because we know very little about the age at which AAE forms emerge, it is difficult to determine at what age a clinician should expect to see AAE forms in a child's language sample. Preliminary investigations by Cole (1980) and Reveron (1978) indicated that AAE forms probably emerge at approximately 4 years of age. Both studies examined the development of AAE forms in African American children 3–6 years of age. Before age 4, the children's use of AAE forms was minimal or nonexistent. If future developmental research supports these findings, how then will the clinician characterize an African American client 3 years of age or younger who is not yet using AAE forms? As an SAE speaker? If so, when AAE forms emerge a year later, does it render the test results obtained at age 3 invalid? Alternatively, if the child's caregivers use AAE forms, should the clinician assume that this child will use AAE forms in the future as well? If so, should standardized tests be used with this child? The answers to these questions are unclear. Terrell and Terrell (1993) recommend using the young child's parents as a barometer of future language use. Accordingly, if the parents are observed to use AAE forms, then the clinician should assume that the child will also be an AAE speaker and avoid assessment instruments inappropriate for AAE speakers. In addition, periodic language reassessments should be scheduled to monitor the child's language development until a clearer picture of dialect usage emerges.

Beyond characterizing the child's AAE forms, further analysis of the language sample raises a different set of issues. Several investigations have presented language sample analysis procedures that are potentially appropriate for children who use AAE forms. Among the procedures most widely recommended are language-probing techniques (Holland & Forbes, 1986; Leonard & Weiss, 1983; Seymour, 1986b; Terrell & Terrell, 1993; Vaughn-Cooke, 1986), criterion-referenced assessment (Leonard & Weiss, 1983; Seymour, 1986; Stockman, in press; Terrell & Terrell, 1993; Vaughn-Cooke, 1986), and analysis of complex syntax (Craig & Washington, 1994).

Language Probing Language-probing techniques have been recommended and used extensively with children who use SAE (Berko, 1958; Leonard, Schwartz, Morris, & Chapman, 1981; MacWhinney, Bates, & Kliegl, 1984). They involve identifying a linguistic structure with which the child seems to be having difficulty, creating obligatory contexts for use of the structure, and probing for the child's ability to use the structure in each of the obligatory contexts. Language probing appears to hold some promise as a procedure for collecting data designed to describe and characterize the linguistic productions of African American children. However, little information exists addressing what variables influence a child's decision to delete or to exclude a linguistic structure. If it is unknown what constitutes an obligatory context for AAE forms, then it would seem that any linguistic structure that has the potential to be influenced by AAE should be excluded from the language-probing process. An assessment technique that cannot address the child's primary linguistic system has limited potential as a diagnostic tool. Consequently, the utility of language probing as an assessment technique will remain unclear until we understand more fully the variables that influence inclusion and exclusion of AAE forms.

Criterion-Referenced Assessment Criterion-referenced assessment procedures have been examined as a promising alternative to standardized testing with African American children who use AAE (Leonard & Weiss, 1983; Seymour, 1986; Stockman, in press; Terrell & Terrell, 1993; Vaughn-Cooke, 1986). These procedures involve establishing a present criterion level that represents mastery of a given linguistic structure and examining the child's use of the structure to determine whether it meets the established criterion. Whereas norm-referenced measurements compare the child's performance with the performance of other children, criterion-referenced measurements compare the child's performance with an operationalized performance criterion.

Several different criteria have been used with SAE speakers to indicate mastery of a structure, including three or more uses of a structure within a 100-utterance language sample (Watkins & Rice, 1991) and use of the structure in obligatory contexts with 90% accuracy (Bloom & Lahey, 1978; Paul, 1981). These criteria are based on well-established developmental data that allow the clinician or researcher to establish expectations for the SAE-speaking child's language functioning. In the absence of comparable data for African American children, it is difficult to establish valid criteria for mastery of the language forms that characterize AAE. Using SAE criteria in the absence of criteria for AAE is potentially biased and certainly arbitrary and is not recommended (Seymour, 1986b).

When valid data are unavailable for establishing language performance criteria and the child produces immature language patterns that do not match those of the parent or caregiver, Terrell and Terrell (1993) recommend that a true language disorder should be suspected. Whereas using the parents' patterns of AAE usage to determine whether the child will eventually use AAE appears both logical and reasonable, making a judgment about typical versus disordered language status using this criterion involves an entirely different set of assumptions. In order to accept Terrell and Terrell's recommendation, one must assume that the linguistic productions of African American children should mirror those of African American adults and that the normal developmental data established for SAE speakers constitute an acceptable model for characterizing AAE forms. It is not clear that we can accept either of these assumptions without empirical evidence.

Stockman (in press) introduced the Minimal Competency Core (MCC) as a means by which criteria for performance might be established with African American children who speak AAE. Stockman defined the MCC as representing the least amount of linguistic knowledge that the child must exhibit in order to be considered to be without a language disorder. The basic assumption of the MCC is that a child with a language disorder should be less competent than the least competent speaker of the same age who is developing language without impairments. Identifying a core of linguistic features that are exhibited by apparently typically developing AAE-speaking children at a given age should therefore provide the necessary criteria for identifying children who are not developing language typically. For example, in a study of consonant development, Stockman and Settle (1991) identified a core of 15 word-initial consonants that were produced correctly by all of their 3-year- old subjects ($n = 7$) at least four times in a 2-hour conversational language sample. Using these 15 consonants as a reference point, they evaluated the speech of a 3-year-old boy who was later determined to have speech and language impairments. They found that this child was able to meet the productivity criterion (4 times in a 2-hour sample) for only 6 of the 15 consonants identified as a part of the consonant core. His limited consonant repertoire severely affected speech intelligibility. Using this procedure Stockman (in press) also established semantic, pragmatic, and morphosyntactic function cores for these same seven children.

The concept of the MCC holds promise for establishing performance criteria in AAE-speaking children and for identifying those children who are developing language impairments. The MCC needs to be established for a wider range of linguistic behaviors and age groups to gain widespread acceptance and validity. However, it appears to offer clinicians a means by which they can identify African American children who are functioning differently from their peers in specific speech and language areas.

Complex Syntax Analysis   Craig and Washington (1994) identified analysis of complex syntax production as a potentially important assessment technique for use with African American children. They examined production of 12 types of complex syntax by a sample of 45 low-income, African American boys and girls apparently without language impairments. The complex structures examined ranged from simple infinitives with the same subject to the use of embedded clauses and clauses with subordinated relationships. They found that most of the subjects used complex syntactic structures to varying degrees. In addition, the frequency of use of these structures correlated positively with the percentage frequency of AAE forms evident in a child's sample.

Craig and Washington (1994) identified complex syntax as a potentially important analysis for two major reasons. First, the development of complex syntax has been identified as an important benchmark in a child's development of linguistic competence (Paul, 1981). Infrequent use of complex structures or absence of use of these structures helps identify SAE-speaking children who have language deficits. Second, as proposed by Craig and Washington, complex syntax analysis seems to avoid some of the pitfalls that have been encountered with other analysis procedures when assessing children who use AAE forms. Complex syntax analysis uses the clause as the unit of analysis, and the morphosyntactic nature of AAE forms renders the clause largely unaffected by AAE. It should be possible to determine whether a child who uses AAE forms is developing language typically by identifying atypical use of complex syntactic structures. Craig and Washington presented preliminary norms for the use of complex syntax by African American children without language impairments who are poor and living in large urban settings. More information about the atypical language user is needed, however, to fully characterize complex syntax skills in children who use AAE.

Summary Only two analysis procedures discussed here, the MCC and complex syntax analysis, appear to hold promise for *immediate* use as culturally fair assessment approaches. The absence of normative data for African American children who speak AAE severely limits clinicians' choices, even where nonstandardized assessment is concerned. Stockman (in press) appropriately cautions that language sample is "no less affected by the lack of adequate normative data on minority speakers than are standardized tests" (p. 8).

CONCLUSION

This chapter examined language assessment for African American children who use AAE forms. The picture that has emerged offers some promise, but also underscores the critical need to develop standardized assessment instruments for African American children who speak AAE.

Although we have reported since the 1970s that most standardized assessment instruments are invalid for these children, little has been done to improve the outlook. Attempts to renorm or adjust existing tests have met with little success, and no new tests are available for use. In addition, the continued lack of language developmental data for AAE forms also complicates our ability to interpret data obtained through nonstandardized assessment approaches, although specific criterion-referenced assessment procedures appear to have some promise for immediate application.

In short, our knowledge of language use and development in this population remains critically incomplete. Without this knowledge base, attempts to assess the linguistic skills of African American children will continue to meet with little success and much controversy. This knowledge gap has implications not only for clinical assessment and intervention services, but also for research.

From a research standpoint, the gaps in our knowledge identified in this chapter seem to indicate that a fruitful agenda for future research should focus on 1) obtaining a more complete characterization of AAE forms used by young African American children, 2) understanding how AAE forms are acquired, and 3) developing normative profiles of language development in AAE speakers.

From a clinical standpoint, developing culturally fair assessment techniques, both standardized and nonstandardized, is imperative to identify and diagnose correctly language impairments in African American children. With no developmental information or culturally fair testing instruments apparent on the horizon, however, clinicians will continue to be faced with hard case-management decisions about African American clients who have suspected language impairments. Until this information becomes available, what are the alternatives?

First, by using the procedures recommended by Leonard and Weiss (1983) it is possible for the clinician to determine whether an African American child client uses AAE forms. Comparing the child's linguistic productions with a list of adult-derived AAE forms has limited usefulness for characterizing all of the child's non-SAE utterances or for diagnosing language disorders. However, research indicates that this procedure is useful for clarifying whether or not a client is a user of AAE forms (Leonard & Weiss, 1983; Washington & Craig, 1994). Once a client has been identified as such, however, it is recommended that standardized assessment instruments be avoided unless the clinician is confident that the results obtained have been consistently reliable with African American clients.

Second, distinctions should be made among those children who do not use AAE, those who have language problems secondary to a primary medical condition such as Down syndrome, and those who use AAE but have no identified medical condition that predisposes them to language disorders. For the first two groups, assessment and subsequently intervention are straightforward. There are appropriate assessment tools for these children. For the third group, however, valid and reliable assessment alternatives are few. Stockman (in press) and Craig and Washington (1994) have described some nonstandardized assessment alternatives with this population. Unfortunately, however, until more developmental data become available, African American children who use AAE forms likely will continue to be overidentified for language intervention services.

REFERENCES

Adler, S., & Birdsong, S. (1983). Reliability and validity of standardized testing tools used with poor children. *Topics in Language Disorders, 3,* 76–88.

Arnold, K.S., & Reed, L. (1976). The grammatic closure subtest of the ITPA: A comparative study of black and white children. *Journal of Speech and Hearing Disorders, 41,* 477–485.

Baratz, J.C. (1969). *Teaching black children to read.* Washington, DC: Center for Applied Linguistics.

Baratz, J.C. (1970). Educational considerations for teaching standard English to Negro children. In R.W. Fasold & R.W. Shuy (Eds.), *Teaching standard English in the inner city* (pp. 223–231). Washington, DC: Center for Applied Linguistics.

Berko, J. (1958). The child's learning of English morphology. *Word, 14,* 150–177.

Blake, I.K. (1984). *Language development in working-class black children: An examination of form, content, and use.* Unpublished doctoral dissertation, Columbia University, New York.

Bloom, L., & Lahey, M. (1978). *Language development and language disorders.* New York: John Wiley & Sons.

Boehm, A.E. (1971). *Boehm Test of Basic Concepts.* New York: The Psychological Corporation.

Bridgeforth, C. (1984). *The development of language functions among black children from working class families.* Paper presented at the presession of the 35th Annual Georgetown University Round Table on Language and Linguistics, Georgetown University, Washington, DC.

Brown, R. (1973). *A first language.* Cambridge, MA: Harvard University Press.

Bureau of Census. (1990). *Statistical abstract of the United States* (110th ed.) Washington, DC: Author.

Carrow, E. (1973). *Test for Auditory Comprehension of Language.* Boston: Teaching Resources Corporation.

Carrow, E. (1974). *Carrow Elicited Language Inventory.* Boston: Teaching Resources Corporation.

Chapman, R.S., Kay-Raining Bird, E., & Schwartz, S.E. (1990). Fast mapping of words in event contexts by children with Down syndrome. *Journal of Speech and Hearing Disorders, 55,* 761–770.

Chapman, R.S., Schwartz, S.E., & Kay-Raining Bird, E. (1991). Language skills of children and adolescents with Down syndrome: I. Comprehension. *Journal of Speech and Hearing Research, 34*(5), 1106–1120.

Cole, L. (1980). *Developmental analysis of social dialect features in the spontaneous language of preschool black children.* Unpublished doctoral dissertation, Northwestern University, Evanston, IL.

Craig, H.K., & Washington, J.A. (1986). Children's turn-taking behaviors: Social-linguistic interactions. *Journal of Pragmatics, 10,* 173–197.

Craig, H.K., & Washington, J.A. (1994). The complex syntax skills of poor, urban, African-American preschoolers at school entry. *Language, Speech, and Hearing Services in Schools, 25,* 181–190.

Dillard, J. (1972). *Black English.* New York: Random House.

Dunn, L. (1959). *The Peabody Picture Vocabulary Test.* Circle Pines, MN: American Guidance Service.

Dunn, L., & Dunn, L. (1981). *Peabody Picture Vocabulary Test–Revised.* Circle Pines, MN: American Guidance Service.

Evard, B.L., & Sabers, D.L. (1979). Speech and language testing with distinct ethnic-racial groups: A survey of procedures for improving validity. *Journal of Speech and Hearing Disorders, 7,* 271–281.

Ezell, H.K., & Goldstein, H. (1989). Effects of imitation on language comprehension and transfer to production in children with mental retardation. *Journal of Speech and Hearing Disorders, 54,* 49–56.

Ezell, H.K., & Goldstein, H. (1991). Comparison of idiom comprehension of normal children and children with mental retardation. *Journal of Speech and Hearing Research, 34*(4), 812–819.

Fasold, R.W. (1981). The relation between black and white speech in the South. *American Speech, 61,* 163–189.

Fasold, R.W., & Wolfram, W. (1970). Some linguistic features of Negro dialect. In R.W. Fasold & R.W. Shuy (Eds.), *Teaching standard English in the inner city* (pp. 41–86). Washington, DC: Center for Applied Linguistics.

Goldman, R., Fristoe, M., & Woodcock, R.W. (1970). *Goldman-Fristoe-Woodcock Test of Auditory Discrimination.* Circle Pines; MN: American Guidance Service.

Hall, W.S. (1976). Black and white children's responses to Black English vernacular and Standard English sentences: Evidence for code-switching. In D.S. Harrison & T. Trabasso (Eds.), *Black English: A seminar* (pp. 19–46). Hillsdale, NJ: Lawrence Erlbaum Associates.

Hartley, X.Y. (1982). Receptive language processing of Down's syndrome children. *Journal of Mental Deficiency Research, 26,* 263–269.

Hemingway, B.L., Montague, J.C., & Bradley, R.H. (1981). Preliminary data on revision of a sentence repetition test for language screening with black first grade children. *Language, Speech, and Hearing Services in the Schools, 12,* 153–159.

Holland, A., & Forbes, M. (1986). Nonstandardized approaches to speech and language assessment. In O.L. Taylor (Ed.), *Treatment of communication disorders in culturally and linguistically diverse populations* (pp. 49–66). Boston: College-Hill Press.

Kercher, M.B., & Bauman-Waengler, J.A. (1992, November). *Performances of Black English speaking children on standardized language tests.* Paper presented at the American Speech-Language-Hearing Association Annual Convention, San Antonio, TX.

Kirk, S.A., McCarthy, J.J., & Kirk, W.D. (1968). *The Illinois Test of Psycholinguistic Abilities (rev. ed.).* Urbana: University of Illinois Press.

Kovac, C. (1980). *Children's acquisition of variable features.* Unpublished doctoral dissertation, Georgetown University, Washington, DC.

Labov, W. (1966). *The social stratification of English in New York City.* Washington, DC: Center for Applied Linguistics.

Larson, R., & Olson, L. (1963). A method of identifying culturally deprived kindergarten children. *Exceptional Children, 29,* 130–134.

Lee, L. (1971). *Northwestern Syntax Screening Test.* Evanston, IL: Northwestern University Press.

Lee, L. (1974). *Developmental Sentence Analysis.* Evanston, IL: Northwestern University Press.

Leonard, L.B., Schwartz, R., Morris, B., & Chapman, K. (1981). Factors influencing early lexical acquisition: Lexical orientation and phonological composition. *Child Development, 52,* 882–887.

Leonard, L.B., & Weiss, A.L. (1983). Application of nonstandardized assessment procedures to diverse linguistic populations. *Topics in Language Disorders, 3*(3), 35–45.

MacWhinney, B., Bates, E., & Kliegl, R. (1984). Cue validity and sentence interpretation in English, German and Italian. *Journal of Verbal Learning and Verbal Behavior, 23,* 127–150.

McDavid, R.I., & McDavid, V.G. (1951). The relationship of the speech of American Negroes to the speech of whites. *American Speech, XXVI,* 16–37.

McNeill, D. (1966). The creation of language by children. In C.A. Ferguson & D.I. Slobin (Eds.), *Studies of child language development* (pp. 22–42). New York: Holt, Rinehart & Winston.

McNeill, D. (1970). *The acquisition of language: The study of developmental psycholinguistics.* New York: Harper & Row.

Mecham, M.J., Jex, J.L., & Jones, J.D. (1967). *Utah Test of Language Development.* Salt Lake City, UT: Communication Research Associates.

Miller, W., & Ervin-Tripp, S. (1964). The development of grammar in child language. In U. Bellugi & R. Brown (Eds.), *The acquisition of language.* Monographs of the Society for Research in Child Development, 29(1), Serial no. 92, 1–36. Lafayette, IN: Child Development Publications of the Society for Research in Child Development.

Nelson, N.W., & Hyter, Y.D. (1990). *How to use Black English Sentence Scoring (BESS) as a tool of non-biased assessment.* Short course presented at the American Speech-Language-Hearing Association Annual Convention, Seattle, WA.

Newcomer, P., & Hammill, D. (1977). *The Test of Language Development.* Austin, TX: PRO-ED.

Olswang, L., & Carpenter, R. (1978). Elicitor effects on the language obtained from young language-impaired children. *Journal of Speech and Hearing Disorders, 43,* 76–88.

Paul, R. (1981). Analyzing complex sentence development. In J.F. Miller (Ed.), *Assessing language production in children: Experimental procedures* (pp. 36–46). Austin, TX: PRO-ED.

Ramer, A., & Rees, N. (1973). Selected aspects of the development of English morphology in black American children of low socioeconomic background. *Journal of Speech and Hearing Research, 16,* 569–577.

Ratusnik, D.L., & Koenigsknecht, R.A. (1976). Influence of age on black preschoolers' nonstandard performance of certain phonological and grammatical forms. *Perceptual and Motor Skills, 42,* 199–206.

Reveron, W.W. (1978). *The acquisition of four Black English morphological rules by black preschool children.* Unpublished doctoral dissertation, Ohio State University, Columbus.

Rychman, D.B. (1967). A comparison of information processing abilities of middle- and lower-class Negro kindergarten boys. *Exceptional Children, 33,* 545–552.

Seymour, H.N. (1986). Clinical intervention for language disorders among nonstandard speakers of English. In O.L. Taylor (Ed.), *Treatment of communication disorders in culturally and linguistically diverse populations* (pp. 135–152). Boston: College-Hill Press.

Seymour, H.N., & Miller-Jones, D. (1981). Language and cognitive assessment of black children. In N. Lass (Ed.), *Speech and language: Advances in basic research and practice* (Vol. 4). New York: Academic Press.

Smith, H.W., & May, W.T. (1967). Influence of the examiner on the ITPA scores of Negro children. *Psychological Reports, 20,* 499–502.

Steffensen, M. (1974). *The acquisition of Black English.* Unpublished doctoral dissertation, University of Illinois, Evanston.

Stephenson, B.L., & Gay, W.O. (1972). Psycholinguistic abilities of black and white children from four SES levels. *Exceptional Children, 36,* 705–709.

Stewart, J. (1981). Multidimensional scaling analysis of communicative disorders by race and sex in a mid-south public school system. *Journal of Communication Disorders, 14*(6), 467–483.

Stewart, W. (1970). Toward a history of American Negro dialects. In F. Williams (Ed.), *Language and poverty* (pp. 51–70). Chicago: Markham Publishing.

Stockman, I.J. (in press). The promises and pitfalls of language sample analysis as a tool assessing linguistic minority children. *Language, Speech, and Hearing Services in Schools.*

Stockman, I.J., & Settle, S. (1991, November). Initial consonants in young black children's conversational speech. Presented at the American Speech-Language-Hearing Association Annual Convention, Atlanta, GA.

Stokes, N.H. (1976). *A cross sectional study of the acquisition of negation structures in black children.* Unpublished doctoral dissertation, Georgetown University, Washington, DC.

Taylor, O.L. (1988). Speech and language differences and disorders of multicultural populations. In N.J. Lass, L.V. McReynolds, J.L. Northern, & D.E. Yoder (Eds.), *Handbook of speech-language pathology and audiology* (pp. 939–958). Philadelphia: B.C. Decker.

Terrell, S.L., & Terrell, F. (1993). African-American cultures. In D.E. Battle (Ed.), *Communication disorders in multicultural populations* (pp. 3–37). Stoneham, MA: Butterworth-Heinemann.

Vaughn-Cooke, F.B. (1986). The challenge of assessing the language of nonmainstream speakers. In O.L. Taylor (Ed.), *Treatment of communication disorders in culturally and linguistically diverse populations* (pp. 23–48). Boston: College-Hill Press.

Washington, J., & Craig, H. (1992). Performances of low-income, African-American preschool and kindergarten children on the Peabody Picture Vocabulary Test-Revised. *Language, Speech, and Hearing Services in Schools, 23,* 329–333.

Washington, J., & Craig, H. (1994). Dialectal forms during discourse of urban, African-American preschoolers living in poverty. *Journal of Speech and Hearing Research, 37,* 816–823.

Watkins, R.V., & Rice, M.L. (1991). Verb particle and preposition acquisition in language-impaired preschoolers. *Journal of Speech and Hearing Research, 34*(5), 1130–1141.

Wepman, J.M. (1973). *Wepman Auditory Discrimination Test.* Palm Springs, CA: Language Research Association.

Wiener, F.D., Lewnau, L.E., & Erway, E. (1983). Measuring language competency in speakers of Black American English. *Journal of Speech and Hearing Disorders, 48,* 76–84.

Wolfram, W. (1976). Levels of sociolinguistic bias in testing. In D.S. Harrison & T. Trabasso (Eds.), *Black English: A seminar* (pp. 56–75). Hillsdale, NJ: Lawrence Erlbaum Associates.

Wolfram, W., & Fasold, R. (1974). *The study of social dialects in American English.* Englewood Cliffs, NJ: Prentice Hall.

Wyatt, T. (1990). *Linguistic constraints on copula production in Black English child speech.* Unpublished doctoral dissertation, University of Massachusetts, Amherst.

4

The Importance of Psychological and Sociocultural Factors for Providing Clinical Services to African American Children

Sandra L. Terrell and Francis Terrell

In the early 1970s, when the debate among dialectal deficiency and dialectal difference theorists regarding African American English (AAE) was at its peak, our clinical work with African American children in rural Florida schools made us realize that our rather considerable training in taking into account AAE patterns to achieve nonbiased assessment and intervention services was not enough. At those Florida schools, which serviced migrant farmworkers as well as permanent residents, clinical services frequently took a back seat to the families' more critical concerns, such as food, clothing, shelter, and health care.

Because of the socioeconomic background of many of these children, it was difficult for us to justify pulling them from classroom activities to work on incorrect articulation when their teeth (the ones that remained) were yellow, crooked, or appeared to be rotting. Many African American, and some white, children were placed in self-contained classrooms for children with mental retardation on the basis of the results of an intelligence screening test. However, when observed outside of their classrooms, these same children seemed to function quite well within their environments, as shown by their knowledge, for example, of the best ways to harvest produce or of how babies (both animal and human) are made.

In addition, children who needed speech-language pathology services sometimes came and went with the harvest and may have been seen only during the first and last 3 weeks of the school year. Other children might remain in the area, but would be in the fields performing farm work during school hours.

However, beyond economic conditions, certain sociocultural and psychological factors influence language and other behaviors among many African Americans. With such children dialectal variation alone is not the best assessment criterion for providing clinical services.

This chapter explores the research on some of these factors and shows how they can be used to develop nonbiased assessment and treatment procedures for African American clients. The specific factors considered in this chapter are self-esteem, anger and hostility, and cultural mistrust. There are additional sociocultural and psychological factors, such as religion, that may influence clinical services, but we selected self-esteem, anger and hostility, and cultural mistrust for two major reasons. First, a number of theoretical and empirical studies exist on these factors and their effects on clinical services, particularly in counseling and clinical psychology settings. These studies can provide a solid foundation for investigating how these factors may influence assessment and treatment of speech and language disorders. Second, our own professional experience indicates that these factors may influence assessment and treatment outcomes to a greater extent than other sociocultural and psychological factors.

Even though self-esteem, anger and hostility, and cultural mistrust are discussed separately in this chapter, these three factors may be difficult to differentiate in an African American client; indeed, they are likely to overlap. The client with a high level of self-esteem or cultural identification may feel anger and hostility toward whites in general because of past (or current) injustices and may also harbor a high level of mistrust (i.e., suspiciousness) toward anything or anyone perceived as white or reflecting white dominance. Thus, one or more of these sociocultural or psychological factors could influence a client's performance in assessment and treatment situations.

After reviewing the research on self-esteem, anger and hostility, and cultural mistrust, the chapter concludes with a brief discussion on clinical applications.

SELF-ESTEEM

The variable that has been studied most among African Americans is ethnic identification and the consequent sense of identity, or what is commonly thought of as
self-esteem. *Self-esteem* refers to the regard or value that people place on themselves. *Ethnic identification* means the extent to which a person identifies with
other African Americans. Typically, the extent to which people identify positively
with members of their cultural group reflects positive self-concept. Psychologists
generally agree that individuals, whatever their color, have varying degrees of self-
esteem.

Early in their history in the Americas, many African Americans were led by
whites to believe that they were inferior to them. The white majority needed to
promote such a view to justify both slavery and the second-class citizenship of
African Americans after the abolition of slavery. Fundamental to this myth was
the idea that African Americans were intellectually inferior and basically primitive
or "animal-like" in their expression of basic impulses, such as sex and aggression.
They also were thought to have an inability to delay gratification, a tendency to
be happy-go-lucky, and an inferior form of communication.

Previous literature by African American scholars, such as Kenneth B. and
Mamie P. Clark (1947), indicated that, because an individual's self-concept is based
on experiences and American society had devoted considerable efforts promoting
the idea that African Americans are inferior, many African Americans have internalized this belief. The result is a deficiency in self-esteem. For example, in
one of their studies (1947), the Clarks asked 119 northern and 134 southern
African American children (ages 3–7, both male and female) to choose one of four
dolls (two white, two African American). Like white children, African American
children indicated that they preferred white dolls over black dolls. Such studies
suggested that African American children have a negative evaluative attitude
about a key component of their physical appearance. Other researchers made similar
contributions (Landreth & Johnson, 1953).

Later research (Baughman, 1971; F. Terrell, S.L. Terrell, & Taylor, 1988;
White, 1984) indicated that the sense of self-concept and ethnic identification
among many African Americans has significantly improved. One of the factors
reflecting such improvement in African American self-esteem is culturally relevant social reinforcers, defined as terms of verbal praise that are identified with and
used among African Americans to demonstrate admiration or approval
(F. Terrell, S.L. Terrell, & Taylor, 1988).

In our initial study on culturally relevant social reinforcers (F. Terrell, Taylor, &
S.L. Terrell, 1978), we gave three groups of adolescents an intelligence test.
The adolescents in one group were given tangible reinforcers each time they
answered a question correctly. Another group was given traditional social
reinforcers after each correct answer, and the third group was given culturally
relevant social reinforcers. The tangible reinforcers consisted of an M&M after

each correct response; the traditional social reinforcers consisted of verbal praise suchas "good" and "fine"; and the culturally relevant social reinforcers included phrases such as "good job, blood"; "right on, brother"; and "good job, homeboy." Results of the study indicated that children given either the tangible or the culturally relevant social reinforcers achieved significantly higher scores on the intelligence test than those who were given the traditional social reinforcers. In other words, for these African American adolescents, the cultural social reinforcers were as effective as the candy given to enhance children's intelligence test performance.

In 1981 we replicated the study (F. Terrell, S.L. Terrell, & Taylor) using younger African American children (ages 7–10) who had been diagnosed as having borderline mental retardation. This second study yielded similar results. Furthermore, as a group, the mean scores of the groups given either tangible or culturally relevant social reinforcers improved so significantly that the individuals could no longer be classified as having mental retardation. Instead, the mean scores fell into the low, but average, range.

In another study, we wanted to determine whether there was a relationship between culturally relevant social reinforcers and the race of the examiner (F. Terrell, S.L. Terrell, & Taylor, 1980). In other words, could someone who was white effectively administer culturally relevant social reinforcers? A total of 120 African American males, 9–11 years of age, were selected and assigned to either a white or African American examiner to form two groups. Within each group, children were given no reinforcer, tangible reinforcers, traditional social reinforcers, or culturally relevant social reinforcers after each correct response on an intelligence test. Children given tangible rewards, regardless of the race of the examiner, obtained significantly higher scores than children given no reinforcers or children given traditional social reinforcers. However, children given culturally relevant social reinforcers by an African American examiner obtained significantly higher scores than the children who received culturally relevant social reinforcers from the white examiner.

Among other things, findings from these studies may indicate that African American children who strongly identify with their culture may view testing as irrelevant, and unless appropriate procedures are followed, such as providing meaningful reinforcers and an African American clinician, these children may not demonstrate their full cognitive or educational potential.

ANGER AND HOSTILITY

Grier and Cobbs (1968), analyzing case studies, concluded that as a result of historical racial injustices African Americans tend to harbor angry feelings. These authors relied on basic Freudian or psychoanalytical concepts and argued that African Americans unconsciously act out their anger in symbolic ways and that much of their behavior represents the internal frustration of being dehumanized in a predominantly white society.

Along with Fanon (1968), Grier and Cobbs (1968) also investigated in detail research studies and the theoretical cause of the feelings and unconscious behavioral manifestations of anger and hostility among many African Americans who feel frustrated by their treatment in a predominantly white society. Fanon suggested that the decisions made by those in power are political in that they are ultimately designed to maintain the status quo. In their efforts to maintain the power equation, the majority culture power brokers oppress those who are in the minority and are powerless. In this context, there will continue to be cultural and class conflicts because of efforts by the minority to equalize the distribution of power. Even the definition of crime and the administration of the criminal justice structure is controlled by the powerful, according to Fanon. This is reflected in the fact that the poor who break the law are more likely to go to prison than the rich who "misappropriate funds."

Many white Americans are often surprised to hear that anger is so rampant in the African American community. Typically, white Americans believe that, if anger and hostility exist at all, they are limited almost exclusively to lower-class African Americans. White Americans are usually not surprised to learn that some types of crimes committed by African Americans are a manifestation of this hostility toward whites, as a retaliation against whites for previous, as well as ongoing, injustices or as a means of releasing the frustration of being denied equal opportunity to participate in society.

Whites often mistakenly believe that so-called middle-class African Americans are content. Rarely does the white community associate anger and hostility with middle- and upper-class African Americans. It is assumed that, because these African Americans are successful, they are content with their status in American society. However, a close inspection of events taking place in American society strongly indicates that this is a gross misperception. Perhaps the most telling indication of this discontent is the continuing popularity of organizations such as the National Association for the Advancement of Colored People (NAACP) and the Southern Christian Leadership Conference (SCLC). Membership in these organizations is composed primarily of middle-class African Americans.

In many instances, middle-class African Americans are angrier than poor African Americans. Middle-class African Americans represent the most ambitious, achievement-oriented component of the African American population. They have often worked among whites. They have been exposed to the reward system. Nevertheless, because of their skin color, they have not had equal access to these rewards. Thus, they tend to be more aware than others of the possibilities, as well as the rewards, for success. But they view themselves as not having been given their share of the rewards for their contributions. Because they do not walk around with "doctor," "lawyer," or "teacher" written across their chest, when prominent

African Americans go into grocery stores, ride on buses and airplanes, and deal with various agencies they are treated like any other African American person— that is, in a prejudiced manner. They are angered because they are not treated with the same level of respect as their white counterparts.

Hostility and anger thus appear to be rampant among African Americans regardless of income, prestige of their occupation, region of the country, or religious affiliation. Given the history of African Americans in America and the way in which they continue to be treated, to believe otherwise probably demonstrates a lack of familiarity with African American culture. Yet the myth of the "happy Negro" continues to persist among many Americans. However, when the overt behavior of African Americans begins to threaten the security and possessions of whites, the latter are forced to reexamine some of their simplistic and self-serving assumptions about the former.

An angry person cannot hide this emotion, and this inner feeling is almost always displayed in some way. Frequently, however, the display of anger is quite subtle or indirect. Consequently it is easy for feelings of anger to go unrecognized by people who, for psychological reasons of their own, do not want to see them. Historically, of course, African Americans have always been in a position where it was extremely dangerous for them to express their anger by means of direct aggression against their white counterparts. Yet, although there are fewer restrictions in this regard in contemporary society than there were in the past, it would be a gross distortion to pretend that they no longer exist. Economic reprisals against the "uppity" are still quite common. For example, many African American people, regardless of their status in life, believe that it may not take much provocation, if any at all, for certain police officers to abuse or murder an African American as a threat.

African Americans express anger in a number of ways. First, they may attack the source of their anger directly. This is rarely done because of the futility of this approach. They may also attack other African Americans as a vicarious way of releasing their pent-up hostility, thus displacing their anger.

Another way African Americans may deal with anger is to attempt to remain unaffected and repress the emotion created by situations that elicit anger. This, of course, is difficult, if not impossible. Yet another strategy is to discharge the animosity with wit or humor—in other words, to laugh to keep from crying (S.L. Terrell & F. Terrell, 1993).

Another adaptation among African Americans to expressing anger is the one most likely to manifest within clinical situations. In interactions with white persons, African Americans may appear to be overly compliant because they think this is the way white people expect them to act. The pattern begins in childhood when mothers communicate to children the message that they must be compliant "because this is the only way you will get along with whites." African Americans may renounce gratifications available to others and assume a resigned mask. The objective is to figure out "the man" but keep "the man" from deciphering him or her. This type of behavior is prevalent in the middle and upper classes, but is also found throughout African American subcultures. In short, on the surface the person is passive and compliant. Below the surface, however, a storm is raging.

It should be noted that anger among African Americans is directed not only toward whites but also toward members of their own and other ethnic groups who seem to have internalized white values and traditions. Thus, it is not uncommon for African Americans to manifest hostility toward other African Americans who seem to have adopted white values and behavioral patterns. This animosity has direct and immediate implications for assessment. That is, having an African American examiner assess an African American client may produce results that are no more valid than if the assessment had been done by a white examiner. This may occur if the examinee believes that the African American examiner is simply a black-skinned person with white values and beliefs— an "Oreo." African Americans may also show their anger by refusing to demonstrate their actual ability or potential to perform a task by giving incorrect answers, not answering questions, or terminating sessions.

CULTURAL MISTRUST

Cultural mistrust is defined as the tendency for African Americans to be suspicious of whites. As African Americans identified with their own cultural patterns, they also began to develop an increased suspicion of whites. Grier and Cobbs (1968) pointed out that many African Americans have long been wary of whites. Indeed, in her autobiography *I Know Why the Caged Bird Sings* (1969), Maya Angelou eloquently and reverently described this trait in her grandmother.

The trust–mistrust issue was of special importance during the post-Reconstruction period at the turn of the 20th century. DuBois (1903) was of the opinion that African Americans should not passively surrender and entrust their civil, legal, and political rights to whites, believing that whites would return these rights when the African Americans demonstrated to them that they were ready to assume the responsibilities of full citizenship. The mistrust of whites continues to be a topic of discussion among African Americans in meetings and publications.

It is interesting to note that African Americans with diametrically different philosophies mistrust whites. The Kerner commission (Kerner, 1968), created by the Johnson administration to study the causes of urban unrest, rebellions, and violence in America's black ghettos, documented the history of white racism in America and concluded that African Americans had valid reasons to distrust white institutions, promises, and illusions of significant progress in eliminating racial oppression. Martin Luther King, Jr. (1958, 1967) implied that whites could not be trusted. Because of the consistent mistreatment of African Americans, Native Americans, and other minorities by whites, along with many broken promises, African American revolutionaries, individuals, and organizations all viewed the white culture as decadent and lacking humanistic concern for others.

Research seems to indicate that this mistrust of whites affects the lives of African Americans in a variety of areas, including 1) education and training (Brazziel, 1974; Russell, 1971); 2) politics and law (Kitano, 1974; Warren, 1969); 3) work and business interactions with whites (Baughman, 1971; Rutledge & Gass, 1967); and 4) interpersonal or social contexts (Kitano, 1974; Terrell, Terrell, & Golin, 1977).

The empirical research by Terrell and Miller (1979) strongly suggests that the more times an African American individual had been discriminated against, the more mistrusting of whites he or she is. In addition, African Americans who reported that discrimination was highly disturbing to them also tended to be more mistrustful of whites than those who were less disturbed by it (F. Terrell & S.L. Terrell, 1981).

Given that mistrust does seem to be relatively common among African Americans and that this mistrust seems to originate, at least in part, from racism, an important question is what impact mistrust has on African Americans in clinical, research, and other settings. We developed a questionnaire to measure the level of mistrust among African Americans (see Appendix A) called the Cultural Mistrust Inventory (CMI) (F. Terrell & S.L. Terrell, 1981). In addition, to facilitate longitudinal studies about cultural mistrust among children, we also developed the Children's Cultural Mistrust Inventory (CCMI) (F. Terrell & S.L. Terrell, 1996). (See Appendix B.) The following sections provide a summary of research on several areas in which cultural mistrust is a factor.

Cultural Mistrust and Mental Abilities

A series of studies using the cultural mistrust scales appears to demonstrate that cultural mistrust influences performance by African Americans on intelligence tests. Terrell et al. (1978) administered an intelligence test to African Americans who had high and low levels of mistrust of whites. It was found that individuals with high levels of mistrust obtained lower scores than individuals with lower levels of mistrust. In a similar study (Terrell et al., 1981), we selected a group of adolescents with high and low levels of mistrust of whites. Half of the participants in these two groups were then administered an intelligence test by an African American examiner, and the remaining sample was administered the test by a white examiner. It was found that students with a high level of mistrust who were tested by a white examiner had lower intelligence quotient scores than any other group. This study was replicated using elementary school children, and similar results were found (F. Terrell & S.L. Terrell, 1983). Thus, our findings indicate that being mistrustful of whites can have an adverse effect on intelligence test performance.

Cultural Mistrust and Interpersonal Behavior

The extent to which African Americans mistrust whites also seems to be related to how they interact with whites. One study indicates that African Americans who are mistrustful of whites avoid contact with them. For example, F.Terrell and S.L.

Terrell (1984) found that African Americans who are highly mistrustful of whites refuse to seek counseling if the clinician they are assigned to is white. Similar results have been found in other studies (Watkins & Terrell, 1988; Watkins, Terrell, Miller, & Terrell, 1989). These studies indicate that African Americans experiencing emotional problems might prefer to retain their difficulties rather than attempt to resolve them if that requires interacting with whites.

Cultural Mistrust and Academic and Occupational Expectations

Although the number of African Americans reaching higher socioeconomic levels has been increasing, results of the 1990 U.S. census showed that the actual percentage has declined (Bureau of Census, 1993). African Americans are disproportionately represented in occupations such as sanitation workers, waiters or waitresses, housekeepers, and domestics. Few African Americans tend to be employed as chemists, judges, and officers of large corporations. Several variables also correlate with the academic performance and occupational level of African Americans. These include low achievement motivation (Taylor, 1989), low self-esteem (Terrell et al., 1980), and poor role models (Baughman, 1971). We conducted a study (F. Terrell, S.L. Terrell, & Miller, 1993) to determine whether there was a relationship between educational and occupational expectations of African American adolescents and the extent to which they mistrusted whites. One hundred and thirty-two African American high school students were administered the Cultural Mistrust Inventory (F. Terrell & S.L. Terrell, 1981) and the Two-Factor Index of Social Position (Hollingshead & Redlich, 1958), an inventory used for classifying occupational and educational levels. The students were also asked to select the educational level they expected to attain. No significant relationships were found between educational expectations and mistrust level. However, the results did suggest that African American adolescents who expect to enter less prestigious, lower-paying occupations tended to be more mistrustful of whites. Thus, some African Americans may not seek prestigious occupations at least in part because they do not trust whites. Similarly, African Americans may not seek employment in fields that they do not believe are open to them.

Do these findings mean that being mistrustful of whites is undesirable? There is some controversy among investigators about whether or not cultural mistrust is pathological. On the one hand, Grier and Cobbs (1968) maintain that cultural mistrust is a healthy, adaptive attitude. Others, such as Kardiner and Ovesey (1951), have insisted that the lack of trust is indicative of an unhealthy, pathological personality. It is likely that in some instances mistrust does have survival or facilitative value, but in others it can be counterproductive. Being excessively mistrustful of whites can be potentially harmful to an African American's success. However, we believe that being overly trusting of whites can place African Americans at risk for not achieving optimal success.

In summary, the studies reviewed indicate that the mistrust African Americans have of whites may influence the success of clinical interactions. African

Americans may not be willing to disclose essential information when completing case history questionnaires or interviews. In addition, they may resist initial attempts that clinicians might make to establish rapport. Clinicians must not only be aware of these potential obstacles but also develop effective strategies to deal with them. Clinicians working with African American clients may need to devote additional time to establishing rapport in order to minimize the mistrust level before starting research, evaluation, or intervention procedures.

CLINICAL APPLICATIONS

The psychological and sociocultural factors that may influence the communication behaviors of African Americans need to be considered in selecting assessment procedures and designing treatment programs. Much has been written about the need for nonbiased assessment and treatment procedures (Battle, 1993; Committee on the Status of Racial Minorities, 1983; Taylor & Payne, 1983). Such procedures are especially important when dealing with individuals who may feel anger and mistrust toward the very persons and institutions that provide clinical services.

Because of the complexity of the cultural variables that can affect service delivery, nonbiased management can be achieved only by taking these factors into consideration when providing services to African Americans. Because nonbiased management is a process and professional way of life based on respecting a person's culture, normal linguistic style, family structure, and beliefs, the first critical step for any clinician or researcher is to attempt to evaluate—or at least understand—African Americans from their own cultural viewpoint. This is particularly true if the researcher or clinician is white.

The companion step for nonbiased management, which we also consider critical, is for the researcher or clinician to conduct an honest self-evaluation to determine the existence of discriminatory, racist, or any other attitudes that might impede valid research about or clinical service activities for African Americans. It is necessary for researchers or clinicians to determine whether or not they have the requisite training and skills to conduct valid, scientifically sound studies with African American subjects or to deliver appropriate clinical services to African American clients. After conducting an honest self-evaluation and concluding that either their skills or attitude could influence the research or clinical services, professional researchers should make the appropriate choices to refer, consult, or team with another professional who does have the requisite expertise.

Specific Applications to Speech and Language Services

Little actual research has examined the possible impact that self-esteem, anger, and mistrust have on speech and language behaviors. Research has centered on clinical and counseling psychology contexts. Therefore, the following examples of ways in which clinicians might deal with psychological and sociocultural factors when providing speech and language services to African Americans are based on our clinical internship experiences with the African American children who attended two rural Florida public schools where we interned.

Several years before conducting our research on the correlation between self-esteem and children's reactions to culturally relevant social reinforcers, we concluded that it was possible that many of the African American children in those two Florida public schools had low self-esteem. Even though the schools had been recently desegregated, many of the African American children still experienced segregation within the walls of the self-contained classrooms for children with mental retardation. In addition to intelligence testing biases, because of poverty, parental illiteracy, and lack of dental, basic health care, and personal care products (e.g., adequate clothing, African American hair-care items), the children's worldviews, emotions, and perceptions may have affected their performance at school and in clinical situations.

For several of these children, the use of culturally relevant reinforcers was particularly effective in enhancing their performance, at least within the clinical setting. Culturally appropriate verbal praises were used, as well as appropriate hair-care items (such as styling their hair with Afro-Sheen and a hair pick after a set number of correct responses). This activity served a dual role of reinforcing language learning *and* enhancing personal appearance and self-esteem.

One African American female who was in the self-contained classroom for children with mental retardation spit on the ground when she was angry, which occurred somewhat frequently. She often said that she wished that she could be in the general fourth-grade class with the other children. Her mother was illiterate (she signed the permission to perform services form with an x). The family resided in a very small, run-down home, and the child's body and clothing appeared at times to smell like urine. For this child, the most appropriate reinforcer was to take her home with us for a weekend, with her mother's "signed" permission. We hoped that new clothes and hair-care items, a bath and shampoo, and personal attention and language stimulation from two educated African American role models would give her something that would have been unlikely to occur within the confines of language therapy alone. In addition, by observing this child in this manner, we were able to question the school district's diagnosis of mental retardation as a first step toward a more valid cognitive reevaluation resulting in future participation in a general classroom.

As stated, it appeared somewhat ridiculous to provide therapy for articulation errors while ignoring the children's lack of dental care. We asked and received a donation of dental screening and follow-up services from a professor of dentistry who taught at the university hospital in the region. This professional traveled the 60 miles roundtrip to the school to perform the initial dental evaluations on-site.

Cultural mistrust in the clinical setting was most often seen when case history forms were sent to a child's home to be completed and returned. Case history forms often contain questions that many view with suspicion. Therefore, our case histories were brief, limited to the most essential questions, and conducted only during a face-to-face meeting arranged at the convenience of the parent, legal or unofficial guardian, or anyone else who had primary responsibility for the child, including an older sibling.

Although no empirical studies exist at this time on cultural mistrust in the language research and assessment settings, cultural mistrust may result in restricted linguistic output (i.e., low word production) in African American children. If research or assessment findings are based on language samples from African American children who were highly suspicious of white examiners, then the low word production of these children could be due to their being mistrustful of whites rather than a true reflection of their vocabulary. We therefore recommend that the clinician or investigator spend extra time to develop a rapport with the African American child.

FUTURE DIRECTIONS FOR RESEARCH

Systematic exploration of the influence of sociocultural and psychological factors on the communication behaviors of African Americans is in its infancy, and extensive research is needed. Studies designed to explore these factors within the context of speech, language, and hearing services require immediate attention. To date, such research has centered around clinical and counseling psychology contexts. The effect of the amount of cultural mistrust among African Americans on language productivity, dialect use, assessment, intervention performance, family satisfaction with the clinical services, and race of clinicians should be examined.

Finally, it has long been recognized that many African Americans mistrust not only whites but also other African Americans. Given the push to recruit more minorities as speech-language pathologists and audiologists, particularly to enhance services to minority populations, research examining the extent to which African Americans mistrust other African Americans must be undertaken. Studies exploring ways of ameliorating this tendency should then follow.

CONCLUSION

Over the years, we have engaged in a program of research largely designed to examine the effects of African American consciousness, a trend that began in the 1960s and continued into the 1970s. Our own research in this area seems to indicate that individuals with high levels of cultural mistrust tend to perform better when tested by other African Americans but that their performance deteriorates when they are tested by whites. Studies examining behaviors as a function of other factors in African American cultural identity have been too limited for any firm conclusions to be drawn. However, our preliminary findings and experiences suggest that either the excessive or insufficient presence of these factors is related to poorer levels of functioning.

In conclusion, many African Americans have a heightened sense of awareness and identity. However, researchers must study the effects that differing levels of ethnic identity may have on a variety of behaviors, including language performance.

REFERENCES

Angelou, M. (1969). *I know why the caged bird sings.* New York: Bantam.

Battle, D.E. (Ed.). (1993). *Communication disorders in multicultural populations.* Boston: Andover.

Baughman, E.E. (1971). *Black Americans: A psychological analysis.* New York: Academic Press.

Brazziel, W.W. (1974). Career education and black Americans. In R. Johnson (Ed.), *Black agenda for career education.* Columbus, OH: ECCA Publications.

Bureau of Census. (1993). *1990 Census of population, social and economic characteristics.* Washington, DC: U.S. Government Printing Office.

Clark, K.B., & Clark, M.P. (1947). Racial identification and preference in Negro children. In T.M. Newcomb & E.L. Hartley (Eds.), *Readings in social psychology.* New York: Holt.

Committee on the Status of Racial Minorities. (1983). Position paper on social dialects. *ASHA, 25*(9), 23–24.

DuBois, W.E.B. (1903). *The souls of black folk.* Chicago: McClurg.

Fanon, F. (1968). *The wretched of the earth.* New York: Grove.

Grier, W., & Cobbs, P. (1968). *Black rage.* New York: Bantam.

Hollingshead, A.B., & Redlich, F.C. (1958). *Social class and mental illness: A community study.* New York: John Wiley & Sons.

Kardiner, A., & Ovesey, L. (1951). *The mark of oppression: Explorations in the personality of the American Negro.* New York: Norton.

Kerner, O. (Chairman). (1968). *The report of the National Advisory Commission on Civil Disorders.* New York: Bantam.

King, M.L., Jr. (1958). *Stride toward freedom.* New York: Harper & Row.

King, M.L., Jr. (1967). *Where do we go from here: Chaos or community.* New York: Harper & Row.

Kitano, H.H. (1974). *Race relations.* Englewood Cliffs, NJ: Prentice Hall.

Landreth, C., & Johnson, B.C. (1953). Young children's responses to a picture and insert test designed to reveal reactions to persons of different skin color. *Child Development, 24,* 63–79.

Russell, M. (1971). Erased, debased, and encased: The dynamics of African educational colonization in America. In J.W. Blassingame (Ed.), *New perspectives on black studies* (pp. 40–59). Chicago: University of Illinois Press.

Rutledge, A.L., & Gass, G.Z. (1967). *Nineteen Negro men.* San Francisco: Jossey-Bass.

Taylor, O.L., & Payne, K.T. (1983). Culturally valid testing: A proactive approach. *Topics in Language Disorders, 3,* 8–20.

Taylor, R. (1989). *Assessment of exceptional students: Educational and psychological procedures* (2nd ed.). Englewood Cliffs, NJ: Prentice Hall.

Terrell, F., & Miller, F.S. (1979). *The development of an inventory to measure experience with racialistic incidents among blacks.* Unpublished manuscript.

Terrell, F., Taylor, J., & Terrell, S.L. (1978). Effects of type of social reinforcement on the intelligence test performance of lower-class Black children. *Journal of Consulting and Clinical Psychology, 46,* 1538–1539.

Terrell, F., & Terrell, S.L. (1981). An inventory to measure cultural mistrust among blacks. *Western Journal of Black Studies, 5,* 180–185.

Terrell, F., & Terrell, S.L. (1983). The relationship between race of examiner, cultural mistrust, and the intelligence test performance of black children. *Psychology in the Schools, 20,* 367–369.

Terrell, F., & Terrell, S.L. (1984). Race of counselor, client sex, cultural mistrust level, and premature termination from counseling among black clients. *Journal of Counseling Psychology, 31,* 371–375.

Terrell, F., & Terrell, S.L. (1996). An inventory for assessing cultural mistrust in black children. In R.L. Jones (Ed.), *Handbook of tests and measurements for black populations.* (Vol. 1, pp. 245–248). Hampton, VA: Cobb & Henry Publishers.

Terrell, F., Terrell, S.L., & Golin, S. (1977). Language productivity of black and white children in black versus white situations. *Language and Speech, 20,* 377–383.

Terrell, F., Terrell, S.L., & Miller, F. (1993). Level of cultural mistrust as a function of educational and occupational expectation among black students. *Adolescence, 28,* 573–578.

Terrell, F., Terrell, S.L., & Taylor, J. (1980). Effects of race of examiner and type of reinforcement on the intelligence test performance of lower-class clients. *Journal of Counseling Psychology, 31,* 371–375.

Terrell, F., Terrell, S.L., & Taylor, J. (1981). Effects of type of reinforcement on the intelligence test performance of retarded Black children. *Psychology in the Schools, 18,* 225–227.

Terrell, F., Terrell, S.L., & Taylor, J. (1988). The self-concept level of black adolescents with and without African names. *Psychology in the Schools, 25;* 65–70.

Terrell, S.L., & Terrell, F. (1993). African-American cultures. In D.E. Battle (Ed.), *Communication disorders in multicultural populations.* Boston: Andover.

Warren, R.L. (1969). Politics and the ghetto system. In R. L. Warren (Ed.), *Politics and the ghettos* (pp. 11–30). New York: Atherton Press.

Watkins, C.E., & Terrell, F. (1988). Mistrust level and its effects on counseling expectation in black client-white counselor relationships. *Journal of Counseling Psychology, 35,* 194–197.

Watkins, C.E., Terrell, F., Miller, F.S., & Terrell, S.L. (1989). Cultural mistrust and its effects on expectational variables in black client-white counselor relationships. *Journal of Counseling Psychology, 36,* 447–450.

White, J.L. (1984). *The psychology of blacks: An Afro:American perspective.* Englewood Cliffs; NJ: Prentice Hall.

Appendix A

Revised Cultural Mistrust Inventory (CMI)

Enclosed are some statements concerning beliefs, opinions, and attitudes about Blacks. Read each statement carefully, and give your honest feelings about the beliefs and attitudes expressed. Indicate the extent to which you agree by using the following scale:

0 1	2 3	4 5	6 7	8 9
Not in the least agree	Slightly agree	Moderately agree	Very much agree	Entirely agree

The higher the number you choose for the statement, the more you agree with that statement. For example if you "moderately agree" with a statement, you would choose the numbers 4 and 5 which appear above the label "Moderately agree." If you chose number 5, this means you agree more with the statement than if you had chosen number 4. The same principle applies for the other labels. The higher the number you chose, the more you agree with the statement.

Finally, there are no right or wrong answers, only what is right for you. If in doubt, mark the number that seems most nearly to express your present feelings about the statement. Please answer all items.

1. Whites are usually fair to all people regardless of race. (BW–)
2. White teachers teach subjects so that it favors whites. (ET+)
3. White teachers are more likely to slant the subject matter to make blacks look inferior. (ET+)
4. White teachers deliberately ask Black students questions which are difficult so they will fail. (ET+)

From Terrell, F., & Terrell, S.L. (1981). An inventory to measure cultural mistrust among blacks. *Western Journal of Black Studies, 5,* 180–185; reprinted with minor revisions by permission.

5. There is no need for a Black person to work hard to get ahead financially because whites will take what you earn anyway. (BW+)
6. Black citizens can rely on white lawyers to defend them to the best of his or her ability. (PL−)
7. Black parents should teach their children not to trust white teachers. (ET+)
8. White politicians will promise blacks a lot but deliver little. (PL+)
9. White policemen will slant a story to make Blacks appear guilty. (PL+)
10. White politicians usually can be relied on to keep the promises they make to Blacks. (PL−)
11. Blacks should be suspicious of a white person who tries to be friendly. (IR+)
12. Whether you should trust a person or not is not based on his race. (IR−1)
13. Probably the biggest reason whites want to be friendly with Blacks is so they can take advantage of them. (BW+)
14. A Black person can usually trust his or her white co-workers. (BW−)
15. If a white person is honest in dealing with Blacks, it is because of fear of being caught. (BW+)
16. A Black person can not trust a white judge to evaluate him or her fairly. (PL+)
17. A Black person can feel comfortable making a deal with a white person simply by a handshake. (BW−)
18. Whites deliberately pass laws designed to block the progress of Blacks. (PL+)
19. There are some whites who are trustworthy enough to have as close friends. (IR−)
20. Blacks should not have anything to do with whites since they can not be trusted. (IR+)
21. It is best for Blacks to be on their guard when among whites. (IR+)
22. Of all ethnic groups, whites are really the Indian-givers. (IR+)
23. White friends are least likely to break their promise. (IR−)
24. Blacks should be cautious about what they say in the presence of whites since whites will try to use it against them. (IR+)
25. Whites can rarely be counted on to do what they say. (IR+)
26. Whites are usually honest with Blacks. (IR−)
27. Whites are as trustworthy as members of any other ethnic group. (IR−)
28. Whites will say one thing and do another. (IR−)
29. White politicians will take advantage of Blacks every chance they get. (PL+)
30. When a white teacher asks a Black student a question, it is usually to get information which can be used against him or her. (ET+)
31. White policemen can be relied on to exert an effort to apprehend those who commit crimes against Blacks. (PL−)
32. Black students can talk to a white teacher in confidence without fear that the teacher will use it against him or her later. (ET−)
33. Whites will usually keep their word. (IR−)
34. White policemen usually do not try to trick Blacks into admitting they committed a crime which they didn't. (PL−)

35. There is no need for Blacks to be more cautious with white businessmen than with anyone else. (BW–)
36. There are some white businessmen who are honest in business transactions with Blacks. (BW–)
37. White store owners, salesmen, and other white businessmen tend to cheat Blacks whenever they can. (BW+)
38. Since whites can't be trusted in business, the old saying "one in the hand is worth two in the bush" is a good policy to follow. (BW+)
39. Whites who establish business in Black communities do so only so that they can take advantage of Blacks. (BW+)
40. Blacks have often been deceived by white politicians. (PL+)
41. White politicians are equally honest with Blacks and whites. (PL–)
42. Blacks should not confide in whites because they will use it against you. (IR+)
43. A Black person can loan money to a white person and feel confident it will be repaid. (BW–)
44. White businessmen usually will not try to cheat Blacks. (BW–)
45. White business executives will steal the ideas of their Black employees. (BW+)
46. A promise from a white is about as good as a three dollar bill. (BW+)
47. Blacks should be suspicious of advice by white politicians. (PL+)
48. If a Black student tries, he will get the grade he deserves from a white teacher. (ET–)

Key: PL refers to items composing the Politics and Law subscale. ET refers to items composing the Education and Training subscale. BW refers to items composing Business and Work subscale. IR refers to items composing the Interpersonal Relations subscale. Items followed by a positive sign (+) are positively keyed. Items followed by a negative sign (–) are reverse keyed.

Appendix B

Children's Cultural Mistrust Inventory (CCMI)

Rate the extent to which you agree with each of the statements below using the following scale: "1 = No," "2 = Sometimes," "3 = Yes."

1. Most White children will give your toys back if you lend them to him or her. (C–)
2. Most White teachers can be trusted to give you the grade you deserve. (A–)
3. White policemen will help you if you need it. (A–)
4. A White child will pay your money back if you lend him or her some. (C–)
5. A White store owner will try to cheat you. (A+)
6. Most white children do not keep their promise. (C+)
7. Most white people will promise you one thing and then do something else. (A+)
8. A White child will keep a secret. (C–)
9. White children cannot be trusted. (C+)
10. White children usually do not tell the truth. (C+)
11. Most white children cheat when they play games. (C+)
12. A white child will accuse you of something you didn't do. (C+)
13. A White child will try to steal your toys. (C+)
14. Most White people are honest. (A–)
15. Most White people do not keep their promises. (A+)
16. White policemen will accuse you of something you didn't do. (A+)
17. Most White people tell fibs. (A+)
18. If you work for a White person and they promise to pay you for the work, they will keep their word. (A–)
19. If you lose something and a White child finds it, he will try to return it. (C–)

Key: C refers to mistrust of White children. A refers to mistrust of White authority figures. Items followed by a positive sign (+) are positively keyed. Items followed by a negative sign (–) are negatively keyed.

From Terrell, F., & Terrell, S.L. (1996). An inventory for assessing cultural mistrust in black children. In R.L. Jones (Ed.), *Handbook of tests and measurements for black populations* (Vol. 1, pp. 245–248). Hampton, VA: Cobb & Henry Publishers; reprinted with minor revisions by permission.

5

Issues in Service Delivery to African American Children

Lynda R. Campbell

The expectations and demands placed on children in schools are congruent with the values, traditions, and behaviors of the middle-class mainstream society. Hence, schools in the United States are designed to prepare middle-class children to participate in their own cultures (Iglesias, 1985a; Saville-Troike, 1979). The curricula and instructional approaches in schools are organized so that the academic skills that middle-class children have learned at home are reinforced and practiced. Thus, middle-class children have significant school-comparable experiences prior to entrance (Heath, 1982, 1991). They would not be as successful in school if instruction were in a language variety other than their own and if the curriculum content, instructional procedures, and classroom interaction rules were incompatible with those from their home community culture (Iglesias, 1985a). The African American culture often has been viewed by educational institutions as inferior and interfering with the intellectual and emotional development of children and hindering the development of lifestyles and values typical of mainstream U.S. culture (Ramirez, 1988). Educational practices based on the assimilationist melting pot philosophy disregard cultural and linguistic differences and require conformity. Instead of reinforcing and utilizing children's diverse culture and languages, most practices in schools either ignore or attempt to eradicate them while imposing their own.

73

A child's primary language or dialect is the variety the child learned first in the home. For many children from the African American culture, this variety is termed African American English (AAE) and is also referred to as Black English Vernacular, Black Dialect, Black English, and Ebonics. Educational practices based on a culturally pluralistic philosophy regard children's home community culture and linguistic variety as legitimate systems to be maintained. In addition, the school setting is seen as providing opportunities and strategies to acquire the linguistic standard, school discourse variety, and other appropriate services to achieve academic success. Children who speak AAE are currently described as speaking a different dialect or language in comparison to Standard American English (SAE). Although "language difference" has replaced "language deficit," when the language difference is AAE it is often treated as a deficit. Furthermore, Ogbu (1982) and others (Baugh, 1995; Smitherman, 1988) have stated that although linguistic variations may be categorized as "differences" not all varieties are perceived as equal: Some provide access (or the perception of access) to educational, economic, and social rewards, whereas others, such as AAE, do not.

Competence in the linguistic standard and school discourse is a strong indicator of the likelihood of eventual academic success. Many children from the African American culture either are not successful academically or are not achieving their maximum potential. This lack of academic success is a contributor to African American children's increased failure to complete high school or their completion of high school with marginal competencies in those skills expected to have been acquired through the educational system (Gay, 1993). Thus, strategies are needed to ensure that AAE-speaking students will not fail academically because of linguistic differences.

Barriers to the provision of quality educational services to children from the African American culture include ethnocentric attitudes of professionals; low expectations and negative attitudes toward African American students, their families, and communities; lack of professional training regarding cultural and linguistic diversity; test bias and misdiagnosis; monocultural educational materials and curricula; inappropriate and inadequate instructional techniques; and differential disciplinary and reward systems (Campbell, 1986, 1993, 1994; Campbell, Brennan & Steckol, 1992; Campbell & Taylor, 1992a, 1992b; Ford, 1992; Gay, 1989, 1993; Menyuk & Menyuk, 1988; Ogbu, 1982; Ramirez, 1988).

A goal of Goals 2000: Educate America Act of 1994 (PL 103-227) is for 90% of the U.S. population to graduate from high school. Because language and communication skills are the foundation for learning, adequate proficiency in these areas is crucial for the achievement of Goals 2000 (American Speech-Language-Hearing Association, 1993). This goal can be achieved only if barriers to academic success are removed and educational practices are improved. School practices that provide children from the African American culture, both with and without communication disorders, access to quality educational opportunities and experiences must be developed and systematically adopted.

THE KEY ROLE OF SPEECH-LANGUAGE PATHOLOGISTS IN EDUCATIONAL OUTCOMES

Speech-language pathologists delivering services to children from the African American culture in educational settings will likely function in diagnostic, therapeutic, and access roles in various situations at different points based on students' needs. Speech-language pathologists employed in schools are frequently required to determine whether children have speech and language disorders that may be causing or contributing to their academic difficulties. When African American children struggle academically, teachers often suspect that they have special education needs and refer them to speech-language pathologists for testing. On the one hand, African American children may do poorly on standardized language tests because of linguistic and cultural differences and thus may be inappropriately placed based on such measures, resulting in overdiagnosis—that is, the inclusion in special education of children without communication disorders. On the other hand, African American children may have communication disorders that are interpreted as communication differences because current tests and practices are not sensitive enough to distinguish cultural and linguistic differences from disorders, resulting in underdiagnosis—that is, failure to include children with communication disorders.

When speech-language pathologists perform an access role, service delivery focuses on analyzing the situation (e.g., the classroom) and then working within it to design ways in which a child, given the communication difference, disorder, or both, can function satisfactorily. Access services may include the development of prompting strategies, environmental modifications, modification of how information is presented in the context in which the child must function, supporting others (teachers, aides, related-services providers, and families), advocacy, and coordination. As the child moves from grade to grade, needs for communication access will change.

The diagnostic role requires speech-language pathologists to distinguish cultural and linguistic differences from disorders of communication. Most developmental data available are based on typical white, mainstream children from middle-class backgrounds. Speech-language pathologists should be aware of the limitations of using these data as the norm for all children. Definitions of normal and disordered communication should be determined from the perspective of the child's speech community.

Taylor (1986a) provides a conceptual framework for the study of normal and disordered communication composed of four processes and outcomes that operate within the constraints of culture: 1) developmental processes, 2) precursors of communication pathology, 3) assessment and diagnosis, and 4) treatment.

Developmental processes serve as the underlying basis for understanding normal and disordered communication within the cultural group. They include internal and external cultural outcomes. Internal cultural outcomes include adult—

child interactions within the culture; indigenous cognitive acquisition, language, and communication systems; and development of adult language and communicative competence. External cultural outcomes are reflective of the extent to which persons interact outside of their indigenous culture. They may foster a second cognitive, language, and communication system, depending on a number of variables, including age, amount of exposure, and motivation.

Precursors of communication pathology include "culturally defined pathological behaviors" (Taylor, 1986a, p. 14), as well as several biological, nutritional, social, genetic, and psychological etiologies of impaired communication. Assessment, diagnosis, and treatment involve clinical issues of diagnosis and management. The outcomes from these processes must be conceptually formed based on the cultural and linguistic norms of the child's speech community.

When a child's speech and language skills differ significantly from those of peers from a similar cultural and linguistic background, a communication disorder should be suspected. A valid assessment of the child's speech and language is necessary (Wyatt & Seymour, 1990). Because a single sample of a child's speech in any one situation cannot be considered representative of a child's repertoire, speech-language pathologists must examine the child's use of speech and language in a variety of communicative situations with different listeners and tasks. Otherwise, the resulting assessment may be inaccurate and the consequent placement and delivery of services to the child inappropriate.

Figure 1 depicts what may happen to a child with a communication disorder depending on the appropriateness of the clinical decisions made by the speech-language pathologist. A failure to recognize the communication disorder (inappropriate classification) may result in the communication impairment becoming more disabling with the potential for psychological manifestations and reduced academic performance or academic failure. Recognition of the communication disorder (appropriate classification) may be followed by appropriate or inappropriate services. Appropriate services include proper goals, objectives, and techniques based on the communication impairment and needs of the child and will likely result in ameliorating or reducing the communication impairment and improving the potential for increased academic achievement. Inappropriate services include goals, objectives, and techniques that are either not culturally sensitive or not based on the communication impairment and needs of the child and may result in the much the same outcome as an inappropriate classification.

General Assessment Issues

Assessment instruments and procedures used to evaluate and determine "normality" and "abnormality" must be related to an appropriate normative cultural referent. Culturally sensitive valid assessment instruments and procedures are necessary to ensure that African American children who have communication disorders receive the services they need in order to achieve educational success and that those without communication disorders are not penalized because of cultural and

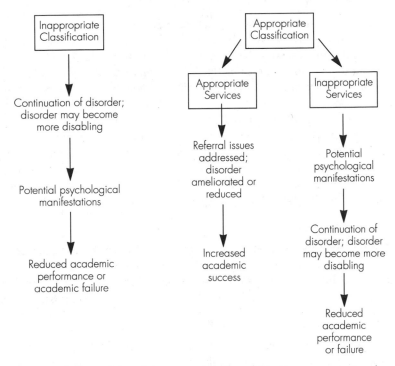

Figure 1.   Potential effects of clinical decision making for a child with a communication disorder.

linguistic differences. Hence, speech-language pathologists providing services to children from the African American culture must be familiar with the African American language and culture as well as norms of the children's local speech community.

Assessment criteria of the speech and language for children from the African American culture should include 1) a description of the children's functional communication skills; 2) a composite description of the children's communication skills, linguistic structures, and functional usage of speech and language in all social domains; and 3) caregiver and teacher interviews conducted regarding the children's communication skills in the home community and classroom situations (supplemented, when possible, by home and classroom observations).

Information obtained from the interviews and observations should be used in conjunction with data on performance on formal and informal measures, including speech and language samples. As stated, a child's performance should be compared with the performance of peers from a similar speech community.

General Testing Issues

A lack of developmental and normative communicative data makes it difficult for speech-language pathologists to differentiate between communication differences and disorders. Most speech and language assessment instruments are designed to measure facility with SAE. An African American child's background and life experiences, as well as school curricula exposure, may differ enough from that of the test standardization sample that the child is penalized for a lack of knowledge outside of his or her realm of experience. Furthermore, a child's cultural communicative norms may differ enough from that of the test developer and examiner that the child may appear "delayed" when, in reality, the child's communicative skills are comparable to those of peers from a similar speech community. Exclusive use of standardized assessment instruments, a lack of familiarity with test-taking situations, and situational, examiner, and format biases are also barriers to be removed in the assessment process (Lund & Duchan, 1993; Roseberry-McKibbin, 1994; Taylor & Payne, 1983).

Assessment Alternative

Instrument Modification A number of researchers have suggested some possible alternatives to formal, standardized testing for assessing the speech and language of children from the African American culture as well as other culturally and linguistically diverse backgrounds (Seymour & Miller-Jones, 1981; Stockman, 1986; Taylor & Payne, 1983; Washington & Craig, 1992). Some have proposed adapting and revising standardized assessment instruments to allow developing local test norms, deleting biased test items, changing bias stimuli to parallel forms that are more appropriate, accepting culturally appropriate responses, and changing scoring to permit dialect alternatives to be considered correct (Taylor & Payne, 1983; Taylor, Payne, & Anderson, 1987; Washington & Craig, 1992). Vaughn-Cooke (1983, 1986) provide an in-depth analysis of the strengths and limitations of various alternatives to traditional standardized assessment instruments.

Modifying testing procedures has also been suggested as a method for improving assessment (Erickson & Iglesias, 1986). Such modifications as suggested in the literature include rewording instructions, allowing additional response time, recording all responses, rescoring and giving credit for linguistic variations, offering continued testing beyond the ceiling, developing practice items, changing stimuli, repeating stimuli more often than specified, completing the test in several sessions, having the child explain why the incorrect answer was selected, and having the child name and point to pictures in receptive tasks (Erickson & Iglesias, 1986; Kayser, 1989).

It is important to realize that each of the alternatives has limitations and must be used with caution when interpreting and using the results. Modifying and adapting a test change the validity and reliability of the original instrument; therefore, original test norms should not be used. Furthermore, the use of an alternative procedure and its limitations should be clearly stated in evaluation reports.

Informal Assessment Researchers have also indicated the importance of using informal assessment procedures. The use of criteria reference testing allows a child's performance to be compared against an identified criterion (Seymour &

Miller-Jones, 1981). Speech and language samples provide the opportunity to examine many parameters of communication (Stockman, 1986). Dynamic assessment provides a measure of the child's ability to learn by identifying problem areas, changing the environment, evaluating over time, and comparing performance and modifiability (Kayser, 1989; Pena, Quinn, & Iglesias, 1992; Roseberry-McKibbin, 1994). Multiple observations in naturalistic contexts and evaluating communication holistically by focusing on functional aspects allow the examination of a child's communication behaviors in daily situations (Cheng & Langdon, 1993; Roseberry-McKibbin, 1993, 1994). Other informal mechanisms for eliciting information about a child's communication behaviors include the use of questionnaires and ethnographic interviews involving teachers and family members.

In educational settings, the goal of assessment is to describe the learner's condition, to make predictions, to make educational placements based on forecasts, and to match educational services. Perhaps assessment instruments and procedures that evaluate children's ability to learn rather than their amount of exposure to, and knowledge of, language will be helpful in alleviating some of the problems with present language tests, methods, and procedures as described. If the focus of assessment changes, then the role of the evaluator will change to one who seeks to evaluate the nature of interventions required to change the status, not the learner's present status and exposure (Hilliard, 1981).

LANGUAGE SOCIALIZATION

To become communicatively competent within the African American culture, children must acquire appropriate communicative forms and knowledge, such as how these forms are expected to vary based on factors such as the speaker and situation. Caregivers in all cultures guide their children's participation in the community and support their learning. Communicative interactions in the home are reflective of child-rearing attitudes and practices (Health, 1991; Iglesias, 1985b). Desirable skills and values vary greatly across cultures. Within and across cultures, different communication skills are viewed as important, different teaching approaches are valued and considered appropriate, and different people and situations are available for participation in teaching (Bauman, 1971; Crago, 1992; Heath, 1991).

Acquiring language and becoming a culturally competent communicator are intertwined processes (Crago, 1992). Although all societies have criteria for categorizing communication on a continuum from appropriate to inappropriate, in order to be considered culturally competent a speaker must use language correctly in terms of social restraints (Gumperz, 1974, 1982). Often, mistakes resulting from not being a culturally competent communicator convey semantic messages that are more than just inaccurate—they may misinform the listener about personal attributes of the speaker. In fact, the criteria for judging linguistic behaviors as polite, insincere, aggressive, stupid, and so forth vary across cultures (Bauman, 1971; Menyuk & Menyuk, 1988).

Through interactions with family, peers, and other persons in their home community, African American children learn the discourse rules of their speech community. Rules regarding who may speak to whom, when to talk and how much to say, what can be talked about, when to be silent, who is allowed to speak first, and what words and structures may be used are all examples of ways of speaking that children must understand and in which they must demonstrate cultural proficiency (Heath, 1982; Ward, 1971). Thus, children must possess knowledge of culturally acceptable behaviors and the consequences of inappropriate ones (Gumperz, 1982; Rees & Gerber, 1992).

Schooling presents African American children with another set of role relationships where competency is required. Participation in the educational process requires most African American children to acquire a second set of cultural and communication norms. Researchers have documented the adverse effects of school culture and practices that are discontinuous with the culture and communication norms of children from diverse backgrounds such as the African American culture (Campbell, 1993, 1994; Cecil, 1988; Crago, 1992; Gee, 1986, 1989; Heath, 1982, 1991; Smitherman, 1988).

Ethnography focuses on studying the culture of a group by examining behavior, knowledge, and artifacts. In educational and clinical settings, ethnography can be used to reveal the culture of the classroom, speech and language therapy sessions, home, community, and other settings. Ethnographic observations and open-ended interviews can provide insights into discontinuities between the cultures of students and their home community and the cultures of students and teachers functioning within the classroom (Kovarsky & Maxwell, 1992; Westby & Erickson, 1992).

USING ETHNOGRAPHIC INTERVIEWS

Speech-language pathologists and teachers can investigate elements of culture by either observing or participating in ethnographic interviews. Based on the information gathered through the interviews and observations, inferences about aspects of a particular culture can be made. However, these inferences should be confirmed or refuted through the use of additional interviews, observations, and triangulation processes by comparing and contrasting information from a variety of data sources (Kovarsky & Maxwell, 1992; Westby & Erickson, 1992).

Ethnographic interviews can be used to gather data as needed throughout the continuum of service delivery. Ethnographic interviews of the student, teacher, and student's family can provide data important to the preassessment through therapeutic intervention or disposition phases for a child who possesses a communication disorder. For a child who is later diagnosed as not possessing a communication disorder, the information collected in the interviews may provide insights regarding institutional needs. Of course, for a child who has a communication disorder, the information collected in the interviews will provide insights and directions for meeting the child's communication needs. Various aspects of the information gained from interviewing parents and teachers must also derive from interaction with the child. The selection of informants (interviewees) must be determined in such a way that the interviewer can "ask the right questions to the right people in the right ways" so that useful and appropriate data can be collected (Westby, 1990, p. 101).

GENERAL ETHNOGRAPHIC INTERVIEW PRINCIPLES

Developing rapport, using descriptive questions, and carefully wording questions are important facets of the ethnographic interview process (Patton, 1980; Spradley, 1979). Developing rapport involves establishing a sense of trust between the interviewer and informant. Restating the purpose of the interview and what the interviewee says, as well as asking questions focusing on discovering communicative use based on the informant's experiences, feelings, perceptions, and perspectives, not meaning, are methods designed to facilitate and maintain rapport. Descriptive questions allow the interviewer to learn what the informants consider important in their world and how they perceive their world. Descriptive questions include grand tour, mini-tour, example, experience, and native language questions. Grand tour questions are designed to encourage the informant to talk about a broad experience. Mini-tour questions are similar to grand tour except that the person is asked to describe a specific experience. Example questions are more specific than grand and mini-tour questions. Example questions take some experience or idea and ask for an illustration. Experience questions ask about experiences in a specific setting and tend to elicit narrations about atypical circumstances. Native language questions ask people to use terms they would most commonly use while the interviewer seeks to understand what these terms mean to the informants.

The wording of questions is crucial and can both facilitate the development and maintenance of rapport and achieve the interview objective (Patton, 1980; Westby, 1990). A major task of the ethnographic interview is to keep the informant talking. Hence, open-ended, rather than closed-ended, questions, as well as presupposition questions, can be used effectively. The interviewer must maintain control of the interview so that the desired information is obtained. Furthermore, the interviewer must ask one question at a time and use transition, summarizing, and direct announcement prefatory formats to alert the informant to the nature of the upcoming question (Patton, 1980). Westby (1990) provides a detailed discussion of developing rapport, the use of descriptive questions, and the wording of questions and their application in a family-focused service-delivery program. In addition to the factors mentioned above, the following factors must be considered during an ethnographic interview (Patton, 1980; Roseberry-McKibbin, 1994; Spradley, 1979; Westby, 1990):

1. The interviewer should make the purpose of the interview clear. The purpose will likely need to be stated several times throughout the interview.
2. The informant must clearly understand the purpose of the interview and feel that some benefit will be received by participating.
3. The interviewer should "ask the right questions to the right people in the right ways" so that data collected can be useful in meeting the determined needs (Westby, 1990, p. 101).
4. The interviewer must appear interested and respectful of the information shared, even if one does not agree with it.
5. During an interview, the interviewer and the informant should have ample opportunities to ask and answer questions—that is, to function as both interviewer and informant.
6. Professionals should be aware of, and attempt to minimize, the potential effect of perceptions and situational variables on the ways interviewers and informants respond to each other.
7. The more intimate the question, the more reserved and cautious the informant may become. Certain information may be excluded from outsiders.

ACQUIRING SCHOOL CULTURE INFORMATION

An ethnographic interview can be used to collect data regarding the culture of a classroom. The informant may be the teacher, aide, or student, depending on the purpose and type of information to be collected. In the diagnostic and therapeutic stages of service delivery, the interview may focus on the behaviors of both the classroom teacher and the particular student. In the clinical service delivery process, an ethnographic interview focusing on the teacher will likely include questions about the classroom norms and rules. Questions regarding the teacher's perceptions and interpretations of the performance of the student referred or receiving services as well as feelings and attitudes toward SAE, AAE, and the African American culture will also likely be included.

An ethnographic interview focusing on a particular student from the African American culture would likely include questions about the language used in the classroom and by whom; the child's perceptions of self-communication skills and behaviors; the child's perceptions of the teachers and peers' perceptions of the child's communication and behaviors; the child's knowledge of classroom rules, discourse, and appropriate behaviors; the child's feelings and attitudes toward English and the home language variety; and attitudes toward the mainstream culture, home community culture, general education, and special education.

ACQUIRING HOME COMMUNITY CULTURE INFORMATION

An ethnographic interview is an important part of the data collection process that allows the interviewer to learn about a child's cultural group. The interview should consider the role of children in their families and how they learn in their home environments (Westby, 1990). The informants, usually parents or a significant other, need to clearly understand the purpose of the interview. An ethnographic interview focusing on an African American child's home community would likely include questions about the language used in the home and by whom; family and community perceptions of the child's communication skills and comparison to peers and siblings; feelings and attitudes toward English; attitudes toward the mainstream culture, general education, and special education; cultural ceremonies, rituals, and other important events; and ways of feeling and thinking (Lund & Duchan, 1993; Roseberry-McKibbin, 1994; Westby & Erickson, 1992).

INTERVENTION

Federal legislation, current philosophy in early childhood education, educational reform proposals, and other initiatives advocate parental partnerships and family-centered intervention to meet the social, emotional, and academic needs of children. Intervention goals, objectives, and techniques for a child from the African American culture who possesses a communication disorder must reflect the child's needs and the family's interests, priorities, and values. Activities and techniques that are culturally appropriate and compatible with the child's learning style preferences and orientations must be used. Many African American children with a communication disorder may also speak AAE. In such cases, intervention goals, objectives, and procedures must reflect the communication components that are impaired. The speech-language pathologist must clearly distinguish those components that are reflective of the communication impairment from those that are features of AAE. Only goals regarding communication impairments are appropriate for intervention. Clinical techniques used in intervention for communication impairments should not jeopardize the integrity of a child's AAE variety (Campbell, 1993, 1994). Hence, bidialectal techniques should be incorporated in intervention procedures for children who are AAE speakers.

Therapeutic intervention targets for communication impairments should be based on the expected linguistic standard for children from the African American culture. On the one hand, it is not appropriate for a speech-language pathologist to teach the child what is assumed to be the child's cultural way of speaking. On the other hand, if a child's response to a target is correct, although it is a feature of AAE and not SAE, the child's response must be viewed as acceptable.

While targeting communication impairments, speech-language pathologists may feel that it is helpful to facilitate acquisition of SAE by requiring children from the African American culture to restate AAE verbalizations in SAE to demonstrate bidialectal proficiency. Speech-language pathologists are cautioned against the use of this practice. Children are enrolled in speech-language therapy because of communication impairments that tend to result in the focus of therapy emphasizing "remediation of errors" (Kovarsky & Maxwell, 1992; Ripich & Panagos,

1985). Because of the speech-language pathologist's frequent role as "evaluator" and the child's role as "error maker" (Kovarsky & Maxwell, 1992; Ripich & Panagos, 1985), requiring a child to code-switch and restate utilizing the linguistic standard will likely result in the child interpreting the AAE variety as an "error" to be corrected.

SERVICE DELIVERY APPROACHES

The principal service delivery approaches described by Miller (1989) within educational settings are applicable if they meet the needs of the child. These approaches include delivery of services in a self-contained classroom, collaborative instruction, one-on-one classroom-based intervention with selected students, and consultant participation. Many of these approaches are used in most schools to deliver speech and language services to children with communication disorders. Staff, curriculum, and program development are also service delivery possibilities. The selection of a particular service delivery approach for a child with a communication disorder from the African American culture should be based on the needs of the child. In fact, these service delivery approaches may be combined as necessary.

The consultant, staff, curriculum, and program development approaches are indirect service delivery possibilities for children from the African American culture. These approaches are applicable for children from the African American culture with as well as without communication disorders. Although not often considered, intervention is needed when children have been referred for special education testing because of cultural communication differences. In such a situation, intervention involving the specific teachers may be conducted through a series of consultations. These indirect approaches afford a venue for speech-language pathologists to provide in-services regarding speech and language disorders and differences, second dialect instruction, and other programs and strategies designed to enhance children's academic success by meeting their needs and the needs of their families and teachers.

Standard English as a Second Dialect Instructional Support

The major role of speech-language pathologists is to provide speech and language services to persons who possess a communication disorder. Speakers of AAE are often mistakenly perceived as having a communication disorder (Bauman, 1971; Campbell, 1992a, 1993, 1994; Taylor & Payne, 1983; Taylor et al., 1987). The Social Dialects Position Paper (American Speech-Language-Hearing Association, 1987) indicates that speech-language pathologists possessing appropriate knowledge and training regarding second dialect instruction may provide elective services for persons who want to become more proficient in SAE. Speech-language pathologists may serve as consultants to assist educators in utilizing features of a dialect to facilitate the learning of SAE as a second dialect. Speech-language pathologists may also provide direct instruction in SAE as a second dialect as an elective service.

With appropriate knowledge and training, speech-language pathologists can collaborate with teachers in teaching the desired competency in SAE without eradicating students' AAE (Campbell, 1993, 1994; Taylor, 1986b; Wolfram, 1993). Because AAE speakers may also have communication disorders, speech-language pathologists must be careful to distinguish linguistic variations from pathological forms.

Teaching Standard English as a Second Dialect

Teaching the linguistic standard as a second dialect for African American children involves increasing children's SAE skills as a second language system—the first system being AAE. The major goals of second dialect instruction utilizing a bidialectal approach are the abilities to speak, write, read, and auditorily comprehend both the first and second varieties (Taylor, 1986b).

Teaching the linguistic standard as a second dialectal variety requires knowledge and competency in the following areas: linguistic rules of the dialect, linguistic contrasting analysis procedures, and the effects of attitudes toward dialects (American Speech-Language-Hearing Association, 1987). The second dialect instructional program must be culturally based; verbal and nonverbal communication must be appropriate for different audiences, situations, and topics taught; and sensitivity to the aspirations and needs of the children must be projected. The instructional program should respect and build on the language, culture, and learning styles of students from the African American culture while responding to the need to transmit specific skills and competencies in SAE. Second dialect instruction must also be based on a model that involves all aspects of the curriculum (Taylor, 1986b). Various models, principles, and techniques developed for teaching SAE as a second dialect consider the learner's culture and facilitate code switching (Campbell, 1993, 1994; Taylor, 1986b; Wolfram, 1993). The second dialect instructional approach selected must be one that is culturally based and meets the needs of the children.

ISSUES ABOUT AFRICAN AMERICAN ENGLISH

Prior to implementing second dialect instruction, speech-language pathologists and teachers must identify and remove any misconceptions regarding AAE (Campbell, 1994). Professionals should be aware of ethnocentric tendencies, such as the tendency to use one's own linguistic variety as the standard, resulting frequently in a negative rating of differences (Campbell, 1994; Taylor, 1990; Westby, 1990). In addition, professionals may harbor myths and other inaccurate beliefs about SAE and AAE. These must be identified and removed prior to beginning second dialect instruction (Campbell, 1993, 1994; Campbell et al., 1992; Taylor, 1986b).

Instruction should also be linked to specific communicative purposes and situations for which the targeted skills can be used. Campbell (1993, 1994) suggests that the following practices may jeopardize the integrity of students' AAE by drawing a negative portrayal and interpretation of this variety compared with the school's form: using disordered terminology when referring to AAE; implying that AAE is an imperfect attempt at the linguistic standard; using stereotypical statements; using the linguistic standard as the only targeted variety; presenting information in a dichotomous manner; and providing reinforcement only for productions of the linguistic standard.

UNDERSTANDING AND INVOLVING FAMILIES

When working collaboratively with families, professionals must be prepared to encounter a variety of family structures, cultural traditions, gender role and status expectations, communication styles and norms, child-rearing practices, values, beliefs, attitudes, goals, and aspirations. For example, in some African American families, an older sibling may have certain educational and child-rearing responsibilities. In some families, parents may not "play" with the child; however, abundant interactions may be observed during other activities, such as meal preparation (Thomas, 1994). By knowing with whom the child interacts, the style of interaction, and the topics, professionals will likely develop appropriate goals and procedures that will fit into the family's routine.

Family structure is an important consideration in the development of home–school partnerships. Much research focuses on the disproportionate number of African American children in female-headed, single-parent families. Although such families are often defined as dysfunctional on the basis of marital status, a single-parent family structure in itself does not constitute dysfunctionality (Thomas, 1994). Another important area in the development of home–school partnerships is the interdependence and multigenerational character of many African American families. The involvement of extended family members and other kinship networks in child rearing within the African American culture requires that these persons be included in the structure of a parent–school partnership.

Families transmit and shape cultural attitudes, behaviors, and patterns. Effective home–school partnerships allow for the construction of a bridge to better meet the needs of the child, family, and school. Speech-language pathologists and teachers may establish collaborative relationships with the family of a student from the African American culture in order to identify and develop culturally appropriate educational and clinical goals and practices (Crago, 1992). Communication and collaboration with families must be respectful and mutually beneficial. Figure 2 depicts assumptions underlying communicative interactions between professionals and children from the African American culture and their families. Professionals should be aware of potential differences in knowledge, experience, and cognitive preferences. Differences in social rules and roles, as well

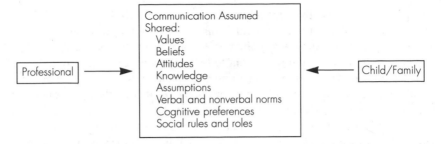

Figure 2.   Assumptions underlying communicative interactions.

as verbal and nonverbal communication rules used by professionals and children and their families, may adversely affect interpersonal dynamics. Professionals must become knowledgeable of each family's culture, including communication behaviors and norms, values, beliefs, and assumptions.

The involvement of African American families may span a continuum with information sharing at one end and actual family training at the other end. Caregivers, as a result of their experiences with educational systems, make assumptions about the communication and academic skills that will be required of their children in schools. Consciously or unconsciously, parents tend to teach these skills in interactions with their children (Iglesias, 1985a). These assumptions may or may not be comparable with the norms of the caregiver's community or educational institutions. Effective home–school collaboration can help alleviate this discontinuity.

Barriers to Successful Collaboration with Families

Ethnocentrism and Stereotyping   Each family is different. The degree of assimilation into and participation in the mainstream culture will vary by family. Professionals must recognize that variations exist within cultural groups and avoid stereotyping and ethnocentrism. If stereotypes are wrongly applied, their ability to identify the diversity of contributions families can make to their children's education becomes limited.

One-Way Notions of Differences   Collaborative relationships will likely result in professionals recognizing aspects of a student's family culture that differ from the school or professional culture. Professionals must be aware of one-way notions of differences. Just as aspects of a family's culture may appear different to professionals, aspects of professionals' culture may also appear different to the family. In most instances, differences are shades of similarities.

Unidirectional Relationships   The lack of recognition of the strength and validity of diverse cultures by many professionals has resulted in many home–school relationships being exclusively unidirectional (Bauman, 1971; Crago, 1992; Nelson, 1994). Typically, children and families from diverse backgrounds have borne the strain of change (Crago, 1992). Professionals who are able to alter their practices in ways that recognize the strength and validity of a family's culture will be able to create a successful family–school–child relationship.

Assumptions of Knowledge of School Professionals must be aware of the tendency to assume that families ought to be knowledgeable of school-appropriate behaviors and practices and be willing and able to incorporate these practices into their relationships. Parents are often unaware of the school discourse and communication demands placed on their children (Iglesias, 1985a). Most families want their children to succeed, even though they may not know how to assist. Professionals who know how to include families will have an increased likelihood of success (Nelson, 1994).

Hierarchical Authority Professionals should be aware of the tendency to propose solutions and strategies that are their own and not the family's. Professionals often enter relationships with families from a hierarchical position of authority. This fact may be due to a number of factors, including the specialized instructional training professionals receive and the organizational structure of schools. These factors have contributed to a belief that professionals are more knowledgeable and objective than parents; hence, parents may be expected to defer educational decision making to professionals and to take suggestions, often without question (Thomas, 1994). Such a hierarchical relationship ignores the adult nature of parent–teacher relationships and the wealth of knowledge and information that can be shared.

Potential Cultural Biases in Language Intervention Parent-Training Programs

Most normative studies of parent–child interactions have focused on white, middle-class, two-parent families. These normative studies shape the philosophy, goals, and techniques of most parent-training programs. In conversationally based parent-training programs, parents are taught strategies that are designed to encourage children's communication development. These strategies are based on parent–child research that relies on a number of assumptions regarding parent–child interactions (van Kleeck, 1994). One assumption is that parents are the child's primary contact and that the prevailing pattern of interaction in the family is dyadic. Another assumption is that the family values children talking a lot and initiating and directing conversations with adults. It is also assumed that the family believes adults should make conversational accommodations to young children and that children learn best as "equal" participants. These assumptions are illustrative of the cultural bias implicit in most parent–child interaction goals (Crago, 1992; Heath, 1991; Schieffelin & Eisenberg, 1984; Scollon & Scollon, 1981; van Kleeck, 1994; Ward, 1971). Furthermore, professionals may erroneously assume that the underlying assumptions of parent-training programs—which are based on white, middle-class studies of parent–child interactions—reveal natural, rather than culturally learned, behaviors and that the resulting goals are appropriate for all families (Ochs & Schieffelin, 1984; van Kleeck, 1994).

The factors briefly discussed here reflect issues that need to be addressed in conversationally based parent-training programs. Van Kleeck (1994) provides an extensive critique of potential cultural biases and clinical implications in conversationally based parent-training programs. Her critique explores parent–child interactions in the areas of social organization, value of talk, status, beliefs regarding intent, and teaching language to children.

Most conversationally based parent-training programs have been developed to reflect values, beliefs, and child-rearing behaviors not shared by all cultural groups (Crago, 1992; Heath, 1991; van Kleeck, 1994). In view of the limitations of these parent-training programs, van Kleeck (1994) offers three options. One option is for the parent-training program to remain unchanged and for the speech-language pathologist to determine its suitability for a particular family. A second option is to create a parent-training program designed to fit the family. A third option is to alter a current parent-training program to better fit a particular family. Professionals must use caution when applying the principles and strategies of conversationally based parent-training programs to parents from the African American culture as well as other diverse backgrounds. Of course, a fourth option is to not use a conversationally based parent-training program at all. Several other service delivery models are available and may be appropriate. Professionals should select the model that is most appropriate for meeting the needs of the child and family.

CONCLUSION

Although internal variation occurs, children acquire the cognitive, social, linguistic, and communicative behaviors and values of their culture. All cultures have criteria for categorizing various dimensions of communication on a continuum. Definitions of normal and disordered communication can be determined only from the perspective of a child's home community culture. A culturally appropriate valid assessment of a child's communication is necessary to distinguish between a communication disorder and communication difference. Such an assessment process should include both formal and informal measures and home and classroom cultural data. Techniques such as ethnographic interviews and observations can be used to gather home and classroom cultural data from the perspective of the informant. Beyond the assessment process, these data can be used throughout the continuum of service delivery based on the needs of the child.

Speech-language pathologists need to develop and maintain collaborative relationships with caregivers, teachers, and other specialists so that the needs of students can be met. Effective home–school partnerships provide an opportunity to bridge the gap between home and school to better meet the needs of the child, family, and school.

Language and communication skills are the foundation for learning. The development and adoption of service delivery practices that provide children from the African American culture, both with and without communication disorders, access to quality educational opportunities are essential. Challenges provide opportunities for change and thereby possibilities for improvement. Professionals can view their task as providing children from the African American culture the opportunity to learn and demonstrate newly acquired competencies while maintaining the development of the children's home community culture.

REFERENCES

American Speech-Language-Hearing Association, Committee on the Status of Racial Minorities. (1987). Social dialects position paper. *Asha, 29* (1), 45.

American Speech-Language-Hearing Association, Ad Hoc Committee on Changes in Education Policies and Practices. (1993). *Trends in changes in school reform and their effects on speech-language pathologists, audiologists, and students and communication disorders.* Unpublished technical report. Rockville, MD: Author.

Baugh, J. (1995). The law, linguistics, and education: Educational reform for African American language minority students. *Linguistics and Education, 7*(2), 87–105.

Bauman, R. (1971). An ethnographic framework for the investigation of communicative behaviors. *Asha, 3*(6), 334–340.

Campbell, L.R. (1986). A study of the comparability of master's level training and certification and needs of speech-language pathologists (Doctoral dissertation, Howard University, Washington, 1985). *Dissertation Abstract International, 46,* 10B. (University Microfilms No. 85–28, 727)

Campbell, L.R. (1993). Maintaining the integrity of children's home communicative variety: Speakers of Black English vernacular. *American Journal of Speech-Language Pathology, 2*(1), 11–12.

Campbell, L.R. (1994). Discourse diversity and Black English vernacular. In D.N. Ripich & N.A. Creaghead (Eds.), *School discourse problems* (pp. 93–131). San Diego, CA: Singular Publishing Group.

Campbell, L.R., Brennan, D.G., & Steckol, K.F. (1992). Preservice training to meet the needs of people from culturally diverse backgrounds. *Asha, 34,* 29–32.

Campbell, L.R., & Taylor, O.L. (1992a). ASHA certified speech-language pathologists: Perceived competency levels with selected skills. *Howard Journal of Communication, 3*(3 & 4), 163–176.

Campbell, L.R., & Taylor, O.L. (1992b). Perceived competencies of speech-language pathologists relative to the provision of services to culturally and linguistically diverse children. *Texas Journal of Audiology and Speech Pathology, 18,* 31–34.

Cecil, N.L. (1988). Black dialect and academic success: A study of teacher expectations. *Reading Improvement, 25*(1), 34–38.

Cheng, L.L., & Langdon, H.W. (1993, July). *Best practices in working with second language learners with possible language/learning problems: A collaborative approach between the clinician, school staff and the student's family.* Paper presented at the annual University of the Pacific Summer Colloquium, Stockton, CA.

Crago, M.B. (1992). Ethnography and language socialization: A cross-cultural perspective. *Topics in Language Disorders, 12*(3), 28–39.

Erickson, J.G., & Iglesias, A. (1986). Assessment of communication disorders in non-English proficient children. In O.L. Taylor (Ed.), *Nature of communication disorders in culturally and linguistically diverse populations* (pp. 181–217). San Diego, CA: College-Hill Press.

Ford, B.A. (1992). Multicultural education training for special educators working with African-American youth. *Exceptional Children, 59*(2), 107–114.

Gay, G. (1989). Ethnic minorities and educational equality. In J.A. Banks & C.A. McGee Banks (Eds.), *Multicultural education: Issues and perspectives* (pp. 167–188). Boston: Allyn & Bacon.

Gay, G. (1993). Ethnic minorities and educational equality. In J.A. Banks & C.A. McGee Banks (Eds.), *Multicultural education: Issues and perspectives* (2nd ed., pp. 171–194). Boston: Allyn & Bacon.

Gee, J.P. (1986). Orality and literacy: From the savage mind to ways with words. *TESOL Quarterly, 20,* 719–746.

Gee, J.P. (1989). Two styles of narrative construction and their linguistic and educational implications. *Discourse Processes, 12,* 287–307.

Goals 2000: Educate America Act of 1994, PL 103–227. 20 U.S.C.§ 5801 *et seq.*

Gumperz, J. (1974). Linguistic and social interaction in two communities. In B.G. Blount (Ed.), *Language, culture, and society* (pp. 250–266). Cambridge, MA: Winthrop Publishers.

Gumperz, J. (1982). *Discourse strategies: Studies in interactional sociolinguistics I.* New York: Cambridge University Press.

Heath, S.B. (1982). What no bedtime story means: Narrative skills at home and school. *Language and Society, 11,* 49–76.

Heath, S.B. (1991). *Ways with words: Language, life, and work in communities and classrooms.* New York: Cambridge University Press.

Hilliard, A.G., III. (1981). *Non-discriminatory testing of African-American children.* Washington, DC: Proceedings of the 1981 National Conference on the Exceptional Black Child, Council for Exceptional Children. (ERIC Document Reproduction Service No. ED 215 459)

Iglesias, A. (1985a). Communication in the home and classroom: Match or mismatch? *Topics in Language Disorders, 5*(4), 29–41.

Iglesias, A. (1985b). Cultural conflict in the classroom: The communicatively different child. In D.N. Ripich & F.M. Spinelli (Eds.), *School discourse problems* (pp. 79–96). San Diego, CA: College-Hill Press.

Kayser, H.G. (1989). Speech and language assessment of Spanish-English speaking children. *Language, Speech, and Hearing Services in Schools, 20*(3), 226–244.

Kovarsky, D., & Maxwell, M.M. (1992). Ethnography and the clinical setting: Communicative expectancies in clinical discourse. *Topics in Language Disorders, 12*(3), 76–84.

Lund, N.J., & Duchan, J.F. (1993). *Assessing children's language in naturalistic contexts* (3rd ed.). Englewood Cliffs, NJ: Prentice Hall.

Menyuk, P., & Menyuk, D. (1988). Communicative competence: A historical and cultural perspective. In J.S. Wurzel (Ed.), *Toward multiculturalism: A reader in multicultural education* (pp. 151–161). Yarmouth, ME: Intercultural Press.

Miller, L. (1989). Classroom based language intervention. *Language, Speech, and Hearing Services in Schools, 20,* 153–169.

Nelson, N.W. (1994, September). School-age language: Bumpy road or super-expressway to the next millennium? *American Journal of Speech-Language Pathology, 3*(3), 29–31.

Ochs, E., & Schieffelin, B.B. (1984). Language acquisition and socialization: Three developmental studies and their implications. In R.A. Shweder & R.A. LeVine (Eds.), *Culture theory: Essays on mind, self, and emotion* (pp. 276–322). New York: Cambridge University Press.

Ogbu, J. (1982). Cultural discontinuities and schooling. *Anthropology and Education Quarterly, 13*(4), 390–397.

Patton, M. (1980). *Qualitative evaluation methods.* Beverly Hills, CA: Sage Publications.

Pena, E., Quinn, R., & Iglesias, A. (1992). The application of dynamic methods to language assessment: A nonbiased procedure. *The Journal of Special Education, 26*(3), 269–280.

Ramirez, M., III. (1988). Culture and thought: Cognitive styles and cultural democracy. In J.S. Wurzel (Ed.), *Toward multiculturalism: A reader in multicultural education* (pp. 198–206). Yarmouth, ME: Intercultural Press.

Rees, N.S., & Gerber, S. (1992). Ethnography and communication: Social-role relations. *Topics in Language Disorders, 12*(3), 15–27.

Ripich, D.N., & Panagos, J.M. (1985). Accessing children's knowledge of sociolinguistic rules for speech therapy lessons. *Journal of Speech and Hearing Disorders, 50,* 335–346.

Roseberry-McKibbin, C. (1993). *Bilingual classroom communication profile.* Oceanside, CA: Academic Communication Associates.

Roseberry-McKibbin, C. (1994, September). Assessment and intervention for children with limited English proficiency and language disorders. *American Journal of Speech-Language Pathology, 3*(3), 77–88.

Saville-Troike, M. (1979). Culture, language, and education. In H.T. Trueba & C. Barnett-Mizrahi (Eds.), *Bilingual multicultural education and the professional: From theory to practice* (pp. 139–148). Rowley, MA: Newberry House.

Schieffelin, B., & Eisenberg, A. (1984). Cultural variation in children's conversations. In R. Schiefelbusch & J. Pickar (Eds.), *The acquisition of communicative competence* (pp. 377–420). Baltimore: University Park Press.

Scollon, R., & Scollon, S. (1981). *Narrative, literacy, and face in interethnic communication.* Norwood, NJ: Ablex.

Seymour, H.N., & Miller-Jones, D. (1981). Language and cognitive assessment of black children. *Speech and Language: Advances in Basic Research and Practice, 6,* 203–263.

Smitherman, G. (1988). Discriminatory discourse on Afro-American speech. In G. Smitherman & T. Van Dijk (Eds.), *Discourse and discrimination* (pp. 144–175). Detroit, MI: Wayne State University Press.

Spradley, J. (1979). *The ethnographic interview.* New York: Holt, Rinehart & Winston.

Stockman, I.J. (1986). Language acquisition in culturally diverse populations: The black child as a case study. In O.L. Taylor (Ed.), *Nature of communication disorders in culturally and linguistically diverse populations* (pp. 117–155). San Diego, CA: College-Hill Press.

Taylor, O.L. (1986a). Issues, historical perspectives and conceptual framework. In O.L. Taylor (Ed.), *Treatment of communication disorders in culturally and linguistically diverse populations* (pp. 3–19). San Diego, CA: College-Hill Press.

Taylor, O.L. (1986b). Teaching standard English as a second dialect. In O.L. Taylor (Ed.), *Treatment of communication disorders in culturally and linguistically diverse populations* (pp. 153–195). San Diego, CA: College-Hill Press.

Taylor, O.L. (1990). *Cross cultural communication: An essential dimension of effective education.* (ERIC Document Reproduction Service No. ED 325 593)

Taylor, O.L. (in press). Clinical practice as a social occasion: An ethnographic model. In L. Cole & V.R. Deal (Eds.), *Communication disorders in multicultural populations.* Rockville, MD: American Speech-Language-Hearing Association.

Taylor, O., & Payne, K. (1983). Culturally valid testing: A proactive approach. *Topics in Language Disorders, 3,* 8–20.

Taylor, O., Payne, K., & Anderson, N. (1987). Distinguishing between communication disorders and communication differences. *Seminars in Speech and Language, 8,* 415–427.

Thomas, D. (1994). Family-school partnerships in a pluralistic society. In B.C. Epanchin, B. Townsend, & K. Stoddard (Eds.), *Constructive classroom management: Strategies for creating positive learning environments* (pp. 70–97). Pacific Grove, CA: Brooks/Cole.

van Kleeck, A. (1994, January). Potential cultural bias in training parents as conversational partners with their children who have delays in language development. *American Journal of Speech-Language Pathology, 3*(1), 67–77.

Vaughn-Cooke, F.B. (1983). Improving language assessment in minority children. *Asha, 25*(9), 29–34.

Vaughn-Cooke, F.B. (1986). The challenge of assessing the language of nonmainstream speakers. In O.L. Taylor (Ed.), *Treatment of communication disorders in culturally and linguistically diverse populations* (pp. 23–48). San Diego, CA: College-Hill Press.

Ward, M. (1971). *Them children: A study in language learning.* Prospect Heights, IL: Waveland Press.

Washington, J.A., & Craig, H.K. (1992). Articulation test performances of low-income, African-American preschoolers with communication impairments. *Language, Speech, and Hearing Services in Schools, 23*(3), 203–207.

Westby, C.E. (1990). Ethnographic interviewing: Asking the right questions to the right people in the right ways. *Journal of Childhood Communication Disorders, 13*(1), 101–111.

Westby, C.E., & Erickson, J. (1992). Prologue. *Topics in Language Disorders, 12*(3), v–viii.

Wolfram, W. (1993). Research to practice: A proactive role for speech-language pathologists in sociolinguistic education. *Language, Speech, and Hearing Services in the Schools, 24,* 181–185.

Wyatt, T.A., & Seymour, H.N. (1990, summer). The implications of code-switching in Black English speakers. Language and discrimination (special ed.). *Equity & Excellence, 24*(4), 17–18.

Acquisition of the African American English Copula

Toya A. Wyatt

Child language researchers and speech-language pathologists have strug-
gled for years with the issue of distinguishing between difference and
disorder in African American English (AAE) child speech. Part of this
struggle is associated with the fact that many of the linguistic forms considered to be characteristic of normal dialect use in AAE such as the zero
(absent) copula and past tense -ed, plural -s, and possessive -s markers can
also be viewed as indices of disorder in mature Standard American English
(SAE) speech. Although it is common for preschool-age SAE-speaking
children to produce sentences during the early stages of language development where these forms are variably absent, children who persist in the
use of these variable forms past the age of 3 or 4 years are usually identified having a language delay. The same criteria, however, cannot be applied to children acquiring AAE as their first dialect, given the fact that
variable absence of the same grammatical forms is a normal part of both
child and adult AAE grammar.

There is an inherent problem, therefore, in using an SAE developmental framework for evaluating the linguistic competence of AAE-
speaking children. Yet the majority of speech and language tools utilized
by speech-language pathologists are based on developmental information
obtained almost exclusively from SAE-speaking children. This has gen-

erally resulted in the overreferral of AAE-speaking children for special education and speech-language intervention services.

A number of scholars have proposed several solutions to address this problem. These range from focusing on the more universally shared aspects of language development such as semantics and pragmatics (Stockman, 1986a, 1986b; Stockman & Vaughn-Cooke, 1982; Stockman, Vaughn-Cooke, & Wolfram, 1982) to focusing on the more non–dialect-specific aspects of English grammar and phonology (California Speech-Language-Hearing Association Task Force on the Assessment of the African-American Child, 1994; Stockman & Settle, 1991).

Although such solutions enable clinicians to avoid some of the pitfalls encountered when testing children from nonstandard English backgrounds, they still continue to rely on the use of language analysis frameworks originally developed for SAE-speaking children. As a result, SAE continues to serve as the standard for evaluating the linguistic performance of AAE-speaking children. As Seymour (1986) notes, this type of comparative approach can lead to erroneous assumptions about the communicative competence of AAE-speaking children, primarily because it provides a "distorted and incomplete view of their language" (p. 53).

This overreliance on existing SAE norms and theories of language development contributes to the lack of research into those aspects of AAE grammar that, although different, can still provide useful information for distinguishing between dialect and disorder. If researchers were to take the time to study those intricacies of AAE grammar that are not compatible with or easily analyzed by existing theories of language, they might find that they are able to provide new insights on the child language-acquisition process for both AAE- and other English-speaking child populations. They may also discover language universals that characterize the early language development of all English-speaking children but that have not yet been considered.

THE COPULA IN AAE

One aspect of AAE grammar that may help to highlight a universal feature of developing English language grammar is the zero (absent) copula. For years, sociolinguists have been interested in the "inherent variability" (Labov, 1969) of AAE grammar and what impact this variability has on feature use. One of the most widely studied variable features of AAE grammar has been the AAE copula.

Much of the research on the copula has focused on the ways in which production of this verb form in AAE differs from that in SAE. In SAE, for example, the copula can take one of only two possible forms: 1) the full form, where it appears as an uncontracted verb (i.e., "She is sick"); or 2) the contracted form (i.e., "She's sick"). In contrast, the AAE copula can take at least five different forms: 1) the full form (i.e., "She is sick"); 2) the contracted form (i.e., "She's sick"); 3) the nonstandard agreeing verb form (i.e., "They is sick"); 4) the zero form (i.e., "She sick"); and 5) the "go" copula form (i.e., "Here go a sick one") (Wyatt, 1991a).

Another form of the verb "to be" that has also been characterized as a possible variant of the AAE copula but that will not be addressed in this chapter is the habitual or aspectual "be" (i.e., "She be sick"). Some linguists have suggested that "be" operates as an equivalent form of the verbs "is," "are," and "am," but others, such as Fasold (1972) and Green (1993, 1995), have argued that "be" cannot be considered an equivalent form of the copula. They have provided support for their claim by highlighting the differing semantic and syntactic status of these two verbs. For example, in contrast to the copula verbs "is," "are," and "am," which are used to mark a presently occurring state of being in both AAE and SAE, the aspectual "be" is frequently used to mark an ongoing or continuous state of being. Therefore, when an AAE speaker says "She be sick," it is implied that the female to |which he or she is referring ("she") is in the habit of frequently being sick. In other words, not only is she sick right now, but she has frequently been sick in the past and she is likely to be sick in the future. In contrast, the AAE speaker who says "She is sick," "She's sick," or "She sick" is generally referring to the fact that the woman in question is currently sick, with no reference to her future or past state of health. This distinction has led to the classification of the habitual "be" as an aspectual marker that differs in semantic use from the verb forms "is," "are," and "am."

Green (1993, 1995) further distinguishes these two verbs by providing linguistic evidence of their differing syntactic roles in yes–no questions, tag questions, and negatives. For example, if one wishes to transform the sentence "She is sick" into a yes–no question in SAE, the resulting question form would be "Is she sick?"; the resulting tag question form would be "She is sick, isn't she?"; and the resulting negative form would be "She isn't sick." In AAE, however, it would be ungrammatical to produce a yes–no question beginning with the verb "be" (i.e., "Be she sick?"). The most appropriate transformation would be "Do she be sick?" Similarly, the most appropriate tag question form would be "She be sick, don't she," and the most appropriate negative sentence form would be "She don't be sick." Therefore, not only does the aspectual "be" differ in meaning from other forms of the copula, but also it adheres to different grammatical rules for question and negative formation. Given these differences, the aspectual "be" will be excluded from all discussions of the AAE copula in this chapter.

The high degree of variability in copula and other feature use in AAE grammar has traditionally led to the depiction of AAE as being less rule governed than SAE. In addition, the variability of feature use has been characterized as being "random" in nature. In the 1960s, however, Labov, Cohen, Robins, and Lewis (1968) challenged this assertion by demonstrating that copula absence in AAE occurs as a function of several systematic grammatical rules that delineate when it is permissible for the copula to be "deleted" in AAE sentences.

In a preliminary analysis of AAE copula production patterns, Labov et al. (1968) and Labov (1969) hypothesized that use of the zero copula form is permitted in AAE in those linguistic contexts that allow for contraction of the copula in SAE. These same researchers also suggested that there is an underlying copula form in the deep structure of AAE grammar that undergoes a process of contraction and eventual deletion before occurring as a zero (absent) form in the surface structure of AAE sentences. Given the apparent relationship between deletion and contraction (the fact that the copula can only be deleted in those contexts where it can also be contracted), Labov et al. (1968) and Labov (1969) further suggested that copula deletion and contraction are "dependent" processes in AAE. That is, copula deletion depends on prior operation of a verb-contraction rule.

A number of scholars, however, challenge Labov's assertion that the zero copula form in AAE occurs as a result of dependent contraction and deletion processes. Some, such as Mufwene (1983, 1991), suggest that the deep structure of AAE grammar does not possess the copula form and that the presence of the copula in surface structure occurs as a function of a grammatical rule that adds rather than deletes a present copula. Such scholars, therefore, tend to view copula absence and contraction as independent processes. Under this analysis, absence of the copula in AAE's surface structure grammar is explained by the existence of an underlying zero copula in the deep structure and not as the result of dependent contraction and deletion processes.

Labov (1969) also delineated those linguistic contexts where zero copula use in AAE is more likely to occur. For example, Labov observed that in AAE the zero copula form occurs more often when 1) it follows a pronoun subject versus a full noun subject, 2) it precedes locative or adjective versus noun predicate, 3) it follows voiced versus voiceless consonants, and 4) it precedes words beginning with consonant versus vowels sounds. He also noted that the zero copula is rarely absent in some environments, including those where past tense "was" and "were" forms are expected, the final positions of clauses, and during emphatic speech.

Since Labov's original (1969) analysis, other scholars have proposed the existence of other constraints on copula use. Wolfram (1969), for example, noted that the zero copula is rarely produced in the first-person singular (e.g., "am") contexts and after the subject pronouns such as "what," "that," and "it." He also noted that the zero copula is more common in the second-person singular and in the plural ("are") than in the third-person singular ("is"). A complete summary of Labov's (1969) and Wolfram's (1969) findings can be found in the appendix at the end of this chapter.

In addition to detailing the environments in which the zero copula is more likely to occur, Labov (1969, 1972) also presented a model of AAE grammar that specifies those grammatical factors (e.g., preceding grammatical context, following grammatical context, preceding phonological context) playing the greatest role in zero copula use. Using this model, Labov (1969) determined that the single most important factor influencing whether or not the zero copula is likely to occur is the nature of its preceding subject. Based on these findings, Labov et al. (1968) proposed a variable-rule grammar model that not only specifies the grammatical and phonological contexts in which the AAE zero copula is able to occur but also ranks these contexts in terms of their relative impact on zero copula use.

THE ACQUISITION OF VARIABLE RULES BY AAE-SPEAKING PRESCHOOLERS

Variable Rules and Communicative Competence in Child Speech

Labov (1969), Labov et al. (1968), and Wolfram (1975) have all suggested that knowledge of these variable rules by speakers of AAE represents an important aspect of communicative competence. According to Labov (1969), competent speakers of any language must understand not only the ways in which grammatical structures are used in their language but also the linguistic conditions that favor, disfavor, or mandate the presence of these structures. Wolfram and Fasold (1974) consider such knowledge to be intuitive. In addition, some scholars such as Sankoff (1973) have provided evidence that children in a speech community have an early developing knowledge of these rules. For example, when Sankoff (1973) utilized a variable-rule framework to examine the production of a future marker ("bai") by child and adult speakers of Tok Pisin, a language spoken in New Guinea, she found no differences between child or adolescent and adult speakers' production of this future marker. Both groups displayed similar knowledge of the grammatical constraints on feature use. Sankoff concluded that child Tok Pisin speakers acquire an understanding of the variable-rule constraints of this future marker at the same time that the marker begins to emerge in their speech.

These findings have significant implications for the study of zero copula use in AAE child speech. The majority of studies on preschool-age AAE-speaking children's productions of the copula and other English grammatical forms have utilized an SAE-based framework for evaluating their use of these forms. As a result, the grammatical productions of these children have generally been examined only from an SAE-based perspective. Such a perspective, however, does not make accomodations for the use of variable-feature forms. As a result, the copula production patterns of AAE-speaking children have been analyzed in terms of how well they conform to the rules of SAE. In contrast, few studies have examined whether or not preschool-age AAE child speakers possess knowledge of the variable rules that govern copula production in their native dialect. This type of information, however, would be invaluable for evaluating the linguistic competence of children acquiring AAE as their first language.

Another limitation of previous research on the copula in child speech is that, even when a more appropriate analysis framework has been utilized, it has rarely been used to study the speech patterns of AAE-speaking children below the age of 8 years. The lack of attention to the speech characteristics of younger speakers can be attributed partly to the widespread belief that AAE child speakers produce "age-graded" features that are not representative of adult grammar. The term *age grading* is used to refer to age-group differences in the use of grammatical, phono-logical, or lexical features or to the social stratification of a feature across different age levels. According to Dillard (1972), age grading is a "near-universal" phe-nomenon (p. 236) that occurs in all speech communities. In SAE speech commu-nities, for example, several vocabulary items used by toddlers and preschoolers, such as "night-night" for "bed" and "choo-choo" for "train," are considered socially acceptable up until a certain age (Owens, 1992). Such items would be considered examples of age grading. Dillard (1972), however, suggests that age grading occurs to a greater extent in the AAE community than in other English speech communities. He further hypothesizes that language age grading in the African American speech community is the result of African socialization prac-tices that have been used for centuries in Africa for marking the passage of chil-dren through several stages of social development, or age grades, and that have continued to survive in the African American community. Wolfram (1974), how-ever, has proposed that the hypothesized "age-graded" differences in the speech of African American children are the results of normal developmental language processes, and he cautions against the labeling of these differences as simply age-graded phenomena. Regardless of what these child language differences are based on, because of their desire to develop a model of AAE adult grammar, most AAE scholars have generally ignored the developing grammar of younger child speak-ers because of these potential age-grading influences.

Syntactic Constraints on AAE Copula Production in Child Speech

The few studies that have examined the copula production patterns of elementary school-age AAE speakers have generally supported the findings of adult research studies. Bailey and Maynor (1987) conducted an examination of language data collected by Loman (1967) on four 10-year-old African American children liv-ing in the Washington, D.C., area. They found that, as with older AAE speakers, Loman's child subjects produced the zero copula more frequently in the second-person singular and plural versus the third-person singular and that it was rarely used in the first-person singular. Legum, Pfaff, Tinnie, and Nicholas (1971), who studied the copula production patterns of African American kindergarten, first-, second-, and third-grade speakers, also found that the zero copula was used more often in the second-person singular and plural (50%–100%) than in the third-person singular (16%–35%). In addition, they noted that the zero copula was never used in the first-person singular.

Only three studies (Kovac, 1980; Steffensen, 1974; Wyatt, 1991a, have ex-amined preschool-age speakers' acquisition of AAE's variable copula rules. Stef-fensen's (1974) study focused on the emergence of several morphological forms (e.g., the plural -*s*, possessive -*s*, third-person singular -*s*, past tense -*ed*, the cop-ula) in the speech of two African American toddlers over a 10-month period (from 18 to approximately 27 months of age). Steffensen found that for both of her sub-jects the copula stabilized in sentence final positions and in emphatic copula contexts by 21 months of age. She also noted that the copula emerged in nominative or labeling contexts before emerging in locative and attributive contexts. In addition, by 23 months of age, the copula was more likely to be produced before vowels than before consonants. With respect to person and number, the copula emerged in the first-person singular before it emerged in the plural and third-person singular.

Steffensen's findings provide empirical and theoretical support for some of the copula production patterns noted in adult AAE speech. For example, Steffensen observed that stable and consistent use of the copula initially occurred in those contexts where the present copula is required in adult AAE (e.g., final clause position, emphatic contexts). The copula also began to emerge in those linguistic contexts where the copula is more frequently used in adult AAE speech (e.g., nominative predicate contexts) before emerging in those contexts when it is less frequent in adult AAE speech.

In 1980, Kovac conducted a similar type of investigation where she compared the copula production patterns of twenty-six 3-, 5-, and 7-year-old African American middle-class and working-class children with the copula production patterns of twenty-three 3-, 5-, and 7-year-old white middle-class and working-class children. Overall, Kovac found a higher frequency of zero copula use among the African American child subjects than among white child subjects. She also found that working-class African American children used the zero copula more often than middle-class African American children at 5 and 7 years. Interestingly, Kovac also noted a decrease in the use of the zero copula by working-class African American children between the ages of 5 and 7 years.

Kovac also studied the effect of preceding and following linguistic context on the copula production patterns to determine whether those of her preschool-age subjects were similar to those reported for adults. She was primarily interested in determining whether copula contraction and deletion were dependent grammatical processes as reported by Labov (1969). In contrast to Labov's findings, Kovac found different patterns of copula contraction and deletion than those of older AAE speakers. She concluded that copula contraction and deletion operate as independent, rather than dependent, processes in child speech.

Syntactic, Semantic, and Pragmatic Constraints on Copula Production in Child Speech

Wyatt (1991a) examined the combined influence of syntactic, semantic, and pragmatic constraints on zero copula use by ten 3- to 5-year-old AAE-speaking children. All children were enrolled in one of two child care programs in a low- to middle-income urban northeastern community where the majority of residents were from African American or Puerto Rican backgrounds. The majority of children participating in the study came from single-parent homes where the family income was $15,000 or less and where the mothers either were unemployed or worked part-time.

In order to qualify for the study, each child had to demonstrate evidence of 1) normal language development, 2) moderate to heavy use of AAE features, 3) emerging Late Stage V/Post Stage V grammatical form use in accordance with Miller's (1981) profile of language development, and 4) emerging Phase 8 semantic and pragmatic category use in accordance with Lahey's (1988) profile of language development. Final candidates for the study were selected on the basis of language data obtained through 1) an informal 10- to 15-minute screening of their articulation and language abilities; 2) an examination of syntactic, semantic, and pragmatic level using data from a 30-minute language sampling session; and 3) a rating of AAE feature use in a representative 3-minute spontaneous conversation sample. The latter was determined with a rating scale developed for evaluating the degree of feature use and based on previous models of AAE community use proposed by Taylor (1971) and Hoover (1978) (see Figure 1).

Each of the 10 selected subjects was seen for six videotaped language sampling sessions with an age-peer in his or her child care setting. All six sessions were conducted over a 6-week period to minimize the possibility of developmental growth. Each session lasted for 30 minutes and involved structured and unstructured play interactions between the subject and one age-peer. Each session also followed a standard, predictable format consisting of 1) a brief 2- to 3-minute opening dialogue with the examiner; 2) a 5- to 10-minute puzzle play activity; 3) a 5- to 10-minute Colorform activity; and 4) 15–20 minutes of unstructured play with a variety of different toys such as fashion dolls, play food sets, life-size baby dolls, toy care, and basketball action play figures.

At the conclusion of the language sampling process, all conversational interactions between subjects and their dyad partners were transcribed word by word using an adapted version of Bloom and Lahey's (1978) video transcription procedures. The verbal utterances of subjects and accompanying nonverbal actions were then identified and transcribed.

During the first stage of analysis, all transcribed copula productions were identified and classified in terms of the following information: 1) utterance type (e.g., declarative, question); 2) nature and form of copula variant (e.g., zero copula, full present copula, contracted present copula); 3) preceding linguistic context (e.g., noun phrase, pronoun subject); 4) following linguistic context (e.g., adjective, locative, noun phrase predicate); 5) person-number context (e.g., third-person singular, first-person singular, second-person singular); 6) underlying semantic content (e.g., nominative, locative action, locative state); 7) speech act focus (e.g., comment, report/inform function); and 8) discourse function (e.g., negate, respond, initiate). An analysis of the children's copula production patterns within several targeted linguistic environments was then conducted.

The grammatical contexts examined in this study were partially derived from previous studies of the AAE copula. For example, the preceding, following, and person-number grammatical contexts analyzed were similar to those used in the studies of Labov (1969), Wolfram (1969), and others. Selected semantic contexts

Rater's Initials_____

Subject #_____

Rating of AAE Feature Use:

| Heavy AAE | | | | | | | Little or No AAE |

Heavy
AAE ——————————————————————————— Little or No
     1   2   3   4   5   6   7   AAE

Possible Dimensions of Feature Use:

    Syntax
    Lexicon
    Phonology
    Stress/Intonation

Rating Key: 1 = Heavy use of AAE on 3–4 dimensions
    2 = Heavy use of AAE on 1–2 dimensions
    3 = Occasional use of AAE on 3–4 dimensions
    4 = Occasional use of AAE on 1–2 dimensions
    5 = Little use of AAE on 3–4 dimensions
    6 = Little use of AAE on 1–2 dimensions
    7 = No evidence of AAE use

Figure 1. African American English Rating Scale. (Adapted from Wyatt, 1991a).

were taken from the semantic category taxonomies developed by Bloom and Lahey (1978) and Lahey (1988). Only those semantic categories considered to be most productive for copula use were considered. In addition, in those cases when more than one semantic category could be assigned to an individual utterance, only one (the one that appeared to capture the most significant meaning expressed by that utterance) was used. The pragmatic contexts examined were adapted from Lahey's (1988) taxonomy of language functions. A slightly different organizational scheme, however, was used with each utterance being analyzed for both discourse function of the utterance (e.g., respond, imitate, negate) and underlying speech act focus (e.g., comment, report/inform). The taxonomy used was also expanded by adding a new category (elaborate) to accommodate utterances produced by children that elaborated on some aspect of a preceding utterance. Only those pragmatic categories determined to be most productive for copula use were retained. In addition, each copula utterance was assigned to only one pragmatic category.

A total of 1,148 copula tokens were identified and analyzed. The specific linguistic contexts examined are as follows:

1. *Grammatical context*
   a. Preceding subject: noun phrase, personal pronoun, "this," "it/that," "there/ here"
   b. Following predicate: noun phrase, adjective, locative
   c. Person-number context: third-person singular, second-person singular or plural
2. *Semantic context:* locative state, attributive state, quantity, possessive state, nomination, specification
3. *Pragmatic context*
   a. Discourse function: routine, repair, imitation, initiation, response, negation, elaboration
   b. Speech act: comment, report/inform

Results revealed findings similar to those reported for adults about the probability and actual frequency of zero copula use in targeted linguistic environments. For example, results showed that the zero copula was used by the children more often 1) after pronoun (56%) than noun (21%) subjects; 2) before locative (35%) and adjective (27%) than noun (18%) predicates; and 3) in second-person singular or plural (45%) than third-person singular (19%) predicates (see Figures 2A–2C). In addition, in accordance with findings from previous studies of adult copula production patterns, preceding context was found to be the most important factor for determining zero copula use, as has generally been observed in adult speech.

The role of semantic context on zero copula use was less clear because of an apparent interaction between semantic and grammatical (syntactic) context. Specifically, an analysis of frequency data revealed semantically based patterns of copula use that paralleled those already obtained in a grammatical analysis of copula production. For example, there was a strong parallel between zero copula production patterns noted for the semantic context of locative and the grammatical context of locative predicate. Similarly, the pattern of zero copula use in attributive semantic contexts paralleled the one for predicate adjective contexts. Zero copula use in nominative semantic contexts paralleled that of noun phrase predicate contexts (see Figure 2D).

There appeared to be little difference in the percentage of zero copula use across the seven examined discourse contexts. Overall, zero copula use ranged from 21% to 31% in the five categories examined, with less than 15% use observed in the negate and elaborate categories (see Figure 2E).

One interesting pattern of zero copula use did emerge when speech act context was considered. For example, the zero copula form was used 24% of the time in comment contexts; however, it was never used in report/inform contexts (see Figure 2F).

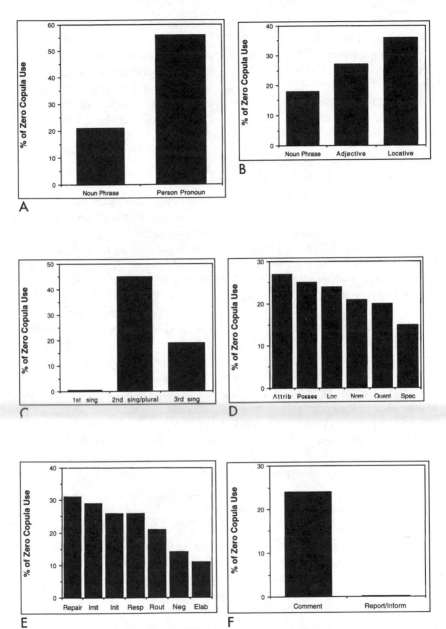

Figure 2. Zero copula use by AAE preschool-age speakers. Group data. (A–C: From Wyatt, T. [1991a]. Linguistic constraints on copula production in Black English child speech. *Dissertation Abstracts International, 523 (2)*, 781B. [University Microfilms No. DA9120958]. D–F: From Wyatt, T. [1991b, April]. *Pragmatic constraints on copula production in Black English child speech*. Paper presented at the National Black Association for Speech, Language, and Hearing, Los Angeles, CA.; reprinted by permission.)

In addition to examining zero copula production patterns in variable linguistic contexts (those where the zero copula is possible in AAE), Wyatt (1991a) examined copula production patterns in those contexts where the use of the zero copula is generally not permitted. These include contexts previously identified by Labov (1969) and Wolfram (1969) as rare for zero copula use, such as emphatic, past tense, first-person singular, and final clause contexts. Once again, findings were similar to those reported for adults, with child subjects using the zero copula form less than 1% of the time in these contexts.

Toward a Theory of Pragmatic Constraints on AAE Zero Copula Use in Child Speech

Relying on findings from the pragmatic analysis of zero copula patterns in the preceding study, I hypothesize that both pragmatic and syntactic influences play a strong role in AAE-speaking children's zero copula use. For example, reduced use of the zero copula form in elaborate discourse contexts by the preschoolers in Wyatt (1991a) may have occurred because the children were attempting to provide their listener(s) with new or additional information. Reduced use within the report/inform speech act contexts could have been similarly influenced by the fact that the children were talking about objects outside of the immediate speaking context. In both cases, there was a need for increased communicative effectiveness, and according to Lahey (1988) one of the most effective ways for accomplishing the latter is to use linguistic redundancy. The AAE-speaking subjects in my study may have been using the copula as a linguistically redundant marker, considering that, as Brown (1973) notes, the present tense English copula contributes little to the underlying meaning of utterances.

The zero copula form in report/inform contexts may also have been less frequent because the present copula was serving as a marker of the narrative past. The majority of the children's report/inform utterances seemed to occur when they were talking about nonpresent or past events. Consider the following example:

> Mmmm-mm . . . cuz everytime when I walk around and I have a little dress and I . . . an' I don't know it if it's my cousin Keisha's . . . an' they just, they say 'little baby' cuz it. . . . cuz they think . . . cuz it . . . cuz it's little. (Wyatt, 1991a, p. 157)

The classification of the present copula as a marker of the narrative past is supported by the research findings of Myhill and Harris (1986) and Labov and Harris (1986), who observed increased use of the third-person singular -s marker in narrative versus nonnarrative contexts in their studies of younger AAE speakers. These researchers concluded that adolescent and young adult AAE speakers use the third-person singular -s marker as a marker of narrative past. Given the results from my study, it is possible that AAE-speaking preschoolers may be using the present copula in a similar manner.

The zero copula was also rarely used within negate discourse contexts. Limited use of the zero copula form in this context, however, was most likely related to the emphatic nature of most negate utterance exchanges. Consider the following example from an exchange that occurred when two girls were arguing over the labeling of a Colorform piece:

KT: "Dat's a piece of *girl*."
KH: "Dat's a piece of *furniture*." [negates KT's utterance]
KT: "Piece of *girl*, I said!" [negates KH's utterance]
KH: "It's a piece of *furniture!*" [negates KT's utterance] (Wyatt, 1991a, p. 157)

Labov (1969) has previously stated that emphatic stress plays a significant role in the use of AAE copula forms. Specifically, he noted that the copula is almost always present in emphatic contexts such as "Allah *is* God" and "He *is* a expert." Although the children in my study did not always use primary stress on the copula verb in their productions, their negate utterances generally occurred in emphatic contexts. Therefore, the more frequent use of the present copula during negate utterance exchanges may be due to the emphatic nature of most of these exchanges.

IMPLICATIONS FOR THE DIFFERENTIATION BETWEEN DIFFERENCE AND DISORDER IN AAE CHILD SPEECH

It is evident from the previously cited studies that when the copula production patterns of young preschool-age children are examined from an AAE-based, rather than an SAE-based, framework of analysis, a wealth of information about grammatical feature use can be obtained about children's degree of grammatical rule knowledge. If variable rules do indeed constitute a critical aspect of grammatical knowledge in AAE, this type of information can be very important for determining a child's level of linguistic competence. Such information helps to determine not only how well AAE-speaking children acquire the language-specific features of their dialect but also how knowledgeable they are about the rules for variable-feature use. The research reviewed in this chapter provides evidence that typically developing young AAE child speakers do in fact know these variable-rule constraints. However, it would be interesting to examine whether language-impaired AAE speakers possess the same grammatical knowledge.

It would also be interesting to determine whether AAE children with language impairments exhibit the same general percentage of zero copula use as speakers without impairments. The relative frequency or percentage of overall zero copula use may differ for AAE child speakers with and without language impairments. Support for this theory can be found in the research of Wyatt and Bates (1992), who examined the overall rate of auxiliary verb omissions produced by AAE child speakers with and without impairments. When the total number of "be," "can," and "do" auxiliary verb omissions in children's *wh-* and yes–no questions was tabulated, we found that subjects with language impairments omitted these verbs 43% of the time in comparison to their age-peers without impairments, who omitted these verbs 35% of the time. Wyatt and Bates's (1992) findings were based on a data corpus of 291 questions from the children without language impairments and 456 questions from the children with such impairments.

In a similar study, Seymour, Bland, and Green (1992) examined the overall rate of copula and auxiliary verb omissions in the speech of kindergarten and first-grade speakers. However, in contrast to the findings of Wyatt and Bates (1992), Seymour et al. (1992) actually found a higher percentage of auxiliary and copula verb omissions among their subjects without language impairments than their subjects with impairments. However, the number of copula and auxiliary verb tokens ($n = 117$) collected by Seymour et al. (1992) was much smaller than the 741 tokens (291 from children without impairments and 456 from children with impairments) in the Wyatt and Bates study.

One major problem with attempting to delineate a criterion-based level of acceptable zero copula use is the range of language diversity that exists among individual AAE child speakers. The issue has been addressed by a number of different scholars, including Baugh (1983), Burling (1973), Hoover (1978), Taylor (1971), and Washington and Craig (1994). I also observed this same range of language diversity in my study. For example, of the 19 children who were initially identified as potential subjects, only 12 were considered to be moderate to heavy users of dialect features (demonstrating AAE feature use on 40% or more of their speaking turns), even though all of the children resided in the same lower-class community and came from similar socioeconomic backgrounds.

I also found that when the overall zero copula production patterns of the 10 children participating as final subjects in the study were examined individually, the amount of zero copula use varied from child to child. Although all children had been labeled as moderate to heavy users of AAE by three expert judges, their individual level of zero copula use ranged from approximately 5% to 45% (see Figure 3). The overall group average of zero copula use was 25%.

A second way in which to compare the copula production patterns of child speakers with and without language impairments is by examining relative linguistic context influences. As stated, group studies of both adult and preschool-age AAE speakers have shown that AAE speakers tend to produce the zero copula more frequently in certain environments than others. AAE child speakers with language impairments may display a differing hierarchical ranking of these environments than speakers without impairments.

As with the first approach (the examination of overall zero copula use), however, there may be problems in using hierarchical rankings as the basis for differentiating between speakers with and without impairments when looking at children on an individual basis. Although the children in my study (Wyatt, 1991a), as a group, produced the zero copula more often after pronouns versus nouns, before adjective and locative versus noun predicates, and in second-person singular and plural versus third-person singular contexts, there was some

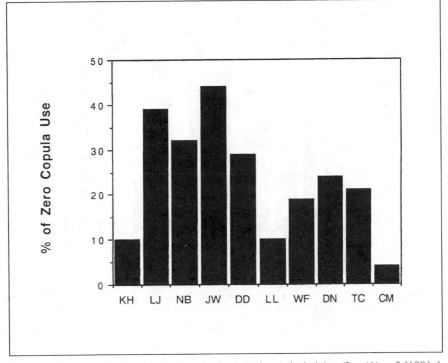

Figure 3.   Overall zero copula use by AAE preschool-age speakers. Individual data. (From Wyatt, T. [1991a]. Linguistic constraints on copula production in Black English child speech. *Dissertation Abstracts International, 523*[2], /81B. [University Microfilms No. DA9120958]; reprinted by permission.)

degree of individual variation with respect to the relative ranking of these environments (see Figures 4–6).

Finally, existing normative information on AAE-speaking children's zero copula production patterns can be used for identifying children with language impairments by examining how they use zero copula forms when such use is generally prohibited. For example, the children without impairments in my study used the zero copula form in the first-person singular context less than 1% of the time, but AAE-speaking children who have language impairments may violate this important grammatical constraint. This type of approach would be similar to that used for identifying language impairments in children from SAE-speaking communities. The only difference is that an AAE-determined definition of obligatory context rather than the SAE-based definition of obligatory context would be used.

CONCLUSIONS

The lack of appropriate research on the developing grammar of AAE-speaking children has often led to an inaccurate and incomplete examination of their lan-

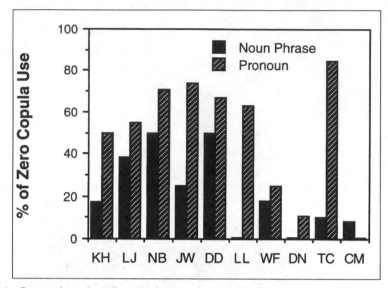

Figure 4. Zero copula use by AAE preschool-age speakers. Preceding grammatical context. Individual data. (From Wyatt, T. [1991a]. Linguistic constraints on copula production in Black English child speech. *Dissertation Abstracts International, 523*(2), 781B. [University Microfilms No. DA9120958]; reprinted by permission.)

guage abilities. In addition, few studies have attempted to delineate the systematic nature of seemingly variable and random feature use. However, attention to even the most variable aspects of AAE could potentially provide important diagnostic information for evaluating the linguistic competence of AAE child speakers and lead to a more accurate description of their language abilities. Such analyses may also help shed light on those aspects of AAE child grammar that are common to the developing grammar of other English-speaking child populations during the earliest stages of language development.

This chapter presented findings from several studies of copula production in AAE child speech based on a variable-rule–based analysis framework. In general, findings from these studies have demonstrated that there are systematic grammatical constraints on the use of the AAE zero copula similar to those reported for adult speakers. In addition, these studies reveal the operation of additional pragmatic constraints that help explain the conditions for zero copula use. These findings have important implications for the differential diagnosis of language impairment in AAE-speaking children. They also highlight the value of using alternative analysis frameworks for examining the language skills of this population. It may seem more pragmatic to develop diagnostic procedures based on existing SAE analysis frameworks, but the continued use of these procedures is likely to ignore the validity and beauty of AAE's rich language grammar.

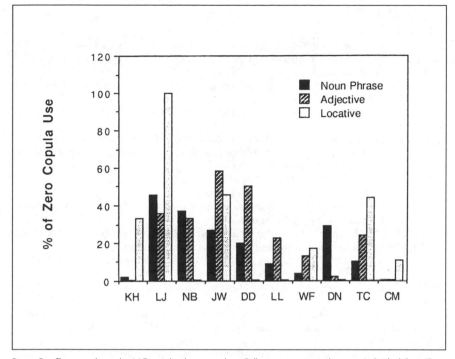

Figure 5. Zero copula use by AAE preschool-age speakers. Following grammatical context. Individual data. (From Wyatt, T. [1991a]. Linguistic constraints on copula production in Black English child speech. *Dissertation Abstracts International, 523(2)*, 781B. [University Microfilms No. DA9120958]; reprinted by permission.)

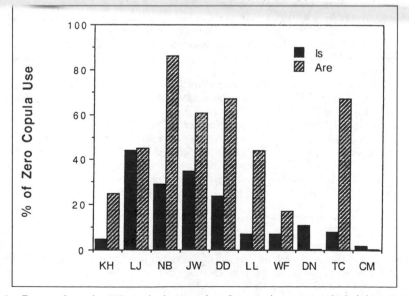

Figure 6. Zero copula use by AAE preschool-age speakers. Person-number context. Individual data. (From Wyatt, T. [1991a]. Linguistic constraints on copula production in Black English child speech. *Dissertation Abstracts International, 523*[2], 781B. [University Microfilms No. DA9120958]; reprinted by permission.)

REFERENCES

Bailey, G., & Maynor, N. (1987). Decreolization. *Language in Society, 16,* 449–473.
Baugh, J. (1983). A survey of Afro-American English. *Annual Review of Anthropology, 12,* 335–354.
Bloom, L., & Lahey, M. (1978). *Language development and language disorders.* New York: Macmillan.
Brown, R. (1973). *A first language: The early stages.* Cambridge, MA: Harvard University Press.
Burling, R. (1973). *English in black and white.* New York: Holt, Rinehart & Winston.
California Speech-Language-Hearing Association Task Force on the Assessment of the African-American Child. (1994, November). CSHA position paper: Assessment of the African-American child. *CSHA, 21*(3), 1–17.
Dillard, J.L. (1972). *Black English.* New York: Vintage.
Fasold, R. (1972). *Tense marking in Black English: A linguistic and social analysis.* Washington, DC: Center for Applied Linguistics.
Green, L. (1993). *Topics in African American English: The verb system analysis.* Unpublished doctoral dissertation, University of Massachusetts, Amherst.
Green, L. (1995). Study of verb classes in African American English. *Linguistics and Education, 7*(1), 65–81.
Hoover, M. (1978). Community attitudes toward Black English. *Language in Society, 7,* 65–87.
Kovac, C. (1980). Children's acquisition of variable features. (Doctoral dissertation) *Dissertation Abstracts International, 42*(02), 687A. (University Microfilms No. AAC8116548)
Labov, W. (1969). Contraction, deletion, and inherent variability of the English copula. *Language, 45,* 715–762.
Labov, W. (1972). *Language in the inner city.* Philadelphia: University of Pennsylvania Press.
Labov, W., Cohen, P., Robins, C., & Lewis, J. (1968). *A study of the nonstandard English of Negro and Puerto Rican speakers in New York City.* Final report, Cooperative Research Project No. 3288. Washington, DC: U.S. Office of Education.
Labov, W., & Harris, W. (1986). De facto segregation of black and white vernaculars. In D. Sankoff (Ed.), *Diversity and diachrony* (pp. 1–24). Amsterdam: John Benjamins Publishing.
Lahey, M. (1988). *Language disorders and language development.* New York: Macmillan.
Legum, S., Pfaff, C., Tinnie, G., & Nicholas, M. (1971). *The speech of young black children in Los Angeles.* Technical Report No. 33. Inglewood, CA: Southwest Regional Laboratory. (ERIC Document Reproduction Service No. ED 057 022)
Loman, B. (1967). *Conversations in a Negro-American dialect.* Washington, DC: Center for Applied Linguistics. (ERIC Document Reproduction Service No. ED 013 455)
Miller, J. (1981). *Assessing language production in children.* Austin, TX: PRO-ED.
Mufwene, S. (1983). *Some observations on the verb in Black English Vernacular.* Papers, Series 2, No. 5. Austin: African and Afro-American Studies and Research Center, The University of Texas at Austin.
Mufwene, S. (1991). Why grammars are not monolithic. In G. Larson, D. Brentari, & L. MacLeod (Eds.), *The joy of grammar: A festschrift for James D. McCawley.* Amsterdam: John Benjamins Publishing.
Myhill, J., & Harris, W. (1986). The use of the verbal -s inflection in BEV. In D. Sankoff (Ed.), *Diversity and diachrony* (pp. 25–31). Amsterdam: John Benjamins Publishing.
Owens, R. (1992). *Language development: An introduction.* New York: Macmillan.
Sankoff, G. (1973). Above and beyond phonology in variable rules. In C.J.N. Bailey &

R.W. Shuy (Eds.), *New ways of analyzing variation in English* (pp. 44–61). Washington, DC: Georgetown University Press.

Seymour, H. (1986). Alternative strategies for the teaching of language to minority individuals. In F. Bess, B. Clark, & H. Mitchell (Eds.), *Concerns for minority groups in communication disorders* (pp. 52–57). ASHA report No. 16. Rockville, MD: American Speech-Language-Hearing Association.

Seymour, H., Bland, L., & Green, L. (1992, April). *A description of language disorders in African-American children.* Paper presented at the National Black Association for Speech, Language, and Hearing Convention, Chicago.

Steffensen, M. (1974). The acquisition of Black English. *Dissertation Abstracts International, 35*(07), 4489A. (University Microfilms No. AAC7500442)

Stockman, I. (1986a). The development of linguistic norms for nonmainstream populations. In F. Bess, B. Clark, & H. Mitchell (Eds.), *Concerns for minority groups in communication disorders* (pp. 101–110). ASHA report No. 16. Rockville, MD: American Speech-Language-Hearing Association.

Stockman, I. (1986b). Language acquisition in culturally diverse populations: The black child as a case study. In O. Taylor (Ed.), *Nature of communication disorders in culturally and linguistically diverse populations* (pp. 117–155). San Diego, CA: College-Hill Press.

Stockman, I., & Settle, S. (1991, November). *Initial consonants in young black children's conversational speech.* Poster session presented at the annual convention of the American Speech-Language-Hearing Association, Atlanta, GA.

Stockman, I., & Vaughn-Cooke, F. (1982). Semantic categories in the language of working-class black children. In C.E. Johnson & C.L. Thew (Eds.), *Proceedings of the Second International Child Language Conference, 1,* 312–327.

Stockman, I., Vaughn-Cooke, F., & Wolfram, W. (1982). *A developmental study of Black English—Phase I* (Final Report). Washington, DC: Center for Applied Linguistics. (ERIC Document Reproduction Service No. ED 245 555)

Taylor, O. (1971). Response to social dialects and the field of speech. In *Sociolinguistics: A cross disciplinary perspective* (pp. 13–20). Arlington, VA: Center for Applied Linguistics. (ERIC Document Reproduction Service No. ED 130 500)

Washington, J., & Craig, H. (1994). Dialectal forms during discourse of poor, urban, African-American preschoolers. *Journal of Speech and Hearing Research, 37*(4), 816–823.

Wolfram, W. (1969). *A sociolinguistic description of Detroit Negro speech.* Washington, DC: Center for Applied Linguistics.

Wolfram, W. (1974). The relationship of white Southern speech to Vernacular Black English. *Language, 50*(3), 498–527.

Wolfram, W. (1975). Variable constraints and rule relations. In R. Fasold & R. Shuy (Eds.), *Analyzing variation in language* (pp. 70–88). Washington, DC: Georgetown University Press.

Wolfram, W., & Fasold, R. (1974). *The study of social dialects in American English.* Englewood Cliffs, NJ: Prentice Hall.

Wyatt, T. (1991a). Linguistic constraints on copula production in Black English child speech. *Dissertation Abstracts International, 523*(2), 781B. (University Microfilms No. DA9120958)

Wyatt, T. (1991b, April). *Pragmatic constraints on copula production in Black English child speech.* Paper presented at the National Black Association for Speech, Language, and Hearing, Los Angeles, CA.

Wyatt, T., & Bates, K. (1992, April). *Question formation in normal and disordered African-American English (AAE) child speech.* Paper presented at the annual convention of the National Black Association for Speech-Language-Hearing, Chicago.

Appendix A

Linguistic Constraints on Zero Copula Use in AAE (Adapted from Wyatt, 1991a)

According to Labov (1969) and Labov et al. (1968), copula "deletion" in AAE occurs as the result of the same grammatical and phonological factors that influence contraction of the copula in colloquial SAE. Specifically, Labov (1969) proposed that the copula in AAE can be "deleted" only in those linguistic contexts where a contracted copula form can also be used in SAE. In those contexts where contraction of the copula is not permitted, the zero copula form cannot occur. Labov (1969) and Wolfram (1969) also made the following observations about some of the additional constraints on copula use.

Contexts That Favor Use of the Zero Copula

The single most important constraint on copula contraction and deletion in AAE is whether the preceding subject is a pronoun or noun phrase. Contraction and deletion are more frequent when the preceding subject is a pronoun than when it is a noun:

"<u>He</u> (is) real big now" versus "<u>John</u> is real big now."

The copula is more likely to be contracted and deleted when it precedes a predicate adjective or locative than when it precedes a noun phrase:

"That ball (is) <u>red</u>" versus "That's a <u>ball</u>."

The copula is more likely to be contracted and deleted after voiced versus voiceless consonants:

"This ba<u>g</u> (is) too full" versus "This ba<u>t</u> is too heavy."

The copula is most likely to be contracted and deleted when it precedes a consonant versus when it precedes a vowel:

"He (is) never bad like that" versus "He's always bad like that."

The copula is more frequently absent in the plural and second-person singular versus the third-person singular:

"They (are) bad" versus "She's bad."

Contexts That Discourage Use of the Zero Copula

The copula is rarely absent in the following contexts:

- Past tense contexts ("He was big")
- When it follows a modal ("He's supposed to be goin'")
- When it is in clause final position ("Yes, he is")
- In emphatic utterances ("Girl, he is fine")
- In the first-person singular context ("I am bad")
- After subject pronouns "what," "that," "it" ("That's what I said")

7

Phonological Development and Disorders in African American Children

Ida J. Stockman

Phonology is the study of the inventory and patterning of speech sounds in a spoken language. Simply put, it encompasses what speakers need to know in order to match the conventional pronunciation of words in a language. Phonology is important to the description of language dialect differences. Sound pattern or *accent* long has been used to distinguish one dialect from another. *Accent* differences among regional dialects can be observed even when other linguistic features (e.g., grammar, vocabulary) are identical. Likewise, the phonological features of a social dialect like African American English (AAE) often are preserved (e.g., the word "ask" is pronounced as [æks]) when common AAE grammatical patterns are absent. Such observations suggest that phonology is an aspect of language that is particularly vulnerable to dialect differences.

Although phonology, like other aspects of language, is concerned with the rule-governed patterns of speakers' mental representation of a grammar, it is set apart by the interface with the physical aspects of speech perception and production. Physical factors both *diversify* and *constrain* pronunciation patterns. Pronunciation is diversified because babies first hear speech sounds in their local linguistic environments. Local auditory input may especially tailor the speech sounds with imprecise articulatory gestures (e.g., vocalic and prosodic sounds). *Regional* dialects of English differ more on vowel than consonant sounds. Language-specific influence on vowels apparently shows up as early as 10 months in babbled speech (Boysson-Bardies, Halle, Sagart, & Durand, 1989). Jusczyk (1992), noting that strong evidence for "babbling drift" had not come from consonant-focused studies, hypothesized that "native language effects may show up sooner in the production of vowels than consonants" (p. 34). Ingram (1995), arguing against a universal theory of prosodic input to infants, proposed that prosodic input is tailored to cultural and language-specific conventions.

Pronunciation patterns also are *constrained* or at least tempered by the physical nature of speech production and perception. Sounds seldom are produced in isolation of each other in meaningful speech. A given sound inevitably is modified by its coarticulated context. Pronunciation is constantly challenged by the types of words that we happen to bring together to create messages. The resulting movement configurations are modulated by a biomechanical system that sets natural limits on the rapidity and efficiency of speech sound articulation. In some cases, conventional pronunciation is sacrificed to naturalness. Dialects differ in how much pronunciation patterns cater to natural tendencies (Wolfram, 1991). Speakers of languages like AAE, which are not written down, may be more susceptible to natural tendencies than are speakers of written languages like Standard American English (SAE).

Perhaps it is the inability to escape the physical effects of speech perception and production that makes pronunciation so vulnerable to dialect differences. Maybe this is why scholars have devoted less attention to African American children's phonological patterns than to other aspects of their dialect. Yet it is the speaker's pronunciation that first alerts one to a communication problem. Parents are more likely to be concerned early on about a child's speech if words cannot be understood. To judge whether a child has an impairment, however, the speech-language pathologist needs information about speech behavior in the linguistic community and resources to conduct an adequate phonological assessment. Surveys show that many speech-language pathologists do not have the information and resources for delivering services to speakers of a minority dialect like AAE (Campbell & Taylor, 1992).

This chapter summarizes what is known about the phonological characteristics of AAE and its acquisition by African American children and offers guidelines for phonological assessment, intervention, and research with this population.

CHARACTERISTICS OF AAE PHONOLOGY

African American English refers to the social and ethnic dialect spoken by mature, native U.S. African Americans who share a slave ancestral history. The dialect is assumed to have a pidgin or creole origin (Dillard, 1972).

According to Edwards and Shriberg (1983), phonological competency requires knowledge at four levels (Figure 1). First, speakers must know the inventory of segmental phonemes, namely, the consonant and vowel sounds that contrast word meanings (b̲a̲t̲/p̲a̲t̲; ba̲t̲/be̲e̲t̲; ba̲t̲/ba̲d̲). Second, speakers must know the morpheme structure rules—that is, how phonemes are arranged to make words. Such rules specify the phoneme's syllable or word position, the number and sequence of consonants that can occur within the same syllable of a word, and so on. The /w/ and /j/ sounds in English occur only in initial and medial word positions while /ŋ/ occurs only in medial and final positions. Third, speakers must know the rules governing the predictable sound changes that occur when morphemes are combined into words. *Morphophonemic rules* specify the pronunciation changes required when words are transformed by adding bound morphemes to lexical stems (cf. "ins̲a̲ne" vs. "ins̲a̲nity" or "tack̲e̲d" vs. "tagg̲e̲d"). Fourth, speakers must know the rules governing the predictable sound changes that occur when phonemes are combined into words. *Allophonic rules* specify the pronunciation required when the production of the same sound is predictably altered by the surrounding phonetic context (e.g., the phoneme /t/ is aspirated in initial word position [e.g., "t̲oe"], flapped in medial position [e.g., "but̲t̲er"], and imploded in final position [e.g., "pot̲"]. Such low-level phonetic changes do not alter word meaning, but they contribute to the sound of native-like speech.

A comprehensive description of a phonological system also includes the suprasegmentals, another layer of sound patterning in a language. *Suprasegmentals* are the *paralinguistic,* prosodic features that are "superimposed on" or "distributed over" a string of segments, syllables, or words (Lehiste, 1970, as cited in Edwards & Shriberg, 1983, p. 20). Some prosodic features in English, such as stress and intonation, occur with enough regularity to mark semantic contrasts between words and between phrases or sentences with identical segmental phonemes. For example, "des̲s̲ért" and "désert" are distinguished by syllabic stress. *Intonation* or *pitch contour* can differentiate between the same sentence spoken as a question (e.g., "You are John?") or a statement of fact (e.g., "You are John.").

When one considers the number of different aspects entailed in the phonological description of a language, it is clear that more is known about some AAE features than others. Scholars have focused mainly on the inventory of phonemes and the rules governing their systematic and variable distribution in words (i.e., morpheme structure rules). There are virtually no formal descriptions of AAE's morphophonemic and allophonic rules or its suprasegmental features. The next section summarizes phonological features that are commonly cited in descriptions

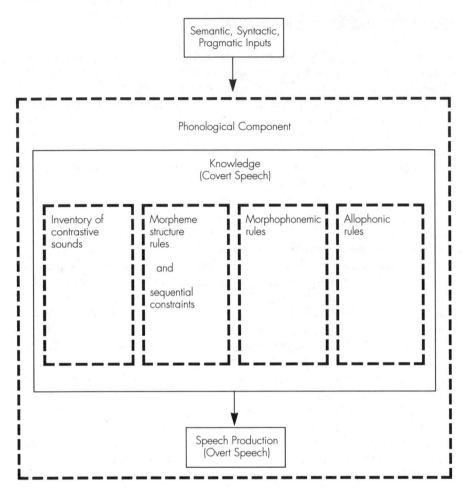

Figure 1. The phonological component of a language or language user. (From Edwards, M., & Shriberg, L. [1983]. *Phonology: Applications in communicative disorders.* San Diego, CA: College-Hill Press, Figure 2.4, p. 37; reprinted with permission.)

of AAE (Baugh, 1983; Labov, 1972; Luelsdorff, 1975; Proctor, 1994; Williams & Wolfram, 1977; Wolfram, 1969, 1991, 1994).

Segmental Characteristics of AAE

Inventory of Phonemes Single vowels and consonants can be compared for SAE and AAE in Tables 1 and 2, respectively. Every vowel shown for SAE is present in AAE except for the three phonemic diphthongs /aɪ/, /aʊ/, and /ɔɪ/. The phonological process of *ungliding* reduces them to single vowels in some contexts. Every consonant in SAE occurs in AAE, except for the interdental fricatives. The

Table 1. SAE and AAE vowels in medial or interconsonantal context (dialect differences in bold)

SAE	AAE	Example word	Comment
Front			
/i/	/i/	beet	
/ɪ/	**/ɪ/**	**pit**	/ɪ/ between sibilants (e.g., sister)
/e/	/e/	bait	
/ɛ/	**/ɛ/**	**bet**	/ɪ/ before nasals (e.g., [pin] for pen)
/æ/	/æ/	bat	
Central			
/ɝ/	**/ɜ/**	**bird**	
/æ/	**/ə/**	**butt<u>er</u>**	
/ʌ/	/ʌ/	butt	
Back			
/u/	/u/	boot	
/ʊ/	/ʊ/	foot	
/ɔ/	/ɔ/	bought	
/o/	**/o/**	**boat**	or /ə/ in unstressed syllables "hollow"
/ɑ/	/ɑ/	pot	
Dipthongs			
/aɪ/	**/ɑ/**	**ice**	/aɪ/ & /ɑ/ neutralized; ice = ass
/aʊ/	**/ɑ/**	**out**	/aʊ/ & /ɑ/ neutralized; out = at
/ɔɪ/	**/ɔ/**	**oil**	/ɔɪ/ & /ə/ neutralized; oil = all

Because few studies have focused on vowels in AAE, reported similarities to SAE are mainly inferential. That is, vowel similarity in the two dialects is inferred in the absence of evidence to the contrary. However, the reported observations in this table can be corroborated by casual observation of AAE speakers.

voiced sound, /ð/, is virtually absent because it often is realized as /d/ in initial word position and as either /d/ or /v/ in medial and final positions, whereas the voiceless sound, /θ/, is realized as /t/ and/or /f/. However, speakers may articulate the /θ/ in the initial position of words.

Morpheme Structure Rules Both AAE and SAE use the same rules for combining phonemes into words. The dialects differ on the positional distribution of particular consonants in initial, medial, and final word positions and on the frequency of their use in a given position.

Single Phonemes A comparison of Tables 1 and 2 reveals more consonant than vowel differences between the dialects. Differences between AAE and SAE consonants can be observed in one or more word positions for every major phoneme class shown in Table 2. Medial and final consonant differences are more prominent than initial ones. The voiceless interdental fricative /θ/, for example, may occur in the initial position, but often is realized as /f/ in medial and final positions (e.g., bathtub→bæftub/; bath→bæf/). Compared with SAE sound changes, AAE sound changes most often involve phoneme substitutions and weakening

Table 2. Single consonants in SAE and AAE by word position (dialect difference in bold)

SAE consonant[a,b]	AAE word position Initial		Medial		Final		COMMENT
Sonorants							
/m/	m-	man	-m-	ha<u>mm</u>er	-ø	ha<u>m</u>	variable final absence
/n/	n-	<u>n</u>eck	-n-	mo<u>n</u>ey	-ø	ca<u>n</u>e	variable final absence
/ŋ/ᵐ/ᶠ			-ŋ-	si<u>ng</u>er	**-ŋ**	**so<u>ng</u>**	ŋ → n in unstressed syllables variable final absence
/w/ⁱ/ᵐ	w-	<u>w</u>eek	-w-	Dar<u>w</u>in			
/j/ⁱ/ᵐ	j-	<u>y</u>ou	-j-	ba<u>y</u>ou			
/r/ⁱ/ᵐ	r-	<u>r</u>ock	-r-	a<u>rr</u>ow			
/l/ⁱ/ᵐ	l-	<u>l</u>ie	-l-	ye<u>ll</u>ow	ø/ə	be<u>ll</u>	
Obstruents							
/b/	b-	<u>b</u>et	-b-	bu<u>bb</u>le	-ø	ca<u>b</u>	variable final absence
/p/	p-	<u>p</u>et	-p-	ha<u>pp</u>y	-ø	ta<u>p</u>	variable final absence
/d/	d-	<u>d</u>ebt	-d-	da<u>dd</u>y	-ø	pa<u>d</u>	variable final absence
/t/	t-	<u>t</u>ape	ʔ	ci<u>t</u>y	-ø	po<u>t</u>	variable final absence
/g/	g-	<u>g</u>ate	-g-	do<u>gg</u>ie	-ø	ho<u>g</u>	variable final absence
/k/	k-	<u>c</u>ap	-k-	ba<u>k</u>er	-ø	ca<u>k</u>e	variable final absence
/v/	v-	<u>v</u>ote	-v-	fa<u>v</u>or	-ø	sa<u>v</u>e	variable final absence
/f/	f-	<u>f</u>ood	-f-	ta<u>ff</u>y	**-f**	sa<u>f</u>e	v → b before nasals, (e.g., se<u>v</u>en)
/ð/	**d-**	<u>th</u>y	**-d-**	o<u>th</u>er	**-v**	ba<u>th</u>e	/d/ or /v/ may alternate
/θ/	**θ/t-**	<u>th</u>igh	**-nf-**	ba<u>th</u>room	**-f**	ba<u>th</u>	
/z/	z-	<u>z</u>oo	-z-	o<u>z</u>one	-ø	ha<u>z</u>e	variable final absence
/s/	s-	<u>s</u>oup	-s-	si<u>ss</u>y	-s	bus	
/ʒ/ᵐ/ᶠ			-ʒ-	mea<u>s</u>ure	**-ø/dʒ**	bei<u>g</u>e	variable final absence
/ʃ/	ʃ-	<u>sh</u>ow	-ʃ-	fi<u>sh</u>ing	-ʃ	ca<u>sh</u>	
/h/ⁱ/ᵐ	h-	<u>h</u>at	-h-	be<u>h</u>ave			
/dʒ/	dʒ-	<u>j</u>oke	-dʒ-	bu<u>dg</u>et	-dʒ	ju<u>dg</u>e	
/tʃ/	tʃ-	<u>ch</u>ick	-tʃ-	ki<u>tch</u>en	-tʃ	ma<u>tch</u>	

Adapted from Labov (1972); Luelsdorff (1975); Williams and Wolfram (1977); and Wolfram (1969, 1991, 1994).
ᵃAll consonants occur in all word positions unless otherwise specified in superscript as initial (i), medial (m), or final (f) position. The /hw/ was excluded because it alternates with /w/ for many speakers.
ᵇThe /r/ in final position is treated as a vowel and not included here as a true consonant (e.g., see final /r/ in butt<u>er</u> or bee<u>r</u>).

processes due to segment omission or devoicing. Although deletion processes affect final consonants most often, any consonant or vowel segment is vulnerable to deletion in an unstressed syllable of a word.

Consonant Clusters   Table 3 shows the clusters that occur in SAE and AAE. The inventory includes only monomorphemic consonant sequences that are blended within the same syllable. Thus, medial sequences are excluded, as are bimorphemic blends formed by adding inflections such as /s/ or /z/ to the end of a word. Table 3 shows that SAE and AAE have the same consonant clusters in *initial* word position with few exceptions, namely, /θr/, /ʃr/, and /str/. One of these three clusters, /θr/, is reduced to a single phoneme. The two remaining clusters involve substitutions that either create a non-English cluster /ʃr/→/sr/ or replace an existing cluster /str/→/skr/. In contrast to initial clusters, most final ones involve segment deletion, with few exceptions. In unstressed syllables, however, every single consonant and consonant cluster is vulnerable to deletion regardless of its word position.

Frequency and Variable Rules of Phoneme Use in Words It is well known that many AAE features, including final consonant deletion, also occur in SAE varieties, but less often. The variable rules governing such quantitative differences may be the most remarkable difference between AAE and SAE. Wolfram (1991) pointed out that the frequency of a feature is determined by language-external factors (i.e., social conditions for using a given feature including code-switching rules) and language-internal factors. The latter appear to be much better specified than the former. Final consonant absence is most likely to occur under the following conditions:

1. The final consonant is either a nasal or oral stop.
2. The final consonant or consonant cluster precedes a word that begins with a consonant, especially an obstruent (e.g., "right food"; "best buy") as opposed to a vowel (e.g., "right on"; "best of").
3. The final consonant occurs in a word whose contrastive status can be maintained in its absence; semantic contrast can be maintained by lengthening or nasalizing the preceding vowel more than usual (e.g., "bad," "bean"); semantic clarity can be preserved without the final consonant by relying on redundant grammatical forms when words are inflected for number, case, or time. The plural -s inflection in *"shoes"* may be absent in *"I have two shoes,"* where quantity is already marked by the word *"two,"* but not in *I have shoes,* in which prior reference to quantity is absent.
4. The final consonant occurs in a monomorphemic cluster (e.g., *"sent"*) as opposed to a bimorphophonemic cluster (e.g., *"can't"*).

Thus, AAE is not an open-syllable dialect despite its higher frequency of final consonant absence relative to socially preferred SAE dialects.

Morphophonemic Rules Bound morphemes are characteristic of AAE, although the full range of pronunciation changes that occur when they are added to lexical stems has not been described systematically. There is reason to expect morphological and phonological features to interact in the dialect. AAE speakers commonly delete inflections for tense (-ed), quantity (-s), and case (i.e., possessive -s and third-person singular -s). Inflectional absence reduces phonetic complexity created when bound markers are added to a word. Adding an /s/ plural marker to a word ending in a final consonant /s/ creates bisegmental and trisegmental consonant clusters (e.g., "pets," "pests"). Since such consonant clusters are

Table 3. Initial and final consonant clusters in SAE and AAE (dialect differences in bold)

Initial			Final		
SAE	AAE	Example word	SAE	AAE	Example word

BISEGMENTALS

Obstruent + Sonorant			Sonorant + Obstruent		
br-	br-	break	-lm	-m	film
pr-	pr-	pray	-lm	-n	kiln
dr-	dr-	dry	-lp	-p	help
tr-	tr-	try	-ld	-d	held
gr-	gr-	grow	-lt	-t	lilt
kr-	kr-	cry	-lk	-k	elk
fr-	fr-	fry	-lf	-f	elf
θr-	**θ-**	throw	-lv	**v/ø**	solve
ʃr-	**sr-**	shred	-lθ	**f/t**	health
bl-	bl-	bleed	-ls	-s	false
pl-	pl-	plea	-ltʃ	tʃ	mulch
gl-	gl-	glue	-ldʒ	-dʒ	bulge
kl-	kl-	climb	-mp	**-mp/m**	trump
fl-	fl-	fly	-mf	**-mp**	triumph
sl-	sl-	sleep	-nt	**-nt/n**	bent
dw-	dw-	dwarf	-nd	**-n**	land
tw-	tw-	twin	-ns	-ns	fence
kw-	kw-	queen	**-nz**	**-ns**	lens
gw-	gw-	Gwen	-nθ	**-nf/nt**	tenth
sw-	sw-	swine	-ntʃ	-ntʃ	lunch
mj-	mj-	mule	-ndʒ	-ndʒ	change
bj-	bj-	beauty	**-ŋk**	**-ŋ**	sink
pj-	pj-	pew			
kj-	kj-	cute			
vj-	vj-	view			
fj-	fj-	few			
hj-	hj-	huge			
sm-	sm-	smile			
sn-	sn-	snake			

Obstruent + Obstruent			Obstruent + Obstruent		
sp-	sp-	spot	-sp	**-s**	wasp
st-	st-	stop	-st	**-s**	west
sk-	sk-	sky	-sk	**-s/ks**	ask
			-pt	**-p**	kept
			-kt	**-t**	act
			-ft	**-f**	left
			-ps	-ps	corpse
			-ks	-ks	box
			-ts	-ts	quartz
			-dθ	**-t/f**	width

(continued)

Table 3. (continued)

TRISEGMENTALS

Obstruent + Obstruent + Sonorant			Sonorant + Obstruent + Obstruent		
spr-	spr-	sprite	-mpt	-mp	tempt
str-	skr-	strike	-mps	-mps	mumps
skr-	skr-	scratch	-ŋkθ	-nf	strength
spl-	spl-	splash	-ŋks	-ns	larynx
skl-	no information	schlera	-kst	-ks	next
			-ksθ	-st/ks	

Adapted from Labov (1972); Luelsdorff (1975); Williams and Wolfram (1977); and Wolfram (1969, 1991, 1994). 1994).

reduced in AAE (e.g., "te*st*"→/tɛs/), the plural of words is formed by using the syllable addition rule, which yields /tɛəz/ instead of /tests/. Although there is no such word as *"tesez"* in SAE, the same addition rule is used whenever the /s/ inflection is added to a word that ends in an /s/. For example, in SAE the plural of *"fence"* is /fɪnsəz/. Speakers of SAE and AAE do not follow a different phonological rule. Speakers of AAE simply apply the same rule to a broader range of words than is observed in SAE because of the final cluster reduction patterns in the dialect.

Much less is known about pronunciation changes that occur when derivational morphemes are added to words. Derivational morphemes can change the grammatical class of the word to which they are attached, in contrast to inflectional morphemes, like -'s or -ed, which do not. A noun (e.g., *"profanity"*) can be changed into an adjective (e.g., *"profane"*) or an adjective (e.g., *"strong"*) can be changed to a noun (e.g., *"strength"*) or verb (e.g., *"strengthen"*) and so on. Shifts in grammatical class can be accompanied by changes in the vowel, stress pattern, and so on. Just one study (Luelsdorff, 1975) has attempted to describe the nature of morphophonemic vowel alternation rules in AAE. The subject was an African American male adolescent residing in Washington, D.C. His conversational speech was taped over a 10-month period. Luelsdorff listed one or more different lexical examples of 94 affixes used by the subject to derive new words. None of these examples required use of a vowel alternation rule. Just two examples of vowel alternation were observed (cf. wise and wizard; deep and depth). Luelsdorff concluded that the database did not justify incorporating the vowel shift rule in AAE phonology.

Allophonic Rules Allophonic rules are not singled out in common descriptions of AAE features, but it is reasonable to expect differences here too, given the lexical distribution of some phonemes (e.g., /θ/ and /f/). Allophonic rules specify context-sensitive changes in the production of a given phoneme that do not alter word meaning (Edwards & Shriberg, 1983). The production of /θ/ or the voiceless interdental consonant in initial word position can be in complementary allophonic distribution with /f/ in medial and final positions. In such cases, the underlying phonological competency of AAE speakers would allow /f/ to replace /θ/

in certain positions without changing word meaning. That is, the word *teeth* is understood by AAE speakers to refer to the same thing regardless of its pronunciation with a final /θ/ or /f/ (Seymour & Ralabate, 1985). If so, then AAE has complex allophonic rules relative to SAE. Its allophones not only include phonetic variants of the same phoneme, but different phonemes also can be treated as semantically irrelevant under certain conditions.

Suprasegmental Features of AAE

Wolfram (1994) briefly mentioned two AAE prosodic characteristics. Stress is placed on the first syllable of some words (e.g., "po̲lice," "De̲troit") that typically are unstressed in other dialects. Speakers of AAE use "a higher pitch range and more rising and level final contours" than do speakers of other English varieties (p. 238).

The fundamental frequency of the voice, which corresponds to perceived pitch, is lower among African Americans than white Americans. (See Dejarnette & Holland's [1993] review.) Less is known about the relationship of perceived pitch to speech intonation patterns. In a comparative study of the conversational patterns of African American ($N = 7$) and white ($N = 8$) adolescents living in Seattle, Washington, Tarone (1975) observed that, compared with whites, African American 1) used higher and more varied pitches; 2) used more level and rising final pitch contours on all sentences in informal situations; 3) used level and *falling* pitch contours on questions, which typically generate a rising contour; and 4) used nonfinal intonation contour to mark "if" clause dependency when the "if" word was absent. Tarone (1975) attributed the majority of AAE's intonational characteristics to the use of language in the particular context of "Black street culture" and not to inherent AAE and SAE differences in intonation rules.

SUMMARY

The preceding discussion revealed that AAE phonological features do *not* differ from those of SAE in every respect. What emerged from the description is that AAE and SAE differ mainly in the positional distribution of phonemes in words and not in the phoneme inventory, with few exceptions. Dialect differences occur most often in the medial and final positions of words. Given the variable rules governing the context dependency of medial and final consonants in AAE, its phonological differences are mainly quantitative and not qualitative.

Among the features that mark AAE dialect as different from SAE, few, if any, are used exclusively by African Americans. Many AAE characteristics can be observed among speakers of other dialects (Fasold, 1981). White Southern and New England speakers also drop the postvocalic /r/. It is common to hear word/ syllable final consonant deletion in the English spoken as a second language by Asian immigrants who have learned native languages, such as Cantonese and Mandarin, which have few final consonants. Consequently, it is inappropriate to conclude that a Vietnamese speaker, who deletes final consonants, is speaking AAE or, conversely, that an AAE speaker with the same feature is speaking Vietnamese English. These speakers simply share a feature. Every AAE feature difference identified may be observed in some other dialect under certain conditions. This observation is to be expected, given the overlapping nature of dialects belonging to the same language. Even among AAE speakers, the type and frequency of features displayed will vary in relation to social class, region, and gender (Wolfram, 1969, 1991).

PHONOLOGICAL PATTERNS OF AFRICAN AMERICAN CHILDREN

Language is learned over time. It is not enough for clinicians to know the AAE dialect spoken by mature African Americans. They also need to know about African American children's phonology at different developmental stages. However, most studies have not had the goal of describing their typical or atypical phonological development. Two types of studies have been done. One type has aimed to describe how well African American children perform on prestructured elicitation tasks relative to a cohort of white children or standardized test norms. Elicitation procedures have targeted either a specific set of AAE pronunciation features (Ratusnik & Koenigsknecht, 1976) or broadly sampled speech sound articulation in the initial, medial, and final positions of isolated words in response to pictured stimuli (Bleile & Wallach, 1992; Cole & Taylor, 1990; Haynes & Moran, 1989; Seymour & Seymour, 1981; Simmons, 1988; Washington & Craig, 1992a).

Another set of studies has focused more narrowly on a single phonological pattern or set of phonemes as produced typically in conversational speech. In some studies, African American children were studied to explore a broad theoretical issue (Stockman, 1993; Stockman & Stephenson, 1981; Vaughn-Cooke, 1976). In other studies (Moran, 1993; Seymour, Green, & Huntley, 1991; Stockman, 1993; Stockman & Settle, 1991; Wolfram, 1989), a description of phonological performance was the end goal, although they did not uniformly focus on describing developmental change. Just one study (Seymour et al., 1991) had anything to say about atypical development.

Taken together, these two sets of studies permit broad inferences about African American children's phoneme inventory and morpheme structure rules. They offer little or no information about the morphophonemic, allophonic, or suprasegmental characteristics of their speech.

Phonological Segments in AAE Development

Elicited Articulation Test Performance The earliest studies compared African American children's responses to prestructured elicitation tasks with those of white children. Ratusnik and Koenigsknecht (1976) studied the relationship of articulation performance to race, social class, and age. Half of the 120 subjects were African American and half were white. Each racial group included four subgroups: younger (median age = 4;5) and older (median age = 5;10) children in the lower and middle classes as determined by residential neighborhood in Chicago and its suburbs. In addition to spontaneous speech, responses were elicited to paragraph completion and sentence repetition tasks designed to tap 12 nonstandard English features, which included 9 phonological features: prevocalic, intervocalic, and postvocalic voiceless *th;* voiced *th;* voiced *v;* postvocalic consonant clusters; and postvocalic *l* and *r* plus the vowel /æ/.

Regardless of whether the sounds occurred in initial, medial, or final word position, mean scores for nonstandard usage were consistently higher for African American than white children. Within each racial group, such scores were higher for younger than older children and higher for those from the lower than the middle class.

Subsequent studies relied on standardized articulation tests, but varied the comparative reference point used. African American children's test responses were compared with those of white children (Seymour & Seymour, 1981; Simmons, 1988), test norms (Cole & Taylor, 1990; Simmons, 1988; Washington & Craig, 1992a), and teacher judgments (Bleile & Wallach, 1992; Washington & Craig, 1992a).

Seymour and Seymour (1981) administered the Goldman-Fristoe Test of Articulation (GFTA; Goldman & Fristoe, 1986) to typically developing white and African American children in child care centers of Springfield, Massachusetts. The 80 children in each racial/ethnic group were equally distributed in number and gender at ages 4 and 5. The two ages were pooled in each racial group for all analyses. The contrastive consonant analysis revealed primarily quantitative rather than qualitative group differences. From the data, it can be inferred that the two groups had the same consonant inventory. But African American children made the most errors on every consonant, except /r/, /l/, /dʒ/, and /tʃ/. Eight of each group's 10 most frequently erred consonants were the same: /θ/, /ð/, /v/, /s/, /z/, /dʒ/, /tʃ/, and /r/. Substitutions were the most common error type for both groups, but omissions due largely to word-final stops comprised a larger percentage of the errors made by African Americans than whites. Common substitutions (/ɟ/ to /d/, / θ/ to /f/), which have been identified as AAE features, also were twice as frequent for African Americans as whites. The Seymours concluded that, except for final stop consonant omission, "norm referenced criteria for English consonants used in the testing of 4- and 5-year-old Black children would differ little from that used for other children" (p. 279).

Simmons (1988) used the Fluharty Preschool and Language Screening Test (Fluharty, 1978) to screen 166 African American and 94 white children (ages 3-6 years) for Head Start programs in the southern rural United States. Only the responses to the articulation subtest are summarized here. Simmons reported that African Americans erred more than whites on nine consonants (/t/g/k/f/θ/d/ŋ/z/s/) in medial and final positions. No information was given about the error patterns used. Still, when compared with test norms, African Americans did not fail the subtest more often than whites. It was concluded that the test is not racially biased.

Haynes and Moran (1989) administered the GFTA to 222 African American preschoolers in rural eastern Alabama. None was receiving speech-language treatment or exhibited any problems. In this cross-sectional developmental study, there were 45–50 children at each grade level from preschool through third grade (ages 3;5–9;11). Unlike Seymour and Seymour's (1981) traditional segment-by-segment analysis of GFTA responses, a phonological process analysis was done in this study. This type of analysis aims to reveal systematic sound changes that affect multiple segments. For example, the deletion of /b/, /d/, and /g/ in word-final position represents a single pattern labeled as final voiced stop deletion instead of three separate articulation errors. All 13 phonological patterns targeted focused on consonantal errors.

It was reported that most of the children never exhibited all 13 of the phonological processes targeted by the test at any age. Final consonant deletion was most prevalent, followed by velar fronting, cluster reduction, and later stopping. Voiced stops were most often deleted, as Seymour and Seymour (1981) observed earlier. The percentage of children who exhibited each pattern decreased systematically across age for every process. Nonetheless, the children persisted in final consonant deletion beyond third grade compared with test norms.

Cole and Taylor (1990) also tested African American children in the southern United States. They were concerned about the validity of standardized tests for identifying phonological impairment. The 10 subjects (5 males and 5 females) were first-graders enrolled in a Lafayette County public school in Mississippi. All subjects were of a low socioeconomic class, as determined by their participation in the school's free lunch program. None had a speech therapy history. Each child was given The Templin-Darley Tests of Articulation (TDTA; Templin & Darley, 1969), The Photo Articulation Test (PAT; Pendergast, Dickey, Selmar, & Soder, 1969), and The Arizona Articulation Proficiency Scale Revised (AAPS; Fudala, 1974) in counterbalanced order. The total scores on each test were calculated first using the procedures described in the manual and then recalculated by giving credit on items that are known to mark AAE features. The percentage of all such items was determined to be 29% (29/141) on the TDTA, 19% (13/67) on the AAPS, and 14% (13/91) on the PAT. Raw scores were elevated when dialect-sensitive items were not counted as errors. If these adjustments had not been made, 70% of the 10 children would have been identified as disordered on the AAPS, 60% on the TDTA, and 30% on the PAT. When score adjustments were made for dialect-sensitive items, none of the children showed up as delayed on the PAT, and no more than 20% did so on the two remaining tests.

Although the AAPS (Fudala, 1974) turned out to be the most negatively biased test in Cole and Taylor's (1990) study, Washington and Craig (1992a) observed a different outcome when they administered its second edition (Fudala & Reynolds, 1986) to metropolitan Detroit children. Their 28 low-income African

American subjects included boys and girls between ages 4;6 and 5;3 who were enrolled at schools designed for children at risk. Although none had a history of speech or language intervention services, all had been judged by classroom teachers to be poor communicators because of either poor articulation patterns ($N = 8$) or poor grammar ($N = 20$). Washington and Craig (1992a) wanted to determine how well the AAPS predicted a child's placement in the group with speech impairments when credit was given for dialect-sensitive items. Subject responses were scored first using the normative data and procedures in the test manual. Scores were adjusted to allow credit for 12 test items (Items 10, 14, 17, 20, 22, 25, 28, 33, 38, 46, 47, and 48), which Cole and Taylor (1990) had identified as dialect sensitive. Washington and Craig (1992a) noted that the test already gave credit for some dialect-sensitive items without using Cole and Taylor's score adjustment. The mean scores for the children with speech impairments, as identified by teachers, were significantly lower than those of children without speech impairments regardless of whether the children were credited for dialect-sensitive items. Nonetheless, significant score gains resulted from crediting each group with correct responses on 12 such items. However, these score changes were not large enough to alter the group placement of 89% or more of the 28 children who took the test. Washington and Craig (1992a) concluded that the revised AAPS can yield a fair articulatory assessment of African American children, but conceded that the test may be less biased toward northern than southern speakers.

Bleile and Wallach (1992) set out to determine whether responses to the PAT predicted Head Start teachers' judgments of which children had trouble speaking and which did not. Three teachers judged the speech of 27 African Americans between ages 3;6 and 5;6. The male and female children were healthy with no hearing loss or oral-motor deficits. The No Trouble Speaking (NTS) group included 12 children (ages 3;7–5;3) and the Trouble Speaking (TS) group had 15 children (ages 3;7–5;3). The authors pointed out that girls outnumbered boys in the NTS group and suggested that the male sex bias associated with developmental disability in other groups also is present for African Americans. The subjects' articulation responses to the PAT were transcribed phonetically and analyzed to reveal patterns that differentiated the NTS and TS groups.

Both groups exhibited test responses that reflected common AAE dialect features (e.g., θ/f and ð/d substitutions). Noticeable group differences were revealed in the number and pattern of errors. The TS group exhibited consonant errors in the *initial* position of words in addition to medial and final word positions that are characteristic of AAE. The TS group also exhibited nasal errors, more than one or two stop consonant and fricative errors, and five or more consonant cluster errors and failed to produce /r/ in at least one context. Bleile and Wallach (1992) concluded that the PAT is capable of revealing articulatory patterns that predict whom community informants are likely to judge as having trouble speaking.

Selected Phonemes or Phonological Patterns In contrast to the global sampling of articulation or phonological patterns in the studies described, other studies have focused more narrowly on a single phonological pattern or subset of sounds (usually consonants). The patterns often studied have been those that commonly differentiate AAE and SAE.

Initial Unstressed Syllables Unstressed syllable deletion is a common AAE feature. Vaughn-Cooke (1976, 1986) focused on this phonological process in the initial word position as attested to in words such as "away," "before," "admit," and so on. She set out to show that cross-generational age shifts in the variable deletion of unstressed syllables in AAE reflected an evolving phonological pattern that is best explained by a theory of language change. Although southern African American and white speakers were studied, only the results pertaining to African Americans are presented here. Instances of initial unstressed syllable deletion were taken from the conversational speech of typical speakers in rural Mississippi (the primary samples). They represented three age groups: 8–20 ($N = 29$), 40–59 ($N = 5$), and 60–92 years ($N = 6$). More than half (59%) of the 29 subjects in the youngest group were between 8 and 12 years and still in the formative stages of language development. Analyses focused on five classes of words as distinguished by the phonological shape of the unstressed syllable: single vowel (v) as in "about"; a vowel + consonant (vc) as in "until"; consonant + vowel (cv) as in "remember," which cannot cluster; consonant + vowel (cv) as in "believe," which can cluster to yield *"blieve"*; and a double consonant cluster + vowel (ccv) as in "pretend." Subanalyses of each syllable shape focused on the word's membership in a grammatical class, its number of syllables, and the preceding phonetic context.

The frequency of syllable deletion increased as subjects got older, although the process occurred variably in every age group. The pattern of findings yielded by the combination of factors explored leads to the following inferences. Initial unstressed syllables are most likely to be deleted by African American speakers when 1) the syllable shape consists of a single vowel (e.g., "away"); 2) the preceding word ends in a vowel (e.g., "go away"); and 3) the target word belongs to a closed grammatical class (e.g., conjunction, preposition) that typically is unstressed in natural speech (cf. "awáy" and "áble"). Unstressed syllables are most likely to be present when 1) the syllable has a cv shape that cannot be clustered with the initial consonant of the second syllable (cf. "beside" and "belong"→"blong"); 2) the preceding word ends in a vowel (e.g., "my divorce"); 3) the target word belongs to an open grammatical class (e.g., nouns, verbs, adjectives) that typically is stressed in natural speech (cf. "begin" vs. "before"); and 4) the word has three syllables (e.g., *"depression"*) as opposed to two (e.g., *"divorce"*). These findings essentially showed that initial unstressed syllable deletion occurs variably but with patterned regularity.

Initial Consonants In contrast to Vaughn-Cooke's (1976) study of older children, Stockman and Settle (1991) examined very young children's single consonant repertoire in initial word position. The seven subjects were typically developing African American children (three males and four females) between 33 and 36 months of age in the Center for Applied Linguistics (CAL) database (see

Stockman & Vaughn-Cooke [1989] for a description of the database). Initial consonants were targeted because they present fewer AAE and SAE differences than do medial and final consonants. Words that are spoken with initial consonants in AAE were targeted in a 2-hour speech sample. An initial consonant was counted in a child's inventory when four correct productions relative to AAE rules had been produced, and these instances included two different words (e.g., "boat," "bath"). This criterion was met by every child on a range of 17–21 different consonants, which included a common core of 15 consonants: /m/n/b/p/d/t/g/k/w/l/r/j/f/s/h/. This minimal consonant core corresponds roughly to the expected consonant repertoire at about 3 years of age based on published studies, as summarized by Newman and Craighead (1989, p. 81).

Medial Consonants   Medial or intervocalic consonants occur at syllable junctures. Scholars have debated whether they should be regarded as either phonetically unique or as another instance of syllable-initial or final consonants. Medial consonants are not included in some articulation tests. Medial consonant sequences, in particular, are complex because some correspond to the phonotactic structure of initial and final clusters (e.g., "basket"), whereas others do not (e.g., "napkin"). In two related studies (Stockman,1993), Stockman & Stephenson, 1981; it was hypothesized that 1) some medial consonant sequences function like syllable-internal initial clusters (e.g., "basket"), whereas others do not (e.g., "napkin"); and 2) consonant performance varies with the number and type of medial consonants in a sequence.

Speakers of AAE are ideal subjects for testing hypotheses about medial consonant sequences. Rules in AAE allow speakers to retain most word-initial clusters and to delete segments in final ones, particularly when they precede another consonant. The medial consonant sequence in bisyllabic words like "fifteen" often is reduced by deleting the postvocalic consonant (e.g., fifteen→[fItin]). Despite tendencies to delete in AAE, medial consonant sequences with the phonotactic structure of initial clusters (e.g., -sk- in "basket") should not be reduced if they continue to function like syllable-initial clusters (e.g., sk- in "skit").

Stockman and Stephenson (1981) designed a nonsense word repetition task to explore whether perceived articulation errors vary with the number of medial consonants in a sequence and the sequence's conformity with the phonotactic structure of initial clusters. Medial consonant stimuli structured around /s/ included four types of items as illustrated here: bisab, bistab, bitsab, and bitstab. The subjects were typically developing 4-year-old African Americans in Washington, D.C., who were learning AAE. The children represented three levels of /s/ proficiency based on number of correct contexts on the Screening Deep Test of Articulation (McDonald, 1968).

Fewer medial consonant errors were observed at high (8–10 correct contexts) than at lower proficiency levels. At all three levels, fewer errors occurred on /s/ as a single medial consonant than on consonant sequences with /s/. Medial consonant sequences that conformed to word-initial clusters (e.g., bistab) were reduced less often than those that did not (e.g., bi<u>ts</u>ab, bi<u>tst</u>ab). Cluster reduction often was achieved by deleting the postvocalic consonant (e.g., bi<u>s</u>tab; bi<u>s</u>ab; bi<u>t</u>stab). Children at the highest /s/ proficiency levels deleted the postvocalic consonant less often in consonant sequences with the phonotactic structure of word initial blends (e.g., bi<u>st</u>ab) than in those without it (e.g., bi<u>ts</u>ab, bi<u>tst</u>ab). It was hypothesized that medial consonant sequences like -*st*- functioned like word-initial clusters. The syllable boundary should come before such medial sequences (bitstab) but between segments in nonconforming sequences (bittsab).

In a larger follow-up study, Stockman (1993) explored whether articulatory performances on initial and medial consonants actually were comparable. Single and sequenced consonants in initial and medial nonsense words were elicited from African Americans using the same stimulus paradigm developed by Stockman and Stephenson (1981). The 106 typically developing children from Washington, D.C., ranged from 36 to 96 months in age. They spanned six age groups, each with male and female subjects.

Judges perceived fewer errors in any context as the children's ages increased. Neither frequency nor type of error distinguished initial and medial performance on /s/ as a single consonant (e.g., <u>s</u>ibib vs. bi<u>s</u>ib). In both positions fewer errors occurred on single than sequenced consonants (e.g., <u>s</u>ibib and <u>st</u>ibib; bi<u>s</u>ib and bi<u>st</u>ib or bi<u>ts</u>ab). As children got older, they performed the same on initial clusters (e.g., <u>st</u>ibib) and comparable medial consonant sequences (e.g., bi<u>st</u>ib). Neither cluster was often in error. By contrast, errors continued to occur at every age on medial sequences that violated the phonotactic structure of word-initial clusters (e.g., bi<u>ts</u>ib). Most errors were due to postvocalic consonant deletion (e.g., bi<u>t</u>sab). The results showed that African American children are sensitive to the rule-governed regularity of initial consonant clusters and respect this regularity even in medial position. It was concluded that initial consonant performances are better predictors of performance on some medial consonants than others.

Final Consonants The selective deletion of final consonants is a common AAE feature. Among the deleted consonants are those for which word contrasts can be maintained by altering the preceding vowel in some way. Nasal consonants represent such a subsystem. Final nasal consonant absence occurs in such languages as French where lexical contrast is retained by nasalizing the preceding vowel. Wolfram (1989) explored whether African Americans exhibited the same pattern. In two analyses, final nasals were sampled in an hour-long conversational speech sample taken from each of 12 subjects in the CAL database (Stockman & Vaughn-Cooke, 1989). This database includes only low-income native English speakers from Washington, D.C.

In the first analysis, four children were observed at three age cross-sections, each with males and females: 18 months, 36 months, and 48 months. The words that potentially can end in an /m/ or /n/ were identified in their speech and transcribed phonetically. The *ng* was excluded because it often is realized as /n/ in

AAE. The 18-month-old subjects did not produce enough words to show stable or consistent final nasal consonants in their speech. There was no evidence that the preceding vowel was nasalized either. At the two older ages, there were enough lexical tokens to infer that a *variable* pattern of final /m/ and /n/ absence coexisted with extensive vowel nasalization. The /n/ was more often deleted than /m/. Both consonants were less likely to be absent when a vowel began the succeeding word or syllable instead of a consonant or no word followed at all.

These patterns were corroborated by the longitudinal analysis of one child in the cross-sectional sample. Her performance was tracked monthly from 18 to 29 months of age. Final nasal absence was observed at the earliest developmental stage with clear bias toward /n/ as opposed to /m/ deletion. Both consonants were more likely to be present when they preceded vowels than consonants. Wolfram (1989) concluded that final nasal consonant absence operates in AAE just like it does in nasalized languages such as French.

Stockman (1991) explored whether the alveolar segment bias, which Wolfram (1989) had observed for final nasals, also applied to final voiceless oral stops with parallel points of articulation. Words that potentially can end in a /p/, /t/, or /k/ according to AAE rules were identified in the conversational speech of seven typically developing African Americans in the CAL database (Stockman & Vaughn-Cooke, 1989). These same children were among Wolfram's (1989) subjects. They ranged in age from 33 to 36 months. An analysis of their phonetically transcribed words showed more frequent deletion of /t/ than of /p/ or /k/, and /p/ was the least often deleted. Each consonant was more likely to be deleted when it preceded another consonant than a vowel in the adjacent word. It was concluded that final consonant deletion in AAE is influenced by an alveolar segment bias.

Moran (1993) examined final stop consonant deletion in relation to the preceding vowel's duration and clinicians' transcription proficiency. The subjects were 10 African Americans in rural Alabama ranging between ages 4;2 and 9;10. Males and females were included. None was enrolled in speech therapy. All the children deleted final consonants 20% of the time in their conversational speech. Each subject twice said the names of 40 pictures to yield 80 responses for analysis. Natural speech was encouraged by having subjects put the stimulus word in a standard carrier phrase, "This one is. . . ." The stimulus list included 20 minimal word pairs that contrasted in the presence or absence of a final voiced or voiceless stop (e.g., "boat" vs. "bow"; "cab" vs. "cap"). Tape-recorded speech responses were judged by white female graduate students in communication disorders. Acoustic analysis of vowel length was done only for the words in which the final consonant was perceived to be absent by all three judges.

The measured duration of the preceding vowel was significantly longer for stops that were perceived as absent than for those that were not. Voiced stops had longer preceding vowels than voiceless stops and were more often judged as absent. Clinicians perceived fewer instances of final stop deletions after phonetic training than before it. It was concluded that the length of the preceding vowel influences the perception of final stop absence.

Phonological Patterns of Children with and without Speech Impairments
It is important to summarize Seymour et al.'s (1991) study here because it focused on whether the kind of phonological patterns described earlier in this chapter could distinguish African Americans with speech delay from those without it. Consonant cluster reduction and final consonant deletion were among the five phonological processes targeted in their study of conversational speech. Vowels were not analyzed. The children ranged in age from 5;6 to 8;6. The nonclinical group included six children. The seven children in the clinical group were enrolled in articulation therapy but were of normal intellectual functioning based on the Columbia Mental Maturity Scale (Burgemeister, Blum, & Lorge, 1972). A certified speech-language pathologist used a variety of toys and pictures to elicit a 30-minute conversational speech sample from each child at school. Three people phonetically transcribed the speech samples, and 1,589 words, pooled across all subjects, were analyzed.

No group difference was observed in total number of utterances produced, number of words, percentage of words with nonstandard pronunciation, or the consonant inventory. Both groups omitted single final consonants, alveolar ones in particular. Both groups reduced final clusters, although the clinical group did so more often. Group differences were most remarkable for liquid simplification. All subjects with impairments but one simplified liquids, whereas no one did so in the nonclinical group. Omission errors by both groups were influenced by the type of succeeding sound and the grammatical class to which the target word belonged. The results showed that clinical and nonclinical groups are not distinguished by consonant deletion patterns, which are characteristic of AAE.

Suprasegmental Features in AAE Development

Little research has focused on the suprasegmental features of AAE. African Americans have been shown to have a lower fundamental frequency than whites (Dejarnette & Holland, 1993). A vocal pitch difference is reliably detected as early as 27 months of life (Tull, 1973). Most of the work on young children has been done in the context of narrative discourse, where the goal has been to determine if and how prosodic features may be used to mark discourse organization (Champion, 1995). Tull (1973) is an exception to this trend. In one of the few studies of African American children's early vocal patterns, Tull compared African American and white children in Ohio at 19 months and 27 months on six physical measurements related to fundamental frequency, pitch contours, and duration. Neither the African American nor the white high school student judges could reliably associate distinctive vocal characteristics with African American babies at 19 months, but both groups of judges did so at 27 months. The physical measurements revealed that final syllable inflection was lower for white than African American children. Voiced segments were longer, and the percentage of voicing within an utterance was longer for African Americans than for whites. Syllable duration decreased between 19 and 27 months for African Americans.

SUMMARY

There are big gaps in the research on the normal and abnormal phonological development of African American children. Few studies have primarily aimed to describe developmental changes in natural speech beginning at an early age. Enough has been done to permit broad inferences about the phoneme inventory and its lexical distribution, but virtually nothing is known about allophonic and morphophonemic rules or suprasegmentals. Nonetheless, some aspect of phonology now has been studied for African Americans in virtually every major U.S. geographic region. These studies permit the following tentative conclusions:

1. African American children's phonological articulatory patterns change across age and vary with social class and geographic region.
2. African American children produce the same phoneme inventory as speakers of native SAE dialects with few exceptions. They differ primarily in the distribution and frequency of phoneme use in particular contexts. However, they differ less on phonemes in initial word position than on those in medial and final positions. The use of single word-initial consonants in conversational speech at 36 months should approximate what is expected of SAE speakers at the same age.
3. African American children are not open-syllable users. The variable absence of medial and final consonants is rule governed. Children are more likely to delete a) final nasal and oral stops than fricatives, b) final alveolar than labial stops in the same class, c) final consonants preceding a consonant than a vowel, and d) final consonants in monomorphemic clusters than in bimorphemic ones. There also is evidence that deletion patterns are influenced by whether consonants are embedded in words belonging to a closed as opposed to an open grammatical class.
4. African American children may use alternative ways to mark lexical contrasts when a final consonant is absent (e.g., the preceding vowel may be nasalized or lengthened more than usual).
5. Standard articulation tests vary in the number of dialect-sensitive items included and are likely to reveal persistence of final consonant deletion beyond the age at which it typically is present in SAE speakers.

CLINICAL MANAGEMENT: ASSESSMENT AND TREATMENT THEMES

Diagnosing Phonological Disorders

African American children with phonological problems have been identified (Seymour et al., 1991), and community informants do differentiate between children who have trouble speaking and those who do not (Bleile & Wallach, 1992; Washington & Craig, 1992a). But the incidence of phonological disorders among African Americans is unknown (Taylor & Peters, 1986). Identifying such an impairment is not problematic in cases of obvious or frank organic insult. African Americans' speech can be impaired by the same factors (e.g., hearing loss, oral-structural and neuromotor damage) that affect other groups. Identifying impairment is problematic because the cause of phonological impairment usually is unknown. Most children with delayed speech and language look typical, and they see, hear, and move their bodies at will. Too often, the most definitive, although obvious, thing that can be said is that the child presents with a developmental disorder or, worse, a functional one.

Distinguishing a normal phonological difference from a developmental phonological disorder is all the more difficult for two other reasons. First, normative data on speakers of minority dialects are inadequate. Second, the kind of articulation difficulties typically associated with delayed speech (e.g., final consonant deletion, cluster reduction) are the same features that already characterize dialect differences and normal developmental errors (Wolfram, 1994). The fact that AAE phonology converges with developmental phonology is not indicative of retardation among African Americans, as Wolfram (1994) pointed out. The explanation is to be found "in the universal set of phonological naturalness and marking principles that guide phonological variation and change toward a more natural state in different types of language situations" (p. 238).

It is standard clinical practice to base clinical judgments on the results of a standardized articulation test, a language sample analysis, and/or a parent referenced-criterion procedure. There are several issues to consider when using each procedure to identify phonologically impaired AAE speakers.

Standardized Tests   Standardized tests obviously are useful for identifying pathology. They are intended to provide controlled observation conditions across different speakers. As a result, clinicians ought to be able to conclude that differences between a child's score and that of a peer-group sample are due to a disorder and not to the testing procedures.

The use of standardized tests can compromise judgments about AAE speakers. Their peer-group samples may not adequately represent AAE speakers, even when African Americans are included in proportion to their representation in the general U.S. population (Washington & Craig, 1992b). Test authors do not offer much detail about the characteristics of the African American speakers included in a sample. At the same time, articulation tests typically are not designed to sample the contexts in which all aspects of AAE phonological competency can be displayed. For example, consonants are sampled in the initial, medial, or final positions of isolated words. This sampling format does not account for the fact that AAE speakers are less likely to produce a final consonant in isolated words than in a multiword context in which it precedes a word beginning with a vowel. Given that speech sounds are equally weighted in the scoring, standardized tests do not account for segment deletion bias in AAE either. Therefore, there is the potential to make erroneous judgments about the phonological competency of AAE speakers.

Although we attempt to eliminate or minimize negative test bias by not counting an alternative dialect response to an item as an error (Cole & Taylor, 1990), this strategy need not result in adequate assessment either. After allowances are made for dialect-sensitive items, there may not be enough remaining items for a valid assessment. Deep tests of articulation are good examples to use here. This testing method should be advantageous for sampling the final consonants in AAE. A deep test does not sample consonant production in single isolated words like traditional articulation tests. It elicits many more productions of the same consonant than do single-word tests and does so in abutting contexts like those found in connected speech. Using the long version, the production of a consonant can be sampled before every English consonant (e.g., "bus fish"; "bus lock") and after each one (e.g., "fish sun"; "lock sun"). However, a word-final consonant preceding a word that begins with another consonant (e.g., "bus fish") is precisely the kind of context that is so vulnerable to deletion by AAE speakers. After making allowances for dialect differences, there may be too few remaining items to judge final consonant production in different contexts. Of the 10 contexts sampled for each consonant in The Screening Deep Test of Articulation (McDonald, 1968), as many as six items are dialect-sensitive for four of the nine sounds tested: /r/, /ts/, /θ/, and /ʃ/. Once the alternative normative dialect responses on six items are excluded, the four remaining items hardly constitute a deep test of articulation for these sounds. Local norms would not result in a more adequate test.

A test loaded with dialect-sensitive items is not useful for predicting impairment. Such items elicit different normative responses from those given by the standardization sample. Consequently, they do not help clinicians differentiate language differences from disorders, unless speakers offer a different response than typically is expected for the minority dialect. For example, a speaker could say the word *"bath"* as [bak] or [bas] instead of [baf].

Conversational Speech Sampling Ideally one should not diagnose a speech problem before listening to a sample of spontaneously generated speech, dialect issues aside. Production of elicited single words or even short phrases on standardized tests may not exemplify habitual speech. It is easier to produce careful speech or to code-switch altogether when the responses are simple and do not have to be selectively retrieved. If nothing else, a conversational sample allows the clinician to observe how well articulatory patterns are preserved when attention must be shared with all the other aspects of language production, including its coexisting prosodic and kinesic features. Stockman (in press) observed further that a spontaneously generated language sample is likely to be less negatively biased toward speakers of minority languages than are other procedures because "the speaker chooses the words and how they are said."

However, if clinicians cannot gloss the words that speakers generate themselves, then intelligibility becomes an issue. In habitual speech, AAE speakers may alter the production of even initial consonants under some conditions. For example, the initial /d/, which replaces /ð/ in words like "that," may be absent when the preceding word ends in a nasal consonant. For example, "ran there" /ræn dɛə/ can become [ræ nɛə]. In fact, sound changes affecting successive words in the flow of speech can make some words difficult to recognize, as is the case for words with adjacent unstressed syllables. For example, the phrase "talking about" can be reduced to [ta: ba:] or [ta: ma:]. Intelligibility can be decreased further in connected speech because there are so many opportunities for abutting consonant contexts (e.g., "take food") that favor final consonant deletion by AAE speakers. Intelligibility also is likely to be affected by the fact that listeners must resolve grammatical and lexical differences at the same time as phonological ones.

Parental Input Ignorance about minority dialects has forced clinicians to rely on the knowledge of community informants when making diagnostic judgments. In fact, clinicians who are not knowledgeable about the dialect community should be very careful about diagnosing a child as having a speech disorder when family members do not consider the child to have a problem. Terrell, Arensberg, and Rosa (1992) proposed a procedure that uses the parent's speech as the criterion reference point for judging delay. Both the child and the parent are given the same test. The clinician identifies the child's pronunciation patterns that match and those that do not match the parent's productions. Matched patterns are considered normative. Nonmatched patterns are considered signs of pathology if the child is older than the age at which the pattern is expected to occur.

The use of parents as the yardstick for evaluating a child's speech does not replace the need for normative data on young African American children. Every child acquires the native dialect over time. The younger the child, the less we can expect typical patterns to match those of the parents. Although older school-age children should match parental pronunciation patterns better than younger children, mismatches still may occur more often than expected. This is because older children may be more influenced by the SAE in schools than are their parents. The extent to which child and parent normative patterns match also varies with the level of parental education. Nothing is known about this area. The need for research on language change issues is discussed on page 147.

Some Guiding Assessment Principles

The preceding discussion suggests that it is a challenge to diagnose a phonological problem in African American children. It clearly is advantageous to use multiple assessment procedures. Proctor (1994) offers many helpful hints for maximizing clinical observations of phonology when dealing with speakers of minority languages and dialects. I identify guidelines for interpreting phonological/articulatory behavior regardless of which assessment procedure is used. These guidelines exploit Wolfram's (1994) hypothesis about how phonological impairment may be expressed in AAE given its similarities and differences relative to SAE.

According to Wolfram (1994), phonological impairment may be expressed in one of three ways. A Type I impairment involves violation of AAE features that are qualitatively and quantitatively like SAE features. Other levels of impairment involve violation of features that differ from SAE either qualitatively (Type II) or quantitatively (Type III). An implicational relationship is assumed to hold among these levels such that a Type I impairment implies or predicts Type II and III impairments and a Type II impairment implies or predicts a Type III impairment. The implicative assumption is based on the expectation that nonstandard and standard dialects are likely to differ on the most marked or complex features of the language (Wolfram, 1991). Hence, a dialect-specific feature will be delayed if the simpler dialect-shared features are also delayed.

Wolfram's (1994) framework offers a useful heuristic not only for determining whether the AAE speaker has an impairment but also for estimating the severity of impairment. The implied multilevel approach to the identification task suggests that clinicians should determine first if AAE speakers are delayed on phonological features that do not differ from SAE. Such features, which include initial single consonants and clusters along with point vowels (/i/, /æ/, /u/, and /a/), are among the most basic English features. A speaker, for example, who misarticulates oral and nasal consonants in the initial position of words exhibits a Type I impairment. This level of impairment is likely to be associated with severe phonological difficulty and to involve AAE features that differ from SAE as well (i.e., if the implicative assumption holds). By focusing on initial consonants, one can at least determine whether there is a phoneme inventory constraint (all consonants except /ŋ/ and /ʒ/ occur in this position) and whether the child has discovered consonant sequencing rules. Most standard articulation tests permit a broad sampling of single consonants and consonant clusters in initial word position.

Wolfram's (1994) view of impairment predicts that performance can be age appropriate on commonly shared AAE and SAE features, but still be impaired on features that mark the dialect as different or nonstandard. To identify a Type II impairment, the child's performance may be compared with a parent's repertoire or, better still, with other African American children in the same age range and linguistic community. Clinicians also should use their own knowledge of AAE patterns to judge when they are violated. A child could be at risk if the voiceless interdental *th* is replaced by a /k/ or /p/ instead of an /f/, the expected AAE variant. Similarly, a child could be at risk if a liquid consonant (e.g., /l/) replaces the voiced interdental *th* instead of the /d/ or /v/, the expected AAE variants.

Finally, a Type III impairment may be identified on quantitative grounds alone, if nothing turns up at Types I or II. Type III impairment involves violation of the expected AAE and SAE differences on those features that are qualitatively shared between dialects but differ quantitatively. Quantitative differences reflect rule-governed variability (Wolfram, 1991). Speakers of AAE and SAE both use final consonants, but AAE speakers do so in fewer contexts. Final consonant use in AAE depends on a variety of factors, including the type of sound and its phonetic context. The clinician must determine whether the child applies a pronunciation pattern (e.g., final consonant deletion) in a wider range of predictable contexts than does the typical AAE speaker. For example, AAE speakers without impairments are not expected to delete a final single consonant before a vowel, but an AAE speaker with impairments may do so. Diagnostic screening could be streamlined further by focusing just on particular consonants, such as labial stops, which are deleted less often than are alveolar ones. A 36-month-old child who never says a final consonant in any context is likely to be delayed in phonological development. To identify a Type III impairment, clinicians must know about variable AAE rules and choose diagnostic contexts that favor feature use for speakers without impairments.

Most standardized tests sample articulation performances broadly enough to identify impairment on commonly shared AAE and SAE features (i.e., a Type I impairment) and possibly a Type II impairment. They typically target most word-initial single consonants and commonly occurring consonant clusters. Apparently, even the entire AAPS–Revised can validly identify speech delay among low-income African American children in the northcentral U.S. region (Washington & Craig, 1992a), whereas the Fluharty Preschool and Language Screening Test is diagnostically valid for Southern speakers (Simmons, 1988). The PAT also appears to be useful for screening the articulation of African American children. According to Cole and Taylor (1990), it did not misdiagnose any of the Southern African American children in their sample after allowances were made for dialect-sensitive items. In addition, the PAT's use of real photographs allows the test stimuli to be more easily recognized than do tests with line-drawn pictures (Madison, Kolbeck, & Walker, 1982). The PAT can reveal response patterns that predict community informants' judgments about which children have trouble speaking and which ones do not (Bleile & Wallach, 1992).

Standard articulation tests, however, cannot be used so easily to identify a Type III impairment—namely, impairment resulting from the speaker's violation of features that differ quantitatively from SAE. These features are governed by variable rules. These rules, for example, specify the contexts for segment deletion, which operate across single-word boundaries.

Phonological Intervention Issues

Once an African American child is identified as having a phonological disorder, we should expect general intervention principles to be the same for them as for other groups of speakers (Seymour, 1986). It must be pointed out, however, that all intervention occurs in a cultural context and that service delivery models are culturally constructed as well. Because African Americans comprise less than 3% of the clinicians certified by the American Speech-Language-Hearing Association, there usually is a culture and language mismatch between African American children and the clinicians who treat them. We know little about the impact of this situation on the effectiveness of service delivery to the African American community. It is reasonable to expect treatment effectiveness to be affected by the extent to which therapy respects 1) the cultural and individual differences in learning style and pace, 2) the cultural relevance of stimulus contexts and vocabulary used in the performance context, and 3) the need for an empathic and trusting relationship between clinician and client (Terrell & Terrell, 1993). The same factors should influence phonological treatment for any group of speakers.

Specifying intervention goals for African Americans bears further discussion on two fronts. One issue concerns the teaching of AAE features and the other one concerns the teaching of SAE.

AAE as an Intervention Goal   Clinicians seem to have grasped the notion that AAE should be the reference point for identifying AAE speakers with impairments until they ask whether one should work on AAE or SAE when treating the disorder. The answer is that, of course, AAE should be the reference point for treating a disorder as well. The concern about using AAE as the reference point stems partly from a narrow view of its linguistic features. It is most often viewed as a dialect that differs categorically from SAE. How can a clinician possibly give the child a word to imitate without putting on the final consonant? It is important to point out that AAE and SAE phonology share many of the same features. Intervention with AAE speakers can never involve teaching the child a strange new speech sound inasmuch as AAE and SAE have virtually the same phoneme inventory. Treating the child's whole phonological system requires attention to those AAE features that do not differ from SAE in addition to those that do. Furthermore, dialect-specific patterns (e.g., substitutions, as in the case of the voiced *th*→/d/ or the voiceless *th*→/f/), represent a subset of possible natural responses to SAE input. These same patterns are produced by children who are in the process of learning SAE and by adults who learn SAE as a second language.

A multilevel system can be used to prioritize intervention goals. First, clinicians should target AAE patterns that affect phonemes in ways that do not differ from SAE. Shared features are likely to reflect basic competencies that critically affect intelligibility. Initial consonant errors impair intelligibility. Next, they should focus on phonological patterns that violate dialect-specific features. Intervention goals for qualitatively different dialect features have been met when the child gives a dialect-appropriate response to SAE input. For example, the child is assumed to have reached the behavioral goal if she or he says /f/ in response to the clinician's modeling of voiceless *th* in words like "ba*th*tub" or "ba*th*."

Intervention for impairment of quantitatively different dialect features (e.g., final consonant deletion) should target just those contexts (e.g., preceding a vowel) in which a final consonant is expected to occur in AAE. These are the same contexts in which final consonants also occur in SAE varieties.

SAE as an Intervention Goal   Although speech-language pathologists are certified to deal with clinical pathology, they also grapple with the issue of if and how to serve people without speech impairments whose native dialect has been judged to be a handicap. Pronunciation patterns can be so noticeable that they often contribute to the judgment that normal speech is handicapping. A handicap exists whenever communicative patterns impede adequate functioning in a particular context. It can be a temporary condition that reflects a speaker's relation to a particular context of speech use. In contrast, a communication disorder presumably reflects an organismic or constitutional problem in the speaker that is neither context specific nor temporary. While speech-language pathologists most often deal with communication disorders that also are handicaps, the two need not be linked. On the one hand, a person with a speech impairment (e.g., stuttering) may not be handicapped or impeded in achieving life goals. On the other hand, speakers without speech impairments can be handicapped if their dialect is judged to be inadequate for a particular work or educational setting. Likewise, clinicians can be professionally handicapped when their SAE does not allow them to communicate effectively in a clinical context involving speakers of a minority language or dialect.

Intervention for speakers without speech impairments who are perceived as speech handicapped is popularly known as *accent reduction.* This type of intervention raises two questions: 1) Should AAE speakers without impairments change their speech patterns? 2) If so, are speech-language pathologists qualified to do the intervention? In response to the first question, clinicians may be tempted to tell nonstandard speakers that services are not needed because their speech is simply different, not disordered. But the reality is that speakers of minority dialects and languages can be functionally handicapped by their normal communication patterns. Employers are less likely to hire African Americans who speak vernacular AAE than those who do not (Terrell & Terrell, 1983). When speech patterns interfere with achieving life goals, speakers are wise to expand their linguistic repertoires.

Changing the linguistic repertoire for a speaker without impairments does not necessarily mean that the existing dialect or language must be abandoned. Intervention goals should be guided by whether the existing dialect is a native or nonnative tongue. For native speakers of nonstandard English dialects like AAE, SAE should be learned and used as an alternative second dialect when the communicative context warrants it (Taylor, 1986; Wolfram, 1991). Altering the code or style of speaking to accommodate different situations is a natural part of pragmatic communicative competency. In some cases, code switching amounts to little more than a style shift, as is the case for SAE speakers. For minority groups, it may be necessary to shift dialects or even languages to accommodate a particular communicative context. The question of whether AAE speakers should learn SAE should be viewed in the context of shifts in communication registers. This means that intervention should be geared toward expanding, not replacing, the existing native language. In contrast, accent reduction therapy for speakers of English as a second language aims to replace the existing English with more native-like English. Nevertheless, meeting this goal does not require the speaker to abandon the non-English native language.

In response to the second question, it is not clear that speech-language pathologists are suitably educated to teach SAE to nonstandard English speakers. This is not a scope-of-practice issue. Speech-language pathologists generally are concerned with facilitating communicative competency, which includes the pragmatics of modifying speech to suit different situations. The issue is whether they are adequately prepared to deal with dialects as a code-switching phenomenon. Clinicians need to operate with a quite a bit of knowledge about the cultural conditions for speaking in order to properly guide the intervention. Until 1995, accreditation standards of the American Speech-Language-Hearing Association did not require educational programs to expose students to issues in cultural diversity. And even now that it does, students often are exposed to dialects in a piecemeal fashion, given the popularity of the infusion instructional model. Most students are not required to take a course on language dialects or on issues pertaining to culture and communication.

Moreover, behavioral *eradication* underlies clinical models for changing disordered behavior. An eradication approach aims to rid the speaker of existing behavior and replace it with new behavior. Such approaches, while compatible with the goal of eliminating nonnative English accents, are not compatible with the goal of teaching a coexisting, *alternative* code to speakers of a native nonstandard English dialect. Standard American English is meant to complement, not replace, the native nonstandard English dialect. It is questionable whether speech-language pathologists are prepared to meet the latter kind of intervention goal.

RESEARCH OUTLOOK

Research on the phonology of child speakers of AAE has been limited in quantity and investigative scope. Much of the research has been motivated by the urgent need to solve practical clinical problems. The validity of existing assessment procedures has been determined by sampling performance on standardized tests, which are best suited for use with older children. Furthermore, prestructured elicitation procedures, which require one to already know what to assess, have been used without the benefit of much normative data on African Americans. Developmental studies of African American children's phonology in natural speaking situations beginning at an early age are practically nonexistent.

Much of what is known even about mature AAE speakers is based on a narrow population—namely, young urban teen males interacting in very selective social contexts. This subgroup is not likely to represent the speech patterns of all AAE speakers, who vary widely on factors known to cause dialect differences (e.g., social class, education, geographic region). We have paid so much attention to how SAE and AAE speakers differ that we know little about the range of normal variability among AAE speakers.

We need to know more about the normative phonological patterns of AAE speakers on all fronts. A comprehensive description demands a research focus on the AAE features that are like SAE in addition to those that are not. The questions and methods also must be theoretically grounded in ways that reveal the acquisition process and connect it to what is known about human learning in general.

Investigating Common AAE and SAE Phonological Features

Expanding Developmental Descriptions of AAE   Research has focused less often on AAE features that are like SAE than on those that differ. This bias undoubtedly reflects the fact that many commonly shared features are basic English features that already have been studied in some detail. Replication studies usually are not encouraged unless the goal is to reveal a different outcome. It is reasonable to expect the existing knowledge base to be applicable to all the children who learn dialects of the same language, particularly in respect to their commonly shared features. However, replication studies with African Americans are warranted for several reasons.

First, African Americans seldom have been subjects in developmental research studies (Graham, 1992). Generalizing existing developmental findings to them often is tempered by continuing suspicion that they either do not develop as much language as other groups or do so at a slower rate (see, e.g., Hart and Risley's 1995 study of vocabulary). Only empirical observations can determine whether this view is myth or reality.

Second, a comprehensive description demands the inclusion of commonly shared AAE and SAE features. In the absence of empirical documentation, even the assumptions about which features are shared remain tentative. This is especially the case for vowel and prosodic sounds. Table 1 in this chapter gives the impression that there are few vowel differences between AAE and SAE, but the fact is that we know very little about vowels in AAE. Past studies have focused on consonants. Research is likely to turn up AAE and SAE vowel differences, given the argument that vowels are particularly susceptible to the local listening environment. Labov (1987) has hypothesized that vowels are shifting across time in different directions for vernacular AAE speakers and for SAE speakers.

Third, identical phonological features in two dialects do not guarantee the same developmental schedule. African American children's acquisition of shared AAE and SAE phonological features is likely to be mediated not only by different language input conditions but also by interactions between the features that are similar and dissimilar to SAE. Indeed, studies have turned up differences between child speakers of SAE and AAE in the frequency of error on particular phonemes (Seymour & Seymour, 1981). African Americans do not always make more errors. For example, they appear to make fewer errors on the consonantal /r/ than do SAE speakers (Seymour & Seymour, 1981). The word-initial /r/ met the criterion for inclusion in a minimal competency core as early as 33 to 36 months in Stockman and Settle's (1991) study. Normative data based largely on white children typically show /r/ as a later developing sound. However, late /r/ development may be due to the use of standard single word articulation tests instead of conversational speech samples as used by Stockman and Settle (1991). Larkins (1983), using connected speech samples, showed that the /r/ was correctly produced more than 90% of the time by 3-year-old white children. Although /r/ performance was not represented by word position, still African American children with speech impairments differed from those without speech impairments in liquid simplification (Seymour et al., 1991) and correct production of /r/ in at least one context (Bleile & Wallach, 1992). Mowrer and Burger (1991) concluded that monolingual South African Xhosa-speaking preschoolers had overall earlier articulatory development than white South African preschoolers who were monolingual English speakers. Group differences were more common on some sounds than others. When compared on what appeared to be perceptually equivalent sounds, for example, Xhosa speakers made fewer errors on fricatives like /s/, /z/, and /ʃ/ than did their white English-speaking counterparts.

No readily available explanation comes to mind for what seems like advanced learning of some speech sounds among speakers with African lineage. In the case of U.S. speakers, however, the simplicity of the AAE phonological system in certain respects encourages speculation about the distribution of perceptual-cognitive resources in learning a language. The word "simplicity" refers to the fact that AAE as the target language allows simpler sounds (e.g., /f/, /d/) to replace phonetically more complex ones (e.g., interdental fricatives). Final consonants can be deleted as singletons and in clusters, and the /r/ does not have the vocalic (/ɝ/ in "bird"; /ɣ/ in "butter") or postvocalic (/r/ in "beer") allophones. There are grammatical simplification patterns as well (Wolfram, 1991). These observations raise a number of questions about the acquisition process. How are cognitive resources used when the target language allows speakers to operate with simpler or more natural sound patterns? Does this mean that more attention can be devoted to perfecting the production of the more difficult consonants like prevocalic /r/ and /l/? Or is a phonetic gain offset by the added cognitive resources that may be required to figure out variable as opposed to nonvariable rules in the dialect?

Implications for Linguistic Theory Research on commonly shared AAE and SAE dialect features is relevant to evaluating theoretical assumptions about linguistic universals and the possible biological basis for language. Bickerton (1984) is among scholars who have gone so far as to argue that the acquisition of pidgin and creole grammars, in particular, can offer unique evidence for the biological substrates of language. Phonology is especially suited to the study of language universals, given its interface with the physical aspects of speech perception and production. Cross-linguistic parallels in phonology have been revealed (Locke, 1983; Locke & Pearson, 1992). However, studies most often have compared different languages rather than dialects. The exclusion of nonstandard dialect speakers like those who acquire AAE is surprising. The cultural context and language socialization experiences of African Americans have been viewed as different from those of other U.S. ethnic groups, and rightfully so (Battle &

Anderson, 1993). Furthermore, it has been argued that frequency and type of familial language input influence the language of African American children (Hart & Risley, 1995). Consequently, cross-dialect research on shared features ought to be done, if for no other reason than to determine whether the same speech sound acquisition schedule is preserved despite different input conditions. If so, then very robust developmental features would be revealed to the advantage of clinicians. It would allow them to use the same guidelines to evaluate speakers from different linguistic and cultural backgrounds, including those who speak SAE.

Investigating AAE and SAE Phonological Differences

Expanding the Developmental Description of AAE   There is strong reason to continue documenting how AAE and SAE child speakers differ. First, a comprehensive description of African American children's normative patterns across age must include such differences. Given the narrowly focused research on AAE phonology, there still is much to learn about their dialect-specific features. As discussed, suspected differences in the vocalic and prosodic aspects of speech have been neglected in research, as have morphophonemic and allophonic AAE rules. Admittedly, the nonlinear aspects of phonology have been neglected in the study of all groups (Stoel-Gammon, 1992).

Second, regardless of which phonological dimension is studied, research should aim to reveal not only categorical or qualitative AAE/SAE differences, as done in the past, but also quantitative ones. In fact, the phonology of a decreolizing dialect like AAE may be best distinguished from SAE by its quantitative feature differences. That is, AAE and SAE speakers use the same features, but differ in frequency of use. Research should continue to capitalize on the variable-rule paradigm, which has allowed scholars to account for such quantitative variability. Although much remains to be learned about the rules that condition the differential distribution and use of speech sounds across age, we know enough already to expect multiple linguistic factors to be important.

Third, in the earlier part of this chapter, it was shown that final consonant deletion is influenced by the type of speech sound produced, the type of succeeding consonant, the type of word in which consonants are embedded, and so on. But we do not know if or how such contingencies are developmentally ordered nor how they may interact to influence performance for any one speaking event. Does performance respect a rule hierarchy when competing factors operate to influence the presence or absence of a speech sound in a given context? What happens, for example, when the final consonant occurs in a word preceding a consonant, a context that favors deletion, but the word belongs to an open grammatical class, a context that does not favor deletion (e.g., "beet juice")? Is a variable-rule dialect inherently more difficult or easier to learn than a dialect that lacks a wide range of such variability? To get at such causal or interacting performance factors, research has to have more than a normative descriptive goal. It also must be guided by broad questions about language learning mechanisms.

Implications for Linguistic Theory
Theories of Language Change The study of AAE/SAE phonological differences also is relevant to theories of language change and markedness. Cross-
generation comparisons of AAE speakers can reveal information about the rate,
direction, and cause of language change (Vaughn-Cooke, 1986, 1987). Although
all dialects change across time, AAE may be changing more rapidly than others.
Language is a barometer of social change. Since the mid-1970s, school desegre-
gation, particularly in Southern states, has changed the language input for many
African American children. The impact of such input on children's speech is
likely to particularly affect word pronunciation, an easily observed and monitored aspect of spoken language. The implications are that clinical assessment
must be tempered by the possibility that 1) the existing normative descriptions of
AAE may not be entirely accurate, and 2) parental speech patterns may not be
ideal criteria for judging the normative dialect patterns of school-age children.
The question of if and how fast AAE may be changing is not being addressed.

Scholars are at least paying attention to the *direction* of language change in
AAE. This work has been relevant to evaluating the claims of Labov's (1987) divergence hypothesis, namely, the claim that AAE is becoming less like SAE across
time. The issue is far from settled. Vaughn-Cooke (1987) has argued that time-
apparent data are needed. The comparative study of AAE and SAE speakers across
successive generations is expected to be important testing ground for the divergence hypothesis.

Theories of Markedness Patterns of diachronic language change in a decreolizing dialect like AAE can offer evidence for "markedness" principles in
phonological theory. These principles have been used to scale articulatory complexity in terms of natural constraints (Edwards & Shriberg, 1983) and support
the assumption of implicative relationships among sounds. Markedness theory has
been used to explain why some speech sounds are present or absent more often than
others in languages, why some speech sounds change before others within a language across time, and why some speech sounds are acquired earlier than others
in ontogenetic development. Such explanatory power is clinically useful because
it allows clinicians to scale the severity of phonological impairment and prioritize
intervention goals. For example, severe problems would be associated with failure
to produce easy or less marked phonological features. The scaling of articulatory
complexity theory along naturalness lines optimally should allow clinicians to
predict performance on untested sounds from the performance on the tested ones.
For example, errors would be expected to occur on marked phonological features
if they were observed on less marked ones.

The study of AAE and SAE dialect differences could offer further support
for markedness theory inasmuch as they appear to be patterned along naturalness
lines. Variable rules for consonant deletion, for example, cater to natural phonological tendencies. Consonants are most often deleted in the marked word-final
position. The greater tendency to delete final stops than fricatives also may re-

flect naturalness principles. Kent's (1982) observation that fricatives are more often correct in the word-final than initial position during typical SAE development suggests that fricatives are easier to say in final than initial position. The tendency to retain the final consonant before the vowel reflects the preservation of the highly favored canonical cvcv structure in the languages of the world. Vaughn-Cooke's (1976, 1986) insightful, cross-generational study of unstressed syllable deletion suggested that AAE is changing across successive generations in the direction of becoming progressively more phonologically complex like SAE. Older speakers did not omit the initial unstressed syllables in what could be regarded as phonologically less marked or easier contexts. Speakers at all ages were likely to say unstressed syllables when their phonological shapes and phonetic contexts did not violate the canonical cvcv pattern. Younger subjects also produced unstressed syllables in words with more marked phonological shapes. Such observations point to language changes that are patterned to respect naturalness principles. It would be valuable to explore whether markedness principles predict cross-generational dialect changes on other AAE features (e.g., final consonant deletion) and whether such shifts parallel the direction of developmental changes among children with typical or delayed speech. Parallels between AAE features and children's language development have been observed. But as Ferguson (1992) noted, "studies that compare diachronic sound change with children's phonological development in a point-by-point fashion. . . are relatively rare" (p. 490).

Need for Clinical Research

Although basic research on AAE phonology is expected to inform and strengthen clinical research, applied issues should continue to be investigated in their own right. Descriptions of abnormal phonological systems among African Americans are conspicuously absent. Studies need to show whether Wolfram's (1994) multi-level framework for describing phonological impairment in a nonstandard English dialect actually holds up when applied to a population of children. The implicative assumption of this model motivates several questions. Do AAE child speakers with Type I impairment also exhibit Types II and III impairments? Is there a relationship between intelligibility ratings and degree of impairment represented as Types I, II, or III? Does intervention with a Type I impairment lead to symptom reduction for Types II and III impairments?

Researchers should make limited use of existing standardized tests when seeking an *initial* description of a developing system, but diagnostic validity studies of standardized tests will continue to be valuable. The use of community informants as the reference point for validating tests should be encouraged in particular (Bleile & Wallach, 1992).

SUMMARY

This chapter has offered an overview of the issues concerned with AAE phonology. It was argued that phonology is particularly susceptible to dialect differences. The Edwards and Shriberg (1983) model of phonological competency was used as a framework for describing AAE and SAE differences and similarities and for summarizing studies of African American children's phonology. The survey of children's phonological patterns was organized around studies have focused on a broad sample of performance using standardized tests and those that have focused on particular phonological subsystems, as revealed most often in a language sample. Clinical assessment issues were reviewed in terms of the use of standardized tests, conversational speech samples, and parent-referenced criterion procedure for doing a phonological evaluation. Guidelines for interpreting performance outcomes were structured around Wolfram's (1994) multilevel framework for describing phonological impairment in a nonstandard dialect like AAE. Intervention issues related to teaching AAE and SAE to African American children were addressed. Finally, theoretical and clinical research issues that affect the study of similarities and differences between AAE and SAE were identified.

REFERENCES

Battle, D., & Anderson, N. (1993). Cultural diversity in the development of language. In D. Battle (Ed.), *Communication disorders in multicultural populations* (pp. 158–185). Boston: Andover.

Baugh, J. (1983). *Black street speech: Its history, structure and survival.* Austin: University of Texas Press.

Bickerton, D. (1984). The language bioprogram hypothesis. *Behavioral and Brain Sciences, 7,* 173–221.

Bleile, K., & Wallach, H. (1992). A sociolinguistic investigation of the speech of African-American preschoolers. *American Journal of Speech-Language Pathology, 1*(2), 54–62.

Boysson-Bardies, B. de, Halle, P., Sagart, L., & Durand, C. (1989). A cross-linguistic investigation of vowel formants in babbling. *Journal of Child Language, 16,* 1–17.

Burgemeister, B., Blum, L., & Lorge, I. (1972). *Columbia Mental Maturity Scale.* New York: Harcourt Brace Jovanovich.

Campbell, L., & Taylor, O. (1992). ASHA certified speech-language pathologists: Perceived competency levels with selected skills. *The Howard Journal of Communication, 3*(3–4), 163–176.

Champion, T. (1995). *A description of narrative production and development in child speakers of African American English.* Unpublished dissertation, University of Massachusetts, Amherst.

Cole, P., & Taylor, O. (1990). Performance of working-class African-American children on three tests of articulation. *Language, Speech, and Hearing Services in Schools, 21*(2), 171–176.

Dejarnette, G., & Holland, W. (1993). Voice and voice disorders. In D. Battle (Ed.), *Communication disorders in multicultural populations* (pp. 212–238). Boston: Andover.

Dillard, J.L. (1972). *Black English: Its history and usage in the United States.* New York: Random House.

PHONOLOGICAL DEVELOPMENT IN AAE / 151

Edwards, M., & Shriberg, L. (1983). *Phonology: Applications in communicative disorders.* San Diego, CA: College-Hill Press.

Fasold, R.W. (1981). The relation between black and white speech in the south. *American Speech, 56,* 163–189.

Ferguson, C. (1992). Implications of models and research. In C. Ferguson, L. Menn, & C. Stoel-Gammon (Eds.), *Phonological development: Models, research implications* (pp. 487–492). Timonium, MD: York Press.

Fluharty, N.B. (1978). *Fluharty Preschool Speech and Language Screening Test.* New York: Teaching Resources.

Fudala, J.B. (1974). *Arizona Articulation Proficiency Scale: Revised.* Los Angeles: Western Psychological Services.

Fudala, J.B., & Reynolds, W.M. (1986). *Arizona Articulation Proficiency Scale* (2nd ed.). Los Angeles: Western Psychological Services.

Goldman, R., & Fristoe, M. (1986). *Goldman-Fristoe Test of Articulation.* Circle Pines, MN: American Guidance Service.

Graham, S. (1992). Most of the subjects were white and middle class. *American Psychologist, 47,* 629–639.

Hart, B., & Risley, T. (1995). *Meaningful differences in the everyday experience of young American children.* Baltimore: Paul H. Brookes Publishing Co.

Haynes, W., & Moran, M. (1989). A cross-sectional developmental study of final consonant production in southern black children from preschool through third grade. *Language, Speech, and Hearing Services in Schools, 20*(4), 400–406.

Ingram, D. (1995). The cultural basis of prosodic modifications to infants and children: A response to Fernald's universalist theory. *Journal of Child Language, 22,* 223–233.

Jusczyk, P. (1992). Developing phonological categories from speech signals. In C. Ferguson, L. Menn, & C. Stoel-Gammon (Eds.), *Phonological development: Models, research implications* (pp. 17–64). Timonium, MD: York Press.

Kent, R. (1982). Contextual facilitation of correct sound production. *Language, Speech, and Hearing Services in Schools, 13,* 66–76.

Labov, W. (1972). *Language in the inner city.* Philadelphia: University of Pennsylvania Press.

Labov, W. (1987). Are black and white vernaculars diverging? Papers from the NWAVE XIV Panel Discussion. *American Speech, 62,* 5–12.

Larkins, P. (1983). Development at 3 years. In J. Irwin & S. Wong (Eds.), *Phonological development in children 18 to 72 months.* Carbondale: Southern Illinois Press.

Lehiste, I. (1970). *Suprasegmentals.* Cambridge, MA: MIT Press.

Locke, J. (1983). *Phonological acquisition and change.* New York: Academic Press.

Locke, J., & Pearson, D. (1992). Vocal learning and the emergence of phonological capacity: A neurobiological approach. In C. Ferguson, L. Menn, & C. Stoel-Gammon (Eds.), *Phonological development: Models, research implications* (pp. 91–129). Timonium, MD: York Press.

Luelsdorff, P.A. (1975). *A segmental phonology of Black English.* The Hague: Mouton.

Madison, C., Kolbeck, C., & Walker, J. (1982). An evaluation of stimuli identification on three articulation tests. *Language, Speech, and Hearing Services in Schools, 13,* 110–115.

McDonald, E. (1968). *The Screening Deep Test of Articulation.* Pittsburgh, PA: Stanwix House.

Moran, M. (1993). Final consonant deletion in African American children speaking Black English: A closer look. *Language, Speech, and Hearing Services in Schools, 24,* 161–166.

Mowrer, D., & Burger, S. (1991). A comparative analysis of phonological acquisition of consonants in the speech of 21/2- to 6-year-old Xhosa- and English-speaking children. *Clinical Linguistics and Phonetics, 5*(2), 139–164.

Newman, P.W., & Craighead, N.A. (1989). Assessment of articulatory and phonological disorders. In N. Craighead, P. Newman, & W. Secord (Eds.), *Assessment and remediation of articulatory and phonological disorders*. Columbus, OH: Charles E. Merrill.

Pendergast, K., Dickey, S., Selmar, J., & Soder, A. (1969). *The Photo Articulation Test.* Danville, IL: Interstate Printers.

Proctor, A. (1994). Phonology and cultural diversity. In R.J. Lowe (Ed.), *Phonology: Assessment and intervention: Applications in speech pathology* (pp. 207–245). Baltimore: Williams & Wilkins.

Ratusnik, D., & Koenigsknecht, R. (1976). Influence of age on black preschoolers' nonstandard performance of certain phonological and grammatical forms. *Perceptual and Motor Skills, 42,* 199–206.

Seymour, H. (1986). Clinical principles for language intervention for language disorders among nonstandard speakers of English. In O. Taylor (Ed.), *Treatment of communication disorders in culturally and linguistically diverse populations* (pp. 153–178). San Diego, CA: College-Hill Press.

Seymour, H., Green, L., & Huntley, R. (1991). *Phonological patterns in the conversational speech of African-American Children.* Poster presented at the national convention of the American Speech-Language-Hearing Association, Atlanta, GA.

Seymour, H., & Ralabate, P. (1985). The acquisition of a phonologic feature of Black English. *Journal of Communication Disorders, 18,* 139–148.

Seymour, H., & Seymour, C. (1981). Black English and Standard American English contrasts in consonantal development for four- and five-year-old children. *Journal of Speech and Hearing Disorders, 46,* 276–280.

Simmons, J.O. (1988). Fluharty Preschool and Language Screening Test: Analysis of construct validity. *Journal of Speech and Hearing Disorders, 53,* 168–174.

Stockman, I. (1991, November). *Constraints on final consonant deletion in Black English.* Poster presented at the annual convention of the American Speech-Language-Hearing Association, Atlanta, GA.

Stockman, I. (1993). Variable word initial and medial consonant relationships in children's speech sound articulation. *Perceptual and Motor Skills, 76,* 675–689.

Stockman, I. (in press). The promises and pitfalls of language sample analysis as an assessment tool for linguistic minority children. *Language, Speech, and Hearing Services in Schools.*

Stockman, I., & Settle, S. (1991, November). *Initial consonants in young black children's conversational speech.* Poster presented at the annual convention of the American Speech-Language-Hearing Association, Atlanta, GA.

Stockman, I., & Stephenson, L. (1981). Children's articulation of medial consonant clusters: Implications for syllabification. *Language and Speech, 24*(2), 185–204.

Stockman, I., & Vaughn-Cooke, F. (1989). Addressing new questions about black children's language. In R. Fasold & D. Schiffrin (Eds.), *Language change and variation* (pp. 274–300). Amsterdam: John Benjamins Publishing.

Stoel-Gammon, C. (1992). Overview: Research on phonological development: Recent advances. In C. Ferguson, L. Menn, & C. Stoel-Gammon (Eds.), *Phonological development: Models, research implications* (pp. 273–282), Timonium, MD: York Press.

Tarone, E. (1975). Aspects of intonation in Black English. *American Speech, 48,* 1–2, 29–36.

Taylor, O. (1986). Teaching English as a second dialect. In O. Taylor (Ed.), *Treatment of communication disorders in culturally and linguistically diverse populations* (pp. 153–178). San Diego, CA: College-Hill Press.

Taylor, O., & Peters, C. (1986). Speech and language disorders in blacks. In O. Taylor (Ed.), *The nature of communication disorders in culturally and linguistically diverse populations* (pp. 157–180). San Diego, CA: College-Hill Press.

Templin, M., & Darley, F. (1969). *The Templin-Darley Tests of Articulation* (2nd ed.). Iowa City: Bureau of Educational Research and Service, Division of Extension and University Services, University of Iowa.

Terrell, S., Arensberg, K., & Rosa, M. (1992). Parent–child comparative analysis: A criterion-referenced method for the nondiscriminatory assessment of a child who spoke a relatively uncommon dialect of English. *Language, Speech, and Hearing Services in Schools, 23,* 34–42.

Terrell, S., & Terrell, F. (1983). Effects of speaking Black English on employment opportunities. *ASHA, 25,* 27–29.

Terrell, S., & Terrell, F. (1993). African-American cultures. In D. Battle (Ed.), *Communication disorders in multicultural populations* (pp. 3–37). Boston: Andover.

Tull, B.M. (1973). *Analysis of selected prosodic features in the speech of black and white children.* Unpublished dissertation, The Ohio State University, Columbus.

Vaughn-Cooke, F. (1976). The implementation of a phonological change: The case for re-syllabification in Black English. *Dissertation Abstracts International, 38*(01), 234A. (University Microfilms No. AAC7714537)

Vaughn-Cooke, F. (1986). Lexical diffusion: Evidence from a decreolizing variety of Black English. In M. Montgomery & G. Bailey (Eds.), *Language variety in the south* (pp. 111–130). Tuscaloosa: University of Alabama Press.

Vaughn-Cooke, F. (1987). Are black and white vernaculars diverging? *American Speech, 62,* 12–32.

Washington, J., & Craig, H. (1992a). Articulation test performances of low-income, African-American preschoolers with communication impairments. *Language, Speech, and Hearing Services in Schools, 23,* 203–207.

Washington, J., & Craig, H. (1992b). Performances of low-income, African-American preschool and kindergarten children on the Peabody Picture Vocabulary Test-Revised. *Language, Speech, and Hearing Services in Schools, 23,* 329–333.

Williams, R., & Wolfram, W. (1977). A linguistic description of social dialects. *Social dialects. Differences vs disorders.* Rockville, MD: American Speech-Language-Hearing Association.

Wolfram, W. (1969). *A sociolinguistic description of Detroit Negro speech.* Washington, DC: Center for Applied Linguistics.

Wolfram, W. (1989). Structural variability in phonological development: Final nasals in vernacular Black English. In R. Fasold & D. Schiffren (Eds.), *Current issues in linguistic theory: Language change and variation* (pp. 301–332). Amsterdam: John Benjamins Publishing.

Wolfram, W. (1991). *Dialects and American English.* Englewood Cliffs, NJ: Prentice Hall.

Wolfram, W. (1994). The phonology of a sociocultural variety: The case of African American vernacular English. In J. Bernthal & N. Bankson (Eds.), *Child phonology: Characteristics, assessment, and intervention with special populations* (pp. 227–244). New York: Thieme.

8

Orofacial, Physiological, and Acoustic Characteristics

Implications for the Speech of African American Children

Marlene B. Salas-Provance

This chapter has been difficult to conceptualize. Initially, ideas for chapter development came easily. I would write about orofacial anomalies and sickle-cell disease. Many professionals in the field of speech pathology and audiology know that African American individuals have a low incidence of cleft lip and palate and a high incidence of sickle-cell disease, so biological facts provided a locus for study. But after a survey of the literature was completed, the pressing question of "why?" remained. Why is it necessary to discuss orofacial, physiological, and acoustic characteristics as they relate to the speech of African American children? Should we expect factors inherent to a particular race or culture to be the "cause" of speech disorders? Thinking in biological terms, has there been any evidence that shows that African Americans are biologically different from whites? In fact, there has been much discussion that denounces race as a biological category (Barkan, 1994; Cavalli-Sforza, 1995), although some individuals claim otherwise (Herrnstein & Murray, 1994). If biological differences do not exist among people, then orofacial, physiological, and acoustic normative data acquired from white children should be applicable to children from all cultures and races. Yet, as the world becomes increasingly diverse, it becomes clearer that the information we now have is not applicable to all children and that we are missing a big piece of the puzzle when research with individuals from other races and cultures is ignored.

In the early years of our profession, similar questions were asked, not about race but about speech (Perkins & Curlee, 1969). The questions then were several: What causes hearing problems? What causes voice problems? What causes poor articulation? Speech-language pathologists were searching for functional relationships such as that between a poor voice and high muscle tension and a good voice and low muscle tension. Are we now also looking for a simple causal relationship between race and disordered speech production? *Organic* is a term "frequently used in speech pathology to mean that a disorder is *caused* by a defect in the anatomy or physiology of the speech regulating system" (Perkins & Curlee, p. 233). If a speech disorder is not learned (i.e., functional), then it is organic. However, a speech disorder may be both organic and functional. Many times, when the explanation is obvious (the association of nasality and cleft palate), we do not look further than the organic cause. After the cleft is repaired, however, the child may continue to produce nasality; now the disorder (nasality) has a functional or learned component. In the same way, we also must look beyond structure when we study speech production deviations in various races. We must not limit ourselves to the notion of a structural basis for impaired speech production but remember that physiogenic and psychogenic are interrelated. It is necessary to study the orofacial, physiological, and acoustic characteristics of individuals from other races and cultures because speech is not explained simply from a single structural framework (which may or may not be the same for different races). But the psychological factors particular to each ethnic or racial group are equally as important as the physiological components are to explaining speech. Furthermore, intellectual, behavioral, and environmental factors also contribute to this delicate product called speech. Taylor (1980) speaks to this issue when he states, "it may seem reasonable to some to question the tenability of the concept of an African American communication disorder . . . from a sociocultural perspective . . . all communication—normal or pathological—can only be defined, studied, or discussed from a cultural orientation" (p. 63).

There is a limited amount of research related to orofacial structure and physiology and to acoustic characteristics of speech in culturally diverse groups. Many of the existing studies tend to focus on prevalence data on organic-based speech disorders (Siegel, 1975; Vanderas, 1987). Although acoustic analysis of speech is favored as a sophisticated clinical and research approach, it has been used to study the speech of individuals from a variety of races and cultures by only a few researchers (Mayo, 1990; Mayo, Manning, & Hudson, 1989; Walton & Orlikoff, 1994). In 1986, Cole pointed out the need for research in the areas of psychoacoustics and organically based communication disorders with minority populations. In the 1990s, we have only begun to answer this call.

Several factors may lead both to a lack of information and to misinformation on structural and functional characteristics of the speech in African American populations. Early medical research that identified the biological differences between African American and white children often undertaken was to show the superiority of one race over the other (Barkan, 1994; Blakley, 1987; Lewis, 1942; Lewontin, 1972; Pirie, 1950; Stanton, 1960). History reveals that racism dictated assumptions made by many biologists, social scientists, and to a greater degree by physical anthropologists (Brace, 1964, 1982). Although there have been attempts to identify biological factors that distinguish one race from another (Herrnstein & Murray, 1994), many biologists, geneticists, social scientists, and physical anthropologists reject race as a biological category (Barkan, 1994; Lewontin, 1972; Montagu, 1942, 1964; Morganthau, 1995). Indeed, there may be more genetic similarities between persons of different races than there are in persons of the same racial group (Begley, 1995; Cavalli-Sforza, 1971, 1995).

Research efforts with minority populations are further complicated because race is difficult to define biologically due to the historical admixture of people in this country and around the world (Garn & Coon, 1968; Glass, 1955; Goodman, 1973; Herskovits, 1928; Montagu, 1964). Racial markers such as skin color, hair texture, and shape of the eyes, nose, or mouth are superficial and may be misleading. In fact, other factors are more apt to affect biological and structural characteristics, such as parent size, birth order, diet, and history of illness (Moore, 1970).

In addition to the problems inherent in defining and studying race, there are issues regarding the terminology used to describe various groups. For many years subject information was limited to age and sex. Until 1981, when more specific racial categories were added, race was noted only as "White" or "Other" (Chavez, Cordero, & Becerra, 1988). As recently as the mid-1980s, physicians (e.g., Negre, 1985) were arguing that the racial distinction of patients was "litigious, improper, and useless . . . therefore must be banished . . . except in rare cases wherein it contributes to a better understanding of disease" (p. 1310).

This chapter discusses the orofacial structures, speech physiology, and acoustic characteristics of speech of African American children. Historically, African American children have been studied using a comparative model. This traditional model is potentially biased because it assumed that one group was better or lesser than the other. Yet there are times when it is important to differentiate between groups. For instance, the fact that African Americans have a high incidence of sickle-cell disease allows medical professionals to make appropriate differential diagnosis. There also are important sociocultural and environmental factors that should be considered when evaluating children with speech and hearing disorders. These issues will be further explored by surveying research from various disciplines such as anthropology, medicine, dentistry, and genetics, as well as information from speech science and communication disorders. Literature pertinent to organic-based speech and hearing disorders, normal structure and function of the orofacial mechanism, and speech acoustics is reviewed.

ORGANIC-BASED SPEECH DISORDERS

Developmental Factors

Preterm and Premature Birth   Delivery of a healthy baby sets the stage for the development of normal speech and language in a child. Yet some mothers may unknowingly place their unborn children at risk for prenatal or birth trauma by consuming alcohol and drugs or by their poor prenatal care (Adams, 1989). A Kaiser-Permanente birth defects study (Shiono & Klebanoff, 1986) of 28,330 middle-class African American, Mexican American, Asian American, and white women reported that ethnicity (referring to African American, Mexican American, and Asian American women) was the strongest predictor of preterm delivery. This study, controlling for maternal age, education, socioeconomic status (SES), marital status, smoking, and drinking during pregnancy, as well as gestational age at initiation of prenatal care, revealed that the African American women had the highest rates of preterm (<37 weeks) and very preterm (<33 weeks) deliveries. The women in the three ethnic groups were at a higher risk of preterm delivery than the white women. Factors associated with the preterm births were being under 20 years of age, being unmarried, having three or more induced abortions, participating in heavy drinking or smoking, and seeking late (>9 weeks) prenatal care. The maternal age factor is significant and relates to the fact that the majority of teenage mothers are single and poor, with 60% receiving welfare (Sidel, 1986). Racial minorities also are overrepresented in this group (Friede et al., 1987). Poverty, more than biological age of the mother, may account for the difficulties experienced by these babies and their teenage mothers.

It seems that controlling for risk factors, such as age and education, does not entirely eliminate the gap between the mortality rate for African American and white infants (Kleinman & Kessel, 1987). A study by Schoendorf, Hogue, Kleinman, and Rowley (1992), in which SES, education, and age variables were controlled, reported that African American infants born to college-educated parents have higher mortality rates than white infants born to parents from a similar background. This was primarily due to the higher rates of very low birth weight among African American infants, which may have a physiological base, such as a possible association between urinary tract and uterine infections in mothers with premature labor. Maternal urinary tract infection is one of the chief treatable causes of preterm labor (Anderson & Merkatz, 1991). There also may be a genetic effect, where a mother's weight may predict her children's birth weight. In the Kaiser-Permanente birth defects study (Shiono & Klebanoff, 1986), African American newborns were found to be smaller than white newborns at each gestational age. Thus, differences in intrauterine growth and gestation also may account for low birth weight rates. The National Center for Health Statistics (1983) reported that for the years 1970–1983 African American infants were twice as likely to have low birth weight than white infants. Many factors can contribute to low birth weight, including maternal age (<20 or >34), hypertension of the fourth decade, diabetes mellitus, low SES, environmental influences, history of preterm births, presence of a uterine anomaly, and an actual increase in preterm births (Anderson & Merkatz, 1991). Despite correction after SES and behavioral factors (e.g., alcohol, smoking), the gap remains. In general, 42% of all very low birth weight infants (<1,500 gm/<3 lb) have been reported to have congenital anomalies or some neurological handicap (McCormack, 1985). Low birth weight infants (2,500 gms/5.5 lbs.) were 10 times more likely to have mental retardation than normal infants. Some of these infants will require long-term speech and language therapy.

   Culture and Environment   Several studies have shown that certain aspects of the social environment constitute health risks for all children, regardless of race (Kleinman & Kessel, 1987; McGauhey & Starfield, 1993; McLoyd, 1990). One aspect is poverty, where poor children are more frequently ill, more seriously ill, and more likely to have associated problems with their illness. A disproportionate number of African Americans live at or near poverty, the rate being three times as high for African American children as for white children. The rate of poverty for African American children increased from 36% to 41% between the years 1979 and 1985 (Duncan & Rodgers, 1988), compared with an increase from 12% to 13% in white children. Poverty contributes to below-standard medical care for African American children for several reasons, including 1) cost of transportation to doctors' offices, 2) lack of doctors in lower-income communities, 3) lack of medical insurance, 4) reluctance to accept medical assistance, 5) importance of day-to-day survival over the need to seek medical services, 6) high crime and substance abuse, and 7) teenage pregnancy (Cooper, 1990). However, low income alone has not been shown to be a consistent risk factor for poor health among African American children. Other social factors, such as low maternal education and a mother's perception of her own health (i.e., if a mother takes care of her own health, she is more likely to take care of her children's health), increase the risk for poorer health in African American children (McGauhey & Starfield, 1993). It has been reported that teen pregnancy is high among low-SES African American females, and the majority of these teen mothers drop out of school (Randolph & Rivers, 1985; Richardson-Collins & Coleman, 1995). Other studies have reported that approximately 45% of all African American children were living in mother-headed households, that as high as 80% are teen mothers, and that 70% of these children are living in poverty (Bowman, 1990; McGauhey & Starfield, 1993; Staples, 1986). These alarming statistics reveal the importance of providing assistance to these families so they can receive the resources and training necessary for the care of a child with a speech disorder.

   Physical Development   Normative data on weight in normal infants can help identify abnormal weight patterns and possible growth retardation. Verghese,

Scott, Teixeira, and Ferguson (1969) studied 2,632 healthy African American children ages 6 months to 14 years from low-income families. Females weighed slightly more than males at 6 months to 1 year and again between 10 and 14 years of age, but were equal to males in weight from ages 7 to 10. Males were heavier than females after 14 years of age with this trend continuing. One early study (Dunham, Jenss, & Christie, 1939) had indicated that African American infants were smaller at birth than white infants and grew more slowly the first year of life. However, Verghese and colleagues (1969) revealed similar development for African American and white babies during the first year of life.

Owen and Lubin (1973) measured the height and weight of 270 African American children and 1,500 white children ages 1–6 from several socioeconomic levels. They found few statistically significant differences in height and weight. Trends in their data, however, indicated that on the average, although African American babies were smaller at birth than white babies, their growth pattern was equal during the preschool years, and African American children exceed white children in both height and weight thereafter. Interestingly, the investigators felt that the differences were more pronounced when children of similar socioeconomic levels were compared.

Wingerd, Schoen, and Solomon (1971) studied 15,000 African American and white infants in a prepaid health care program. Few differences in growth and development were found in these infants from comparable SES. One is reminded that comparative data should always be taken from children in equivalent SES. Results from studies with children from different SES should be viewed critically as the effects may be due more to the environment than the biological makeup of the child.

Normal growth and development of the head, face, and chest support normal speech development. Fetal studies (Davis et al., 1993) of white and African American infants suggest that there may be differences in body length proportions, with African American infants having shorter trunks. Up to 6 years of age, the chest circumference of African American males was slightly smaller than that of white males in other studies (Meredith, 1978), but beyond this age the chest of the African American males becomes slightly larger. These studies show that the development of the upper torso from birth to 6 years follows a growth pattern that should adequately support respiratory and phonatory function for speech. Other fetal sonographic growth studies (Hadlock, Harrist, Shah, Sharman, & Park, 1990) indicate that there is no difference in fetal measurements of head circumference in white and African American populations from socioeconomically diverse environments.

Neuromuscular Development   Many African American parents have spoken of the excellent body tone of their infants at birth, and research has supported these observations (Cratty, 1986; Masse & Hunt, 1963; Scott, Ferguson, Jenkins, & Cutter, 1955). Scott and colleagues (1955) followed the neuromuscular behavioral development of 250 African American infants from middle and low SES from birth to 8 months of age. Twelve neuromuscular steps were evaluated, including smiling, vocalization, crawling, sitting, and walking alone. Similar results were found in infants from the two socioeconomic groups, which were then combined and compared with a group of 250 white infants from Minnesota. All three groups vocalized at about 7 weeks of age, with the African American infants from the lower SES group being ahead of the other two groups in motor development from the 8th week to the 35th week of life. This advanced motor development has been observed by other investigators (Cratty, 1986; Masse & Hunt, 1963). Unfortunately, all of the investigators attributed this accelerated development to more permissive child care practices by mothers and did not consider the genetically advanced developmental skills characteristic of African American babies.

Masse and Hunt (1963) had an alternative explanation for this precocious development. They felt it may be related to variability in skeletal development and differences in bone density and ossification, or "bone age." Their findings were based on a study of the skeletal maturation in 100 males and 100 females from 10 days to 18 months of age. They reported an accelerated onset of calcification centers in the hands of African infants in the first month of life. Werner (1974) found that some African American infants who are born prematurely show motor development similar to that of children of normal gestational age who have not experienced negative prenatal factors.

Westby (1989) discusses the work of Brazelton and others (Brazelton, Koslowski, & Tronick, 1976; Geber & Dean, 1957, Lester & Brazelton, 1982; M.C. Warren, 1972), who attribute the precocious motor behavior of African American infants to advanced neuromuscular abilities. Several studies reported that African American infants were able to lift their head from a prone position shortly after birth, had good head control when pulled to a sitting position, and walked before 1 year of age. Reflex testing found African American infants to be more advanced than white, Chinese, or Navajo infants in descending order of most to least responsive. African American infants were more active and exhibited extreme state changes in comparison to the Navajo babies. These biological differences in African American infant neuromotor development can be used as a reference for normal development within the racial group. Of course, variation exists both within the individuals and across the racial or cultural group; therefore, it should not be assumed that all children will respond in this manner. Furthermore, although we are more familiar with the development pattern of white infants, that pattern should not be considered the norm (Westby, 1989).

Implications for the Speech-Language Pathologist Many African American children are born into poverty (McGauhey & Starfield, 1993), and many of these children are at risk for speech disorders related to factors associated with low SES, including poor prenatal care, poor nourishment, greater exposure to lead, greater exposure to infection, noncompliance with vaccinations or well-baby checkups, and lack of education. Poor prenatal care may result in increased numbers of infants born with craniofacial anomalies, congenital anomalies, mental retardation, or other developmental disabilities. Many African American children born into nurturing and caring environments, however, reportedly may have precocious neuromuscular development in the first year of life and normally developing speech.

Orofacial Anomalies

Cleft Lip and Palate　Clefting takes several forms including cleft of the lip and palate, isolated cleft lip, isolated cleft palate, and cleft uvula (Fogh-Anderson, 1942). These forms can be grouped into two separate entities including 1) cleft lip with or without cleft palate and 2) cleft palate alone. Their incidence rates are recorded separately.

There are conflicting reports regarding the incidence of cleft lip and palate in African American children. The variation in incidence may be related to a difference between racial or genetic factors and racial or natural selection factors. Congenital cleft lip with or without cleft palate is rare in African Americans in the United States. Depending on the survey, the incidence varies from approximately 1 per 2,500 to 1 per 6,000 live births. This low rate may reflect a natural selection. The incidence of cleft lip with or without cleft palate for whites ranges from 1 per 600 to 1 per 1,000 live births (Altemus, 1966; Altemus & Ferguson, 1965; Cole, 1980; Datubo-Brown, 1989; Erickson, 1976; Ivy, 1962; Vanderas, 1987). The frequency of isolated cleft palate appears to be similar for both white and African American children, approximately 1 per 2,000 and 1 per 2,500 live births respectively (Altemus, 1966; Owens, Jones, & Harris, 1985). According to Richardson (1970), the incidence of cleft uvula was 1 per 369 in a group of 3,319 African American college students. The incidence of cleft uvula among white children also is high, occurring in 1 per 76 live births. The high occurrence of cleft uvula can be explained by the high survival rate of children with minor anomalies such as cleft uvula.

Three natural selection factors recur in the literature and by word of mouth to account for the low incidence of craniofacial anomalies in African American children. They were initially set forth by Millard and McNeill in 1965 to explain the low prevalence of this anomaly found in Jamaican babies. However, these three theories have yet to be proven valid. The first explanation is that the practice of infanticide in some African tribes may have decreased the numbers of deformed infants in the population, therefore decreasing genetic transmission of cleft lip and palate. Second, supposedly, the physically weak were not selected during slave market trading; thus, individuals with obvious impairment who may have been considered "ill" were excluded. The third explanation relates to the institution of slavery itself, which may have eliminated all but the strongest African Americans. It could be argued that individuals with orofacial anomalies were not as healthy as others and therefore may not have withstood slavery.

The incidence of cleft lip and palate for individuals of African descent who remained in Africa appears to be higher than for African Americans, supporting a strong genetic component in this group of individuals. This variation found in African Americans and African natives may help explain the conflicting reports on prevalence found in the literature. David, Edoo, Mustaffah, and Hinchcliffe (1971) tell of the Adamarobe villagers in southern Ghana who have a high incidence of maxillofacial anomalies with an accompanying congenital deafness. Nigerian children were studied by several researchers (Gupta, 1969; Oluwasanmi & Adekunle, 1970; Oluwasanmi & Kogbe, 1975) who found that in the western region of Nigeria 1 in every 1,055 infants is born with a facial cleft. These figures are similar to those for white children. The incidence rate in Trinidad is 1 per 1,888 (Robertson, 1964).

Datubo-Brown (1989) describes seven African children with craniofacial anomalies. Because there is a "social taboo attached to the birth of grossly malformed babies" (p. 342), severe underreporting occurs. The author speculates that the African babies may have more atypical clefts than other infants. In fact, other investigators have found that significantly more African American infants than all other infants have additional mid-line birth defects associated with their maxillofacial problems (Donahue, 1965; Siegel, 1975). Cleft palate alone has been associated more often with other craniofacial anomalies in whites (Gorlin, Cervenka, & Pruzansky, 1971). Clefts of all types will occur more often in African American females than in African American males. The opposite occurs with white children; clefts occur more often in males. Cleft lip and palate occur five times more often in lower socioeconomic status (SES) in African Americans (Cole, 1980).

The effects of a repaired complete or incomplete cleft lip may be more visible on the African American child. Cole (1980) describes three physical characteristics of African Americans following surgery for cleft lip, including 1) defects of the nasal structure, 2) deficiency of tissue in the upper lip, and 3) appearance of postoperative scar. Features of the African American nose such as the short columella, the obtuse nasal arch, and a wide base seem to exaggerate the cleft lip deformity. The upper lip tissue deficiency is in marked contrast to a fuller lower lip, and hypertrophic scarring or keloid formation may occur following surgical correction of the cleft lip (Alhady & Sivanantharajah, 1969; Kitlowski, 1953; Murray, 1963). Keloid formation does not occur on mucosal tissue and therefore would not affect repair of a cleft of the palate (Ketchum, Cohen, & Masters, 1974).

Implications for the Speech-Language Pathologist Because infants with cleft lip and palate require extensive medical care and consistent long-term follow-up, speech-language pathologists should be aware of the factors that might preclude adequate medical service. Of immediate concern for poor children are potential feeding problems. Good postnatal care is important to provide adequate nourishment to the infant. Malnourishment may have a negative effect on growth and development (Cunningham, 1995; Dreizen, Spirakis, & Stone, 1967; Holliday, 1978), which in turn may affect speech and language development. The family must also have the resources necessary to obtain cleft palate team care and the training necessary for the long-term care of a child with cleft lip and palate.

There are no reported studies regarding the articulation skills of African American children with cleft lip and palate. However, they would be expected to experience speech and hearing problems similar to those of white children with cleft lip and palate, including compensatory articulations, otitis media, and possibly conductive hearing loss (Paradise, Bluestone, & Felder, 1969; Peterson-Falzone, 1982; Trost, 1981; VanDenmark, Morris, & VandeHaar, 1979).

Fetal Alcohol Syndrome

Studies indicate that anywhere from 10% to 40% of mothers who have consumed dangerous amounts of alcohol during pregnancy give birth to infants with fetal alcohol syndrome (FAS) (Adams, 1989; Coles, 1992; Zetterstrom & Nylander, 1985). The prevalence of FAS is 1–3 per 1,000 live births (Coles, 1992). There is no clear evidence of a genetic predisposition to alcohol on a racial level but more of a familial or cultural one (Barnes, 1987). All children, including African American children, born into environments where the use of alcoholic beverages is widespread are at a higher risk of acquiring FAS. Children with FAS may often exhibit symptoms that include growth deficiencies, dysmorphic characteristics (orofacial anomalies), and central nervous system disturbances (Sokol & Clarren, 1989).

Gir, Aksharanugraha, and Harris (1989) completed cephalometric measurement of 15 African American children between 3 and 12 years of age who were diagnosed with FAS (Figure 1). The characteristics found in African American children are similar to those found in white children with FAS. Compared with children without FAS, children with FAS were perceived as having mid-face hypoplasia, although the mid-face was structurally normal. The perception of a flat mid-face may be related to the features that are apparent in a newborn with FAS, including an indistinct philtrum, a broad nasal base, and short palpebral fissures. The children with FAS presented with statistically significant differences in "frontal prominence, depressed posterior palate, elongated mandibular corpus, and proclined maxillary incisors" (p. 322).

Digit sucking was common in the children with FAS. The significance of this finding has not been explored. Many typically developing children engage in thumb sucking. The higher incidence of anterior open bite in the children with FAS may be associated with the thumb sucking that persists beyond 5 or 6 years of age and the eruption of permanent dentition (Popovich & Thompson, 1973; Subtelny & Sakuda, 1964). Orthodontic problems, including anterior open bites, proclined incisors, and palatal slant, were present. Hearing problems along with inner-ear abnormalities associated with the low set and rotated ears often are found in these children (Church & Gerkin, 1988). The speech-language pathologist should be alert to any speech or hearing problems in African American children with FAS.

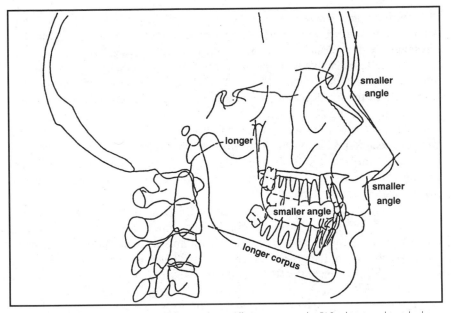

Figure 1. Diagrammatic representation of the significant differences among the FAS subjects and matched controls. (From Gir, A.V., Aksharanugraha, K., & Harris, E.F. [1989]. A cephalometric assessment of children with fetal alcohol syndrome. *American Journal of Orthodontic and Dentofacial Orthopedics, 95,* 319–326; reprinted by permission.)

Hearing Disorders

Middle-Ear Disease. As early as the 1920s (Roy, 1920) African natives were found to have good hearing with a low incidence of otitis media and inner-ear problems. Roy attributed these findings to large eustachian tubes in African natives. He provided no evidence to support this finding. Doyle (1977) identified differences in the length, width, and angle of the eustachian tube in the skulls of African Americans and whites, with length and width being greater in the African American skulls. More recently, researchers (Bush & Rabin, 1980; Griffith, 1979; Lindeman, Holmquist, & Shea, 1981; Robinson, Allen, & Root, 1988) have reported that African American children have a lower prevalence of middle-ear disease. Robinson et al. (1988) performed infant tympanometry on 65 African American and white infants ages 6–13 months. Middle-ear dysfunction was found 33% of the time in the African American babies compared with 53% of the time in the white babies. They concluded that "the racial difference may indicate a mechanical/anatomical difference that allows the middle ear to drain more readily in African Americans" (p. 345). Bush and Rabin (1980) designed a protocol to investigate the effects of drug intervention on otitis media. Unintentionally, they found that at one center, where most of the children were African American, the rate of otitis media was 15 per 1,000 versus 155 per 1,000 at another center where most of the children were white. They attributed this to a real difference by race. However, the lower rate of otitis media in the African American children could be a result of underreporting related to the underutilization of physician services (McGauhey & Starfield, 1993; White, 1977).

It is well known that otitis media occurs almost universally in white children with cleft palate (McWilliams, Morris, & Shelton, 1990); however, there is no information on the incidence of otitis media in African American children with a cleft palate. The high incidence of otitis media in children with a cleft palate is related to the eustachian tube dysfunction associated with clefting. Therefore, one would expect that African American children with a cleft palate would have incidence rates similar to those of white children with a cleft palate. The hearing and middle-ear function of African American children with a cleft palate should be investigated in future studies.

Lindeman and colleagues (1981) studied the relationship of mastoid air cell system size and middle-ear disease in African American children. Significant differences were found between children with and without middle-ear effusion (MEE) in the size of the mastoid air cell system. The mastoid air cell system was smaller in the children with MEE. Results for healthy African American children versus African American children with MEE were 7.0 versus 2.3 cm^2 at age 3; 7.9 versus 2.6 cm^2 at age 4; and 7.5 versus 3.2 cm^2 at age 5.

Inner-Ear Disease The speech-language pathologist and audiologist should be aware of the neurological impairment and hearing disorders that may accompany sickle-cell anemia in African American children. The normal disc-shaped red blood cell assumes a sickle shape, making it difficult for blood cells to travel through the small blood vessels, especially the small vessels in the brain. Approximately 7.8% of African Americans possess the trait or have sickle-cell disease (Coker & Milner, 1982). One in every 10–12 African Americans can expect to carry the disease trait, and 1 in 600 will have the disease (Williams, 1975).

The effect of sickle-cell disease on hearing has been documented by numerous investigators (Buchanan, Moore, & Counter, 1993; Morgenstein & Manace, 1969; Sharp & Orchik, 1978). The anemia and thrombosis associated with the sickle-cell crisis seem to be the two major factors contributing to hearing loss. The hearing loss is usually sensorineural and may be related to decreased blood supply to the cochlea. The hearing loss appears to worsen with each episode of the disease and is progressive and degenerative.

Implications for the Speech-Language Pathologist Early research indicates that African American children may have fewer episodes of otitis media than that reported for white children. It is important, however, to keep in mind the underutilization of medical services and underreporting of medical problems by some African American families, especially those living in poverty (White, 1977). Otitis media at critical periods of speech development may lead to phonological disorder or other speech and language impairment (Menyuk, 1986). Because of the high incidence of sickle-cell disease in African American children, regular hearing screenings should be completed to identify sensorineural loss in these children.

Speech pathology services should be provided for problems related to their hearing loss.

Medical Conditions and Differential Diagnosis: Skin Features

Because more and more speech-language pathologists work with children who have medical problems, it is important for them to know about health and illness. The following section offers an overview of some medical conditions the speech-language pathologist may encounter when working with the African American child.

Skin color changes serve as valuable clues in the diagnosis of many medical conditions (Kostelnik & Ditre, 1994; Polednak, 1989; Williams, 1975). These skin changes may be absent, obscured, or modified in dark skin, making problems more difficult to identify, but experienced dermatologists have learned to recognize skin color differences (Grimes & Stockton, 1988). Reportedly, there are only two color changes in dark skin, pallor and increased pigmentation. Pallor occurs when there is stretching of skin, as in edema. Pallor is an absence of the underlying red tones, so the skin of the African American child will appear ashen gray. Hyperemia, increased blood in a part or organ, can be detected in inflammatory conditions as areas of dark purplish color.

Inflammation   Inflammation or erythema in very dark skinned children is often very difficult to determine, especially in exanthematous diseases such as measles, rubella, scarlet fever, chickenpox, and smallpox. Inflammation can be detected by fingertip palpation. In a cyanotic child, the lips and tongue become ashen gray. Cyanosis also can be suspected when the palms are pressed and the blood return is slow and the color does not return to normal in one second.

Jaundice   Some diseases, such as jaundice, are identified by changes in skin color. Jaundice, a sign of disease of the liver and biliary tree (Fishman, Hoffman, Klausner, Rockson, & Thaler, 1981), is well known to most parents as many newborns become jaundiced within hours after birth. Discoloration of the skin, sclera, and mucous membranes occurs and the infants acquire a yellowish hue. Major color changes occur at the junction of the hard and soft palate, allowing easy diagnosis. However, correct diagnosis is compromised in African American babies who show a muddy-yellow or greenish color instead of the classical yellow hue. Inaccurate diagnosis could result in brain damage.

Sickle-Cell Disease   A slightly yellow sclera related to anemia in sickle-cell disease is found in African Americans. The red blood cell count is decreased progressively with remissions and relapses. Infection and anemia are usually the two causes of death from sickle-cell disease, with the former being the primary cause. The jaundice expression of the destruction of red cells may reveal itself by a greenish-yellow tinge of the sclera, although many healthy people, especially those of darker skin, have a slightly yellow color of the sclera. Children with sickle-cell disease are at increased risk for pneumococcal pneumonia. A lowered resistance to infection may make the children more susceptible to infections such as meningitis that can result in neurological damage (Davies, 1989). When children with sickle-cell anemia present for elective surgeries such as tonsillectomy and/or adenoidectomy it is important for physicians to provide appropriate management to prevent vaso-occlusive events during general anesthesia and surgery (Coker & Milner, 1982). A consequence of vaso-occlusion is cerebral infarction in young children with sickle cell. These children would be at a high risk for stroke and its associated communication disorders. Coker and Milner suggest a three-pronged protocol to include 1) preoperative transfusion and hydration, 2) intraoperative prevention of hypothermia and maintenance of blood volume, and 3) postoperative oxygen therapy and hydration.

Oral Cavity Pigment   When completing an oral examination, it is important for the speech-language pathologist to recognize abnormal pigment characteristics in the African American child. At birth oral pigmentation is sparse, but if found later it may be associated with amalgam tattoo (tooth filling), chronic irritation, heavy metal deposits, or melanoma (malignant tumor) (Brauner, 1994). Appropriate differential diagnosis is critical. The pigment may be light-brown irregular areas over the palatal and lingual aspects of the gums. Pigment varies from brown to blue to a generalized hyperpigmentation, and as age increases oral pigment increases. Pigment lesions are usually seen on the gingival tissue (81%), buccal mucosa (40%), hard palate (38%), tongue (33%), soft palate (26%), and floor of the mouth (25%) (Grimes & Stockton, 1988; Williams, 1975). Oral leukoderma is another normal variant characterized as pearly, whitish-gray thickened plaque on the buccal mucosa. Its consistency is either granular or wet. It is found in 90% of African American adults and 51% of African American children and shows no sex preference (Kostelnik & Ditre, 1994). It is not premalignant.

Nail Pigment   Nail pigmentation also is used as a source of medical diagnosis for a variety of problems. These include nevi (birthmark), benign overgrowth of melanin-forming cells, melanoma, trauma, and pigmentation due to drugs. Nail pigment lesions are usually acquired rather than congenital and increase with age. Pigmentation is seen often in the fingernails occurring in longitudinal stripes running the length of the nail usually in the center or lateral portions. No pigmentation is observed in the nails of children at birth, but pigmentation occurs as early as 3 years of age. About 23% of children below age 10 have been found to have pigmentation of the fingernails.

Cleft Lip   Although cleft lip with or without cleft palate rarely occurs in African American children, there are nevertheless some important factors to consider in terms of lip repair and skin color changes. African American children with a cleft lip may have lip repair within the first month of life (McWilliams, Morris, & Shelton, 1990). Although the main concerns in these early stages are for the health of the child and maintaining adequate nutrition, the parents also should be informed about potential pigmentation problems as the lip heals. Unpredictable pigmentation can occur in the cleft lip scar for two reasons. First, complete destruction of the melanocytes in the area may occur. Second, interference with the melanin-forming capacity is possible (Cole, 1980). The depigmentation can be treated by a superficial covering of cosmetics or by dermal inoculation of the scar with dye, which is variable and nonreversible. Most of these treatments are reserved for adults, but may be considered for children if the depigmentation is of concern (Murray, 1963).

Implications for the Speech-Language Pathologist Although the speech-language pathologist cannot make a medical diagnosis, it is important to understand common signs that may signal a medical problem. Appropriate and timely referral may minimize or avoid a potentially serious situation. For example, knowing that the skin of an African American baby with jaundice will not be yellow but have a greenish hue could prevent potential brain damage. The greenish color in the scalar of the eyes of a child with sickle-cell disease may indicate that the child is anemic. Inflammation associated with an upper respiratory infection may appear as a purple hue on the mucous membranes instead of red. Parents should be aware that in African American children with a cleft lip, there is a chance that a keloid may form or depigmentation may occur at the cleft lip site following repair of the lip.

Normal Structure and Function of the Orofacial Mechanism

Measurement of Facial Structures Speech-language pathologists, as well as professionals in dentistry and orthodontics, are concerned about the development of oral structures. Although the dental problems found in normally developing children rarely affect speech permanently (Peterson-Falzone, 1982; Vallino & Tompson, 1993; Witzel & Vallino, 1992), the speech-language pathologist should have normative data on craniofacial structures to identify children who fall outside the norm and who may need to be referred for professional dental care. Although comparing the craniofacial profiles of African American children with profiles of white children is typically of little value, it becomes important when normative data derived from white children are inappropriately used to make diagnostic treatment decisions for African American children. Of course, there is no standard profile for either group, as a great deal of individual variation may be found in both groups.

Over the years, cephalometric studies have shown conflicting results (Alexander & Hitchcock, 1978; Connor & Moshiri, 1985; D'Aloisio & Pangrazio-Kulbersh, 1992; Drummond, 1968; Enlow, Pfister, Richardson, & Kuroda, 1982; Farrow, Zarrinnia, & Azizi, 1993; Fonseca & Klein, 1978; Flynn, Ambrogio, & Zeichner, 1989; Kapila, 1988; Nummikoski et al., 1988), but generally suggest that before adolescence African American and white children show minor differences in craniofacial dimensions, whereas adults show marked differences in head, face, and dental structures (Drummond, 1968). Cephalometric measurements were completed for a group of 60 inner-city African American children from Tennessee ages 4–9 years (Richardson & Malhotra, 1974). Measurements were taken of head height or cranial vault size (Bregma-Sellion), bony nasal height, or upper facial height (N to ANS), and lower facial height (ANS-Me) (see Figure 2). Mean annual increase in head height decreased with age for both sexes. Over the 6-year period, head size ranged from 100.92 mm to 103.39 mm in males and 98.38 mm to 101.03 mm in females, with male head heights always being larger at each age. Bony nasal height increased by 8.29 mm for males (from 35.81 at age 4 to 44.10 at age 9) and by 9.43 mm for females (from 35.93 mm at age 4 to 45.36 mm at age 9). Both sexes showed a large amount of individual variation in nasal height. Lower facial height for females at age 4 was 55.29 mm and changed by only 6.81 mm to 62.10 mm at age 9. Males had a similar growth spurt of lower facial height by 7.99 mm from 54.16 to 62.15 mm over the same time.

Similar measurements on a group of white children from rural Iowa did not reveal statistically significant differences. The only difference was that the poor African American children from Tennessee grew more slowly than the middle-class white children from Iowa. Because most of the poor African American children were in the school lunch program and the white Iowa children were not, the authors suggest a relationship between undernourishment (inferred from school lunch program participation) and delayed growth. However, the delayed growth

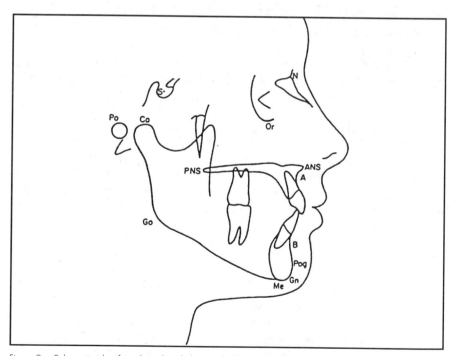

Figure 2.   Schematic identifying lateral cephalometric hard-tissue landmarks. S, Sella turcica; N, nasion; Or, orbitale; ANS, anterior nasal spine; A, subspinale; B, supermantale; Pog, pogonion; Gn, gnathion; Me, menton; Go, gonion; PNS, posterior nasal spine; Co, condylion; Po, porion. (From Connor, A.M., & Moshiri, F. [1985]. Orthognathic surgery norms for American black patients, *American Journal of Orthodontics*, 87, 119–134; reprinted by permission.)

of the African American children also may be related to other factors, such as effects from poor prenatal care, or other medical problems, or normal family growth patterns.

Altemus (1959) studied 80 African American adolescents with typical occlusal relationships (no cross-bites, tooth anomalies, or maligned teeth) from a sample of approximately 3,000 children. The investigator found longer lower facial height, greater dental protrusion, larger absolute head size, and greater soft-tissue thickness of the lower lip and chin than in available norms of white adolescents. Other investigators (Rhine & Campbell, 1980) reported that thickness of facial tissues was found to be greater in a sample of 39 adult African American cadavers than in white and Japanese cadavers. The greatest differences were related to the lips and lower and lateral edges of the orbits. The researchers further clarify that the differences in tissue thickness could not be completely attributable to race, however, as whites now show thicker tissue than did turn-of-the-century whites.

Twenty years after the study by Altemus (1959), similar craniofacial profiles were found in 50 African American children between 8 and 13 years of age from Catholic schools in Alabama (Alexander & Hitchock, 1978). The children selected for the study had the "best" occlusions in the groups, no prior orthodontic treatment, and typical profiles (no obvious craniofacial anomalies). Radiographs, photographs, and impressions were made of all subjects. An average profile was derived and a z-score chart was developed. The findings were compared with cephalometric norms of white children and revealed that the African American children in this study had 1) protrusive and procumbent upper and lower incisors, 2) facial plane (S to N angle) similar to whites (see Figure 2), 3) greater skeletal measurements but usually less than one standard deviation, 4) more anteriorly based maxilla, and 5) less frequent Class II and Class III malocclusions.

Cephalometric studies were also completed on older children and adults (Connor & Moshiri, 1985; Flynn et al., 1989) to obtain normative data on white and African American adults ages 17–48 years. Statistically significant differences were found in the African American adults, including greater facial convexity, maxillary skeletal protrusion, maxillary length, and lower incisor proclination. According to the investigators, racially specific cephalometric values can allow for more accurate diagnosis and treatment planning by orthodontists and oral surgeons as numerous studies appear to support the presence of differences by race in the craniofacial complex.

Measurement of Nasal Structures   There are functional cross-cultural differences in nasal configuration. Long, narrow noses are most common in high, cold, dry climates (increasing the surface area and period of time over which inspired air is warmed and moistened), and flat, wide noses are prevalent in moist, warm climates (decreasing the area). The geographic area of origin of an ethnic group is associated with nasal size and shape and is one explanation for nasal form distribution (Carey & Steegmann, 1981). Awareness of appropriate nasal parameters for the noses of African American children is necessary because adolescents with cleft lip and palate may require nasal reconstruction necessitating the correct anatomical measurements of nasal structures (Baker, 1990; Lindsay & Farkas, 1972). A study of 52 African American, 52 white, and 22 Hispanic college students and adults (Calhoun, House, Hokanson, & Quinn, 1990) found that nasal length was not statistically different among the three groups. But mean columella length was shorter in the African American subjects (45.9 mm) than in Hispanic (47.6 mm) and white (47.8 mm) subjects. Mean nasal width was greater in African American subjects (36.8 mm) than in Hispanic (31.4 mm) and white (30.1 mm) subjects. Others have made similar findings in African American adults (Bernstein, 1975; Matory & Falces, 1986; Ohki, Naito, & Cole, 1991).

Implications for the Speech-Language Pathologist Cephalometric measurements may be a predictive tool to identify certain speech and voice characteristics. Variations in the craniofacial complex may result in acoustics differences in the speech and voice of African American and white children. Vigorous research should be undertaken in this area, including direct examination of the physical characteristics of African American children and their associated formant frequency values. Data from radiography and magnetic resonance imaging would be helpful to image the vocal tracts of African American children and develop normative data on vocal tract characteristics.

Articulatory Function

The majority of articulation studies with African American children (Bleile & Wallach, 1992; Cole & Taylor, 1990; Seymour & Ralabate, 1985; Seymour & Seymour, 1981; Washington & Craig, 1994) focus on phonological skills or dialect differences. This area is covered in Chapter 7 in this book. However, studies describing articulation and speech motor abilities are rare. One early study (Everhart, 1953) that investigated the articulation skills of African American and white children found similar errors for both groups of children. A study by Robbins and Klee (1987) included 11 African American children and 79 white children to assess the oral and speech motor abilities of normally developing children ages 2;6-6;11. Cephalometric measurements revealed that the structure of the vocal tract did not change significantly during this time; however, speech and oral motor performance did move toward a more adultlike target by 6 years of age for both groups. Dialectal variations were taken into consideration in speech screenings completed on approximately 1,000 children from Harlem ages 3–17 (Haller & Thompson, 1975). About 18% of the children failed the speech screening (62.9% of the errors were articulation errors). The types of articulation errors were not given. Articulation disorders are estimated to occur in 7%–12% of the population at large (Perkins, 1977). A 2-year review of records of 320 African natives from Kenyatta National Hospital Speech and Hearing Clinic (Lumba, Oduori, & Singh, 1977) found that 12% (41) had "defective articulation" related to hearing disability (30), cleft lip and palate (2), cleft palate (5), tongue tie (1), and tongue thrust (3). According to the authors, the results of speech therapy for this group were "disheartening" due to poor follow-up.

Many early studies have reported an association between advanced motor abilities and good articulation skills (Albright, 1948; Bilto, 1941). Dickson (1962) showed that the gross motor proficiency of children in first through third grades who retain functional articulation errors was inferior to those who outgrew their articulation errors. It is tempting to speculate then that because African American children have been shown to have precocious neuromuscular development (from early Gesell tests by Geber & Dean, 1957, and from 12 neuromuscular patterns of behavior by Scott et al., 1955) their articulation skills also would be advanced. Other investigators have not found an association between articulation and motor skills, however. Several studies showed that oral structural and neuromuscular abnormalities do not distinguish children with articulation disorders from children without such disorders (Dworkin & Culatta, 1985; Guyette & Diedrich, 1981). Instead, structural and neuromotor development may be only one of numerous factors, including intellectual, behavioral, physiological, and environmental, that may determine an individual's articulation abilities.

Implications for the Speech-Language Pathologist   Normally developing African American children should be expected to develop appropriate articulation skills. The speech-language pathologist must differentiate between functional articulation errors and phonological features of African American English (AAE) to provide appropriate services to African American children. The use of AAE phonological features was considered to be a pathology by early investigators (Raph, 1967), but these features have since been shown to be part of normally developing AAE phonology (Seymour & Seymour, 1981; Stockman, Vaughn-Cooke, & Wolfram, 1982).

Respiratory Function

Normative data regarding lung function are especially important in light of the high susceptibility to respiratory diseases, especially tuberculosis (TB) and pneumonia, in minority populations (Hakim & Grossman, 1995; Jereb et al., 1991). In 1992, approximately 71% of TB cases occurred in minorities, with case rates being seven times higher in African Americans than in whites (Jereb et al., 1991; "Tuberculosis," 1987). There are over one million pediatric cases of TB worldwide, and there has been a 39% increase in TB for children under 5 years of age since the mid-1980s in the United States. African American children at risk include those living in poverty, in urban centers in the South, along the North Atlantic seaboard, and in southern California (Onorato, Kent, & Castro, 1995). Compromised breathing in children with TB may result in respiratory and phonatory problems that could affect speech production; however, there has been little research in this area to support this concept. Some investigators have found conflicting data regarding respiratory function in African American populations. Early research, completed with less sophisticated equipment than is available today, supplied some limited information on vital capacity (Abramowitz, Leiner, Lewis, & Small, 1965; Smillie & Augustine, 1926; Wilson & Edwards, 1921). In all studies, a lower vital capacity (up to 15%) was found in African American males and females than in established norms for whites. A lower vital capacity was accidentally found in 2,000 6- to 16-year-old African American children than in white children, as their growth and development were followed long-term for evidence of hookworm (Smillie & Augustine, 1926). The groups were matched for age, sex, and SES. The authors suggested an association between lower vital capacity and the shorter trunk lengths they found in their African American subjects. Similar findings were made when the vital capacities of 160 adult male inmates were measured in the same study. Other investigators (Roberts & Crabtree, 1927), however, found no significant differences in sitting height vital capacities of white and African American children. More recently, Schwartz, Katz, Fegley, and Tockman (1988a, 1988b) reported the results of a National Health and Nutrition Examination Survey. Spirometric measurements were taken from 1,963 healthy African American and white subjects 6–24 years of age. Lung function was found to be lower in African Americans for measures of forced vital capacity and forced expiratory volume; however, the differences decreased with age.

Nasal airflow and resistance measurements may provide important information for the diagnosis of velopharyngeal incompetence resulting from cleft palate or neurological disease (Warren & DuBois, 1964). These measures also are valuable in assessing nasal airway impairment, which may affect nasal airflow rate, and for the clinical evaluation of nasal obstruction (McCaffrey & Kern, 1979; Warren, 1984; Warren, Hinton, Pillsbury, & Hairfield, 1987). Calhoun and colleagues (1990) measured differences in nasal airflow and resistance in 130 adult African American, Hispanic, and white subjects. Anterior rhinomanometry measurements before and after insufflation of ephedrine sulfate revealed no relationship between external nasal configuration and nasal airflow or resistance measurements, although external nasal parameters (columella length, nasal width, and nasolabial angle) were found to be significantly different between the Hispanics and whites and the African Americans.

Implications for the Speech-Language Pathologist The limited data on the respiratory capacity of African Americans indicate a potentially lower lung vital capacity than for whites. Breathing for speech, however, only requires about 7% of our lung volume (Hixon, 1973), and it is unusual for normally developing children to have insufficient lung volume for speech purposes. Some very sick children or those with multiple system abnormalities may have respiratory problems that endanger their life. Breathing problems that occur during speech production, however, may be the result of inefficient use of air or uncoordinated cycles of inhalation and exhalation. The speech-language pathologist may encounter these problems in children who have cerebral palsy, neurological impairment, or voice disorders. Professionals also should remain alert to the potential of compromised breathing in African American children who have TB, an area that requires further study. A referral to the appropriate medical specialist is an important part of good speech pathology treatment.

SPEECH ACOUSTIC CHARACTERISTICS

Acoustic analysis can be used to identify speakers by age and sex and to differentiate between normal and pathological conditions (Angelocci, Kopp, & Holbrook, 1964; Kent, 1979; Kent & Rosenbek, 1983; Weinberg & Bennett, 1971). Unfortunately, the majority of reported acoustic data do not include African American subjects. Mayo (1985) reviewed articles published from 1977 to 1984 on the communication abilities of African Americans. Of the 5,505 published articles, only three perceptual studies focused on identifying speaker race and only two highlighted spectral characteristics of adult speakers. A similar lack of pertinent work is apparent over the next 10 years and more significantly so in the area of child research.

Perceptual Features

Individuals are often prejudged simply by the sound of their voice. There appear to be perceptually salient physiological features in speech as well as linguistic aspects that can help in identifying the age, gender, health, psychological state, physical attractiveness, and even economic status of a speaker (Firestone & Lehtnin, 1978). Several investigators have used voice samples from children to identify attributes such as gender (Bennett & Weinberg, 1979; Ingrisano, Weismer, & Schuckers, 1980; Weinberg & Bennett, 1971), personality and social status (Bryden, 1968), resonance (Blood & Hyman, 1977), nasality (Colton & Cooker, 1968), and sound intensity (Carter, Ricker, & Corsini, 1972). It is unknown if any of the children in the previous studies were African American. A questionnaire study (Saniga & Carlin, 1991) to identify the perception of vocal behaviors of 3- to 6-year-old African American and white children was completed by 640 parents. The findings indicated that African American boys and girls and white boys were considered the most vocally aggressive.

Some research has focused on identifying race in adult speakers (Bryden, 1968; Lass, Tecca, Mancuso, & Black, 1979; Walton & Orlikoff, 1994). Lass and colleagues found that the race of the speaker could be identified at a greater than 50% accuracy from recorded speech of increasing complexity. The identifying factors were described as cultural differences that were most likely dialectal features or intonation patterns. However, listeners may have been attending to other acoustic cues in speakers who did not exhibit dialectal variation. These cues could include vowel duration, formant transition, or vocal fundamental frequency. In fact, acoustic cues were used to identify racial differences (Bryden, 1968). The voice samples of 47 African American and 44 white adult subjects were identified with 97% accuracy from a recorded reading passage. Subsequent acoustic analysis revealed a trend of lower vowel formants in African American speakers.

Walton and Orlikoff (1994) expanded the study of Lass et al. (1979). In Walton and Orlikoff's study of 50 African American and 50 white male inmates, the race of the speaker was identified with 60% accuracy. The findings revealed that the African American speakers had greater frequency and amplitude perturbation. Significant differences, between the two groups however, were found only for amplitude perturbation. The range for both groups was similar to normative data identified in the literature. Fundamental frequency and vowel formant patterns were similar between the two groups. The mean fundamental frequency (f_0) of 108.85 Hz for the African American male voice samples was similar to the mean f_0 of 107.55 Hz found for the voice samples of white males. The investigators felt that the listeners relied on spectral noise (cycle-to-cycle frequency and amplitude variability and additive noise) to distinguish the speakers as a lower mean-harmonics-to-noise ratio was found for the African American males.

Unfortunately, the limited information available on adults cannot be used to describe the voices of children because of the anatomical and physiological differences in the vocal mechanisms between children and adults. Future studies with African American children should provide information on speaker identification and normative data of the acoustic characteristics of normal and abnormal voices of African American children.

Fundamental Frequency

The rate of vocal fold vibration (fundamental frequency) indirectly reveals information about the anatomic size and physiology of the larynx. For example, children have short and thin vocal folds that vibrate fast compared with those of adult males who have long, more massive vocal folds that vibrate more slowly (Kahane, 1988). Boshoff (1945) completed the only study to date on racial differences in laryngeal structure. This study of 102 Bantu South African black cadaveric male and female larynges found racial differences in vocal fold length. In over 90% of the cases, the vocal fold of both male and female adult South African cadavers was 4–5 mm longer than that of the larynges of 23 white South Africans. Other differences included thinner thyroid cartilages in males and females with a less protrusive thyroid notch in males in the South African larynges.

Fundamental frequency (f_0) is the acoustic representation of the rate of vocal fold vibration and varies according to age. It may be as high as 500 vibratory cycles per second (Hz) in the infant and as low as 90 Hz in the adult male. In adolescence, male f_0 lowers to 180 Hz, but female fundamental frequency remains as high as 280 Hz. Adult females average 230 Hz and adult males 120 Hz. Normative data for comparing normal and abnormal fundamental frequency values are available for white adults and children (Baken, 1987; Hollien & Shipp, 1972; Wilson, 1987) but not for other racial or ethnic groups.

A few investigators have studied the fundamental frequency of African American children and young adults. Hollien and Malcik (1962) found a lower fundamental frequency in adolescent African American males ages 10, 14, and 18

than in white males. A lower reading fundamental frequency also was found by Hudson and Holbrook (1981) in 200 African American male college students with fundamental frequencies ranging from 21 Hz to 27 Hz. Lower fundamental frequencies have been found for African American children and adults from 6 to 18 years of age (Bennett, 1983; Eguchi & Hirsh, 1969; Hudson & Holbrook, 1982; Steinsapir, Forner, & Stemple, 1986; Wheat & Hudson, 1988). However, Mayo (1990) found no fundamental frequency differences between African American and European American college students matched for age and sex.

Formant Frequencies

The supralaryngeal cavity includes the pharyngeal, nasal, and oral cavities. Sound generated at the level of the larynx makes its way through these cavities and is modified by the articulators. During vowel production, the resonating cavities will provide varying degrees of obstruction to this column of air arising from the larynx, filtering certain frequencies and enhancing others. The enhanced frequencies are called the resonant frequencies, or formants. Listeners perceive a vowel according to its formant structure. The important formants for vowel recognition are F1, F2, and F3. The formant frequency is affected by the length of the vocal tract, the location of the constrictions in the vocal tract, and the degree of narrowness of the constriction (Pickett, 1980). Children have higher formant frequency values than adults because of their shorter vocal tracts. Adultlike frequency values will be reached by 12 years of age (Angelocci et al., 1964).

The craniofacial complex accounts for variation of formant frequencies and perceived vowel production. Although normative data are available on formant values for white children and adults (Peterson & Barney, 1952), none are available for other racial or ethnic groups. Early reports from cephalometric data showed racial differences in vocal tract size and cross-section area (Altemus, 1959; Drummond, 1968), suggesting the possibility of racial differences in formant frequency values as a product of the variation in the craniofacial structure. However, few investigators have studied formant structures across racial or ethnic groups.

In a study of 40 African American young males and 40 young females, Mayo, Manning, and Hudson (1989) found that 58% of the mean vowel formant patterns were lower in the African American males than published norms for white males and 75% were lower for African American females than for white females. These findings may imply differences in vocal tract structure between African Americans and whites. However, cultural-linguistic effects from the sentence-level stimuli also may influence the results. It was suggested that the use of isolated vowel or consonant-vowel stimuli instead of sentence-level stimuli in future studies could potentially control for cultural-linguistic effects on vowel formant values.

Mayo followed his initial study (Mayo et al., 1989) with a more comprehensive study of the acoustic parameters in speech of African American and

white populations (Mayo, 1990). He compared the f_0 and formant frequency values (F1, F2, F3) during the isolated vowel productions of 60 young adult African American males and females and their age-matched white peers. There was no significant race effect for f_0, but there were significant effects for vowel formant frequency. African American males had lower mean F1 values of /i/, /u/, and /ae/; lower mean F2 values of /i/ and /u/; and lower mean F3 values of /a/ and /I/. Lower means also were found for African American females for F1 values of /a/, /u/, and /ae/; for F2 values of /i/, /u/, and /ae/; and F3 values of /a/, /I/, and /ae/.

Implications for the Speech-Language Pathologist As researchers continue the study of the acoustic characteristics in African Americans, it will be important to consider dialect variation and its influence on fundamental frequency and formant structures. Some directions for future research include 1) normative data on fundamental frequency and on vowel formant frequency for African American children at different ages and by sex, and 2) normative data on acoustic characteristics of the speech of African American children with various pathologies.

CONCLUSIONS

The area of orofacial, physiological, and acoustic characteristics in the speech of African American children is ripe for research. A call was made by Cole (1986) to engage in research with individuals from diverse groups and to provide normative data from across cultures. That call has now become a cry that can be ignored no longer. It is evident that research with African American children is long overdue and should have a high priority. In many areas of speech-language pathology the existing database is not representative of our racially and ethnically diverse population. There is a crucial need for normative data on structural, physiological, and acoustic characteristics of diverse populations. These data are fundamental for providing appropriate speech and language services.

REFERENCES

Abramowitz, S., Leiner, G.C., Lewis, W.A., & Small, J. (1965). Small vital capacity in the Negro. *American Review of Respiratory Diseases, 92,* 287–292.

Adams, J. (1989). Prenatal exposure to teratogenic agents and neurodevelopmental outcome. In N.W. Paul (Ed.), *Birth defects: Original article series: Vol. 25. Research in infant assessment* (pp. 63–72). Baltimore: Williams & Wilkins.

Albright, R. (1948). Motor abilities of speakers with good and poor articulation skills. *Speech Monographs, 15,* 164–172.

Alexander, T.L., & Hitchcock, H.P. (1978). Cephalometric standards for American Negro children. *American Journal of Orthodontics, 74,* 298–304.

Alhady, S.M., & Sivanantharajah, K. (1969). Keloids in various races. *Plastic and Reconstructive Surgery, 44,* 564–566.

Altemus, L.A. (1959). Frequency of the incidence of malocclusion in American Negro children aged twelve to sixteen. *Angle Orthodontics, 29,* 189–196.

Altemus, L.A. (1966). The incidence of cleft lip and palate among North American Negroes. *Cleft Palate Journal, 3,* 357–361.

Altemus, L.A., & Ferguson, A.D. (1965). Comparison of incidence of birth defects in Negro and white children. *Pediatrics, 36,* 56–61.

Anderson, H.F., & Merkatz, I.R. (1991). Preterm labor. In S.H. Cherry & I.R. Merkatz (Eds.), *Complications of pregnancy: Medical, surgical, gynecologic, psychosocial, and perinatal* (4th ed., pp. 1104–1125). Baltimore: Williams & Wilkins.

Angelocci, A.A., Kopp, G.A., & Holbrook, A. (1964). The vowel formants of deaf and normal-hearing eleven- to fourteen-year-old boys. *Journal of Speech and Hearing Disorders, 29,* 156–170.

Baken, R.J. (1987). *Clinical measurement of speech and voice.* Boston: Little, Brown.

Baker, H. (1990). Anatomical and profile analysis of the female Black American nose. *Journal of the National Medical Association, 81,* 1169–1175.

Barkan, E. (1994). The retreat of scientific racism: Changing concepts of race in Britain and the United States between the world wars. *American Journal of Physical Anthropology, 89,* 502–510.

Barnes, H.N. (1987). The etiology and natural history of alcoholism. In H.N. Barnes, M.D. Aronson, & T. L. Delbanco (Eds.), *Alcoholism: A guide for the primary care physician* (pp. 16–25). New York: Springer-Verlag.

Begley, S. (1995, February 13). Three is not enough. *Newsweek,* pp. 67–69.

Bennett, S. (1983). A 3-year longitudinal study of school-aged children's fundamental frequency. *Journal of Speech and Hearing Research, 26,* 137–142.

Bennett, S., & Weinberg, B. (1979). Acoustic correlates of perceived sexual identity in preadolescent children's voices. *Journal of the Acoustical Society of America, 66,* 909–1000.

Bernstein, L. (1975). Rhinoplasty for the negroid nose. *Otolaryngology Clinics of North America, 8,* 783–795.

Bilto, E. (1941). A comparative study of certain physical abilities of children with speech defects and children with normal speech. *Journal of Speech Disorders, 6,* 187–203.

Blakley, M. (1987). Skull doctors: Intrinsic social and political bias in the history of American physical anthropology with special reference to the work of Ales Hrdlicka. *Critique of Anthropology, 7, 7* 35.

Bleile, K.M., & Wallach, H. (1992). A sociolinguistic investigation of the speech of African American preschoolers. *American Journal of Speech-Language Pathology, 1,* 44–52.

Blood, G.W., & Hyman, M. (1977). Children's perception of nasal resonance. *Journal of Speech and Hearing Disorders, 42,* 446–448.

Boshoff, P.H. (1945). The anatomy of the South African Negro larynx. *South African Journal of Medical Sciences, 10,* 113–119.

Bowman, J.E. (1990). Keynote address: Genetic services for underserved populations. In N. Paul & L. Kavanaugh (Eds.), *Birth defects: Original article series: Vol. 26. Proceedings from a National Symposium on Genetic Services for Underserved Populations* (p. xxx). Washington, DC: National Center for Education in Maternal Child Health.

Brace, C.L. (1964). A nonracial approach towards the understanding of human diversity. In A. Montagu (Ed.), *The concept of race* (pp. 103–152). New York: The Free Press.

Brace, C.L. (1982). The roots of the race concept in American physical anthropology. In F. Spencer (Ed.), *A history of American physical anthropology* (pp. 11–29). New York: The Free Press.

Brauner, G.J. (1994). Pigmentation and its disorders in blacks. In N. Levine (Ed.), *Pigmentation and pigmentary disorders* (pp. 439–464). Ann Arbor, MI: CRC Press.

Brazelton, T.B., Koslowski, B., & Tronick, E. (1976). Neonatal behavior among urban Zambians and Americans. *Journal of the American Academy of Child Psychiatry, 15,* 97–107.

Bryden, J.D. (1968). *An acoustic and social dialect analysis of perceptual variables in listener identification and rating of Negro speakers.* Doctoral dissertation, University of Virginia, Charlottesville.

Buchanan, L.H., Moore, E. J., & Counter, S. A. (1993). Hearing disorders and auditory assessment. In D. Battle (Ed.), *Communication disorders in multicultural populations* (pp. 256–279). Boston: Andover.

Bush, P.J., & Rabin, D.L. (1980). Racial differences in encounter rates for otitis media. *Pediatric Research, 14,* 1115–1117.

Calhoun, K.H., House, W., Hokanson, J.A., & Quinn, F.B. (1990). Nasal airway resistance in noses of different sizes and shapes. *Otolaryngology Head & Neck Surgery, 103,* 605–609.

Carey, J.W., & Steegmann, A.T. (1981). Human nasal protrusion, latitude and climate. *American Journal of Physiological Anthropology, 56,* 313–319.

Carter, A.L., Ricker, K.S., & Corsini, D.A. (1972). Relational judgment of sound intensity by young children. *Perception Psychophysiology, 11,* 1–4.

Cavalli-Sforza, L.L. (1971). *The genetics of human populations.* San Francisco: W. H. Freeman.

Cavalli-Sforza, L.L. (1995). *The great human diasporas: A history of diversity and evolution.* Reading, MA: Addison-Wesley.

Chavez, G.F., Cordero, J.F., & Becerra, J.E. (1988). Leading major congenital malformations among minority groups in the United States, 1981–1986. *Morbidity and Mortality Weekly Report, 37,* 17–24.

Church, M.W., & Gerkin, K.P. (1988). Hearing disorders in children with fetal alcohol syndrome: Findings from case reports. *Pediatrics, 82,* 147–154.

Coker, N.J., & Milner, P.F. (1982). Elective surgery in patients with sickle cell anemia. *Archives of Otolaryngology, 108,* 574–576.

Cole, L.T. (1980). Blacks with orofacial clefts: The state of the dilemma. *Asha, 33,* 557–560.

Cole, L.T. (1986). The social responsibility of the researcher. In F.H. Bess, B.S. Clark, & H.R. Mitchell (Eds.), *Concern for minority groups in communication disorders.* (pp. 93–100). ASHA Report No. 16. Rockville, MD: American Speech-Language-Hearing Association.

Cole, P.A., & Taylor, O.L. (1990). Performance of working-class African-American children on three tests of articulation. *Language, Speech, and Hearing Services in Schools, 21,* 171–176.

Coles, C.D. (1992). Prenatal alcohol exposure and human development. In M.W. Miller (Ed.), *Development of the central nervous system: Effects of alcohol and opiates* (pp. 9–36). New York: Wiley-Liss

Colton, R.H., & Cooker, H.S. (1968). Perceived nasality in the speech of the deaf. *Journal of Speech and Hearing Research, 11,* 533–559.

Connor, A.M., & Moshiri, F. (1985). Orthognathic surgery norms for American black patients. *American Journal of Orthodontics, 87,* 119–134.

Cooper, P.S. (1990). Unequal opportunity. In. N. Paul & L. Kavanagh (Eds.), *Birth defects: Original Article Series: Vol 26. Proceedings from a National Symposium on Genetic Services for Underserved Populations* (pp. 46–48). Washington, DC: National Center for Education in Maternal Child Health.

Cratty, B.J. (1986). Motor planning abilities in deaf and hearing children. *American Annals of the Deaf, 13,* 281–284.

Cunningham, J.J. (1995). Body composition and nutrition support in pediatrics: What to defend and where to begin. *Nutrition in Clinical Practice, 10,* 177–182.

D'Aloisio, D., & Pangrazio-Kulbersh, V. (1992). A comparative and correlational study of the cranial base in North American blacks. *American Journal of Orthodontics and Dentofacial Orthopedics, 102,* 449–455.

Datubo-Brown, D.D. (1989). Craniofacial clefts in an African black population. *Cleft Palate Journal, 26,* 339–343.

David, J.B., Edoo, B.B., Mustaffah, J.F.O., & Hinchcliffe, R. (1971). Adamarobe—A Deaf village. *Sound, 5,* 70–72.

Davies, P. (1989). Long-term effects of meningitis. *Developmental Medicine and Child Neurology, 31,* 398–406.

Davis, R.O., Cutter, G.R., Goldenberg, R.L., Hoffman, H.J., Cliver, S.P., & Brumfield, C.G. (1993). Fetal biparietal diameter, head circumference, abdominal circumference and femur length: A comparison by race and sex. *Journal of Reproductive Medicine, 38,* 201–206.

Dickson, S. (1962). Differences between children who spontaneously outgrow and children who retain functional articulation errors. *Journal of Speech and Hearing Research, 5,* 263–271.

Donahue, R.F. (1965). Birth variables and the incidence of cleft palate: Part I. *Cleft Palate Journal, 2,* 282–290.

Doyle, W.J. (1977). *A functiono-anatomic description of Eustachian tube vector relations in four ethnic populations—An osteologic study.* Ph.D. Dissertation, University of Pittsburgh.

Dreizen, S., Spirakis, C.N., & Stone, R.E. (1967). A comparison of skeletal growth and nutrition in undernourished and well-nourished girls before and after menarche. *Journal of Pediatrics, 70,* 256–263.

Drummond, R.A. (1968). A determination of cephalometric norms for the Negro race. *American Journal of Orthodontics, 54,* 670–682.

Duncan, G., & Rodgers, W. (1988). Longitudinal aspects of childhood poverty. *Journal of Marriage and Family, 50,* 1007–1021.

Dunham, E.C., Jenss, R.M., & Christie, A.U. (1939). Considerations of race and sex in relation to growth and development of infants. *Journal of Pediatrics, 14,* 156–160.

Dworkin, J.P., & Culatta, R.A. (1985). Oral structural and neuromuscular characteristics in children with normal and disordered articulation. *Journal of Speech and Hearing Disorders, 50,* 150–156.

Eguchi, S., & Hirsh, I.J. (1969). Development of speech sounds in children. *Acta Otolaryngologica, 257* (Suppl.), 5–51.

Enlow, D.H., Pfister, C., Richardson, E., & Kuroda, T. (1982). An analysis of black and Caucasian craniofacial patterns. *The Angle Orthodontist, 52,* 279–287.

Erickson, J.D. (1976). Racial variation in the incidence of congenital malformations. *Annals of Human Genetics, 39,* 315–320.

Everhart, R.W. (1953). The relationship between articulation and other developmental factors in children. *Journal of Speech and Hearing Disorders, 18,* 332–338.

Farrow, A.L., Zarrinnia, K., & Azizi, K. (1993). Bimaxillary protrusion in black Americans—An esthetic evaluation and the treatment considerations. *American Journal of Orthodontic and Dentofacial Orthopedics, 104,* 240–250.

Firestone, H.B., & Lehtnin, R. (1978). Some trait judgments made on the basis of voice alone. *Journal of Auditory Research, 18,* 209–212.

Fishman, M.C., Hoffman, A.R., Klausner, R.D., Rockson, S.G., & Thaler, M.S. (1981). *Medicine.* Philadelphia: J.B. Lippincott.

Flynn, T.R., Ambrogio, R.I., & Zeichner, S.J. (1989). Cephalometric norms for orthognathic surgery in black American adults. *Journal of Oral and Maxillofacial Surgery, 47,* 30–38.

Fogh-Anderson, P. (1942). *Inheritance of harelip and cleft palate*. Copenhagen: A. Busck.

Fonseca, R.J., & Klein, D. (1978). A cephalometric evaluation of American Negro women. *American Journal of Orthodontics, 73*, 152–160.

Friede, A., Baldwin, W., Rhodes, P., Buehler, J., Strauss, L., Smith, J., & Houge, C. (1987). Young maternal age and infant mortality: The role of the low birthweight. *Public Health Reports, 102*, 192–199.

Garn, S., & Coon, C. (1968). On the numbers of races of mankind. In S. Garn (Ed.), *Readings in race* (2nd ed., pp. 9–27). Springfield, IL: Charles C. Thomas.

Geber, M., & Dean, R.F.A. (1957). Gesell tests on African children. *Journal of Pediatrics, 49*, 1055–1065.

Gir, A.V., Aksharanugraha, K., & Harris, E.F. (1989). A cephalometric assessment of children with fetal alcohol syndrome. *American Journal of Orthodontic and Dentofacial Orthopedics, 95*, 319–326.

Glass, B. (1955). On the likelihood of significant admixture of genes from the North American Indians in the present composition of the Negroes of the United States. *American Journal of Human Genetics, 7*, 368–385.

Goodman, J.A. (1973). *Dynamics of racism in social work practice*. Washington, DC: National Association of Social Workers.

Gorlin, R.J., Cervenka, J., & Pruzansky, S. (1971). Facial clefting and its syndromes. In D. Bergsma (Ed.), *The clinical delineation of birth defects* (Birth defects: Original Article Series, Vol. 7,. pp. 3–49). Baltimore: Williams & Wilkins.

Griffith, T. (1979). Epidemiology of otitis media—An interracial study. *Laryngoscope, 89*, 22–30.

Grimes, P.E., & Stockton, T. (1988). Pigmentary disorders in blacks. *Dermatology Clinics, 6*, 271–280.

Gupta, B. (1969). Incidence of congenital malformation in Nigerian children. *West African Medical Journal, 18*, 22–28.

Guyette, T.W., & Diedrich, W.M. (1981). A critical review of developmental apraxia of speech. In N. Lass (Ed.), *Speech and language: Vol. 5. Advances in basic research and practice* (pp. 1–49). New York: Academic Press.

Hadlock, F.P., Harrist, R.B., Shah, Y., Sharman, R.S., & Park, S.K. (1990). Sonographic fetal growth standards: Are current data applicable to a racially mixed population? *Journal of Ultrasound Medicine, 9*, 157–160.

Hakim, A., & Grossman, J.R. (1995). Pediatric aspects of tuberculosis. In L.I. Lutwick (Ed.), *Tuberculosis: A clinical handbook* (pp. 117–153). London: Chapman & Hall.

Haller, R.M., & Thompson, E.A. (1975). Prevalence of speech, language, and hearing disorders among Harlem children. *Journal of the American Medical Association, 67*, 289–301.

Herrnstein, R.J., & Murray, C. (1994). *The bell curve: Intelligence and class structure in American life*. New York: The Free Press.

Herskovits, M.J. (1928). *The American Negro: Study in racial crossing*. New York: Knopf.

Hixon, T.J. (1973). Respiratory function in speech. In F.D. Minifie, T.J. Hixon, & F. Williams (Eds.), *Normal aspects of speech, hearing, and language* (pp. 73–125). Englewood Cliffs, NJ: Prentice Hall.

Holliday, M.A. (1978). Body composition and energy needs during growth. In F. Falkner & J.M. Tanner (Eds.), *Human growth 2: Postnatal growth* (pp. 117–139). New York: Plenum.

Hollien, H., & Malcik, E. (1962). Adolescent voice change in southern Negro males. *Speech Monographs, 29*, 53–58.

Hollien, H., & Shipp, T. (1972). Speaking fundamental frequency and chronological age in males. *Journal of Speech and Hearing Research, 15*, 155–159.

Hudson, A., & Holbrook, A. (1981). A study of the reading fundamental frequency of young black adults. *Journal of Speech and Hearing Research, 24*, 197–201.

Hudson, A., & Holbrook, A. (1982). Fundamental frequency characteristics of young black adults: Spontaneous speaking and oral reading. *Journal of Speech and Hearing Research, 25*, 25–28.

Ingrisano, D., Weismer, G., & Schuckers, G.H. (1980). Sex identification of preschool children's voices. *Folia Phoniatrica, 32*, 61–69.

Ivy, R.H. (1962). The influence of race on the incidence of certain congenital anomalies, notably cleft lip-cleft palate. *Plastic and Reconstructive Surgery, 30*, 581–585.

Jereb, J.A., Kelly, G.D., Dooley, S.W., Cauthen, G.M., & Snider, D.E. (1991 December). Tuberculosis Morbidity in the United States: Final data, 1990. *MMWR CDC Surveillance Summaries, 40*(3), 23–27.

Kahane, J.C. (1988). Anatomy and physiology of the organs of the peripheral speech mechanism. In N.J. Lass, L.V. McReynolds, J.L. Northern, & D.E. Yoder, (Eds.), *Speech language and hearing: Vol. II. Normal processes* (pp. 109–179). Philadelphia: W.B. Saunders.

Kapila, S. (1988). Selected cephalometric angular norms in Kikuyu children. *Angle Orthodontist, 59*, 139–144.

Kent, R. (1979). Isovowel lines for evaluation of vowel formant structure in speech disorder. *Journal of Speech and Hearing Disorders, 44*, 513–521.

Kent, R., & Rosenbek, J. (1983). Acoustic patterns of apraxia of speech. *Journal of Speech and Hearing Research, 26*, 231–249.

Ketchum, L.D., Cohen, I.K., & Masters, M.D. (1974). Hypertrophic scars and keloids: A collective review. *Plastic and Reconstructive Surgery, 53*, 140–153.

Kitlowski, E.A. (1953). Treatment of keloids and keloidal scars. *Plastic and Reconstructive Surgery, 12*, 383–392.

Kleinman, J.C., & Kessel, S.S. (1987). Racial differences in low birth weight: Trends and risk factors. *The New England Journal of Medicine, 317*, 749–753.

Kostelnik, K.E., & Ditre, C.M. (1994). Diseases among black people. In L.C. Parish & L.E. Millikan (Eds.), *Global dermatology: Diagnosis and management according to geography, climate, and culture* (pp. 137–153). New York: Springer-Verlag.

Lass, N.J., Tecca, J., Mancuso, R., & Black, W. (1979). The effect of phonetic complexity on speaker race and sex identifications. *Journal of Phonetics, 7*, 105–118.

Lester, B.M., & Brazelton, T.B. (1982). Cross-cultural assessment of neonatal development. In D.A. Wagner & H.W. Stevenson (Eds.), *Cultural perspectives on child development* (pp. 20–53). San Francisco: Freeman.

Lewis, J.H. (1942). *The biology of the Negro.* Chicago: University of Chicago Press.

Lewontin, R.C. (1972). The appointment of human diversity. *Evolution Biology, 6*, 381–398.

Lindeman, P., Holmquist, J., & Shea, J. (1981). The size of the mastoid air cell system among black and white children with middle ear effusion. *International Journal of Pediatric Otolaryngology, 3*, 251–256.

Lindsay, W.K., & Farkas, L.G. (1972). The use of anthropometry in assessing cleft-lip nose. *Plastic and Reconstructive Surgery, 49*, 286–293.

Lumba, M., Oduori, M.L., & Singh, S. (1977). Speech defects as seen at Kenyatta National Hospital. *East African Medical Journal, 54*, 539–547.

Masse, G., & Hunt, E.E. (1963). Skeletal maturation of the hand and wrist in West African children. *Human Biology, 35*, 3–25.

Matory, W.E., & Falces, E. (1986). Non-Caucasian rhinoplasty: A 16-year experience. *Plastic and Reconstructive Surgery, 72*, 239–251.

Mayo, R. (1985, November). *Trends in research on communicatively-impaired black Americans: 1977–1984.* Paper presented at the annual convention of the American Speech-Language-Hearing Association, Washington, DC.

Mayo, R. (1990). *Fundamental frequency and vowel formant frequency characteristics of normal African-American and European-American adults.* Unpublished doctoral dissertation, Memphis State University, Memphis, TN.

Mayo, R., Manning, W.H., & Hudson, A.I. (1989, November). *Formant frequency characteristics of adult African-American male and female speakers.* Paper presented at the annual convention of the American Speech-Language-Hearing Association, St. Louis, MO.

McCaffrey, T.V., & Kern, E.B. (1979). Clinical evaluation of nasal obstruction. *Archives of Otolaryngology, 105,* 542–545.

McCormack, M. (1985). The contribution of low birth weight to infant mortality and childhood morbidity. *New England Journal of Medicine, 2,* 312–316.

McGauhey, P.J., & Starfield, B. (1993). Child health and the social environment of white and black children. *Social Science Medicine, 36,* 867–874.

McLoyd, V. (1990). The impact of economic hardship on black families and children: Psychological distress, parenting and socioemotional development. *Child Development, 61,* 311–346.

McWillaims, B.J., Morris, H.L., & Shelton, R.L. (1990). *Cleft palate speech* (2nd ed.). Philadelphia: Decker.

Menyuk, P. (1986). Predicting speech and language problems with persistent otitis media. In J.F. Kavanagh (Ed.), *Otitis media and child development* (pp. 83–96). Parkton, MD: York Press.

Millard, D., & McNeill, K. (1965). The incidence of cleft lip and palate in Jamaica. *Cleft Palate Journal, 2,* 384–388.

Montagu, M.F.A. (1942). *Man's most dangerous myth: The fallacy of race.* New York: Columbia University Press.

Montagu, M.F.A. (Ed.). (1964). *The concept of race.* New York: Free Press.

Moore, W.A. (1970). The secular trend in physical growth of urban North American Negro school children. In J. Brozek (Ed.), *Monographs of the society for research in child development. No. 140. 35:7. Physical growth and body composition: Papers from the Kyoto symposium on anthropological aspects of human growth* (pp. 62–73). Chicago: University of Chicago Press.

Morganthau, T. (1995, February 13). What color is black? *Newsweek,* pp. 63–66.

Morgenstein, K., & Manace, P. (1969). Temporal bone histopathy in sickle cell disease. *Laryngoscope, 79,* 2172–2180.

Murray, R.D. (1963). Kenalog and the treatment of hypertrophied scars and keloids in negroes and whites. *Plastic and Reconstructive Surgery, 31,* 275–280.

National Center for Health Statistics. (1983). *Health and prevention profile, United States, 1983.* Hyattsville, MD: U.S. Department of Health and Human Services.

Negre, J. (1985, September). Colors, races, languages, and diseases [Letter to the editor]. *Journal of the American Medical Association, 254,* 1310.

Nummikoski, P., Prihoda, T., Langlais, R.P., McDavid, W.D., Welander, U., & Tronje, G. (1988). Dental and mandibular arch widths in three ethnic groups in Texas: A radiographic study. *Journal of Oral Surgery, Oral Medicine, and Oral Pathology, 65,* 609–617.

Ohki, M., Naito, K., & Cole, P. (1991). Dimensions and resistances of the human nose: Racial differences. *Laryngoscope, 101,* 276–278.

Oluwasanmi, J.O., & Adekunle, O.O. (1970). Congenital clefts of the face in Nigeria. *Plastic and Reconstructive Surgery, 46,* 245–251.

Oluwasanmi, J.O., & Kogbe, O.I. (1975). Rarer clefts of the face in Ibadan, Nigeria. *Medical Journal of Zambia, 1,* 25–28.

Onorato, I.M., Kent, J.H., & Castro, K.G. (1995). Epidemiology of tuberculosis. In L.I. Lutwick (Ed.), *Tuberculosis: A clinical handbook* (pp. 20–53). London: Chapman & Hall.

Owen, G.M., & Lubin, A.H. (1973). Anthropometric differences between black and white preschool children. *American Journal of Diseases of Children, 126,* 168–169.

Owens, J.R., Jones, J.W., & Harris, F. (1985). Epidemiology of facial clefting. *Archives of Diseases in Childhood, 60,* 521–524.

Paradise, J.L., Bluestone, C.D., & Felder, H. (1969). The universality of otitis media in 50 infants with cleft palate. *Pediatrics, 44,* 35–45.

Perkins, W.H. (1977). *Speech pathology: An applied behavioral science* (2nd ed.). St. Louis, MO: C.V. Mosby.

Perkins, W.H., & Curlee, R.F. (1969). Causality in speech pathology. *Journal of Speech and Hearing Disorders, 34,* 231–238.

Peterson, G.E., & Barney, H.L. (1952). Control methods in the study of vowels. *Journal of the Acoustical Society of America, 24,* 175–184.

Peterson-Falzone, S.J. (1982). Articulation disorders in orofacial anomalies. In N.J. Lass, L.V. Reynolds, J.L. Northern, & D.E. Yoder (Eds.), *Speech, language and hearing: Vol. II. Pathologies of speech and language* (pp. 611–637). Philadelphia: W.B. Saunders.

Pickett, J. M. (1980). *The sounds of speech communication.* Baltimore: University Park Press.

Pirie, N.W. (1950). Concepts out of context: Pied pipers of science. *British Journal of the Philosophy of Sciences, 2,* 269–280.

Polednak, A.P. (1989). *Racial and ethnic differences in disease.* New York: Oxford University Press.

Popovich, F., & Thompson, G.W. (1973). Thumb- and finger sucking: Its relation to malocclusion. *American Journal of Orthodontics, 63,* 149–155.

Randolph, L.A., & Rivers, S. (1985). A comparison of selected health indicators for black and white children in New York State. *New York State Journal of Medicine, 85,* 131–134.

Raph, J.B. (1967). Language and speech deficits in culturally disadvantaged children: Implications for the speech clinician. *Journal of Speech and Hearing Disorders, 32,* 203–214.

Rhine, J.S., & Campbell, H.R. (1980). Thickness of facial tissues in American blacks. *Journal of Forensic Sciences, 25,* 847–858.

Richardson, E.R. (1970). Cleft uvula: Incidence in Negroes. *Cleft Palate Journal, 7,* 669–672.

Richardson, E.R., & Malhotra, S.K. (1974). Vertical growth of the anterior face and cranium in inner city Negro children. *American Journal of Physical Anthropology, 41,* 361–366.

Richardson-Collins, A.M., & Coleman, A.A. (1995). Norfolk State University resource mothers program: A community response to adolescent pregnancy. In R.W. Johnson (Ed.), *African American voices: African American health educators speak out* (pp. 115–136). New York: National League for Nursing Press.

Robbins, J., & Klee, T. (1987). Clinical assessment of oropharyngeal motor development in young children. *Journal of Speech and Hearing Disorders, 52,* 271–277.

Roberts, F.L., & Crabtree, J.A. (1927). Vital capacity of Negro children. *Journal of American Medical Association, 88,* 1950–1952.

Robertson, E.L.S. (1964). Racial incidence of cleft lip and palate in Trinidad. In *Transactions of the Third International Congress of Plastic Surgery* (pp. 300–305). Washington, DC: Exerpta Medica Foundation.

Robinson, D.O., Allen, D.V., & Root, L.P. (1988). Infant tympanometry: Differential results by race. *Journal of Speech and Hearing Research, 53,* 341–346.

Roy, J.N. (1920). Syphilis among the Negroes of Africa and its manifestations in otorhinolaryngology. *Annals of Otology, Rhinology and Laryngology, 29,* 79–87.

Saniga, R.D., & Carlin, M.F. (1991). *Perceived voice usage in children aged three to six.* Paper presented at the American Speech-Language-Hearing Association meeting, Atlanta, GA.

Schoendorf, K.C., Hogue, C.J.R., Kleinman, J.C., & Rowley, D. (1992). Mortality among infants of black as compared with white college-educated parents. *The New England Journal of Medicine, 326,* 1522–1526.

Schwartz, J.D., Katz, S.A., Fegley, R.W., & Tockman, M.S. (1988a). Analysis of spirometric data from a national sample of healthy 6- to 24-year-olds (NHANES II). *American Journal of Respiratory Physiology, 138,* 1405–1414.

Schwartz, J.D., Katz, S.A., Fegley, R.W., & Tockman, M.S. (1988b). Sex and race differences in the development of lung function. *American Journal of Respiratory Physiology, 138,* 1415–1421.

Scott, R.B., Ferguson, A.D., Jenkins, M.E., & Cutter, F.F. (1955). Growth and development of Negro infants: V. Neuromuscular patterns of behavior during the first year of life. *Pediatrics, 16,* 24–29.

Seymour, H.N., & Ralabate, P. (1985). The acquisition of a phonologic feature of Black English. *Journal of Communication Disorders, 18,* 139–148.

Seymour, H.N., & Seymour, C.M. (1981). Black English and Standard American English consonantal development of four- and five-year-old children. *Journal of Speech and Hearing Disorders, 46,* 274–280.

Sharp, M., & Orchik, D.J. (1978). Auditory function in sickle cell anemia. *Archives of Otolaryngology, 104,* 322–324.

Shiono, P.H., & Klebanoff, M.A. (1986). Ethnic differences in preterm and very preterm delivery. *American Journal of Pediatric Health, 76,* 1317–1321.

Sidel, R. (1986). *Women and children last.* New York: Viking.

Siegel, B. (1975). A racial comparison of cleft patients in a clinic population: Associated anomalies and recurrence rates. *Cleft Palate Journal, 16,* 193–197.

Smillie, W.G., & Augustine, D.L. (1926). Vital capacity of the Negro race. *Journal of the American Medical Association, 87,* 2055–2058.

Sokol, R.J., & Clarren, S.K. (1989). Guidelines for use of terminology describing the impact of prenatal alcohol on the offspring. *Alcoholism, 13,* 597–598.

Stanton, W.R. (1960). *The leopard's spots: Scientific attitudes towards race in America, 1815–59.* Chicago: University of Chicago Press.

Staples, R. (1986). *The black family: Essays and studies.* Belmont, CA: Wadsworth.

Steinsapir, C., Forner, L., & Stemple, J. (1986, November). *Voice characteristics among black and white children: Do differences exist?* Paper presented at the annual convention of the American Speech-Language-Hearing Association, Detroit, MI.

Stockman, I.J., Vaughn-Cooke, F.B., & Wolfram, W. (1982). *A developmental study of Black English—Phase I.* National Institute of Education; 1982. Publication NIE-G-0135. Final Research Report. (ERIC Clearinghouse on Language and Linguistics no. ED 245556)

Subtelny, J.D., & Sakuda, M. (1964). Open-bite: Diagnosis and treatment. *American Journal of Orthodontics, 50,* 337–358.

Taylor, O. (1980). Communication disorders in blacks. In B.E. Williams & O.L. Taylor (Eds.), *Working papers: International conference on black communication* (pp. 62–94). New York: The Rockefeller Foundation.

Trost, J.E. (1981). Articulatory additions to the classical description of the speech of persons with cleft palate. *Cleft Palate Journal, 18,* 193–203.

Tuberculosis in blacks—United States. (1987, April 17). *Morbidity and Mortality Weekly Report, 36*(14), 212–214, 219–220.

Vallino, L.D., & Tompson, B. (1993). Perceptual characteristics of consonant errors associated with malocclusion. *Journal of Oral Maxillofacial Surgery, 51,* 850–856.

VanDenmark, D.R., Morris, H.L., & VandeHaar, C. (1979). Patterns of articulation abilities in speakers with cleft palate. *Cleft Palate Journal, 16,* 230–239.

Vanderas, A.P. (1987). Incidence of cleft lip, cleft palate, and cleft lip and palate among races: A review. *Cleft Palate Journal, 24,* 216–225.

Verghese, K.P., Scott, R.B., Teixeira, G., & Ferguson, A.D. (1969). Studies in growth and development: XII. Physical growth of North American Negro children. *Pediatrics, 44,* 243–247.

Walton, J.H., & Orlikoff, R.F. (1994). Speaker race identification from acoustic cues in the vocal signal. *Journal of Speech and Hearing Research, 37,* 738–745.

Warren, D.W. (1984). A quantitative technique for assessing nasal airway impairment. *American Journal of Orthodontic and Dentofacial Orthopedics, 3,* 306–314.

Warren, D.W., & DuBois, A.B. (1964). A pressure-flow technique for measuring velopharyngeal orifice area during continuous speech. *Cleft Palate Journal, 1,* 52–71.

Warren, D.W., Hinton, V.A., Pillsbury, H.C., & Hairfield, M. (1987). Effects of size of nasal airway on nasal airflow rate. *Archives of Otolaryngology Head and Neck Surgery, 113,* 405–408.

Warren, M.C. (1972). African infant precocity. *Psychological Bulletin, 78,* 353–367.

Washington, J.A., & Craig, H.K. (1994). Dialectal forms during discourse of poor, urban, African American preschoolers. *Journal of Speech and Hearing Research, 37,* 816–823.

Weinberg, B., & Bennett, S. (1971). Speaker sex recognition of 5- and 6-year-old children's voices. *Journal of the Acoustical Society of America, 50,* 1210–1213.

Werner, P. (1974). Infants around the world: Cross-cultural studies of psychomotor development from birth to two years. *Journal of Cross-Cultural Psychology, 3,* 11–134.

Westby, C. (1989). *Cultural differences affecting communicative development.* Unpublished manuscript.

Wheat, M., & Hudson, A. (1988). Spontaneous speaking fundamental frequency of 6-year-old black children. *Journal of Speech and Hearing Research, 31,* 723–725.

White, E.H. (1977). Cultural and biological diversity and health care: Giving health care to minority patients. *The Nursing Clinics of North America, 12,* 27–40.

Williams, R.A. (1975). *Textbook of black related diseases.* New York: McGraw-Hill.

Wilson, D.K. (1987). *Voice problems of children* (3rd ed.). Baltimore: Williams & Wilkins.

Wilson, M.G., & Edwards, D.J. (1921). Standards for normal vital capacity for children: The lung capacity in certain intrathoracic conditions. *American Journal of Disorders in Children, 22,* 443–449.

Wingerd, J., Schoen, E.J., & Solomon, I.L. (1971). Growth standards in the first two years of life based on measurements of white and black children in a prepaid health care program. *Pediatrics, 47,* 818–825.

Witzel, M.A., & Vallino, L.D. (1992). Speech problems in patients with dentofacial or craniofacial deformities. In W. H. Bell (Ed.), *Orthognathic and reconstructive surgery* (Vol. II, pp. 1686–1735). Philadelphia: W.B. Saunders.

Zetterstrom, R., & Nylander, I. (1985). Children in families with alcohol abuse. In U. Rydberg, C. Alling, & J. Engle (Eds.), *Alcohol and the developing brain: Third International Berzelius Symposium* (pp. 153–159). New York: Raven.

9

Vocabulary Development and Disorders in African American Children

Julia Mount-Weitz

This chapter explores the literature about African American children's vocabulary acquisition and usage and attempts to integrate this knowledge with information about vocabulary assessment and intervention practices in schools and clinics. A large body of literature leads to the conclusion that some African American children, most often those who speak an African American English (AAE) dialect, are likely to score poorly on tests of vocabulary and other standardized measures of language. These vocabulary and other language deficiencies compromise the child's ability to profit from educational opportunities, insofar as the importance of vocabulary in reading, writing, talking, listening, and general academic performance is now recognized.

To be an effective tool in spoken and written language, a person's vocabulary must have both depth and breadth (Irvin, 1990; Kamhi & Catts, 1989; Perfetti, 1985). Vocabulary breadth refers to the number of words an individual knows, whereas depth refers to the number of meanings attached to the words with which a person is familiar (Perfetti, 1985). Breadth and depth of vocabulary knowledge play a central role in oral or written language comprehension (Kamhi & Catts, 1989). Coupled with facility in use, vocabulary knowledge enhances precision in comprehension (Perfetti, 1985). Furthermore, extensive vocabulary knowledge facilitates the acquisition of new vocabulary from context (Perfetti, 1985).

The relationship between vocabulary and schooling is a complex one. Vocabulary acquisition itself is a desired outcome of the educational process, but vocabulary knowledge is fundamental to children's achievement in all areas of the curriculum (Dunn & Dunn, 1981; Seifert & Schwarz, 1991), especially reading (Irvin, 1990; Vacca & Vacca, 1989; Wiig & Freedman, 1993). Good readers, particularly children who read frequently, acquire more and more vocabulary, whereas poor readers, who typically don't read extensively, fall behind in vocabulary. Hence, we find that there is a strong reciprocal relationship among vocabulary knowledge, reading skill, and curricular success.

The chapter is divided into three sections. The first section addresses the issues of what children learn about vocabulary and how they go about the process of lexical acquisition. The focus is on those characteristics of lexical acquisition and knowledge that provide the foundation for assessment and intervention practices. The section also reviews literature about the nature of the AAE lexicon. A second section provides a close examination of vocabulary assessment practices of educators and speech-language pathologists. This includes a discussion of the tasks used, data on AAE-speaking children's performance on vocabulary tests, and alternative procedures for testing AAE-speaking children. A third section focuses on vocabulary teaching strategies that have as their foundation current theories about vocabulary knowledge and acquisition. Particular attention is devoted to instructional practices appropriate for AAE-speaking children.

LEXICAL DEVELOPMENT

What Does It Mean to "Know a Word?"

Knowing a word depends on the relationships that exist in an individual's personal experiences, concepts, and the words that serve to label those concepts (Vacca & Vacca, 1989). Among young children, existing concepts about the world are mapped on to new words (Clark, 1993; Crais, 1990). For older children, novel concepts are likely to be introduced with novel words, as in the learning of scientific concepts (Wiig, Freedman, & Secord, 1992). The former are learned by hearing words embedded in experience, whereas the latter tend to be learned from verbally presented information in instructional contexts (Wiig et al., 1992). Word learning is likely to be incremental. There are degrees or levels of knowing a word, ranging from "do not know" to "somewhat familiar" to "know it well" (Blachowicz, 1986, 1994; Irvin, 1990).

Knowing a word first requires that a child have an entry for any particular word in the mental lexicon. Beyond that, knowing a word involves multiple kinds of information (Carey, 1978; Clark, 1993; Wolfram, 1983/1994): syntactic, semantic, morphological, pragmatic, stylistic, and phonological. In learning the syntactic properties of words, a child must acquire information about the parts of speech of the word and rules about the syntactic structures in which a word may occur. Semantically, the child learns the referential properties of a word, the range of ideas to which a word may be applied, and the word's relationship to other words. In this context, pragmatic constraints involve knowing what information a word entails. Stylistic constraints concern the settings and speaking styles in which a word may be used. Morphological information concerns the internal structure of the word, that is, the number and type of free and bound morphemes in the word. Phonological information involves knowing the acoustic and articulatory phonetic characteristics of a word. Phonological information is used to access word representations when they are needed for both comprehension and production. When a new vocabulary word is acquired, that word, along with all relevant information about the word, is placed in the child's mental lexicon. Presumably, the new word will be connected to other words with related meanings or associations.

How Are Words Represented in Memory?

Psycholinguists are still in the process of determining the nature of memory for words. However, some broad conclusions hold some implications for assessment and intervention targeting lexical knowledge. Two theoretical frameworks of lexical organization are of particular interest.

Network Models Network models of lexical organization assume that individual words are stored in memory with many connections to other words (Collins & Loftus, 1975; Collins & Quillian, 1969). For example, the words *petunia* and *flower* might be stored with strong connections with one another. The connections themselves represent various relationships among words. In the example of *petunia* and *flower*, the relationship would be one of inclusion or class membership (Clark, 1993), in the sense that a petunia is a kind of flower.

In the early models (Collins & Quillian, 1969), the words were organized in a strictly hierarchical relationship. Words higher in the hierarchy include all those lower in the hierarchy. Higher-level words are in a superordinate relationship to those lower in the hierarchy; for example, *animal* is a superordinate of *cat*, which in turn is a superordinate of *Himalayan*. The lower-level words are hyponyms or subordinates insofar as they belong to the class of objects named by the superordinate word; for instance, *Himalayan* is a subordinate of *cat*, which in turn is a subordinate of *animal*. Words at the same level in the hierarchy, such as *Himalayan* and *Siamese*, are co-hyponyms or coordinates. Property information about each word in the hierarchical network is also available. For instance, the property "is carnivorous" is located at the highest applicable node and applies to all of the categories subordinate to that node, so an individual who knows that cats are carnivorous could also infer that Himalayans are carnivorous.

The spreading activation model is an update of the hierarchical network model (Collins & Loftus, 1975). In the spreading activation model, words may be connected hierarchically, but their connections also reflect frequency of association between and among words. For example, someone might mentally connect the word *rabbit* to the word *cat* because of personal experience with the relationships in the physical world of rabbits and cats or from repeated exposure to the two words' co-occurrence (e.g., "Spunky, our cat, brought home another rabbit tonight"). The spreading activation model has been used to account for various effects of lexical items on language processing, including comprehension, memory, and recall data.

Semantic Feature Models   A second type of model of lexical representation is the semantic feature model (Smith, Shoben, & Rips, 1974). According to the semantic feature model, words are stored mentally as bundles of semantic features or semantic components that function like subunits of meaning. Synonyms (e.g., *sofa* and *couch*) share nearly identical semantic features. Words that are antonyms share some features but oppose one another on one feature (e.g., *woman* and *girl* share features of human and female but oppose one another on the feature of age). Other words have shared and unshared components with other words. For example, the words *fly* and *soar* share semantic features of movement through space but do not share other meaning features.

The point here is not to debate the various models of lexical organization. Instead, the importance of these models resides in how they delineate the kinds of knowledge that people have about words and how they contribute to ideas about what the impact of vocabulary is on general language processing. The spreading activation model, for instance, provides clues to explain how the presence of words in an oral or written text might facilitate the understanding of later occurring words. Semantic feature models help explain our knowledge that some words can be synonyms, others have overlapping meanings, and still others are antonyms.

Word Composition   Many words in a language are "knowable"; that is, their meanings can be determined from an analysis of their roots and affixes (Anglin, 1993; Clark, 1993). From a morphological perspective, words may be monomorphemic, bimorphemic, multimorphemic, or idioms (Anglin, 1993). A more useful way of morphologically defining words is to classify them as root words (e.g., *gulp*), inflected words (e.g., *weaving, buttoned*), derived words (e.g., *abandonment*), literal compounds (e.g., *payday, sunrise*), and idioms (e.g., *lady's slipper*) (Anglin, 1993). If children understand individual root words and also possess knowledge of various inflectional and derivational morphemes or rules for compounding, they become capable of using a strategy of "morphological problem solving" (Anglin, 1993) to gain access to the meanings of newly encountered multimorphemic words.

Meaning Relations   Various authors (Clark, 1993; Hamersky, 1993) have detailed the relationships that can exist between words: inclusion (also called class membership); synonymy (also called identity); metonymy (part-whole); incompatibility; overlap; opposite; spatial; temporal; function; and rhyming. These relationships are known and used by individuals as they understand and produce language.

Semantic Fields A semantic field is a group of words that all pertain to the same conceptual domain. For example, there exist numerous words associated with the solar system (Wiig & Freedman, 1993) and a different group of words associated with the abolitionist movement and with African American emancipation. As children's lexicons mature, they build up semantic fields. In addition, they learn new words that differentiate a given semantic field.

All of these aspects of word knowledge and usage need to be considered in assessment of and intervention with vocabulary problems. Unfortunately, there is a scarcity of information about the development of children's semantic networks and their learning of word relationships. We have considerably more insight regarding how word relationships and word usage change as children mature, such as the shift from syntagmatic to paradigmatic associations.

How Is Word Knowledge Acquired?

Incidental Word Learning Most words are acquired through incidental learning. Such learning occurs in the absence of direct instruction. Children learn vocabulary and word meanings without direct instruction from oral contexts in the preschool years and from oral, classroom, and written contexts during the school years. Children must encounter a word many times to gain enough information about the word to truly know it. Formal vocabulary instruction cannot provide detailed information about a word, except for a small number of words (Nagy & Herman, 1987).

Children possess vocabulary acquisition strategies that they employ to map concepts on to linguistic forms (Bedore & Leonard, 1995; Carey, 1978; Clark, 1993; Dockrell, 1981; Dollaghan, 1985). Children are capable of learning a considerable amount of vocabulary by interfacing their own mapping strategies with exposure to vocabulary in naturalistic contexts. Mapping takes place through an interaction of the child's conceptual and linguistic systems when a word becomes associated with a referent or with a conceptual domain. A child's vocabulary in the early years is often facilitated by the presence of an adult or otherwise competent speaker who stimulates the child's vocabulary acquisition and who monitors the child's use of vocabulary (Brown, 1973). Preschool children's lexical development is frequently guided by ostensive definition, such as "That's a bird" or "It's a puzzle" (Crystal, 1987; Kouri, 1994; Ninio & Bruner, 1978). Ostensive naming often will be accompanied by pointing, showing, and giving gestures coupled with gazing at the referent. As children mature, they may learn the meanings of words through the medium of other words (e.g., an ostrich is a kind of bird) (Crystal, 1987), including formal definitions. More often, children infer the meanings of new words as they are exposed to new words embedded in language concerning their daily interactions with others through a process called fast mapping.

Fast-mapping studies have demonstrated that children can learn a wide variety of words incidentally from brief exposure to them in a variety of potential word-learning contexts: during play (Dockrell, 1981; Dollaghan, 1985, 1987; Mount, 1993), in classroom messages (Carey, 1978), from watching video presentations (Rice, Buhr, & Nemeth, 1990), and from reading (Crais, 1987; Dickinson, 1984). A variety of word types (e.g., nouns, verbs, adverbs, adjectives) have been learned in such word-learning contexts (Crais, 1987; Dickinson, 1984; Dockrell, 1981; Dollaghan, 1985, 1987; Mount, 1993; Rice et al., 1990).

Carey (1978) proposed that there is an initial fast-mapping period followed by a more protracted period for learning a particular word. During the initial fast mapping, children lay down a partial mental representation for a word. The representation may include all or some of the semantic, syntactic, morphological, and phonological information available about the new word. As children repeatedly encounter the word in new contexts, their representation for the word is expanded.

In infancy, children encounter words embedded within routines, and the meanings for the words are the objects and actions that are part of the routine. Lexical knowledge is first applied in the here-and-now and only later in the there-and-then. Initially, words become attached to specific referents and only later to classes of referents. As children attach words to concepts and classes of referents, denotative meaning is said to develop (Nelson, 1986). In early childhood, children form semantic fields that become further differentiated as children experience new words and new referents (Carey, 1978; Crystal, 1987). During the school years they learn to express and understand definitions of new words and come to prefer to learn the meanings of new words through definitions (Crystal, 1987; Dickinson, 1984).

Constraints on Word Learning   Certain operating assumptions, or linguistic principles, are believed to guide young children's vocabulary mappings. The "taxonomic assumption" is an expectation that words will refer to entities of the same kind (Markman, 1994). The "whole object assumption" indicates that young children will assume that a word refers to an object rather than some characteristic or movement of the object (Markman, 1994). The "mutual exclusivity assumption" states that children prefer only one label for an entity and will avoid attributing a second label to a given entity (Markman, 1994). Related to the mutual exclusivity assumption is the "principle of contrast" (Clark, 1993), which argues that children expect different linguistic forms to indicate differences in meaning. Young children often do not allow overlap in meanings among their words, referred to as the "no-overlap assumption" (Clark, 1993).

Vocabulary Acquisition of African American Children

Unfortunately, we know considerably less about the vocabulary development of African American children than we do about their morphology and syntax. There are numerous gaps in our knowledge base, partly because African American children have not always been included in research studies. When they have been included, the focus has been very narrow. For instance, a considerable amount of research has examined African American children's performance in comparison with that of mainstream children or national norms on standardized tests of vocabulary. Virtually no attention has been directed toward African American children's vocabulary acquisition strategies or the extent of their vocabulary knowledge.

African American Children's Performance on Measures of Vocabulary Our knowledge about AAE-speaking children's vocabulary acquisition depends on how we go about testing. What we know is extremely limited, based largely on the use of standardized testing. Many AAE-speaking children who do not have language disorders nevertheless may perform poorly on standardized tests of language, including vocabulary tests, and numerous studies have found that African American children as a group scored lower than white children on tests of vocabulary or word concepts (Beal, 1987; Bracken, Sabers, & Insko, 1987; Dunn, 1988; Kresheck & Nicolosi, 1973; Washington & Craig, 1992). On the original Peabody Picture Vocabulary Test (PPVT), lower middle-class African American children scored significantly lower than white children from similar socioeconomic environments matched for age and grade level (Kresheck & Nicolosi, 1973). Eleven items used with this age group were missed regularly by the African American children but not by the white children. The Peabody Picture Vocabulary Test–Revised (PPVT–R) (Dunn & Dunn, 1981) was normed nationally and used stratified normative data by including individuals from different ethnic and socioeconomic backgrounds. However, unimpaired, low-income, urban African American preschool and kindergarten children studied by Washington and Craig (1992) tended to score more than one standard deviation below the mean on the revised test. Some items were missed by over 50% of the AAE-speaking children. Unfortunately, even when each child was given credit for such items that occurred below the child's ceiling, 86% still scored below the national mean and 51% scored more than one standard deviation below the national mean.

When African American children scored relatively poorly on the Iowa Test of Basic Skills (ITBS), researchers in the Denver, Colorado, public schools determined that vocabulary deficits accounted for poor performance (Beal, 1987). The African American students scored below national norms on every item in the Vocabulary subtest and performed poorly on subtests that were loaded with specialized subject-related vocabulary (e.g., Social Studies). Such subtests require the understanding of nonvernacular words and an expanded vocabulary.

At this point in the discussion, it becomes important to consider what factors might account for AAE-speaking children's poorer performance on measures of vocabulary.

Child Variables Affecting Performance These findings do not presuppose a deficit in vocabulary knowledge or inadequate language learning abilities. All that can be said is that AAE-speaking children did not know as many of the same, presumably culture-specific, words as did the normative sample. The reasons for some AAE-speaking children's restricted vocabulary development are discussed in the following sections.

Language Acquisition Capacity There is no reason to believe that AAE-speaking children are uniquely deficient in their ability to learn language. Regardless of culture, the rate of language acquisition is the same (Owens, 1992). Studies of early semantic, syntactic, morphological, and phonological developments indicate more similarity than difference in the acquisition sequence (see reviews in Anderson & Battle, 1993; also Stockman & Vaughn-Cooke, 1982, 1986). Related to the topic of vocabulary acquisition is the finding by Stockman and Vaughn-Cooke (1982) that working-class African American children code the same semantic categories as children learning other linguistic systems. African American children have not been the subjects of research concerning language acquisition strategies, although researchers have shown that the language spoken to some African American infants and toddlers is likely to be different from that to working- and middle-class white children (Hale-Benson, 1986; Heath, 1983; van Kleeck, 1994; Ward, 1971).

Heath (1983) has provided comprehensive descriptions of the early language learning environments of African American children in her ethnography of Trackton, an African American working-class community in the Piedmont Carolinas. Her account contrasts sharply with conventional descriptions of middle-class white child-rearing and language stimulation practices (see Owens, 1992). In Trackton, babies have a continuous presence during the conversations of others, but they are seldom treated as participants. Babies' noises might be used referentially or they might produce words, but no one gives them special attention. Any attention that is provided for early vocalizations or verbalizations tends to be affective rather than linguistic. "Even in contexts where the baby's utterances can be easily linked to objects or events, adults do not acknowledge these utterances as labels. . . . They do not repeat the utterance, announce it as a label for an item or event, or place the "word" in an expanded phrase or sentence. To them, the response carries no meaning which can be directly linked to an object or event; it is just 'noise'" (Heath, 1983, p. 76). The prevailing belief is that babies are not taught language but, instead, come to know language.

Language addressed to some African American children may differ from white middle-class norms. Ward (1971) pointed out that adult language to African American children is often directive. In some cultures, children are not expected to initiate conversation or request information. Children may or may not be expected to perform linguistically. Following the child's lead may not be valued, and so expansions and extensions of the child's language may not be used. Dillard (1977) argues that African American children per se are not "verbally deprived" as was once commonly believed. In African American communities, a considerable amount of communication is directed toward children and considerable encouragement for African American children to use language is present. It is important to keep in mind that generalizations to all African American communities should not be made automatically. Moreover, we should not assume that one language learning environment is necessarily superior to another but merely different and that language addressed to children will reflect the values of their individual communities.

African American English Lexicon Certain terms are used widely in the African American community and are shared by African Americans, and some words, used also by Standard American English (SAE) speakers, have special meanings in AAE (Dillard, 1977; Smitherman, 1977). The AAE lexicon arises from the "common linguistic and cultural history" (Smitherman, 1977, p. 43) of African American people—that is, their origins in Africa, their culture during slavery, religious and spiritual traditions, and music. Children whose primary dialect is AAE will have words from the African American lexicon. This implies that AAE-speaking children will know some words that preempt SAE words and they will attach different meanings to SAE words. These differences will affect AAE-speaking children's performance on vocabulary assessment. The use of the African American lexicon does not imply a vocabulary deficit, only a difference.

Socioeconomic Status Another child variable affecting vocabulary test performance is socioeconomic status (SES). Often AAE-speaking children are economically disadvantaged (Evard & Sabers, 1979). Regardless of race or cultural group, children from lower SES groups in general tend to have lower vocabulary scores. Poverty children are often limited in their knowledge about the world, and "their knowledge deficits are reflected in their smaller vocabularies" (Snow, 1982, p. 259). Some African American children have less exposure than middle class children to material objects that lead to greater proficiency with these objects (Dillard, 1977; Heath, 1983; Hart, 1982) and presumably skill in talking about such objects. It is therefore likely that urban low-income African American children's lower vocabulary scores reflect deficiencies in vocabulary resulting from their impoverished environments (Dillard, 1977; Washington & Craig, 1992). In addition to having limited experiences, children from impoverished homes may hear less language. When low-SES families were compared with more advantaged families, Hart and Risley (1995) determined that children from low-SES (welfare) homes hear fewer words per interaction unit, hear fewer different words, receive less parental affirmative feedback, hear more commands rather than prompts and questions, and have less overall interaction with adults. Professional parents addressed the most words per hour to their children, followed by working-class parents, and then the low-SES parents. Hart and Risley speculated that the average 4-year-old in a welfare family may have experienced perhaps 13 million fewer words than the average child in a working-class family.

Although there is little evidence to suggest that poverty children learn language any differently or at a different rate from middle-class children, there is evidence that there are important differences at the time of school entry. Specifically,

> Certain vocabulary words that are specifically informative about content likely to be encountered in school are present to a greater degree in the speech of middle-class children. . . . There is also some evidence to suggest that middle-class children have more familiarity with verbal abstractions—using language to group and conceptualize more frequently than poor children do. (Farran, 1982, p. 269)

Middle-class children are able to use more formal language, the kind needed when speaking to strange adults. For impoverished African American children there seems to be a discontinuity between expectations for language at home and those valued by the school. A problem is created, not because there is anything wrong with the language of poverty children, but because they must adapt to the school system (Moore, 1982).

Cummins (1981) identified two kinds of language needed by children in schools. There is the language of socialization (basic interpersonal communicative skills; BICS) and cognitive-academic language proficiency (CALP). Cummins also established two continua for describing communication tasks. Tasks may range from cognitively demanding to cognitively undemanding. Furthermore, tasks may have different degrees of contextual support. From this scheme emerge four types of communication activities: cognitively undemanding/context embedded; cognitively undemanding/context reduced; cognitively demanding/context embedded; and cognitively demanding/context reduced. The problem is that, in many cases, some AAE-speaking children may have adequate BICS and use language in cognitively undemanding and contextually supportive contexts but have less experience with the more cognitively demanding and decontextualized uses of language.

In this and the previous section of this chapter, we have considered the nature of vocabulary knowledge and vocabulary acquisition and discussed some of the problems encountered by AAE-speaking children, especially in their efforts to acquire the vocabulary valued in school. We turn now to the issue of how the assessment of vocabulary knowledge might best be conducted. It becomes important to examine what is actually assessed by tests designed to evaluate word knowledge. The next section examines new and traditional vocabulary assessment tools and considers their appropriateness for AAE-speaking children. An important part of the discussion concerns the issue of test bias.

ASSESSMENT OF LEXICAL KNOWLEDGE

There are essentially two approaches for assessing vocabulary knowledge. The most frequent approach uses standardized norm-referenced tests. A second approach calls for nonstandardized criterion-referenced assessments, including language sampling. Which procedures one uses will depend on both the nature of the questions being asked and cultural and individual difference variables. This section addresses the nature of vocabulary deficits in relationship to the kinds of tasks that are available for testing vocabulary and then discusses some of the issues involved in the assessment of African American children, especially those who speak AAE.

The Nature of Vocabulary Deficits in Children

There is a certain constellation of characteristics associated with children who have vocabulary deficits. Late onset of language and slow progress in learning words in the preschool years is common as is difficulty integrating and retaining new vocabulary later in life (Hamersky, 1993). The children's word meanings are likely to lack certain features and the meanings will therefore be too narrow or restricted (Hamersky, 1993; Secord & Wiig, 1991). The children have difficulty understanding word relationships such as synonymy, antonymy, hyponymy (Secord & Wiig, 1991), and other similarities and differences among words (Hamersky, 1993). Their semantic networks are less likely to be organized, and they lack strategies for organizing vocabulary. The children's ability to define words will be restricted (Hamersky, 1993). They will have difficulties with certain classes of words, such as conjunctions and transition words (Secord & Wiig, 1991). Older children may have problems with definitions and word formation rules involving knowledge of affixes. Precision and accuracy of word choice may suffer (Hamersky, 1993). Word-finding and word-retrieval problems are likely to be attributed to inadequately developed representations of vocabulary (Kail & Leonard, 1986). Figurative language may be problematic. Needless to say, assessing lexical knowledge requires a broad scope. There are both standardized and nonstandardized means of evaluating vocabulary. When used alone, neither of the approaches is likely to be satisfactory. The best approach to assessment is to evaluate as many dimensions of vocabulary knowledge as possible to determine a child's strengths and weaknesses in the area of vocabulary. As with other language skills, vocabulary is best appraised in a variety of physical, social, and linguistic contexts.

Assessing Vocabulary with Standardized Tests

Most general tests of language development contain subtests that tap vocabulary, but their scope is usually narrow. Fortunately, tests that explore various features of lexical knowledge have been developed: the Language Processing Test (LPT; Richard & Hanner, 1985); the Test of Word Knowledge (TOWK; Wiig & Secord, 1992); The Word Test (TWT; Jorgensen, Barrett, Huisingh, & Zachman, 1981); The Word Test-Revised-Elementary (Huisingh, Barrett, Zachman, Blagden, & Orman, 1990); The Word Test–Adolescent (TWT–A; Zachman, Barrett, Huisingh, Orman, & Blagden, 1989); and ASSET: Assessing Semantic Skills Through Everyday Themes (Barrett, Zachman, & Huisingh, 1988). Tests such as these offer the professional a variety of formats and a much broader view of a child's vocabulary knowledge and skills. A range of tasks are available for the assessment of vocabulary. Table 1 provides a list of common tasks used during vo-

Table 1. Tasks used to assess lexical knowledge in standardized testing and indications of which tests provide stratified normative samples

Tasks	Tests
Picture vocabulary recognition	ASSET*; BBCS*; PPVT-R*; ROWPVT; TOLD2-P; TOWK*
Picture vocabulary naming	ASSET*; EOWPVT; TOWK*
Producing definitions	ASSET* TOLD2-P; TOWK*; TWT; TWT-A
Understanding definitions	ASSET*
Labeling	LPT*
Stating functions/attributes	ASSET*; LPT*
Associations: words associated with certain nouns	LPT*
Associations: naming what items don't belong and explaining why	TWT
Categorization (finding and/or naming items that belong to specific categories)	ASSET*; LPT*
Similarities	LPT*
Differences	LPT*
Multiple meanings (providing multiple definitions or pointing to pictures)	LPT*, TOLD2-I; TOWK*; TWT
Attributes	LPT*
Speaking and/or writing a word in a meaningful sentence	TOAL-2
Relational meanings (understanding that words do/do not belong together)	TOAL-2
Judging if word pairs are synonyms, antonyms, or unrelated	TOLD2-I
Providing synonyms for single words	TWT; TOWK*
Providing synonyms for words in sentences	TWT-A
Providing an antonym for a given word	TOWK*
Brand names (explaining the suitability of the name)	TWT-A
Explaining signs and their importance	TWT-A
Explaining or correcting absurd sentences	TWT
Conjunctions and transition words	TOWK*

* Attempts have been made to provide a stratified normative sample based on census data.

ASSET = Assessing Semantic Skills Through Everyday Themes (Barrett, Zachman, & Huisingh, 1988); BBCS = Bracken Basic Concept Scale (Bracken, 1984); EOWPVT = Expressive One-Word Picture Vocabulary Test–Revised (Gardner, 1990); LPT = Language Processing Test (Richard & Hanner, 1985); PPVT–R = Peabody Picture Vocabulary Test–Revised (Dunn & Dunn, 1981); ROWPVT = Receptive One-Word Picture Vocabulary Test (Gardner, 1985); TOAL = Test of Adolescent Language (2nd ed.) (Hammill, Brown, Larsen, & Wiederholt, 1987); TOLD2-P = Test of Language Development—Primary (2nd ed.) (Newcomer & Hammill, 1991a); TOLD2-I = Test of Language Development—Intermediate (2nd ed.) (Newcomer & Hammill, 1991b); TOWK = Test of Word Knowledge (Wiig & Secord, 1992); TWT = The Word Test (Jorgensen, Barrett, Huisingh, & Zachman, 1981).

cabulary assessment, along with an indication of some of the standardized tests that employ the particular tasks. Those tests that have attempted to provide a stratified normative sample for their standardization population are indicated. However, the reader is cautioned that the use of stratified normative samples does not guarantee that a test will be reliable and valid for a particular segment of the population.

The different tasks call on different kinds of knowledge about vocabulary words, all of which have the potential to reveal a child's strengths and weaknesses with vocabulary. The child's responses will be affected by both the kinds of information available and the nature of the response required by the test (Crais, 1990). Crais cautions against a correct–incorrect, or an off–on, view of vocabulary. As such, expressive and receptive picture vocabulary tests, which only use plus-minus scoring, offer no procedures for qualitative analysis of a child's answers and are unlikely to reveal the presence of partial word knowledge, for example. Furthermore, the context in which the words are assessed is very limited.

Receptive vocabulary tests typically require the child to point to a picture best associated with the stimulus word in a kind of passive recognition process. Expressive vocabulary tests call on the child to name pictures. Answers are scored by comparison with criteria, and any one of a variety of typical answers is accepted but not unconventional ones.

Another common examination procedure is to ask the child to provide definitions for given words, by responding to questions such as "What does X mean?" The quality of the definitions is scored according to the number or type of key words provided by the child. A definition task is more a measure of the child's formal knowledge about how to phrase definitions and less of a measure of what words a child knows and can use in appropriate situations. Children who have not been exposed to conventions for producing definitions are unlikely to reveal the scope of their vocabulary knowledge with measures of this type. Formal definitions are taught in school and older children do become comfortable with definitions as a means of acquiring vocabulary knowledge and displaying that knowledge (Dickinson, 1984).

Some tests ask children to explain the functions of objects or state attributes of objects when given their names. This task is very likely to tap the knowledge that children, including preschoolers, have acquired about objects in the world. Naturally, children who have limited experience with the world of objects, such as children from poverty backgrounds, will be at a disadvantage with this kind of format, as will children who know alternative lexical items for the ones on the test. The risk is that their vocabularies will be underestimated.

The kinds of word relationships established by a child may be evaluated in a number of ways. Association tasks require children to produce words that "go with" a stimulus word. Synonym and antonym tasks ask the child to produce a synonym or antonym, as appropriate, to a stimulus word. Scoring conventions usually require a comparison of the child's response with a set of "acceptable" answers in the test manual. Although these tasks reveal something about relationships among words in a child's lexicon, atypical answers that are appropriate in the child's dialect may not receive credit on such tests.

Other tasks that evaluate relational meanings are those that ask children to judge whether words belong together, determining if word pairs are synonyms, antonyms, or unrelated; using words in oral or written sentences; and recognizing and correcting absurdities.

Two kinds of tasks evaluate children's hierarchical knowledge about words and the objects they represent. Categorization tasks expect children to identify members of a specific category, either by pointing to pictures or by verbal responses. A related type of task asks children to indicate which word in a list does not belong with the other words provided. The child must infer the superordinate category that accounts for most of the items and then exclude an item that does not belong. Answers to these types of questions are closely aligned with the child's underlying conceptual knowledge.

Similarities and differences subtests require that a child compare two items that are taken from the same semantic field. For instance, on the LPT (Richard & Hanner, 1985), the child is expected to tell how pairs of words are the same and how they are different (e.g., car-bus, ring-necklace, stove-refrigerator, banana-corn). To accomplish this, the child must have experience with the words and their referents and be able to compare and contrast the terms on the basis of semantic features.

Nonstandardized Assessment of Vocabulary

Nonstandardized assessment usually begins with observation in the natural environment and is likely to include the collection of language samples from a child during unstructured conversations. Naturalistic contexts presuppose activities, conversational partners, and linguistic and conversational styles that are culturally congruent for the child. Language sampling may be followed up with probes to evaluate specific kinds of knowledge.

Checklist and Diary Information   Children who are just learning to talk will produce only a limited number of words, and these may occur infrequently. Because vocabulary may be context-specific, their word knowledge may be evidenced only intermittently. Therefore, it is sometimes best to rely on parental reports of language acquisition. Rescorla (1989, 1991) finds it feasible to ask parents to use prepared word lists to indicate what words their child knows. Miller (1981) and Crystal (1987) have both advocated the use of diary information. Miller suggests that one day's worth of diary information, taken during several distinctly different activities, such as bathing, dressing, and feeding activities, suffices at any one period of time. Not only will the diary list specific words known by the child or important in the child's life, but also it will permit an analysis of the semantic fields that the child knows or encounters. Typically, no more than 2 hours is required of parents during a sampling period. Miller offers diary recording forms with the advice that they be posted in all areas where interaction with a child is likely. Crystal (1987) claims that estimates of children's vocabularies are greatly expanded when diary information is considered. Naturally, the ability and willingness of parents to maintain diaries must be considered, but it is generally believed that parents can be accurate informants in this area. An alternative is to ask parents to tape-record exchanges with their children.

Using Language Samples A semantic field analysis is a useful way to examine the vocabulary present in children's language samples. The examiner will want to identify word categories that are present in the sample and the words associated with those categories (Crystal, 1987; Miller, 1981). For example, the examiner may want to determine that a child knows a number of nouns and other words associated with people, clothing, vehicles, family, and buildings, and verbs associated with motion or states (Crystal, 1987; Miller, 1981). For older children, words associated with different academic subject areas will be of interest. Wiig and Freedman (1993) have provided extensive word lists that might be applied to a semantic field analysis of school-age children's vocabulary.

In cases where a language disorder may be causing vocabulary problems, procedures for analyzing language samples are focused on searching for evidence of certain vocabulary deficits (Lund & Duchan, 1993). The language transcript should be inspected for examples of overextension and underextension. Language samples might also contain examples where the child's use of words is different from adult usage. Sometimes the child's application of words to referents will be highly variable and will require a comparison of inconsistent word usage to determine the meaning of the word for the child. Finally, a transcript should be examined for evidence of word deficits, including indefinite terms, descriptions, or gestures that would be functioning to replace more definite terms. In some cases, the child will produce idiosyncratic terms, and these should be analyzed as well. The possibility that there are word deficits for specific word classes (e.g., nouns, verbs, adjectives, adverbs) should be explored by determining if certain word classes are missing from a transcript.

Criterion-Referenced Vocabulary Assessment Assessment of vocabulary knowledge may be carried out in semistructured contexts, somewhat between the standardized test and the language sample in formality. Semistructured contexts are appropriate if a goal of vocabulary assessment is the estimation of a child's vocabulary in a particular semantic field or for particular purposes (Owens, 1992; Paul, 1995). In such cases, parents and teachers may suggest kinds of vocabulary to be targeted and the educator or speech-language pathologist will conduct nonstandardized assessment. Activities that incorporate the lexicon of interest are employed. These may be in the form of games, interviews, "setups" (Lund & Duchan, 1993; Paul, 1995), referential communication tasks, and other relevant contexts for comprehending and producing specific vocabulary. Lund and Duchan (1993) recommend elicitations to determine lexical meanings when words have been used inappropriately and also to see if a child can extend a word to a variety of referents. On occasion, with older children, it will be useful to ask a child to define a term that has been used inappropriately, but, as we all know, it is usually easier to use a word than to define it.

Quantification of Vocabulary A traditional means of estimating an individual's lexical diversity is the type-token ratio (TTR; Miller, 1981; Retherford,

1993; Templin, 1957). The TTR is computed by counting the number of different words in a transcript by the total number of words. An advantage of the TTR is that it is stable across various socioeconomic groups. A TTR of 0.50 is typical for boys and girls between the ages of 3 and 8 years. Retherford (1993) indicates that children younger than 3 years will have lower TTRs. Type-token ratios substantially below 0.50 indicate deficient vocabulary or a lack of diversity in the child's vocabulary. A higher TTR indicates relatively greater lexical diversity. In addition to applying the TTR, examining the child's total number of vocabulary words and the number of different words is also recommended (Retherford, 1993) and may in fact be more sensitive than the TTR (Watkins, Kelly, Harbers, & Hollis, 1995).

Evaluation of Children's Potential to Learn Vocabulary   Instead of relying on static one-time measures, it is possible to use what are known as dynamic assessment procedures, paired with mediation, in evaluating children's vocabulary. Dynamic assessment procedures provide children with a sequence of experiences thought of as test-teach-retest to differentiate children with and without language impairments and to assess a child's language learning ability. Peña, Quinn, and Iglesias (1992) used dynamic assessment and mediated learning with African American and Puerto Rican children in a Head Start program. Children identified as possibly having a language disorder and those thought not to were administered a picture labeling test prior to mediation/teaching and after mediation/teaching. It was assumed that children without disabilities who responded poorly to the test would respond to mediation and achieve higher scores on the retest. Conversely, children with a language disorder would not be expected to respond readily to the mediation and do well on the retest. Mediation emphasized labeling of objects or categories and also included identifying the functions of objects. As predicted, the children without disabilities gained more from the mediation than did the children with a language disorder as revealed by the retest scores. Those gains were maintained over time, as indicated by follow-up testing. Furthermore, interventionists rated the children with a language disorder as less responsive to mediation than the children without disabilities. Peña et al. (1992) concluded that the description task, the mediation, and the interventionists' ratings of the children's responsiveness were more effective in determining group membership than was the static pretest involving a labeling task.

Using Standardized Norm-Referenced Tests with African American Children

Test Bias   A number of arguments and effects convince us that the standardized tests that display African American differences or deficiencies are biased. When specific items are routinely missed by African American children but not white children (Kresheck & Nicolosi, 1973; Washington & Craig, 1992), we have strong evidence that the test is biased. When 86% of a group of African American children without impairments score below national norms and 51% more than one standard deviation below the mean (Washington & Craig, 1992), we again have evidence of test bias. In spite of the fact that some tests, like the

PPVT–R, incorporated ethnic and racial balance in the standardization population, the test directions and the items themselves are based on SAE, and thus they continue to be inappropriate for speakers of AAE (Adler & Birdsong, 1983; Washington & Craig, 1992). Tests that are biased with respect to a certain population are not appropriate or valid for use with that population.

Standardized tests are also seldom appropriate for assessing the full range of an individual's knowledge. Wolfram (1983/1994) points out that norm-referenced tests of language evaluate the more superficial aspects of language and language organization. This is the level at which dialect differences also emerge. Dialects tend to be more similar at deeper levels of language knowledge, such as underlying categories and relationships and the conceptual bases of language capability (Wolfram, 1983/1994). These deeper levels of language are seldom tapped by traditional standardized tests. For example, the PPVT requires only the association of a label with a picture of something that is in a particular semantic arena but does not assess the underlying conceptual information attached to the word. Hence, standardized tests of this type will be inappropriate for users of dialects. Wolfram's ideas are supported in part by studies, using language sampling techniques, that show that the amount of AAE in a child's speech is positively correlated with the use of more complex language in the semantic-syntactic sphere (Craig & Washington, 1994, 1995).

Not everyone agrees that differences in vocabulary scores of African American and white children can be attributed to test bias or a mismatch between language and culture. Bracken et al. (1987), using the Bracken Basic Concept Scale, found that African American children at a mean age of 5.5 years tested one half standard deviation below the subtest and total test means and that their scores were significantly lower than those of the white children with whom they were matched according to age, sex, and father's education. However, because the response patterns of the two groups were similar, the researchers argued that children from the two groups respond similarly to the Bracken Basic Concept Scale but that "a true difference exists between the two groups in their rate of basic concept acquisition" (p. 26).

Task Familiarity Sometimes the task used to assess vocabulary knowledge is inappropriate for AAE-speaking children. Standardized tests often present students with questions that have obvious or known answers. Yet, in some African American cultures, asking and answering known-information questions or test questions is not valued (Heath, 1983). Whereas African American adults will solicit information from children, they typically do not ask children questions when the answer is known to both parties. During book reading with their toddlers, African American mothers do use known-information wh-questions and yes–no questions, but less than white mothers (Hart & Risley, 1994).

Peña et al. (1992) point out that not all cultural or linguistic groups emphasize one-word labeling of objects. For example, in the North Philadelphia community that they observed, there is a high demand for descriptions but not for labels. In such cases, poor performance on vocabulary tests involving labeling reflects a different kind of linguistic experience rather than a language disorder. Peña et al. demonstrated the effects of different kinds of testing on the children's scores. On the Expressive One-Word Picture Vocabulary Test, an expressive labeling test, only 9 out of 50 children (18%) scored within one standard deviation from the mean. Conversely, 30 out of the 50 children (60%) scored within one standard deviation from the mean on a task involving functions, descriptions, and explanations. Children both with and without language disorders achieved lower standard scores on the labeling task and higher standard scores on the description task. Furthermore, the description task discriminated the children with disabilities from those without, whereas the labeling task did not. According to the researchers, "this is consistent with a claim that a test matching the values and experiences of children is a more valid measure of language ability" (Peña et al., 1992, p. 277).

In some cultures, children are not expected to be co-conversationalists with adults and they talk to adults only when spoken to (Schieffelin & Eisenberg, 1984; Ward, 1971). Cultural mistrust when the test administrator is not from the same culture as the child will also affect children's attitudes toward testing and their actual scores (Terrell & Terrell, 1993; see also Chapter 4).

In summary, a child who speaks primarily AAE is likely to be disadvantaged on vocabulary tests because the tests are based on SAE (Adler & Birdsong, 1983; Dillard, 1977; Evard & Sabers, 1979) and some words on the test are culture specific (Adler & Birdsong, 1993; Wolfram, 1983/1994). The tasks demanded of children on standardized tests are unfamiliar in one form or another, more so if the children come from impoverished backgrounds. Therefore, anyone who uses such tests with AAE-speaking children must be careful in drawing conclusions from the testing. The cautious evaluator will combine standardized and nonstandardized measures and use assessment tools that comprehensively determine an individual child's strengths and weaknesses.

Although one must carefully select culturally appropriate assessment procedures, it is also important to use culturally sensitive intervention targets and activities. The following section reviews current instructional procedures for facilitating vocabulary acquisition and discusses how the educator or speech-language pathologist (SLP) might be sensitive to African American children's cultures and learning styles (Crawford, 1993; Nellum-Davis, 1993) during vocabulary instruction.

VOCABULARY ENHANCEMENT

Intervention encompasses the integration of culturally appropriate teaching-learning contexts with theoretically grounded objectives and techniques. Some writers believe that African American children possess learning styles that are different from and incompatible with traditional Eurocentric teaching methods. Consequently, teaching practices that are more appropriate for African American children have been advocated. Therefore, appropriate teaching adaptations will be reviewed before a more specific discussion of vocabulary teaching techniques.

The African American Child in Intervention Contexts

The educator or SLP must keep in mind that children who speak AAE are likely to become bidialectal (Stockman, 1986) and bicultural (Hale-Benson, 1990). Many AAE-speaking children, when they first start school, will have experienced SAE predominantly through television and radio (Stockman, 1986). For many, AAE will continue to be their "mother tongue," but they will receive increased exposure to SAE and the Eurocentric culture as part of their schooling (Hale-Benson, 1990). One of the first tasks for educators and SLPs working with African American children is to help them to respect their own dialects and those of others (Campbell, 1994). AAE-speaking children should not be pressured into using SAE but instead should learn to recognize the points of similarity and difference between AAE and SAE (Campbell, 1994; Hale-Benson, 1990). AAE-speaking children also must learn to recognize situations that mandate code switching (Campbell, 1994).

Acknowledging that one source of academic failure is very likely the discontinuities in behavior between home and school, Crawford (1993) outlines a multicultural perspective: recognize all students' potential for learning; teach in a way that affirms diversity; empower students to be self-learners; recognize different approaches to learning; use culturally based learning styles to facilitate learning; challenge students; offer instruction in the home language; draw on and value students' experiences as bases for learning; view students as active learners; maintain trusting and equitable home–school relationships; respect the home community and culture; avoid practices that attempt to assimilate and acculturate students; include the history and culture of all groups; accept the students' home community; and require changes in curricula, teaching styles, the function of schools, and the structure of schools (pp. 2–3).

Bridging Home and School with Early Literacy Experiences   Intervention ideally starts during the preschool years and involves children's caregivers. Early experiences in the home and preschool will facilitate vocabulary acquisition, as well as other language and literacy developments. Crawford (1993) reminds practitioners that language and literacy achievements in the home language facilitate achievements in the language of school. Early literacy experiences in children's everyday lives are one important means for closing the gap between home and school language. Therefore, valuing literacy in the home, embedding and modeling literacy activities in everyday life, and making literacy materials accessible are important, more so than household income. Even in the face of poverty, parents who recognize the importance of literacy experiences to their children's school success have used free programs, such as libraries and library programs, museums, and university reading clinics, to provide literacy experiences for their children. Crawford recommends that educators "assist parents to create language-rich and literate home environments in keeping with their cultural traditions, beliefs, and values and learn how to help children develop skills and attitudes for success in the transformed school" (p. 26).

Recognizing the Child's Culture At the same time as literacy exposure takes place, educators and SLPs must respect and accommodate the culture and the learning styles of individual AAE-speaking children (Crawford, 1993; Hale-Benson, 1990). Hale-Benson (1990) describes the ways in which an educator in her model program creates an educational culture that recognizes and is compatible with the child's home culture and gives the child pride and identity as an African American:

> The teaching method emphasizes Afro-American culture and integrates it in all of its diversity throughout the curriculum. The children learn about Africa and their rich cultural heritage; they learn about Afro-American and African arts and crafts; they listen to folktales and stories written by Afro-American writers; they listen to music and learn about musicians that emerge from Black culture; they learn about heroes in Black history such as Dr. Martin Luther King, Jr. Afro-American studies is a focal point and is also integrated throughout the curriculum of this model. Every opportunity is used to acquaint the children with the culture, cosmology, and history of Africans of the diaspora. . . . The children are exposed to aspects of African culture appropriate to their level of understanding—foods, geography, fashions, music, instruments, songs, poetry, names, history, and art. (pp. 213–214)

Adapting Instruction to the Child's Learning Style Some African American students do not perform as well in large-group, teacher-centered instructional contexts (Crawford, 1993) as they would in small cooperative learning groups. Many do not respond well to drill activities, such as the type found in workbooks and duplicated materials (Crawford, 1993; Nellum-Davis, 1993). Such activities are divorced from any kind of meaningful context or communicative function. Furthermore, these activities are seldom interesting or highly motivating. Many African American students favor contexts that include opportunities for cooperative learning, discussion, and hands-on experiences (Crawford, 1993).

Hale-Benson (1990) emphasizes the importance of elaborated language and communication skills for African American children's success with the curriculum and with standardized tests and indicates approaches that have been useful in her program:

> Black children are very expressive in the use of oral language. However, there is a need to broaden their skills to include those that are called for as a precursor to reading and writing proficiency. Therefore, speaking, listening, labeling, storytelling, chanting, imitating, and reciting are encouraged. (p. 213)

Methods of Vocabulary Instruction

The most robust approach to the facilitation of more extensive vocabulary knowledge would combine opportunities for incidental learning, strategies for profiting from word-learning opportunities, and direct vocabulary instruction (Nagy

& Herman, 1987). The proper mix of learning contexts will be determined by the child's age, interests, and conceptual development.

To some theorists, definitions provide a limited source for children's learning of new vocabulary. There are at least three explanations for the limitations of definitions: first, a student must know other vocabulary words to understand definitions; second, definitions do not contain enough information; third, word meanings are partially derived from their use in context (Irvin, 1990). Deeply knowing a word involves multiple exposures to a word in many different contexts and a mapping on to underlying concepts, but definitions alone cannot provide such experiences. Instead, definitions supply only a single, but nevertheless meaningful, exposure to a word (Nagy & Herman, 1987). A single definition is probably better than a single encounter with a word in text, but the two approaches together are better than either alone.

Contemporary theorists reject the idea that vocabulary can be truly learned through some traditional activities, such as looking up a word, defining the word, memorizing the word, and using the word in a sentence (Blachowicz, 1986; Vacca & Vacca, 1989) or through the use of isolated word lists, drill and practice activities, or fill-in-the-blank worksheets (Hamersky, 1993). Teaching must bridge outside experiences with what is learned in class and teachers must mediate students' learning. Furthermore, the vocabulary and the activities themselves must be relevant and meaningful to the child's life, and a student should be able to use the skills and the information that he or she is taught (Hamersky, 1993).

Vocabulary acquisition occurs in conjunction with concept development (Wiig, Freedman, & Secord, 1992). Practitioners should assume a reciprocal relationship between concept and vocabulary development. Practitioners must therefore provide children with relevant experiences for learning concepts underlying vocabulary words.

Reading to a child is routinely considered an important avenue for the acquisition of new concepts and for related vocabulary development. Hart and Risley (1994) detailed the kinds of maternal utterances produced by African American mothers during book reading. Many mothers used strategies to direct children's attention to lexical items: wh-questions; yes–no questions; directives or requests; labeling; descriptions; and feedback, including repetition of the child's correct responses.

Because language itself is used to accomplish certain goals, it makes sense that vocabulary instruction should involve contexts that are meaningful and purposeful for the child. The content, form, and use components of language need to be integrated. In other words, children and their conversational partners must have goals that motivate the communication, ideas to convey or receive, and linguistic forms for messages to take. In the preschool years, exposure to new vocabulary will occur in conjunction with experiential and learning activities planned for the child. For instance, sand play can be used to expose children to concepts and words related to size and measurement. A field trip to a zoo is likely to facilitate children's learning of animal names and other related terms. Planting a small vegetable garden provides opportunities to compare seeds, plants, and tastes.

In more academic contexts, vocabulary knowledge should be broadened and deepened within the kinds of preliteracy and literacy experiences provided by whole-language instruction (Damico, 1992; Damico & Hamayan, 1992; Norris, 1991; Norris & Hoffman, 1990) and by the inclusion of vocabulary and other language experiences in content-related classes (Vacca & Vacca, 1989).

Vocabulary comprehension and production should be thought of as reciprocal skills. As a child encounters a lexical entry, the child will often "test" that word by using it in language production (Brown, 1973). Children usually comprehend more words than they can produce, and they also understand and produce words before they fully know the meanings of those words. Therefore, Paul (1995) advocates directing intervention targeted primarily at vocabulary production. The expectation is that comprehension of words will be facilitated simultaneously with the focus on production. However, children will require both comprehension and production experiences in many diverse contexts before they know a word both broadly and deeply.

The Selection of Vocabulary Words   In choosing words for vocabulary instruction, the educator should give some attention to the relevance of the word to the child, whether it will be functional for the child in everyday communicative events, and whether the word is timely and fits in with the child's projected encounter with the word in lessons at school (Hamersky, 1993). In the preschool and early elementary years, children's learning of basic concepts is important to their understanding of the language of classrooms. Other important sources of instructional targets are the content curricula, instructional units, literature to which the children will be exposed, and tests that they will have to take.

Wiig and Freedman (1993) organized word lists around very broad themes: human beings (e.g., body parts, senses, attributes, diseases, life cycle); human society (e.g., government and law, interpersonal relationships, related topics); human invention (e.g., education, language, time, artifacts, transportation); sports, recreation, and the arts (e.g., athletics, recreation, music, performing and visual arts); the natural environment (e.g., air and weather, animals, land, the universe); and number and measurement (e.g., mathematics and calculations, nonspecific number and time, specific number and time, relationships of objects in space, the three dimensions). For each thematic unit, interventionists must identify the difficult vocabulary that is likely to be encountered and related vocabulary words. Wiig and Freedman (1993) recommend that the words identified then be organized in relation to other words. They classify thematically related words as nouns, verbs, and adjectives or adverbs.

Certain vocabulary may be needed for academic purposes, regardless of content area. Hamersky (1993) calls the reader's attention to vocabulary that is used in critical thinking across grade levels and in all areas of the curriculum. The words emphasize the student's thinking skills, both in and out of school. Such words are "analyze, attribute, brainstorm, categorize, classify, compare, contrast, define, demonstrate, describe, estimate, evaluate, fact, figurative, generalize, hypothesize, identify, illustrate, infer, irrelevant, literal opinion, organize, predict, prioritize, relate, relevant, sequence, summarize, and variable" (p. 79). Davey (1983) identified vocabulary used in read-alouds: think, hypothesis, mental images, prior knowledge, monitoring, contradictions, ambiguity, predict, analogy, confusing, and context.

Other vocabulary needed by children to express logical relationships includes the conjunctions that draw multiple clauses into meaningful relationships: *and* (additive); *(and) then, while,* and *when* (temporal); *because, so, therefore,* (causal); *if-then* (causal/conditional). Conjunctions may not be a concern for African American children insofar as Craig and Washington (1994, 1995) reported a positive correlation between urban, low-income African American preschoolers' use of AAE and the use of complex syntax, defined partially as the use of a variety of conjunctions. However, it is important to verify that children are able to use these terms to comprehend and express logical relationships.

Children themselves may be asked to add vocabulary words, especially those they have encountered and that they find difficult and those they are expected to learn for school. Families may be consulted for recommendations (Hamersky, 1993).

Teaching Basic Concept Vocabulary Basic concept terms are used in kindergarten and early elementary grades, when teachers give children directions, and they are found in the curricula and in printed materials (Boehm, 1986; Bracken, 1984; Seifert & Schwarz, 1991). Basic concept terms include words for colors, numbers, shapes, spatial terms, and the like. There are numerous approaches for teaching basic concepts, two of which are described in the following paragraphs.

Seifert and Schwarz (1991) effectively implemented a basic concepts intervention program aimed at a large group of Head Start children between 4 years, 3 months and 5 years, 8 months. The program incorporated direct instruction, interactive instruction, and incidental teaching while covering two basic concepts per week. Direct instruction provided the children with numerous positive and negative examples of each concept. Interactive instruction provided occasions for the children to use the concept terms during a specially designed activity. Incidental teaching involved the teachers' use of the targeted concept terms during naturally occurring classroom activities.

Ellis, Schlaudecker, and Regimbal (1995) demonstrated the effectiveness of teaching a select group of basic concepts through a collaborative consultation approach. The targeted students were an ethnically and racially diverse group of inner-city kindergarten children, the majority of whom were African American children from low-income families. The instruction was provided by the children's kindergarten and physical education teachers with consultation from the school speech-language pathologist and a faculty member in a university physical education program. One basic concept was highlighted per week. The classroom teacher presented the target concept, told a story based on the concept, and provided incidental instruction. The physical education teacher planned activities from the regular physical education curriculum to teach the same concepts. The resulting improvements support the idea that basic concepts can be taught, that large group instruction on basic concepts is effective, and that the teaching can be incorporated into general classroom activities in the public school through collaborative intervention.

Content Area Vocabulary   Mastering the lexicon of a content area is central to mastering the content area itself. As Vacca and Vacca (1989) pointed out,

> Vocabulary is as unique to a content area as finger prints are to a human being. A content area is distinguishable by its language, particularly the special and technical terms which label the underlying concepts of its subject matter. (p. 298)

There are three kinds of vocabulary in content area textbooks: general vocabulary, consisting of widely used everyday vocabulary words with widespread meanings; common vocabulary, which takes on a special meaning when used in a particular content area; and technical vocabulary, words used only in a particular subject area. Special consideration must be given to the development of content-related vocabulary. Students must be shown how words in a content area relate to the underlying concepts, how those concepts relate to one another, how words relate conceptually to one another, and how the meanings of words are revealed through sentences and larger passages (Vacca & Vacca, 1989).

Concepts are learned directly and most easily through interaction with the environment and are most difficult to learn from linguistic input. Concepts are strengthened and vocabulary is built by mapping the vocabulary on to the concepts as they are learned. Once children are exposed to new concepts or new vocabulary, the relationship needs strengthening through various kinds of reinforcing activities. Such activities include individual and group discussions, especially those in which children are able to use their new words meaningfully. Such discussions revolve around an assortment of learning activities that are planned for the students. New words must also be applied to more and more familiar contexts. The following activities are presented by Vacca and Vacca (1989) and can be applied to various content areas.

Comparison, classifying, and generalizing operations help children understand word groupings. "Word sorts" are valuable for developing these skills and can be used for most content areas. For example, children may be involved in a "closed sort"; they are provided with a list of words but know in advance the shared features on which the sorting is based. If done in collaboration with other students, the sorting activity serves as the basis for a discussion and the use of the new vocabulary. In an example based on important African American individuals, students would be given the following names and asked to group them: Frederick Douglass, Marian Anderson, Martin Luther King, Jr., Bessie Smith, Mary

McLeod Bethune, Roy Wilkins, Shirley Chisolm, Count Basie, Harriet Tubman, Maya Angelou, Malcolm X, and so on. The children would be told before the sorting to group the individuals as abolitionists, artists, or 20th-century political leaders.

An "open sort" works similarly, but the students are given a list of terms and are left to discover the properties or relationships on which the sorting is based. In justifying their choices, students are given opportunities for using their new vocabulary words. For example, students would be given the following list: air conditioner, blender, dehumidifier, dishwasher, fan, food processor, freezer, humidifier, microwave, mixer, washing machine. The children would very likely group the words according to food preparation, climate control, and cleaning functions.

Categorizing activities are similar to sorts, but are based on superordinate and subordinate relationships: Students might be asked to identify, from a grouping of words, the one word that includes the other three (e.g., the term *elected officials* incorporates other words like *governor, senator, representative, mayor,* etc.). One categorization scheme, the "concept circle" is a variation of sorting; the teacher provides the vocabulary words, each as a part of a pie, and the children guess at the organizing concept. Parts of the pie can be left empty for the children to complete with an appropriate word or concept. A word or concept that does not belong in a sort or a pie can also be indicated, an operation of "exclusion." In all of these activities, children should be expected to discuss and justify their choices, which is possible only if they are attending to the meanings of the items (Vacca & Vacca, 1989).

In "selecting" operations, students make choices and justify their choices Selecting may involve the use of synonym and antonym relationships or the understanding of multiple-meaning words. In "implying" operations, students establish if-then or cause-and-effect relationships and the use of analogical reasoning. When using word analogies, students must first be instructed in the logic of completing analogies. Students complete analogies and provide reasons for their answers.

In Vacca and Vacca's (1989) approach, children are taught to determine a word's meaning from context. One way to learn meaning from context is the "context puzzle," an activity in which words in a passage are marked in some way. The students are required to guess the word's meaning and indicate the clues that helped them arrive at the meaning. Another way to connect the meaning of words to surrounding sentence context is for students to provide words missing in passages, either before or after reading in a content area. If the activity is done before reading, the student builds a meaning for words used in the actual reading passage. If the activity is completed after reading a passage, the student reinforces concepts developed through the reading passage. In a related activity, "OPIN" (for opinion), students individually supply words to complete sentences on worksheets and must then justify their choices to their own group and to other groups in the class. "Word puzzles" are used to match new vocabulary words to known words or to definitions, and numerous games can be used to make the matching more interesting.

Semantic Mapping and Graphic Organizers Semantic mapping is used extensively in literature-based or whole-language approaches to language learning (Damico, 1992; Norris, 1991; Norris & Hoffman, 1993) and is also recommended for use in multicultural language teaching contexts (Damico & Hamayan, 1992). Also known as semantic webbing or semantic networking (Heimlich & Pittelman, 1986), semantic word maps are visual, graphic representations of word relationships, intended to broaden or extend the meanings of words for children (Hamersky, 1993). Semantic mapping engages students actively in learning (Heimlich & Pittelman, 1986). The importance of semantic mapping is its effectiveness in linking new information to what the child already knows and new words with ones already in the child's repertoire (Hamersky, 1993; Heimlich & Pittelman, 1986; Norris, 1991). Semantic maps are used specifically to develop the meanings of words, their relationships to other words, and their conceptual underpinnings (Damico & Hamayan, 1992) and to enable children to "see old words in a new light" (Heimlich & Pittelman, 1986, p. 3).

Semantic mapping has proved an effective teaching strategy insofar as students learn more words and retain vocabulary longer than children using contextual approaches (Heimlich & Pittelman, 1986). Furthermore, its effectiveness in teaching vocabulary has been demonstrated with children from various racial, cultural, and socioeconomic groups, as well as with children with reading disabilities and with large and small mixed groups of good and poor readers. When used as a prereading activity, semantic mapping improves comprehension of a text (Heimlich & Pittelman, 1986).

Hamersky (1993) describes five kinds of visual maps, or formats: the attribute web, the Venn diagram, the semantic continuum, the multiple-meaning tree, and the associated words format. The *attribute web* is used for identifying critical attributes of a word. A key word will be written in the center of the web, and through a brainstorming process children provide words associated with the key word. These are written around the key word. In a variation of the attribute web, the students may be asked to determine which of the attributes are best associated with the key words and to mark these on the web.

Figure 1 shows an attribute web designed to illustrate the words associated with the key word *Kwanzaa,* a topic that might arise during the Kwanzaa season and as part of a discussion about African American holidays and celebrations. This particular attribute web was developed from the children's story *My First Kwanzaa Book* (Chocolate, 1992).

Students might also group or cluster the attributes themselves and redraw their attribute web to show the added organization. For example, Wiig and Freedman (1993) examine *fruit* from the perspectives of common fruits, distinctive features of fruits, attributes of fruits, and climates in which fruits grow. Heimlich

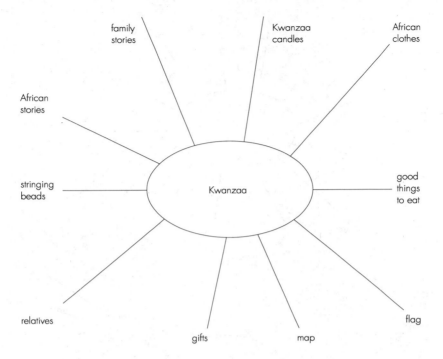

Figure 1.   A simple attribute web for the word *Kwanzaa*.

and Pittelman (1986) illustrate clustered attribute webs for the word concepts related to *stores* (words associated with kinds of stores, people involved, prices, expenses of owning, and problems), *digestion* (words associated with mouth, esophagus, stomach, small intestine, large intestine, and kidneys), and *music* (words associated with melody, form, rhythm, and harmony).

An attribute web illustrating *compost,* presented to children as part of a lesson on ecology, might reflect the kinds of objects associated with a compost pile but could also be redrawn to show subcategories of information associated with the word, as shown in Figure 2. In the second case, more organization is provided to guide the students' mental representation for the word and its relationships.

In a multicultural social studies lesson, children might draw an attribute web showing different kinds of houses and group the houses according to the environments where they are found (see Figure 3).

A *Venn diagram* allows students to understand the relationships between two words or concepts. The Venn diagram is essentially a vehicle for comparison and contrast operations. Venn diagrams are particularly useful in helping children to make distinctions between two words that are closely associated and easily confused. Hamersky's examples include *stain-paint, pyramid-cone, mammals-reptiles,* and *president-dictator.* When using the Venn diagram, students generate their ideas about the two key words. Attributes that describe both of the key words are placed

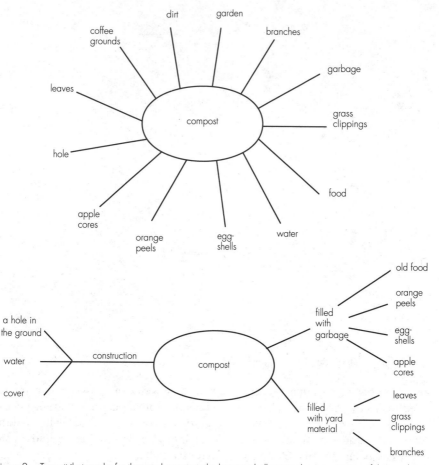

Figure 2. Two attribute webs for the word *compost;* the lower web illustrates the organization of the words.

in the overlapping sections of the two circles, whereas attributes that pertain to only one of the key words are placed in the nonoverlapping, outside sections of the two circles (see Figure 4).

   Multiple-meaning trees are used simply to display the different meanings of words, such as *season, needle, change,* and *spring.* Target words are written at the top of the tree and their different meanings are generated by the students, often mediated by the teacher, and written on the "branches" of the tree (see Figure 5). Hamersky suggests that students then write sentences that illustrate the different meanings of the word.

   A *semantic continuum* is used to show that words are not merely related but can also be ranked between two poles according to attributes pertaining to the word's meaning (see Figure 6). Students may generate words that are then placed on the continuum, or the teacher may generate words and ask the children to rank

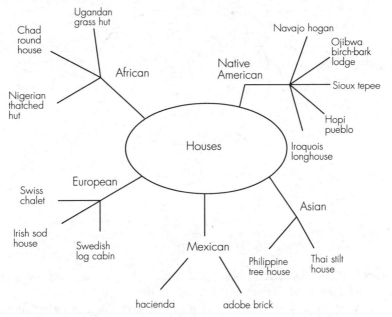

Figure 3. A clustered attribute web from a social studies class.

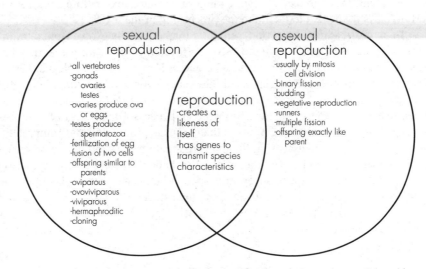

Figure 4. A Venn diagram for comparing and contrasting words with overlapping meanings. (Adapted from Compton's Interactive Encyclopedia [1994/1995].)

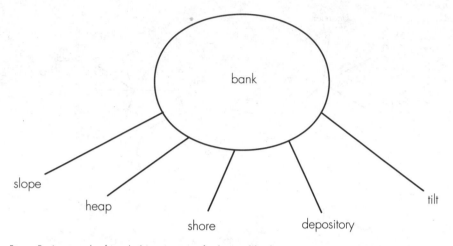

Figure 5. An example of a multiple meaning tree for the word *bank*.

the words. Hamersky offers these examples: *emaciated–obese, dry–soaked, hate–love, solid–liquid, extinct–overpopulated, fiction–fact.*

The semantic map illustrates relationships among words and word concepts, and building it serves language-learning goals. As Norris (1991) noted, "for example, the process of creating the map helps the child learn to develop a topic, form associations, categorize, compare, and make inferences" (p. 74). The map is subsequently used to mediate the reading of a related text, before and/or after certain parts of the text to facilitate the processing of the text.

In before-reading instruction, semantic maps typically evolve from a brainstorming process in which a child or several children generate ideas that they believe to be related to a topic or theme (Damico & Hamayan, 1992; Norris, 1991). The ideas themselves can be classified into subcategories of meaning, labels for the subcategories can be applied, and students can be asked to explain the relationship of a supplied word to the main word (Damico & Hamayan, 1992). A useful byproduct of this kind of activity is the language production and comprehension that evolves from discussing the maps in small groups and before an entire class. Verbalization and discussion among the students, coupled with mediation and scaffolding from the teacher and speech-language pathologist, are key processes. Not only does semantic mapping lead students to learn new words and new word relationships, but also new semantic fields may be developed or expanded (Damico & Hamayan, 1992).

Figure 6. A semantic continuum of words associated with *fear*.

Semantic maps are appropriately used for all curricular subjects and all grades. They can be used as a means of building word and concept knowledge and also to review a particular knowledge domain. They can be expanded indefinitely. Although the development of semantic maps is usually an oral language activity, the maps can later be a source of information for written language work in a whole-language environment (Damico & Hamayan, 1992). For example, Vacca and Vacca (1989) show a clustered attribute web describing the condition of freed slaves after the Civil War that could provide the organization for narrative or expository writing.

Semantic Feature Tasks Another approach used successfully to teach word meanings is *semantic feature analysis.* Semantic features are components of meaning that, in the aggregate, make up the meaning of a word. For example, the words *ewe* and *ram* share the features of animal, mammal, and ruminant, but oppose one another on the feature of gender. Some approaches to vocabulary instruction are based on this concept. Semantic feature analysis enables students to make fine discriminations among related word concepts (Irvin, 1990).

Hamersky (1993) describes an associated words format. In this approach, students are asked to respond with specific types of relationships for a word, based on semantic features. Synonyms share the same features but often have subtle differences in meaning. Subordinate categories possess all of the features of their superordinates but have added features. Antonyms oppose one another on one particular feature but share features as well. Hamersky uses the categories same meaning (synonym); part–whole (analytical perceptions); class name (superordinate); class membership (subordinate); opposite (antonym); spatial information (where); temporal information (when); and function/action. Variations have been proposed by other authors (Wiig & Becker-Caplan, 1984; Wiig & Semel, 1984). Huisingh, Barrett, Zachman, Blagden, and Orman (1988) offer a wide variety of activities and worksheets that address semantic feature relationships among words. In one group activity, Hamersky (1993) has students provide one another with clues to a key word while someone keeps a running list of cues and responses. Students later compare the relationships among the words and decide which were the most effective for guessing the key word.

Crais (1990) describes the use of a grid, or matrix, in which a set of words will be listed on one axis and a list of relevant attributes is presented on the other axis (see Figure 7). Students complete the grids by determining whether a word does or does not have a particular attribute and filling in the grid with + and – marks. This helps children differentiate meanings among related words in a content area.

Word Structure Analysis A strategy of analyzing word structure can be useful in teaching children about finding root words and understanding the changes in meanings or grammatical category brought about by affixes (Crais, 1990). As Vacca and Vacca (1989) point out, "when readers use morphemic analysis in combination with context, they have a powerful meaning-getting strategy at their command" (p. 326). The easiest words to teach are compound words (e.g., *commonwealth, matchmaker*) and words having recognizable stems

	Herbivore	Carnivore	Omnivore	Warm-Blooded	Cold-Blooded	Lay Eggs	Mammal	Insect	Water	Land	Pets	Farm	Jungle	Plain
Badger														
Bird														
Cow														
Crab														
Dolphin														
Fish														
Frog														
Goat														
Gopher														
Groundhog														
Horse														
Kangaroo														
Mouse														
Porpoise														
Rabbit														
Seal														
Sheep														
Snake														
Turtle														
Whale														

Figure 7. An example of a semantic feature grid for animal terms.

to which affixes are added (e.g., *surmountable, deoxygenize, unsystematic, microscope;* Vacca & Vacca, 1989). More difficult to teach are words with Latin or Greek roots and those with irregular pronunciations (e.g., *louver, indictment*).

In some cases, the meanings of the affixes themselves are variable. It is best to teach forms with invariant meanings, for example, words with the following prefixes and suffixes: micro-, mono-, omni-, circum-, intra-, mal-, -graph, -meter, -ess (Vacca & Vacca, 1989). Other affixes with variant forms (e.g., hyper-, neo-, trans-) can be taught, but the interventionist is cautioned to teach children that some affixes have multiple meanings (see Vacca & Vacca, 1989).

In summary, there are a variety of meaningful ways to teach vocabulary to children. It is important to keep in mind that exposure to literate vocabulary is important, even in the preschool years. Vocabulary instruction in schools is best when it incorporates real communication between speaker and listener, writer and reader. To be valuable to children, vocabulary instruction needs to be embedded within all curricular subjects.

CONCLUSION

This chapter has pointed out that some African American children have normal rates of vocabulary acquisition but also possess vocabularies that are different from those commonly appraised with standardized tests. Vocabulary differences in the African American population can be traced to African languages and traditions as well as to present-day cultural differences. Low-income African American children—indeed many low-income children—are most vulnerable to disruptions in vocabulary development, particularly as they are often not exposed to the kinds of vocabulary valued by educational institutions. These children adequately use their vocabulary words for social purposes during the preschool years but experience problems when they must meet the demands of schooling.

The chapter offered a multidimensional approach to assessment. A combination of standardized and nonstandardized procedures is likely to be most informative for diagnostic and intervention purposes. It is especially important to assess children's knowledge of literate, content-related vocabulary.

For low-income African American children and for those who have true language disorders involving vocabulary, a series of approaches to vocabulary instruction based on contemporary ideas about the organization and learning of vocabulary have been reviewed. These activities provide broad-based guidelines for teachers and speech-language pathologists. They can be adapted for nonreading children and for children with language learning disorders. Many of these procedures are best used with groups of children, and, in fact, group discussion is a valued component of vocabulary instruction because children have opportunities to use vocabulary words during such discussions. The procedures are appropriate for regular education environments and adapt nicely to curricular content. Moreover, these procedures are compatible with whole-language philosophies of teaching language. Ultimately, these procedures will expose African American children to many of the vocabulary words needed for successful school achievement, especially in the area of reading, and will provide a foundation for independent vocabulary learning.

REFERENCES

Adler, S., & Birdsong, S. (1983). Reliability and validity of standardized testing tools used with poor children. *Topics in Language Disorders, 3*(3), 76–87.

Anderson, N.B., & Battle, D.E. (1993). Cultural diversity in the development of language. In D.E. Battle (Ed.), *Communication disorders in multicultural populations* (pp. 158–185). Boston: Andover.

Anglin, J.M. (1993). Vocabulary development: A morphological analysis. *Monographs of the Society for Research in Child Development, 58*(10).

Barrett, M., Zachman, L., & Huisingh, R. (1988). *ASSET: Assessing Semantic Skills Through Everyday Themes.* East Moline, IL: LinguiSystems.

Beal, B.B. (1987). *A study to identify items on the Iowa tests of basic skills which are associated with racial or ethnic group membership; to determine possible relationships between instructional needs and these items; and to develop recommendation strategies.* Washington, DC: U.S. Department of Education, Educational Resources Information Center.

Bedore, L.M., & Leonard, L.B. (1995). Prosodic and syntactic bootstrapping and their clinical applications: A tutorial. *American Journal of Speech-Language Pathology, 4,* 66–72.

Blachowicz, C.L.Z. (1986). Making connections: Alternatives to the vocabulary notebook. *Journal of Reading, 29,* 643–649.

Blachowicz, C.L.Z. (1994). Problem-solving strategies for academic success. In G.P. Wallach & K.G. Butler (Eds.), *Language learning disabilities in school-age children and adolescents: Some principles and applications* (pp. 304–322). New York: Merrill.

Boehm, A.E. (1986). *Boehm Test of Basic Concepts—Preschool.* San Antonio, TX: The Psychological Corporation.

Bracken, B.A. (1984). *Bracken Basic Concept Scale.* Columbus, OH: Charles E. Merrill.

Bracken, B.A., Sabers, D., & Insko, W. (1987). Performance of black and white children on the Bracken Basic Concept Scale. *Psychology in the Schools, 24,* 22–27.

Brown, R. (1973). *A first language: The early stages.* Cambridge, MA: Harvard University Press.

BSCS. (1985). *Biological science: A molecular approach.* Lexington, MA: D.C. Heath.

Campbell, L.R. (1994). Discourse diversity and Black English vernacular. In D.N. Ripich & N.A. Creaghead (Eds.), *School discourse problems* (2nd ed., pp. 93–131). San Diego, CA: Singular Publishing Group.

Carey, S. (1978). The child as word learner. In M. Halle, J. Bresnan, & G.A. Miller (Eds.), *Linguistic theory and psychological reality* (pp. 264–293). Cambridge, MA: MIT Press.

Chocolate, D.M.N. (1992). *My first Kwanzaa book.* New York: Scholastic.

Clark, E.V. (1993). *The lexicon in acquisition.* Cambridge, MA: Cambridge University Press.

Collins, A.M., & Loftus, E.F. (1975). A spreading-activation theory of semantic processing. *Psychological Review, 82,* 407–428.

Collins, A.M., & Quillian, M.R. (1969). Retrieval time from semantic memory. *Journal of Verbal Learning and Verbal Behavior, 8,* 240–247.

Compton's Interactive Encyclopedia. (1994/1995). Compton's New Media, Inc.

Craig, H.K., & Washington, J.A. (1994). The complex syntax skills of poor, urban, African American preschoolers at school entry. *Language, Speech, and Hearing Services in Schools, 25,* 181–190.

Craig, H.K., & Washington, J.A. (1995). African-American English and linguistic complexity in preschool discourse: A second look. *Language, Speech, and Hearing Services in Schools, 26,* 87–93.

Crais, E. (1987). *Fast mapping of novel words in an oral story context.* Unpublished doctoral dissertation, University of Wisconsin, Madison.

Crais, E. (1990). World knowledge to word knowledge. *Topics in Language Disorders, 10*(3), 45–62.

Crawford, L.W. (1993). *Language and literacy learning in multicultural classrooms.* Needham, MA: Allyn & Bacon.

Crystal, D. (1987). Teaching vocabulary: The case for a semantic curriculum. *Child Language Teaching and Therapy, 3*(1), 40–56.

Cummins, J. (1981). Empirical and theoretical underpinnings of bilingual education. *Journal of Education, 163*(1), 16–29.

Damico, J.S. (1992). *Whole language for special needs children.* Buffalo, NY: EDUCOM Associates.

Damico, J.S., & Hamayan, E.V. (1992). *Multicultural language intervention: Addressing cultural and linguistic diversity.* Buffalo, NY: EDUCOM Associates.

Davey, B. (1983). Think aloud—Modeling the cognitive processes of reading comprehension. *Journal of Reading, 27,* 44–47.

Dickinson, D.K. (1984). First impressions: Children's knowledge of words gained from a single exposure. *Applied Psycholinguistics, 5,* 359–373.

Dillard, J.L. (1977). *Lexicon of Black English.* New York: The Seabury Press.

Dockrell, J. (1981). *The child's acquisition of unfamiliar words: An experimental study.* Unpublished doctoral dissertation, University of Stirling, Scotland.

Dollaghan, C.A. (1985). Child meets word: "Fast mapping" in preschool children. *Journal of Speech and Hearing Research, 28,* 449–454.

Dollaghan, C.A. (1987). Fast mapping in normal and language-impaired children. *Journal of Speech and Hearing Disorders, 52,* 218–222.

Dunn, L. (1988). *Bilingual Hispanic children on the U.S. mainland: A review of research on their cognitive, linguistic, and scholastic development.* Washington, DC: U.S. Department of Education, Educational Resources Information Center.

Dunn, L.M., & Dunn, L.M. (1981). *Peabody Picture Vocabulary Test—Revised.* Circle Pines, MN: American Guidance Service.

Ellis, L., Schlaudecker, C., & Regimbal, C. (1995). Effectiveness of a collaborative consultation approach to basic concept instruction with kindergarten children. *Language, Speech, and Hearing Services in Schools, 26,* 69–74.

Evard, B.L., & Sabers, D.L. (1979). Speech and language testing with distinct ethnic-racial groups: A survey of procedures for improving validity. *Journal of Speech and Hearing Disorders, 44,* 271–281.

Farran, D.C. (1982). Intervention for poverty children: Alternative approaches. In L. Feagans & D.C. Farran (Eds.), *The language of children reared in poverty: Implications for evaluation and intervention* (pp. 269–271). New York: Academic Press.

Gardner, M.F. (1985). *Receptive One-Word Picture Vocabulary Test.* Austin, TX: PRO-ED.

Gardner, M.F. (1990). *Expressive One-Word Picture Vocabulary Test, Revised.* Novato, CA: Academic Therapy Publications.

Hale-Benson, J.E. (1986). *Black children: Their roots, culture, and learning styles.* Baltimore: The Johns Hopkins University Press.

Hale-Benson, J.E. (1990). Visions for children: Educating black children in the context of their culture. In K. Lomotey (Ed.), *Going to school: The African-American experience* (pp. 209–222). Albany: State University of New York Press.

Hamersky, J. (1993). *Vocabulary maps: Strategies for developing word meaning.* Eau Claire, WI: Thinking Publications.

Hamill, D.D., Brown, V.L., Larsen, S.C., & Widerholt, J.L. (1987). *Test of Adolescent Language.* Austin, TX: PRO-ED.

Hart, B. (1982). Process in the teaching of pragmatics. In L. Feagans & D. C. Farran (Eds.), *The language of children reared in poverty: Implications for evaluation and intervention* (pp. 199–218). New York: Academic Press.

Hart, B., & Risley, T.R. (1994). American parenting of language-learning children: Persisting differences in family–child interactions observed in natural home environments. *evelopmental Psychology, 28,* 1096–1105.

Hart, B., & Risley, T.R. (1995). *Meaningful differences in the everyday experience of young American children.* Baltimore: Paul H. Brookes Publishing Co.

Heath, S.B. (1983). *Ways with words: Language, life, and work in communities and classrooms.* Cambridge: Cambridge University Press.

Heimlich, J.E., & Pittelman, S.D. (1986). *Semantic mapping: Classroom applications.* Newark, DE: International Reading Association.

Huisingh, R., Barrett, M., Zachman, L., Blagden, C., & Orman, J. (1988). *The word book: A program to build expressive vocabulary and semantic skills.* East Moline, IL: LinguiSystems.

Huisingh, R., Barrett, M., Zachman, L., Blagden, C., & Orman, J. (1990). *The Word Test—R Elementary.* East Moline, IL: LinguiSystems.

Irvin, J.L. (1990). *Vocabulary knowledge: Guidelines for instruction.* Washington, DC: National Education Association.

Jorgensen, C., Barrett, M., Huisingh, R., & Zachman, L. (1981). *The Word Test.* Moline, IL: LinguiSystems.

Kail, R., & Leonard, L.B. (March, 1986). *Word-finding abilities in language-impaired children.* ASHA Monographs 25. Rockville, MD: American Speech-Language-Hearing Association.

Kamhi, A., & Catts, H. (1989). *Reading disabilities: A developmental language perspective.* Boston: College-Hill Press.

Kouri, T.A. (1994). Lexical comprehension in young children with developmental delays. *American Journal of Speech-Language Pathology, 3*(1), 79–88.

Kresheck, J.D., & Nicolosi, L. (1973). A comparison of black and white children's scores on the PPVT. *Language, Speech, and Hearing Services in Schools, 4,* 37–40.

Lund, N.J., & Duchan, J.F. (1993). *Assessing children's language in naturalistic contexts* (3rd ed.). Englewood Cliffs, NJ: Prentice Hall.

Markman, E.M. (1994). Constraints on word meaning in early language acquisition. In L. Gleitman & B. Landau (Eds.), *The acquisition of the lexicon* (pp. 199–227). Cambridge: The MIT Press.

Miller, J.F. (1981). *Assessing language production in children: Experimental procedures.* Baltimore: University Park Press.

Moore, E.G.J. (1982). Group versus individual differences. In L. Feagans & D.C. Farran (Ed.), *The language of children reared in poverty: Implications for evaluation and intervention* (pp. 153–255). New York: Academic Press.

Mount, J.A. (1993). *Language disordered and normal children's fast mapping of phonological and semantic information about words under three conditions of explicitness.* Unpublished doctoral dissertation, University of Pittsburgh.

Nagy, W.E., & Herman, P.A. (1987). Breadth and depth of vocabulary knowledge: Implications for acquisition and instruction. In M.G. McKeown & M.E. Curtis (Eds.), *The nature of vocabulary acquisition* (pp. 19–35). Hillsdale, NJ: Lawrence Erlbaum Associates.

Nellum-Davis, P. (1993). Clinical practice issues. In D.E. Battle (Ed.), *Communication disorders in multicultural populations* (pp. 306–316). Boston: Andover.

Nelson, K. (1986). *Event knowledge: Structure and function in development.* Hillsdale, NJ: Lawrence Erlbaum Associates.

Newcomer, P.L., & Hammill, D.D. (1991a). *Test of Language Development—2 Primary.* Austin, TX: PRO-ED.

Newcomer, P.L., & Hammill, D.D. (1991b). *Test of Language Development—2 Intermediate.* Austin, TX: PRO-ED.

Ninio, A., & Bruner, J. (1978). The achievement of antecedents of labelling. *Journal of Child Language, 5,* 1–15.

Norris, J.A. (1991). From frog to prince: Using written language as a context for language learning. *Topics in Language Disorders, 12*(1), 66–81.

Norris, J.A., & Hoffman, P.R. (1990). Language intervention within naturalistic environments. *Language, Speech, and Hearing Services in Schools, 21,* 72–84.

Norris, J.A., & Hoffman, P. (1993). *Whole language intervention for school-age children.* San Diego: Singular Publishing Group.

Owens, R.E. (1992). *Language development: An introduction.* New York: Merrill.

Paul, R. (1995). *Language disorders from infancy through adolescence: Assessment and intervention.* St. Louis, MO: C.V. Mosby.

Peña, E., Quinn, R., & Iglesias, A. (1992). The application of dynamic methods to language assessment: A nonbiased procedure. *The Journal of Special Education, 26*(3), 269–280.

Perfetti, C. (1985). *Reading ability.* New York: Oxford University Press.

Rescorla, L. (1989). The language development survey: A screening tool for delayed language in toddlers. *Journal of Speech and Hearing Disorders, 54,* 587–599.

Rescorla, L. (1991). Identifying expressive language delay at age two. *Topics in Language Disorders, 11,* 14–20.

Retherford, K.S. (1993). *Guide to analysis of language transcripts* (2nd ed.). Eau Claire, WI: Thinking Publications.

Rice, M.L., Buhr, J.C., & Nemeth, M. (1990). Fast mapping word-learning abilities of language-delayed preschoolers. *Journal of Speech and Hearing Disorders, 55,* 33–42.

Richard, G.J., & Hanner, M.A. (1985). *Language Processing Test.* East Moline, IL: LinguiSystems.

Schieffelin, B.B., & Eisenberg, A.R. (1984). Cultural variations in children's conversations. In R.L. Schiefelbusch & J. Pickar (Eds.), *The acquisition of communicative competence* (pp. 377–420). Baltimore: University Park Press.

Secord, W.A., & Wiig, E.H. (1991). *Developing a collaborative intervention program.* Lockport, NY: EDUCOM Associates.

Seifert, H., & Schwarz, I. (1991). Treatment effectiveness of large group basic concept instruction with Head Start students. *Language, Speech, and Hearing Services in Schools, 22,* 60–64.

Smith, E.E., Shoben, E.J., & Rips, L.J. (1974). Structure and process in semantic memory: A featural model for semantic decisions. *Psychological Review, 82,* 214–241.

Smitherman, G. (1977). *Talkin and testifyin: The language of Black America.* Boston: Houghton Mifflin.

Snow, C.E. (1982). Knowledge and the use of language. In L. Feagans & D.C. Farran (Eds.), *The language of children reared in poverty: Implications for evaluation and intervention* (pp. 257–260). New York: Academic.

Stockman, I.J. (1986). Language acquisition in culturally diverse populations: The black child as a case study. In O.L. Taylor (Ed.), *Nature of communication disorders in culturally and linguistically diverse populations* (pp. 73–116). San Francisco: College-Hill Press.

Stockman, I.J., & Vaughn-Cooke, F.B. (1982). Semantic categories in the language of working-class black children. In C. Johnson & C. Thew (Eds.), *Proceedings from the second international congress for the study of child language* (Vol. 1, pp. 312–327). Washington, DC: University Press of America.

Stockman, I.J., & Vaughn-Cooke, F.B. (1986). Implications of semantic category research for the language assessment of nonstandard speakers. *Topics in Language Disorders, 6,* 15–25.

Templin, M.C. (1957). *Certain language skills in children: Their development and inter-relationships.* Minneapolis: University of Minnesota Press.

Terrell, S.L., & Terrell, F. (1993). African-American cultures. In D.E. Battle (Ed.), *Communication disorders in multicultural populations* (pp. 3–37). Boston: Andover.

Vacca, R.T., & Vacca, J.L. (1989). *Content area reading* (3rd ed.). Glenview, IL: Scott, Foresman.

van Kleeck, A. (1994). Potential cultural bias in training parents as conversational partners with their young children who have delays in language. *American Journal of Speech-Language Pathology, 3,* 67–78.

Ward, M. (1971). *Them children: A study in language learning.* Prospect Heights, IL: Waveland Press.

Washington, J.A., & Craig, H.K. (1992). Performances of low-income, African American preschool and kindergarten children on the Peabody Picture Vocabulary Test. *Language, Speech, and Hearing Services in Schools, 23,* 329–333.

Watkins, R.V., Kelly, D.J., Harbers, H.M., & Hollis, W. (1995). Measuring children's lexical diversity: Differentiating typical and impaired language learners. *Journal of Speech and Hearing Research, 38,* 1349–1355.

Wiig, E.H., & Becker-Caplan, L. (1984). Linguistic retrieval strategies and word-finding difficulties among children with language disabilities. *Topics in Language Disorders, 4*(3), 1–18.

Wiig, E.H., & Freedman, E. (1993). *The word book: Developing vocabulary across the curriculum.* Chicago: SRA.

Wiig, E.H., Freedman, E., & Secord, W.A. (1992). Developing words and concepts in the classroom: A holistic-thematic approach. *Intervention in School and Clinic, 27,* 278–285.

Wiig, E.H., & Secord, W. (1992). *Test of Word Knowledge.* San Antonio, TX: The Psychological Corporation & Harcourt Brace Jovanovich.

Wiig, E.H., & Semel, E. (1984). *Language assessment and intervention for the learning disabled.* Columbus, OH: Charles E. Merrill.

Wolfram, W. (1983/1994). Test interpretation and sociolinguistic differences. In K.G. Butler (Ed.), *Cross-cultural perspectives in language assessment and intervention* (pp. 106–119). Rockville, MD: Aspen Publishers.

Zachman, L., Barrett. M., Huisingh, R., Orman, J., & Blagden, C. (1989). *The WORD Test—Adolescent.* East Moline, IL: LinguiSystems.

10

Narratives of Young
African American Children

Eva Jackson Hester

Variability and flexibility in children's language use have been interesting researchers for some time. Early studies of speech style modification revealed that children as young as 4 years old were able to make changes in pitch, syntax, and semantics on the basis of the listener's age and linguistic abilities (Sachs & Devin, 1976; Shatz & Gelman, 1973). Unfortunately, variability in children's language use based on context and content may be overlooked in clinical examinations and may consequently result in faulty assessment of linguistic abilities.

Since the 1980s, attention has focused on variability in children's narrative skills (Heath, 1986; Hicks, 1991; Hudson & Shapiro, 1991; Hyon & Sulzby, 1992; Michaels & Collins, 1984; Preece, 1987). Researchers have recognized that children's narrative skills may vary with different narrative tasks and cultures. Much of the attention on variability in narrative skills has been documented and research results seemingly accepted for mainstream speakers. However, little consideration for such variability and flexibility has been extended to children who speak African American English (AAE). A popular view held by both researchers and clinicians alike is that AAE-speaking children have restricted narrative skills. It has been commonly noted that AAE-speaking children tend to formulate what has been called "topic-associating" narratives that are consistent with the oral culture of AAE speakers (Collins, 1985; Gee, 1985; Michaels, 1981; Nichols, 1989; Westby, 1994).

This chapter proposes some rethinking of the existing position that AAE-speaking children have restricted narrative strategies. However, knowledge of the variable nature of AAE is a prerequisite for understanding the flexibility of communication strategies used by members of the culture. The variability of AAE with regard to both grammatical and phonological features has been discussed extensively in this volume by Wyatt (Chapter 6) and Stockman (Chapter 7) and by other scholars (Abrahams, 1976; Baugh, 1983; Dillard, 1972; Erickson, 1984; Kernan, 1977; Labov, 1972; Smitherman, 1977; Stockman, 1985; Taylor, 1986; Washington & Craig, 1994). There is a consensus among these researchers that AAE features vary according to 1) topic, 2) speaking task, 3) listener characteristics, and 4) the communicative intent of the speaker.

With those key points in mind, I first review existing studies of narrative skills of AAE-speaking children and discuss some of the limitations of previous research approaches. Then, examples of transcripts of narrative texts produced by AAE-speaking children are presented. A basic tenet is that variability and flexibility exist not only in the narratives of one speaker but also among AAE-speaking children. Then the notion of flexibility is explored from the standpoint of code switching and style shifting, with an emphasis on factors that seem to influence the development of these skills. Finally, suggestions are offered to enhance clinical and teaching intervention with AAE-speaking children using knowledge of narrative flexibility.

INVESTIGATIONS OF NARRATIVES OF AAE-SPEAKING CHILDREN

The term *narration* can refer to storytelling, retelling a movie sequence, or relating personal experience. Narratives are ideal for studying language use because they involve units of extended text and are used in both social and educational settings. These texts generally include an introduction, sequence of events, and resolution. Narratives also require the speaker to maintain an oral monologue while the listener assumes a relatively passive role (Roth & Spekman, 1986).

Heath (1986) described narratives in terms of genre. Genre refers to kind or type. There are four basic narrative genres: recounts, eventcasts, accounts, and stories. *Recounts* describe past experiences in which the speaker played one or several roles. This narrative is the most common genre in school performance. *Eventcasts* involve verbal description or explanation of activity presently occurring or to take place in the future. *Accounts* allow individuals to share what they have experienced. This narrative genre is one of the first produced by children and originates from what children have been thinking, and not from what adults wish them to report. The fourth narrative genre is *stories,* which are fictionalized accounts of imagined beings who attempt to attain a goal (Stein, 1982). Story knowledge is derived from listening to stories and from daily experiences with causal relations and various kinds of action sequences (Mandler & Johnson, 1977; Stein & Glenn, 1979). Cultural differences may influence the production of any of these narratives.

Despite the variable nature of AAE and awareness of different narrative genres, investigations of narratives of AAE-speaking children have been generally restricted to recounts or narratives of personal experience. Kernan (1977) was perhaps the first to investigate narratives in this population. Narratives of personal experience were collected from 18 children ages 7–14. The narratives were analyzed for narrative structure and semantic and expressive elaboration. The findings indicated that younger children relied on narrative events to gain audience understanding, whereas older children used more extranarrative elaboration for audience appreciation.

In the 1980s, several researchers began studying AAE narratives in terms of oral and literate language styles (Collins, 1985; Gee, 1985; Heath, 1982; Michaels & Collins, 1984; Nichols, 1989). The oral language style is implicit, which suggests that the meaning of a statement may not be directly expressed. Rather, meaning can be implied through slang, idioms, gestures, or changes in voice and pitch. In addition, the oral language style is contextualized and requires shared knowledge of the participants to be effective. Thus, the oral language style shares features with spoken, rather than written, language.

In contrast, the literate language style has features that are similar to those of written language. This style is explicit and decontextualized. Meaning is expressed using specific vocabulary, complex syntactic structures, and specific cohesive forms (Olson, 1977; Tannen, 1982; Westby, 1985). In this oral-literate framework, some cultures are considered strictly oral, whereas others are considered strictly literate. Many researchers describe AAE speakers as members of an oral culture (Baugh, 1983; Erickson, 1984; Goodwin, 1990; Jarret, 1984; Ogbu, 1987; Smitherman, 1977).

Michaels (1981) conducted one of the first investigations that revealed oral–literate distinctions in the production of children's narratives. This study involved observing "sharing time" activities for African American and white kindergarten students. During the sharing activity, children related personal experiences or described personal items. The narratives that were collected were analyzed for cohesion strategies, syntactic structures, and topic shifts. Michaels found evidence of both oral style narratives and literate style narratives. The oral style narratives were more commonly produced by children who spoke AAE. These narratives were "topic associating" in that they included a series of personal anecdotes without an overall theme. In addition, thematic cohesion was attained through prosodic cues rather than explicit semantic and syntactic forms, such as conjunctions and relative clauses.

In contrast, the white children often produced narratives that were classified as being consistent with a literate style. These narratives were "topic centered" in that they were developed around a central theme. Moreover, the literate style narratives contained specific cohesion forms, such as "because," "so," and "therefore." These narratives also contained relatively more lexical cohesive ties and nominalizations than pronouns. Pronouns were prevalent in the oral style narratives. These findings were supported in subsequent studies (Collins, 1985; Gee, 1985; Michaels & Collins, 1984).

Nichols (1989) found similar oral–literate differences in the story narratives of AAE-speaking children and white fourth-grade children. This study involved collecting stories told in a classroom session. The topics included personal experiences and Halloween themes. The narratives were analyzed for interaction between narrator and audience, thematic development, and cohesive structures. The results indicated that the AAE-speaking children's narratives were characterized by a topic-associating style, audience participation, and implicit cohesive relations, while the white children's narratives were characterized by a single topic, specific lexical references, and explicit relationships between characters. Nichols concluded, however, that the differences in the narrative styles of the two groups were based on cultural traditions rather than oral–literate differences in and of themselves. She further noted that, from a cultural viewpoint, African American children emphasize immediacy, entertainment, and audience participation as important features of storytelling, whereas for white children distance, reporting of events, and moral instruction are important.

The view that AAE-speaking children's narrative skills are restricted to a topic-associating oral style has permeated investigations in both clinical and educational settings (Collins, 1985; Gee, 1989; Westby, 1985, 1994; Wolf, 1984). Why has this narrative style been consistently reported in the literature, given the variable nature of AAE in terms of language and style? First, most of the investigations have used ethnographic methods in studying the narratives of AAE-speaking children. Ethnographic research involves observations of language skills as they occur in a naturalistic environment. The data reflect skills that children routinely *use,* not skills that they may have the *ability to use.* In other words, the prevalent use of personal narratives in noted studies may provide a restricted view of the narrative skills of AAE-speaking children. It is conceivable that narratives that relate a personal experience, such as in a sharing time activity, may elicit more oral style features for AAE-speaking children because of the familiarity with the topic and the experience being conveyed.

The second possible reason for the prevalent reporting of one narrative style is that studies for this population are scant. Only a few studies have actually examined narrative styles in AAE-speaking children. Studies by Hicks (1991) and Hyon and Sulzby (1992) have used different narrative tasks. Although these studies are also few, the findings indicate that AAE-speaking children have more flexible narrative skills than previously reported.

Hicks (1991), for example, investigated different narrative genres in AAE-speaking children and white children in kindergarten and first grade. In this study, 58 children performed three narrative tasks. The subjects were shown a silent film and asked to produce an eventcast, news report, and story about the film. The narratives were analyzed for organizational, grammatical, lexical, thematic, and prosodic features. The findings indicated that the AAE-speaking children displayed a wide range of narrative skills, including temporal sequence, interpretive statements, and descriptive features, and that they varied these skills for each narrative genre. Hicks (1991) concluded that both AAE-speaking children and white children have the ability to shift their narrative styles according to different task demands.

Hyon and Sulzby (1992) also found variations in narrative styles used by AAE-speaking children. This study involved 48 kindergartners who told stories to a familiar adult interviewer. The stories were analyzed for topic-centered and topic-associating features. The results indicated that 16 of the children told topic-centered stories and 28 children told topic-associating stories. The investigators concluded that the findings refuted earlier studies in which AAE-speaking children were found to show a preference for a topic-associating style.

FLEXIBILITY OF NARRATIVES OF AAE-SPEAKING CHILDREN

I have used the term *flexibility* sparingly up to this point and have chosen to refer to *variability* or *variation,* because narrative flexibility with AAE-speaking children requires a twofold approach. First, researchers, clinicians, and teachers must have knowledge of the variability of AAE and the flexibility of narrative styles that can be used by this population. Second, and more important, we must be willing to be flexible in our research, teaching, and clinical strategies when working with children who speak AAE.

The following transcripts are used to illustrate this twofold concept. The transcripts were taken from a larger body of research data involving 60 fourth-grade African American children (Hester, 1994). The two children reported here provide excellent examples of narrative flexibility within and among speakers. The transcripts contain three tasks: 1) conversations with the investigator that include personal accounts, 2) recounts that involve retelling of a movie, and 3) stories that were formulated after a picture was shown for 10 seconds and then removed.

In the present analyses, code switching and style shifting are examined. Although there is some disagreement about a definition of code switching, I have opted to use the broader definition that refers to code switching as alternations of dialects within the same language in the course of a communicative episode (DeBose, 1992; Myers-Scotton, 1993). Specifically, in this discussion, code switching is considered to have taken place when significant changes or a decrease in the number of AAE morphological or phonological features (see Table 1), results in a switch toward a Standard American English (SAE) dialect. At the outset, it should be stated that the analysis to identify code switching is not as complete as it could be; that would be a chapter in itself. However, it is important to begin to

Table 1. Selected grammatical features of AAE

Description	Example
Use of verb forms	
Variable copula use: copula omitted	"She sick."
	"We playing ball."
Use of "be"	"She be fooling with me."
Third-person singular in present tense	"He look at TV."
Absence of past tense forms	"They turn around."
Use of "ain't"	"She ain't had a dress."
Absence of future tense	"She be at the party."
Use of noun forms	
Variable use of plural form	"We make up joke."
Absence of possessive marker	"That Tisha cat."
Pronoun substitution	"They house is green."
Regularization of reflexive form	"He did it hisself."
Pronominal apposition	"My sister, she real nice."
Adjectives and adverbs	
Use of "more" with superlatives	"He more crazier than her."
Omission of -ly on adverbs	"He treat her bad."
Substitution of "it," for "there"	"It was fire in the car."
Sentence patterns	
Double negatives	"Don't nobody talk there."
Use of "at" in "where" question	"Where he at?"

examine AAE narratives in terms of both linguistic and stylistic flexibility to determine the influence, if any, of one on the other. In some instances, as we will see, there is clearly an interplay between these two skills in narrative production.

Style shifting is used here to refer to changes in use of features that constitute a predominantly oral or literate style in narrative production. Table 2 outlines some common features previously mentioned in this discussion and others that have been noted as distinguishing oral and literate language styles (Chafe, 1982; Collins, 1985; Michaels & Collins, 1984; Westby, 1994).

For quick identification, the AAE grammatical features used are underlined in the narratives. Other instances of AAE features characterized by the omission of grammatical forms are noted in parentheses. The story-retelling and story-generation tasks are segmented and numbered by proposition for easy reference during the discussion. The names of the children are fictitious to protect confidentiality. In the conversation, the child's initial is used, and the interviewer is identified by the letter "I."

Child 1: Tisha

Tisha is a fourth-grade student from an inner-city school and low-income family. She demonstrated grade-level reading skills and was described as a good student by her teacher.

Table 2. Selected oral–literate features of narratives

Category	Oral style	Literate style
Syntax	Direct quotes (+)	Direct quotes (−)
	Relative clauses (−)	Relative clauses (+)
Cohesion	Additives (+)	Additives (−)
	Causal markers (−)	Causal markers (+)
	Renaming (−)	Renaming (+)
	Adversatives (−)	Adversatives (+)
Semantics	Formulaic language (+)	Formulaic language (−)
	Emphatic particles (+)	Emphatic particles (−)
	Attributive adjective (−)	Attributive adjective (+)
Narrative structure	Temporal shifts (+)	Temporal shifts (−)
	Location shifts (+)	Location shifts (−)
	Orientation (−)	Orientation (+)
	Coda (−)	Coda (+)

+ indicates a high occurrence of designated feature in narrative style. − indicates a low occurrence.

Conversation Sample

I: Tell me about your family.

T: I got a grandmovuh.
She <u>buy</u> me a lot.
I like my movuh cause she <u>do</u> too.
I like my brovuh cause he (is) smart.
And I teach him how to read and stuff.

I: Tell me more about your brother.

T: He <u>like</u> reading.
Some time, I read wif him.
But sometime, he just read by <u>hisself</u>
cause he <u>know</u> all the words.

I: How old is he?

T: Five.

I: He's really smart then. Did you teach him how to read?

T: He <u>say</u>, "Can I read your book?"
And I <u>say</u>, "You can't read my book because you're not old enough to read the book that I read."
He <u>say</u>, "I can read it."

I: Was he able to read your book?

T: Some words he could, some words he couldn't.

I: Tell me about school.

T: I like school cause it's fun.

I: Tell me about your friends at school.

T: She <u>like</u> me a lot. Her name (is) Monica.

I: Tell me about the things you two do together.

T: When we togevuh, we play hopscotch. We share the same locker. We always have fun togevuh when we (are) playing. We play hopscotch and basketball. When we're in the gym, we sit by each ovuh. And we just make <u>joke up</u> about each ovuh.

Tisha's conversational sample contains a prevalent use of AAE features. There are 13 occurrences of AAE grammatical features that typically involve variable copula use, verb agreement, and pronoun use. Common AAE phonological features also are present, such as the substitution of "th" and "er." Tisha's language use contains both oral and literate features, but it is more consistent with the oral language style. The oral style is indicated by the use of direct quotations and emphatic particles (e.g., "always," "a lot," "just") and the extensive use of pronouns. The most prevalent literate feature used is the causal conjunction "because" to indicate cause-and-effect relationships.

Story Retelling Movie: Cinderella

1.   Cinderella, <u>her</u> muvuh had died
2.   and her favuh had married a stepmovuh
3.   and she had a stepmovuh
4.   and she was very pretty
5.   and one day, the prince <u>come</u> to the ball
6.   so he could marry somebody
7.   and they wouldn't let her go
8.   because she <u>ain't</u> had a dress on
9.   and when the birds and stuff made her a dress
10. her stepsisters tore the dress all up
11. because it was some of their stuff that they had <u>threw</u> away
12. And at the end, she married the prince.
13. And the ugly stepmovuh and the ugly stepsisters, <u>they</u> went to jail.
14. And they lived happily ever after.

In this narrative, we begin to see both code switching and style shifting. Whereas the phonological features remained the same, the instances of AAE morphological features decreased from 13 to 5. The most prominent features used involve verb use and pronominal apposition. However, in general, there is a switch toward more SAE usage than in the conversational task. Similarly, we see a shift toward a literate style of narration. This shift is indicated by the use of relative clauses in proposition 11, P(11), "stuff that they had threw away." There also is an increase in the use of the causal conjunctions "because" and "so," as indicated in P(6), P(8), and P(11). Renaming, that is, using specific lexical terms, also is a prominent literate feature used in this narrative task as opposed to the prevalent use of pronouns in conversation. For example, stepmother and stepsisters are renamed in P(3) and P(13), as opposed to using the pronouns *she* and *they* throughout the story. This explicit lexical renaming strategy aids in the referential cohesion of the story. The use of the passive voice also is a literate style feature present in this narrative as opposed to the active voice used in conversation. Finally, the narrative is topic centered with an explicit orientation and coda denoting the beginning and end of the story. These features are consistent with a literate style, but are reported absent in oral style narratives.

Story Generation from Picture: The Dragon

1. It was a quiet afternoon in the forest
2. When a little boy name Jamal went to play in the woods
3. His movuh told him to be back at 5 for dinner.
4. So, he went out into the woods
5. and he saw this cave
6. So, he went in the cave
7. And he saw some big yellow eyes
8. And he saw some smoke.
9. So he went out the cave
10. and ran home
11. and got his stick
12. And then he came back
13. And then he found a dragon in there
14. and <u>it</u> was fire coming out of the dragon's mouth
15. And the dragon and the little boy <u>was</u> friends
16. when they met
17. And they played a game <u>call</u> hide-n'-seek
18. One <u>hide</u> behind the tree
19. and one <u>hide</u> behind the other one
20. One was going around this way
21. and the other was going around the ovuh way
22. And they hit each ovuh
23. And they played all day
24. And the little boy always remembered the dragon.

Both code-switching and style-shifting tendencies are even more prominent in this narrative. There are only four occurrences of AAE grammatical features. In addition, the narrative is more consistent with a literate style strategy. It is topic centered and contains a prevalent use of many literate style features, such as causal conjunctions, renaming, relative clauses, explicit referential, temporal relationships, and clearly stated orientation and coda. As with the story-retelling task, the past tense is also a prominent feature in the story-generation task.

Summary of Tisha's Narrative Skills   Tisha displayed a wide range of narrative skills in her responses to the three narrative tasks. Both code switching and style shifting were noted as she moved from the less formal conversation to the more formal story-generation task. Furthermore, there appeared to be an interplay between code switching and style shifting for Tisha. Stated more precisely, as Tisha's linguistic features gradually moved toward SAE, her narrative style shifted from oral to a predominantly literate style. Code switching was indicated by a gradual decline in AAE morphological features and a switch to SAE as she progressed from one narrative genre to another. It is noteworthy, however, that the phonological features of AAE remained fairly constant in all narrative productions.

With regard to narrative style, there was a clear transition from using a predominantly oral style in conversation to a literate style in the story-generation task. In the story-generation task, many literate style features were represented, including orientation, causal connectives, attributive adjectives, renaming, codas, and, most of all, a single topic that was developed through explicit lexical terms and thematic coherence.

Child 2: Monique

Monique is a fourth-grade student enrolled in the same inner-city school as Tisha, but in a different class. She has a history of reading and learning problems and has been enrolled in special classes since kindergarten. At the time of this study, her reading skills were 1½ years below grade level.

Conversational Sample

I: Tell me some things that you like to do.

M: Well like to play outside wif my friends. Also, I like to watch TV. There're certain things I like to do and play a lot upstairs in my bedroom.

I: Tell me about your friends.

M: This girl on my block, her name is Felicia. And she play with me and we go to the store.

I: What is she like?

M: She's really kind. If I don't have no money, she give me money. I empty her piggy bank. And she's real, real, real fun to be wif.

I: Do you have any other friends?

M: Yes, my cousin.

I: Tell me about your cousin.

M: She (is) fun but sometime, me and her get in a fight a little. But we always make up and stuff. And my other cousin. My other cousin, we (are) very close like this. [Gestures with two fingers together.]

I: Tell me about her.

M: She (is) only 6 years old, but she's real fun to be wif. We laugh togevuh and she make me funny sometime. And we (are) very close.

I: Do you have a brother or sister?

M: Yeah, I have two sisters and one brovuh.

I: Tell me about them.

M: My sisters and then my brovuh?

I: Yes.

M: Well she (is) 25 years old. She got a little girl and she is real bad. My sister is kind. She like to help out around the house. And my 18-year-old sister, she is fun to be wif and she <u>buy</u> me a lot of stuff. You would have a lot of fun to be wif her. My brovuh, <u>he</u> kinda handicap. I don't know what school he <u>go</u> to. But he's very smart. But sometime, people make fun of my brovuh. I get real mad and tell them about <u>theirselves</u>. And I don't like <u>nobody</u> to make fun of my brovuh.

Monique also prevalently uses AAE features in her narrative. There are 18 occurrences of AAE grammatical forms, and common phonological features also are present. The morphological features used involve variable copula use, pronoun use and apposition, verb agreement, and double negatives. The style is consistent with an oral style of narration as indicated by the extensive use of emphatic particles and pronouns. In addition, the use of conjunctions primarily is limited to the additive "and."

Story Retelling Movie: Naked Gun

1. This is the part I like
2. His wife right? Was coming around
3. And he opened the door, right?
4. And his wife fell down in the water.
5. Alright, this is the way it happened
6. His wife was behind the door
7. and he just opened the door
8. and his wife flew off the gate
9. and went to the floor
10. That's the funniest part.
I: But tell me the whole story.
11. He was trying to help somebody, right?
12. This bad guy was trying to put a bomb in the awards on TV.
13. And he was trying to stop the bomb
14. because the bomb was in the envelope.

In contrast to Tisha's gradual decrease in AAE features in her story recount, Monique code-switched to using primarily SAE features. However, a different tendency emerges when we look at the narrative style. Monique's narrative strategy continues to be consistent with the oral language style used in her conversation. It is characterized by formulaic language, implicit relationships between parts of the narrative, and few lexically explicit referential and temporal relationships. There is only one instance of a causal conjunction to indicate cause-and-effect relations.

Story Generation from Picture: Dragon/Dinosaur

1. Once upon a time, there was a dinosaur
2. He was the meanest dinosaur on earf.
3. Once there was a boy walking in the woods
4. and he saw the dinosaur

5. and the dinosaur was trying to eat the boy up
6. And the boy just grabbed a stick
7. And hit the dinosaur
8. And the dinosaur wasn't mean <u>no</u> more to people.

In this story narrative, Monique continues to use primarily SAE linguistic features. The narrative is topic centered, thereby containing this particular literate style feature. However, many of the other noted literate features continue to be absent, such as causal conjunctions to express cause-and-effect relationships, lexical descriptions to provide more detail, and relative clauses that expand on the actions and roles of the characters. Thus, this narrative may be more closely associated with an oral style of narration than a literate style.

Summary of Monique's Narrative Skills   Like Tisha, Monique demonstrated flexibility in her narrative skills. Code switching was a prominent aspect of narrative productions. In contrast to Tisha, Monique made a rather abrupt switch to SAE in the story-retelling and story-generation tasks. However, her overall narrative style remained consistent with a predominantly oral strategy. For both children, the ability to formulate topic-centered narratives was clearly indicated in the story-generation task. In other story respects, Monique continued to use a predominantly oral language style in her narrative production. It is noteworthy, however, that more literate style features were present in her story-generation task than in the story-retelling task. The most prominent differences between the two narratives were that temporal sequencing and thematic development followed a linear progression in the story-generation task, whereas these features were not as explicit in the story-retelling task.

ORAL AND LITERATE LANGUAGE STYLES: DICHOTOMY OR CONTINUUM FOR AAE-SPEAKING CHILDREN?

The notion of oral and literate cultures has been prevalent in the literature (Heath, 1982; Jarret, 1984; Scollon & Scollon, 1984; Westby, 1985). However, it has been suggested by some researchers that no culture is purely oral or literate. Rather, all cultures use these skills in varying degrees on a continuum according to situational and task variables (Tannen, 1982). The narrative skills demonstrated by Tisha and Monique support this latter view of a continuum rather than a dichotomy for AAE-speaking children. Three major points should be emphasized from the analyses.

First, being a member of an identified oral culture does not restrict one to using only oral style features. Both Tisha and Monique demonstrated the ability to use oral and literate features to varying degrees in their narrative productions. Even more striking is the observation that Tisha not only demonstrated the ability to use literate style features but also shifted from an oral style in conversation to a predominantly literate style in the story-formulation task. The examples illustrated by these two children are inconsistent with the prevalent view that AAE-speaking children are restricted to an oral narrative style by virtue of their culture.

Second, style shifting is task dependent. Both children demonstrated the ability to shift the way that they tell narratives according to the task. Monique shifted from providing an abstract or summary in the story-retelling task to formulating a well-structured narrative in the story-generation task. Although the increase in the number of specific literate style features was minimal in these two narratives, the story-generation task elicited a topic-centered narrative from Monique. In Tisha's case, the task elicited more dramatic differences in her knowledge of narratives. Tisha's use of literate style features gradually increased in the story-retelling task to a predominantly literate style in the story-formulation task.

This observation of variation in narrative skills based on genre also was reported by Hicks (1991). She concluded that shifts in children's narration of events are related to differences in the tasks and differences in the children's interpretation of the tasks. This notion is particularly applicable to Tisha and Monique in that the children seemed to have common interpretations of the story-generation task but viewed the story-retelling task differently. Whereas Monique appeared to view retelling the movie as just talking about main parts, Tisha perceived the task as telling a complete story with a beginning, middle, and end.

Third, children who speak AAE are not restricted to using topic-associating narratives. Despite the prevalent use of the label *topic associating,* a clear definition of this term has yet to be put forth. This narrative style is commonly described as consisting of related topics and anecdotes. This vague description has led researchers to offer varied interpretations of topic associating. Consequently, from examples of stories noted in the literature, topic associating has meant different things to different investigators. What is needed, then, is a story analysis that would clearly identify topic maintenance and development in the stories produced by children who speak AAE. Nevertheless, it is obvious that the stories formulated by Tisha and Monique do not fit even the vaguest description of topic associating. The stories remained centered on the topic with a linear progression of events.

CODE SWITCHING

One of the most interesting observations from the present data is that the two children demonstrated both style shifting and code switching in their narratives. Although the concept of oral and literate language styles has been receiving increasing attention, code switching as a language alternative for AAE speakers has been the focus of interest from scholars since the late 1960s (Adler, 1979; Baratz, 1969; Baugh, 1983; Dandy, 1994; DeBose, 1992; Folb, 1980; Hall, 1976; Riegel & Freedle, 1976; Taylor, 1975; Terrell & Terrell, 1983; Wolfram & Christian, 1989). The impetus for advocating code switching has centered on academic achievement and increased employability. Despite calls for teaching code switching to school-age children, empirical data concerning how to develop this skill are nonexistent. Analysis of the present data is the first attempt to examine systematically code-switching skills in the spontaneous language of AAE-speaking children.

First, code switching is related more to role taking than to literacy. This observation contrasts with data on code switching in adult AAE speakers. Traditionally, code switching has been attributed to well-educated individuals (Payne, 1986; Taylor, 1975). But the present data do not support this position. Recall that Monique demonstrated poor reading skills, whereas Tisha demonstrated normal reading skills. If one equates good reading skills with literacy, it would be predicted that code switching would be demonstrated by Tisha, but not by Monique. The transcripts, however, indicate that both children demonstrated code-switching skills in their story narratives compared with conversational samples.

A primary factor that appeared to facilitate code switching was the child's perception of the speaking task and the role that she played in the communication episode. In conversation, both children appeared to view their communication role as just talking, even though they related short personal accounts. However, as they moved on to story narratives, and particularly the story-generation task, the children seemed to view themselves more as storytellers, perhaps like the teacher who tells stories in their classes. The possibility of the children taking a teacher's role was indicated by a change in pitch and rate as well as grammatical features.

The suggestion that code switching may be somehow linked to schooling is consistent with an earlier conclusion by Hall (1976) that education facilitates code switching in children who speak AAE. However, Hall speculated that code switching may originate from the child's perception of risks involved in speaking a nonstandard dialect in school and the teacher's reaction thereto. Contrary to this view, it is argued here that code switching is facilitated by the children's perception of their role in the speaking task. In storytelling tasks, the children may perceive themselves as the teacher. It is conceivable, then, that in the educational process the child's teacher becomes the role model for imitation.

Second, code switching is task dependent. Although this point was partially discussed in the previous paragraphs, the importance of the speaking task cannot be overemphasized in discussing factors that facilitate code switching. In the earlier sections of this chapter, the variability of AAE depending on speaking task was mentioned. The present data from Monique and Tisha appear to confirm such variability. Clearly, story narrative tasks facilitated code-switching skills in the two children. Recall that, in conversation, both children demonstrated a prevalent use of AAE features. However, in the story-generation task, there was either a marked reduction in AAE features or a switch primarily to SAE. This observation is similar to one made by DeBose (1992) in a case study of the code-switching skills of an African American adult female. He concluded that SAE was used mainly to narrate, whereas AAE was used prevalently in conversational dialogue.

Last, but not least, the ability to code-switch cannot be predicted by the number of AAE features habitually used by the speaker. This final observation also is related to the previous two points. That is, the tendency to code-switch is related more to role-taking and speaking tasks than to the number of AAE features habitually used by the speaker in conversation. This point is important because the language proficiency of AAE speakers is often judged by conversational speech samples. However, evidence from the transcripts suggests that conversation is not a reliable predictor of a child's ability to code-switch. Recall that in conversation, AAE features were quite prevalent for both children. However, Tisha demonstrated a marked ability to code-switch to SAE in the story-generation task with only four occurrences of AAE, whereas Monique made a complete switch to using all SAE features. Hence, it is important to emphasize that prevalent use of AAE features in conversation does not preclude the ability to code-switch to SAE.

RELATIONSHIP BETWEEN CODE SWITCHING AND STYLE SHIFTING

A central question is the degree to which code switching and style shifting are related or influenced by one another. Not surprisingly, the answer to this question is not clear-cut. It seems, however, that the relationship between these two phenomena may be different for different children. Tisha, for example, appeared to demonstrate an interplay of code switching and style shifting as she moved from conversation to story narrative tasks. As mentioned in an earlier section, for Tisha, the AAE features gradually decreased in the story tasks, as her narration took on a more literate style.

In contrast to Tisha, Monique demonstrated an abrupt switch from AAE features in conversation to using SAE features in both story narratives. However, her style of narration remained more consistent with the oral style demonstrated in her conversation. One possible explanation can be offered for the different patterns of the two children. Style shifting may be related more to literacy than to code switching. This speculation is consistent with data from Tisha and Monique and is also supported by studies indicating that the use of a literate style of narration is related to reading ability (Collins, 1985; Michaels & Collins, 1984).

If code switching is not dependent on style shifting and style shifting is not dependent on code switching, then these two skills may occur either independently or in conjunction with each other. Story narratives, however, seemed to facilitate the use of both skills in varying degrees for either child. Certain characteristics of story narratives may be conducive to code switching and style shifting. First, story narratives are often told in past tense, and the use of past tense is an important difference between children's conversations and story narratives. Although the omission of past tense markers is a common feature of AAE, the fact that story events are related in the past tense may increase awareness of past tense forms that are not used consistently. Thus, code switching from AAE to SAE in story-formulation tasks may be a skill used by AAE-speaking children that emerges from their internal knowledge, not use, of SAE.

Second, in the story-formulation task, both children appeared to take on the role of a storyteller, and their rendition is perhaps similar to the way their teacher tells stories to the class. Researchers have noted that narratives require role-taking skills by the speaker (Westby, 1985). However, role taking as described in the literature emphasizes the speaker taking a spectator's role in order to decontextualize the narrative. In the case of AAE-speaking children, role taking may involve more role imitation of the teacher, rather than a spectator's role. However, the end result is the same, a decontextualized narrative. In short, story narratives elicit the use of multidimensional skills that reveal both language performance and language competence.

CLINICAL AND EDUCATIONAL IMPLICATIONS

How can the flexibility of narrative skills demonstrated by Tisha and Monique be elicited when working with AAE-speaking children in therapy or in the classroom? There are probably a variety of approaches to eliciting flexible narrative skills, but important activities should involve role playing and eliciting different types of narratives, including personal narratives, story retelling, and story formulation. In addition, increasing the children's awareness of differences in the narratives that they produce would increase their knowledge of the different forms that they use in different narrative genres. Finally, children with reading problems should be taught to identify specific literate style features in stories that they read and be encouraged to produce either oral or written summaries that contain these features. After the summaries, the children could be instructed on formulating their own stories by including literate style features.

A variety of narrative genres should be elicited from AAE-speaking children in the assessment process. By doing so, we obtain not only a more representative sample of the children's knowledge of narratives but also more extensive information about their proficiency in AAE as well as SAE. This information is particularly relevant for those who advocate bidialectal teaching.

A commonly described approach in teaching SAE to children who speak AAE involves a contrast method (Adler, 1979; Wolfram & Christian, 1989). In this approach, the child is taught SAE forms and then taught to identify differences in SAE and AAE. In view of the present findings, such a direct approach may not be necessary for children who tend to code-switch according to the task. Rather than direct teaching, further assessment of the children's ability to identify differences in the linguistic forms that they use in various narrative productions would be in order. In addition, the assessment process could include various role-playing situations to gain additional knowledge of the child's flexibility in code switching. In this way, the clinician or teacher would have a more expanded base on which to develop a bidialectal program, if needed.

CONCLUSIONS

Knowledge of variability and flexibility of language use is perhaps the single most important factor in working with AAE-speaking children. A twofold approach to flexibility is needed that involves a knowledge of this variability and a willingness by professionals to be flexible in their assessment and teaching methods. In this chapter, both linguistic flexibility and stylistic flexibility were examined in terms of code switching and style shifting. It seems imperative to continue to examine the relationship and commonalities of these skills not only to further our understanding of narrative productions but also to increase our knowledge of the language abilities of AAE-speaking children.

REFERENCES

Abrahams, R. (1976). *Talking Black.* Rowley, MA: Newbury House.

Adler, S. (1979). *Poverty children and their language: Implications for teaching and treating.* New York: Grune & Stratton.

Baratz, J. (1969). A bi-dialectal task for determining language proficiency in economically disadvantaged Negro children. *Child Development, 40,* 889–902.

Baugh, J. (1983). *Black street speech.* Austin: University of Texas Press.

Chafe, W. (1982). Integration and involvement in speaking, writing and oral literature. In D. Tannen (Ed.), *Spoken and written language* (pp. 35–52). Norword, NJ: Ablex.

Collins, J. (1985). Some problems and purposes of narrative analysis in educational research. *Journal of Education, 167,* 57–68.

Dandy, E. (1994). *Black communications: Breaking down the barriers.* Savannah, GA: IRBCO Productions.

DeBose, C. (1992). Codeswitching: Black English and Standard English in the African-American Linguistic Repertoire. *Journal of Multilingual and Multicultural Development, 13,* 157–167.

Dillard, J.L. (1972). *Black English.* New York: Vintage.

Erickson, F. (1984). Rhetoric, anecdote and rhapsody: Coherence strategies in a conversation among Black American adolescents. In D. Tannen (Ed.), *Coherence in spoken and written discourse* (pp. 81–154). Norwood, NJ: Ablex.

Folb, E. (1980). *Runnin down some lines.* Cambridge, MA: Harvard University Press.

Gee, J. (1985). The narrativization of experience in the oral style. *Journal of Education, 167,* 9–35.

Gee, J. (1989). Two styles of narrative construction and their linguistic and educational implications. *Discourse Processes, 12,* 263–265.

Goodwin, M. (1990). *He-said-she-said: Talk as social organization among black children.* Bloomington: Indiana University Press.

Hall, W. (1976). Black and white children's responses to Black English Vernacular and Standard English sentences: Evidence of codeswitching. In D. Harrison & T. Trabasso

(Eds.), *Black English: A seminar* (pp. 201–208). Hillsdale, NJ: Lawrence Erlbaum Associates.

Heath, S. (1982). What no bedtime story means: Narratives at skills, at home, at school. *Language in Society, 11,* 49–76.

Heath, S. (1986). Taking a cross-cultural look at narratives. *Topics in Language Disorders, 7*(1), 84–94.

Hester, E.J. (1994). *The relationship between narrative style, dialect, and reading ability of African-American children.* Unpublished doctoral dissertation, University of Maryland, College Park.

Hicks, D. (1991). Kinds of narrative: Genre skills among first graders from two communities. In A. McCabe & C. Peterson (Eds.), *Developing narrative structure* (pp. 55–87). Hillsdale, NJ: Lawrence Erlbaum Associates.

Hudson, J., & Shapiro, L. (1991). From knowing to telling: The development of children's scripts, stories and personal narratives. In A. McCabe & C. Peterson (Eds.), *Developing narrative structure* (pp. 89–136). Hillsdale, NJ: Lawrence Erlbaum Associates.

Hyon, S., & Sulzby, E. (1992, April). *Black kindergartners' spoken narratives: Style, structure and task.* Paper presented at the annual meeting of the American Educational Research Association, San Francisco, CA.

Jarret, D. (1984). Pragmatic coherence in an oral formulaic tradition. In D. Tannen (Ed.), *Coherence in spoken and written discourse* (pp. 155–172). Norwood, NJ: Ablex.

Kernan, K. (1977). Semantic and expressive elaboration in children's narratives. In S. Ervin-Tripp & C. Mitchell-Kernan (Eds.), *Child discourse* (pp. 91–119). New York: Academic Press.

Labov, W. (1972). *Language in the inner city: Studies in Black English Vernacular.* Philadelphia: University of Pennsylvania Press.

Mandler, J., & Johnson, N. (1977). Remembrance of things parsed: Story structure and recall. *Cognitive Psychology, 9,* 111–151.

Michaels, S. (1981). Sharing time: Children's narrative styles and differential access to literacy. *Language in Society, 10,* 423–442.

Michaels S., & Collins, J. (1984). Oral discourse styles: Classroom interaction and the acquisition of literacy. In D. Tannen (Ed.), *Coherence in spoken and written discourse* (pp. 219–244). Norwood, NJ: Ablex.

Myers-Scotton, C. (1993). *Social motivations for codeswitching.* Oxford: Oxford University Press.

Nichols, P. (1989). Storytelling in Carolina: Continuities and contrasts. *Anthropology and Education Quarterly, 20*(3), 232–245.

Ogbu, J. (1987). Opportunity, structure, cultural boundaries, and literacy. In J. Langer (Ed.), *Language, literacy and culture* (pp. 149–177). Norwood, NJ: Ablex.

Olson, D. (1977). From utterance to text: The bias of language in speech and writing. *Harvard Education Review, 47*(3), 257–282.

Payne, K. (1986). Cultural and linguistic groups in the United States. In O. Taylor (Ed.), *Nature of communication disorders in culturally and linguistically diverse populations* (pp. 19–46). San Diego, CA: College-Hill Press.

Preece, A. (1987). The range of narrative forms conversationally produced by young children. *Child Language, 14,* 353–373.

Riegel, K., & Freedle, R. (1976). What does it mean to be bilingual or bidialectal? In D. Harrison & T. Trabasso (Eds.), *Black English: A seminar* (pp. 25–44). Hillsdale, NJ: Lawrence Erlbaum Associates.

Roth, F., & Spekman, N. (1986). Narrative discourse: Spontaneously generated stories of learning-disabled and normally achieving students. *Journal of Speech and Hearing Disorders, 51,* 8–23.

Sachs, J., & Devin, J. (1976). Young children's use of age appropriate speech styles in social interaction and role playing. *Journal of Child Language, 3,* 81–98.

Scollon, R., & Scollon, S. (1984). Cooking it up and boiling it down: Abstracts in Athabaskan children's story retellings. In D. Tannen (Ed.), *Coherence in spoken and written discourse* (pp. 173–197). Norwood, NJ: Ablex.

Shatz, M., & Gelman, R. (1973). The development of communication skills: Modification in the speech of young children as a function of the listener. *Monographs of the Society for Research in Child Development, 38* (5, Serial No. 152).

Smitherman, G. (1977). *Talkin and testifyin: The language of Black America.* Detroit, MI: Wayne State University Press.

Stein, N. (1982). Story structure versus content in children's recall. *Journal of Verbal Learning and Verbal Behavior, 21,* 196–206.

Stein, N. & Glenn, C. (1979). An analysis of story comprehension in elementary school children. In R.O. Freedle (Ed.), *New directions in discourse processing* (pp. 53–120). Norwood, NJ: Ablex.

Stockman, I. (1985). Language acquisition in culturally diverse populations. In O. Taylor (Ed.), *Nature of communication disorders in culturally and linguistically diverse populations* (pp. 117–156). San Diego, CA: College-Hill Press.

Tannen, D. (1982). The oral/literate continuum in discourse. In D. Tannen (Ed.), *Spoken and written language: Exploring orality and literacy* (pp. 1–16). Norwood, NJ: Ablex.

Taylor, O. (1975). Black language and what to do about it: Some community perspectives. In R. Williams (Ed.), *Ebonics: The true language of black folks* (pp. 29–39). Washington: Georgetown University Press.

Taylor, O. (Ed.). (1986). *Nature of communication disorders in culturally and linguistically diverse populations.* San Diego, CA: College-Hill Press.

Terrell, S., & Terrell, F. (1983). Effects of speaking Black English on employment opportunities. *Asha, 25,* 27–29.

Washington, J., & Craig, H. (1994). Dialectal forms during discourse of poor, urban, African American preschoolers. *Journal of Speech and Hearing Research, 37,* 816–823.

Westby, C. (1985). Learning to talk-Talking to learn. Oral-literate language differences. In C. Simon (Ed.), *Communication skills and classroom success* (pp. 181–212). San Diego, CA: College-Hill Press.

Westby, C. (1994). Multicultural issues. In J. Tomblin, H. Morris, & D. Spriestersbach (Eds.), *Diagnosis in speech-language pathology.(pp. 29–52).* San Diego, CA: Singular Publishing Co.

Wolf, D. (1984). Learning about language skills from narratives. *Language Arts, 61,* 844–849.

Wolfram, W., & Christian, D. (1989). *Dialects and education: Issues and answers.* Englewood Cliffs, NJ: Prentice Hall.

11

Using Oral Narratives to Assess Communicative Competence

Yvette D. Hyter and Carol E. Westby

Communicative competence involves knowing how to put linguistic knowledge to use for various purposes and in various contexts (Gumperz, 1982; Schuler, 1989; Westby, VanDongen, & Maggart, 1989). Research in the use of narrative discourse to assess communicative competence has been based on the development and structure of primarily young children's narratives, and less so on those of older children, such as preadolescents and adolescents. Contrary to popular belief, communicative competence continues to develop through preadolescence and into adulthood. The cognitive development of preadolescents and adolescents enables them to consider a range of possibilities, including abstract relationships (Larson, McKinley, & Boley, 1993; Piaget & Inhelder, 1969).

This period of cognitive and language development is marked by subtle improvements in syntax, semantics, and pragmatics that are important for social and academic success (Damico, 1993; Nippold, 1993). For example, syntactic development is reflected in the use of longer sentences (Scott, 1988), complex sentences containing subordination (Loban, 1976; Scott, 1988), and cohesive devices typically found in literate contexts

(Nippold, 1993). Semantic skills continue to develop as preadolescents and adolescents acquire increased metalinguistic awareness that enables them to infer the meaning of words that have abstract or multiple meanings from linguistic or nonlinguistic contexts (Nippold, 1988). Pragmatics continues to develop as preadolescents and adolescents refine their ability to use syntactic and semantic skills in social and academic contexts. In a variety of communicative contexts, students must be able to describe clearly a sequence of events and express their attitudes about the events in the world while considering the perspective of their listener. To be truly competent, one needs knowledge of social and cultural communication conventions and of various perspectives or points of view (Astington, 1994; Hewitt, 1994; Wolf & Hicks, 1989).

Since the mid-1970s, a shift in the study of communication has occurred from an emphasis on language structure to a focus on semantic and pragmatic aspects of language. With this shift, a greater emphasis has been placed on units of talk that are larger than the sentence, such as those found in narrative discourse. The study of narrative production has been popular because narration is a discourse genre produced in every culture. Narratives are also used by speakers to encode and shape complex events that are central to the organization of their culture (Goodwin, 1990). Furthermore, narratives are important for social and academic success because they reflect a speaker's worldview and lend themselves nicely to the evaluation of communicative competence (Westby, 1994; Westby et al., 1989).

Research in the use of narrative discourse to assess communicative competence has focused primarily on the structure of narrative text. This structural approach describes the general organization and functional units of the narrative. These analyses are overwhelmingly rooted in "unichannel" (lexical channel only) frameworks, although a few "bichannel" (lexical and prosodic or lexical and kinesic channels) frameworks also have been employed. Anthropological and sociolinguistic literature on dialogues and conversations suggest that, in addition to the lexical channel, speakers use prosodic and kinesic channels to convey information (Gee, 1986, 1989c; Gumperz, 1982; Levy & McNeill, 1992; Michaels, 1981; Poyatos, 1983; Westby et al., 1989). Therefore, it is important for researchers to investigate how multiple channels of communication are used to relay information in narrative discourse.

Bruner's (1986) description of narrative events provides a framework with which to investigate communication across multiple channels. This framework of "dual landscapes" (p. 20) has been used to label the description of narrative events, the landscape of action, and the information about the consciousness of the narrator or the story characters' landscape of consciousness. Young children produce narratives that consist primarily of landscapes of actions; that is, they report a series of events. As children mature in social-cognitive skills, which enable them to engage in multiple perspective taking, they increasingly include landscapes of consciousness in their narratives.

Assessment of students' narratives traditionally has focused on developmental changes in structure. Narrative structure depends primarily on the landscape of action or the events occurring in the narratives. The basic structural elements of narratives are fully acquired by around age 10 (Peterson & McCabe, 1983). Little research has explored narrative development beyond that age. In preadolescence and adolescence, narrative development involves the expression of the landscape of consciousness that may include evaluative expressions about the narrator's feelings about the story or the perspectives of the characters of the story. These evaluative expressions may be coded through the linguistic (lexical and prosodic) and/or kinesic channels. When evaluating the narratives of preadolescents and adolescents, it is essential to consider the landscape of consciousness. Because there are cultural variations in the channels (e.g., lexical, prosodic, kinesic) used to express the landscape of consciousness, it is important to consider more than just the lexical coding of consciousness.

This chapter explores how the landscape of consciousness is manifested in the narratives of preadolescents and adolescents. What follows is a review of the narrative analysis frameworks used to determine communicative competence, particularly in African American speakers. Next, the chapter explains how the types of components of landscape of consciousness are coded linguistically (lexically and prosodically) and kinesically. Finally, materials are provided that can help translate the information gathered using this new approach to the clinical setting.

NARRATIVE ASSESSMENT

Damico (1993) suggested that language assessment of preadolescents and adolescents should highlight three areas. First, language evaluations should be conducted in real contexts where the speaker can be observed using language during actual communicative events. Second, these evaluations should be functional; that is, the purpose should be to decide whether speakers show appropriate syntactic and semantic knowledge and the ability to effectively and fluently transmit their message. Finally, results from language evaluations should document the specific communicative problems experienced and the reasons why those problems may exist. Perhaps even more important than determining why communicative problems exist is the need to consider the speaker's strengths, which can be accomplished by identifying the communicative devices the speaker uses to make communication efforts successful.

Research has shown that African American children may develop communication strategies that differ from those typically valued at school (Gee, 1989b, 1989c; Heath, 1983; Michaels, 1981; Michaels & Collins, 1984; Scollon & Scollon, 1981; Shuman, 1986). These strategies may result in different approaches to social interactions, conceptualizing, and narrative production (Gee, 1989c). It has been suggested that communicative strategies lie on a continuum with oral and literate strategies occupying opposite ends (Gee, 1989c; Tannen, 1982). Research has suggested that African American students use more strategies from the oral end of the continuum, whereas schools value strategies used from the literate end of the continuum. Oral communicative strategies are described in the literature as being minimally influenced by linguistic devices used during written communication. These strategies consist of using variations in prosodic, morphological, and syntactic markers to indicate narrative structure and cohesion. On the other end of the continuum are literate strategies that rely exclusively on lexical choice and syntactic structure to convey meaning (Gee, 1986; Tannen, 1982). All speakers operate on this communicative continuum and move closer to one end than the other depending on communicative expectations, experiences, and the communicative context (Gee, 1986).

Narratives emerge in real communicative contexts, such as in conversations between peers, that can satisfy the first goal of language evaluation outlined by Damico (1993). Through the use of narratives, examiners can determine the speaker's ability to use syntactic and semantic skills in his or her own social contexts, meeting the second goal of language evaluation outlined by Damico (1993). Narratives also can be used to observe how information is transmitted across multiple communicative channels (beyond the lexical channel), which is necessary for speakers who provide meaningful information through the prosodic and kinesic channels. Moreover, looking beyond narrative structure into social and cultural conventions and the various perspectives that may be taken by the speaker helps determine the speaker's communicative strengths.

NARRATIVE ANALYSIS FRAMEWORKS

Most narrative analyses have been based on a structuralist approach that focuses on the underlying structure of all stories. Researchers have differentiated the overall organization and order of narrative text from narrative content (van Dijk & Kintsch, 1983). Narratives have been characterized by rule-governed, hierarchical episodes that are composed of several elements: setting, initiating event, response/goal, attempt, outcome, resolution, and ending (Mandler & Johnson, 1977; Rumelhart, 1977; Stein & Glenn, 1979). The primary frameworks, however, that have been used to analyze oral narratives produced by African American speakers are Labov's high point analysis (Labov, 1972; Labov & Waletsky, 1967) and Gee's stanza analysis (Gee, 1986).

Labov's High Point Narrative Analysis

Labov (1972), expanding on Labov and Waletsky's (1967) work, developed a structural model that looked at two different narrative functions. A narrative is defined as a recapitulation of past experiences accomplished by matching the verbal sequence of clauses to the sequence of events that actually occurred (Labov & Waletsky, 1967). The speaker may temporally sequence events with narrative clauses that serve to move the story forward or with free clauses. Free clauses are clauses that are not part of the temporal sequence of events, but that provide comments about the events being reported. In this framework, narratives have two functions, referential (social), for the purpose of relaying events, and evaluative (interactional), for the purpose of relaying why the narrative was told. These functions are conveyed through six elements: abstract, orientation, complicating action, evaluation, resolution, and coda (Labov, 1972).

The *abstract* summarizes the forthcoming narrative and indicates what the narrative will be about. The *orientation* provides information about the characters in the story and about where and when events occurred. *Complicating action* is the component that is required for the text to be considered a narrative. This component chronologically describes past events with narrative clauses and serves as the primary referential function of the narrative. Young children usually produce narratives that are limited to the complicating action, without mentioning why the narrative was told. When the point of the narrative is not expressed, the narrative consists of just a list of facts, which makes the narrative less understandable and not very interesting. Although only this component is required to identify the narrative as a narrative, the other components, particularly the evaluation component, help provide necessary information for the narrative to be understood (Goodwin, 1990).

The *evaluation* explains why the narrative was told. During the evaluation the action of the narrative is suspended. There are two types of evaluations. First, evaluations can be external when the narrator explicitly states what the point of the narrative is. For example, the statement "I was scared" is a description of an emotional state that can be used to indicate the point of a story. Linguistic cues meant to mark external evaluations usually are conveyed through adverbs, adjectives, gratuitous terms, and negatives. *Adverbs* and *adjectives* are evaluative in themselves. For example, the statement "that was funny" uses an adjective to describe the speaker's evaluation of an event. *Gratuitous terms* ("very," "just," "really," etc.) are used to stress (or intensify) the words they modify (Peterson & McCabe, 1983). *Negative* statements are evaluative in that they indicate to the listener the expectations of the speaker or of the characters involved in the narrative that were *not* met. Second, evaluations can be internal when the evaluation is embedded in the narrative text. Embedding can be accomplished by having characters comment on the events, having actions demonstrate the importance of events, and using prosodic or kinesic cues (Goodwin, 1990; Labov, 1972). Embedding helps make the narrative understandable and interesting. As they get older, children use more and more evaluative statements in their narratives.

Resolution recaps events that occur after the high point of the story. In effect, this component describes what happened after the conflict and tells how the conflict was resolved. *Coda* is a formalized ending that also shows the relevance of the story to the present situation (Labov, 1972; Peterson & McCabe, 1983).

In this framework, telling a "good" narrative depends on a sequential order of events and an evaluation. The fact that events may be presented in sequential order does not guarantee that the narrative is presented in a meaningful manner for the listener (Shuman, 1986). It is necessary to examine the evaluation component not only because it makes the narrative more interesting but also because it is an indication that the speaker is able to take the perspectives of others into consideration.

Although Labov's work was the impetus for analyzing stretches of talk larger than the sentence, his framework focuses on the lexical components of narratives. Labov's work did, however, suggest that the social-cognitive skills of the speaker were important for the ability to produce an interesting, coherent narrative. These skills are demonstrated by evaluative statements, which a speaker may make by exploring the perspective of characters in the story.

Gee's Poetic Narrative Analysis

Gee (1986) developed a structural model from a poetic framework. He identified units in narrative discourse by looking at sources of information that are not typically focused on by psycholinguists. These sources of information include oral performances found in oral cultures and oral language in general. Gee (1986) suggested that oral language and oral performances "tend to have rich prosodic and temporal markers of structure" (p. 392). These units of discourse are represented in lines and stanzas. Lines are similar to clauses, but not always, and contain the following attributes:

1. They are relatively short.
2. They start with "and" (or some other conjunction or a verb of saying).
3. They have one pitch glide that terminates the line. *Gee (1986) suggested that some African American speakers may use a nonfalling pitch glide rather than a falling or rising pitch glide.*
4. They often terminate with some sort of junctural phenomena—hesitation, lengthening of final syllables, a short pause, and so forth.
5. They tend to be simple clauses.
6. They display a good deal of syntactic and semantic parallelism with lines adjacent to or near them.

Stanzas are a series of lines about a single topic that are organized rhythmically and syntactically (parallel) to hang together in a particular way. Each change in stanza represents a change in perspective. The following are examples of stanzas:

1. At Grandmother's

I was just up there
I was up my grandmother's house
especially for like like 2 weeks, or 3
well not 2 weeks, 2 days or 3, or more like that
a couple of ah shoot, I should say days

2. Ear Ache

all right, I got this thing
my ear's all buggin me an everything
my ear was all buggin me
and I was cryin
I was all: oooh oooh oooh, oooh oooh
I was doin all that
and my mother put alcohol on though . . . (Gee, 1989b, p. 301).

Gee (1990) suggests that narratives involve more than just communicating about a temporal order of events. Rather, there are several subsystems of language used by all speakers that help the narratives make sense: prosody, cohesion, discourse organization, contextualization signals, and thematic organization.

Prosody is the manner in which words and sentences are stated and includes variations of pitch, loudness, stress, duration of syllables and vowels, hesitations, and pauses. Prosody may be used by a speaker to achieve the perspective desired or to evaluate the actions of the character or the events occurring in the narrative. This can be done by taking on the characters' dialect, speech rate, or speaking style. *Cohesion* refers to the connections between lines and between stanzas and may be achieved through a variety of linguistic devices, such as conjunctions, pronouns, demonstratives, ellipses, repeated words, and phrases. *Discourse organization* refers to the way in which lines and stanzas are organized into higher order units, such as scenes or episodes, that are usually organized according to themes (similar to the stanzas just presented). With *contextualization signals,* the speaker signals to the listener what the context of the narrative event should be. *Thematic organization* is the manner in which the themes in the narrative are similar or contrast.

Gee's work (1986, 1990) incorporated aspects of discourse that have not been typically described in the literature on narratives. Not only does Gee's framework account for information provided by two communicative channels (lexical and prosodic), but also it addresses the social-cognitive aspect of perspective taking on narrative interest and coherence.

INFLUENCES ON NARRATIVES

The variability of narrative production is an important consideration in narrative assessment. Individuals have different experiences listening to and telling stories, and their world knowledge is also different; therefore, narrative production is a by-product of sociocultural and individual differences and influences (Gee, 1990; Gutierrez-Clellen & Quinn, 1993; Scollon & Scollon, 1981; Shuman, 1986). Consequently, the perspective in which a narrative is relayed is influenced by cultural norms. Individuals also express their perspective with linguistic forms available in their native language and dialects (Berman & Slobin, 1994). One's perception of listeners' needs also is influenced by cultural and social experiences.

Narratives are influenced by a variety of psychological and linguistic factors. Without sufficient information on narrative skills across cultures, there is considerable room for erroneous conclusions to be made about the communicative skills of some speakers.

Psychological Influences

The development of social cognition influences one's ability 1) to know that a range of perspectives (voices, points of view) exists; and 2) to achieve multiple perspectives in narrative texts. A perspective, voice, or point of view means that there are different ways of telling a story. More specifically, some aspects of a narrative can be emphasized and others can be deemphasized; some events in the narrative can be interpreted and others can be left to inference (Chatman, 1978). Taking a particular perspective involves being able to coordinate and integrate various psychological perspectives. This particular skill may develop as early as preschool age. It has been documented that, during dramatic play, preschool children have an ability to use multiple voices in narratives (Engle, 1995; Wolf & Hicks, 1989). Wolf and Hicks (1989) found that by age 3 children used three voices to mark narrative text: narrative (describing events), dialogue (portraying the speech of characters), and stage managing (dialogue with the listener). The following text illustrates the aspect of "voice" in narrative text. In the following excerpt, Heather, a 3½-year-old child, demonstrates an ability to juggle "at least three distinct voices in her play narrative" (Wolf & Hicks, 1989, p. 332):

Narrative	Dialogue	Stage managing

[H. plays with a king, queen, and a princess doll, walking each along a table.]

once upon a time
the baby and the mommy and the daddy
they walked through the forest to find a house
and said

        there's a porch . . .

[H. puts the king in the porch, but has trouble fitting the queen in]
and then the baby said

        there's not room enough

[H. looks to the adult]

                there's not enough room
                in this house/can you make
                the porch bigger/people won't
                fit in the porch

[The adult enlarges the porch with blocks. "Tell me some more of the story."] (Wolf & Hicks, 1989, p. 331)

Although young children demonstrate an awareness of and ability to use different voices, as they mature they become better able to integrate more elements and perspectives into a story (McKeough, 1987). As a child's working memory and social cognition develop, he or she can include more detail, more characters, more event sequences (episodes), and obstacles in event sequences. McKeough (1987) suggests that these variabilities are dictated by the speaker's ability to process increasing levels of information, which in turn influences the structure of the narrative.

Bakhtin (1981, as cited in Wertsch, 1991) hypothesized that all texts, whether written or spoken, are subject to various "voices," that is, to a variety of perspectives or points of view. These voices may consist of that of the speaker (narrator), the character(s) being portrayed in the events, and/or the listener, all of which exist in some social context.

The speaker's voice can simply be represented with the words that are uttered. This voice (perspective) has been labeled in the literature as that of the first person, which is more egocentric. (The speaker's voice in this context is equivalent to the narrative clause described by Labov, 1972.) The speaker does not (and at times is unable to) see any view other than his or her own (Quintana, 1994).

The voice of the character can be represented through quoted speech (Goodwin, 1990; Shuman, 1986), variations in prosodic cues (Gee, 1990; Gumperz, 1982), and gestures (McNeill & Levy, 1982). Quoted (reported) speech is differentiated from the speaker's voice through changes in pitch and rate of speech. Specifically, pitch and rate of speech change when the speaker reproduces the character's (or source's) dialect or style. In the following example, the speaker elevates her pitch and increases the rate of her talk (in Clause 3) when inferring what the character may have spoken in response to the actions of the frog (see Appendix A for a key to transcription symbols):

1. an'he (the frog) jumped in on dis man hat # when he was sittin' at da table#
2. so den da lady an' da man had left from dat store
3. an' said dey "*ain't commin' back here no more*" #
4. so den after dat # da boy was crawlin' on da ground (Hyter, 1994, 25f13: 14-15)

In Clause 4 the speaker resumed her habitual pitch and rate of speaking. The speaker also may represent multiple voices simultaneously. Bakhtin (1981, as cited in Wertsch, 1991) uses the term "hybrid construction" to refer to a multi-voiced process, which is "an utterance that belongs, by its grammatical (syntactic) and compositional markers, to a single speaker, but that actually contains mixed within it two utterances, two speech manners, two styles, two languages" (pp. 304-305).

Gestures may be used to reflect the perspective of both the character acting on an object and the object being acted on. Gestures that represent the character's voice first demonstrate the action of the character. The gesture is initiated away from the speaker's body but ends in close proximity to the speaker's body:

An example of a gesture that reflects the agent's point of view is the arm extended upward and forward, the hand forming a grip, then the arm moving downward and toward the self; this appeared with the narrative statement, "and then he bends it way back" (in which "it" refers to a tree). The gesture ironically depicts the movement of the agent. (McNeill & Levy, 1982, p. 282)

When the perspective of the object acted on is being portrayed, gestures represent the actions of the object and are constructed away from the speaker's body (Mc-Neill & Levy, 1982):

> For the same event *(described above)* a gesture reflecting the point of view of the patient *(object*—the tree) would have been different; for example, the arm and hand extended upward and moving downward together, re-enacting the movement of the tree (omitting the agent's grip). An example of such a potent point of view gesture is the right hand extended laterally to the left and rotating around the axis of the arm in a series of circles; this appeared with the statement, "he finished powering the dynamo," and the gesture represents the movement of the armature of the dynamo. (p. 282, italics added)

When the voice of a character (or object) can be represented in a narrative, the speaker is speaking from a second-person perspective. From that perspective, the speaker can see his or her own point of view and that of another. This type of perspective allows the speaker to integrate his or her voice with other voices (Quintana, 1994). These perspectives, then, are dynamic, constantly being formulated during the construction of the narrative (Bakhtin, 1981, as cited in Wertsch, 1991).

To tell a "good" story, a preadolescent or adolescent also needs to have adequate communicative skills, which are reflected in speakers' ability to anticipate listeners' needs. Bakhtin (1981, as cited in Wertsch, 1991) suggested that true meaning cannot exist unless the voice of the listener responds to the voice of the speaker. Speakers can "hear" listeners' voices by the listeners' responses to the speakers' talk. This is demonstrated by whether the talk has been understood by the listener. Speakers' awareness of the listeners' voice is reflected in the way the speakers formulate the story. For example, speakers will supply sufficient background information so that listeners are able to follow their talk. Speakers also will anticipate listeners' needs by clearly referring to events, characters, and so on and by clarifying those references if necessary. Likewise, if there is an assumption of shared knowledge between speakers and listeners, speakers may not refer to events and characters as clearly.

The developmental sequence of acquiring voices is documented by Selman's (1979) theory of social perspective taking (see Table 1). This theory describes the development of the ability to be aware of and to integrate a wide variety of perspectives. He maps the development of reasoning about social activity from preschool to adulthood across a variety of intrapersonal (self-awareness and personality) and interpersonal (interpersonal conflict and group cohesion) contexts.

Selman's stages illustrate the concept that, as individuals mature, their awareness of multiple perspectives develops. This heightened awareness of multiple perspectives allows speakers to represent those perspectives in narratives linguistically (lexically and/or prosodically) or kinesically.

Table 1. Social perspective-taking ability

Domains of social perspectivism	
Levels of social perspectivism	Understanding of persons
Level 0 (2 years–5:11 years): Undifferentiated perspective	Physicalistic conceptions: Understanding of persons in physical terms (e.g., big, tall)
Level 1 (4:6 years–12:4 years): Differentiated, subjective perspective	Conceptions of intentionality: Awareness of nonobservable internal characteristics of persons (e.g., subjective states)
Level 2 (6 years–15:10 years): Self-reflective, social, or reciprocal perspective	Introspective understanding: See self through the eyes of others
Level 3 (11:7 years–adulthood): Third-person or mutual perspective	Stable personality: Understanding of persons with trait conceptions
Level 4 (17 years–adulthood): In-depth or societal perspectives	In-depth conceptions: Integration of diverse aspects of self (e.g., awareness of existence of conscious and unconscious motivations).

From Quintana, S.M. (1994). A model of ethnic perspective-taking ability applied to Mexican-American children and youth. *International Journal of Intercultural Relations, 18*(4), 419–448. Reprinted with kind permission from Elsevier Science Ltd. The Boulevard, Langford Lane, Kidlington OX5 IGB, UK.

Linguistic Influences

Linguistic skills include having command of a range of communicative devices available in one's native language or dialect to construct utterances in a narrative (Berman & Slobin, 1994). For example, English affords the use of nouns, pronouns, and ellipses for character references. It also allows speakers to re-refer to characters by using anaphora or a re production of the previous explicit referent (renominalization) to decrease potential ambiguity of referential terms (Bamberg, 1986; Clancy, 1980; Hyter, 1994; Karmiloff-Smith, 1979).

Linguistic influences may consist of literate or oral communicative strategies. Some literate linguistic devices include the use of conjoined phrases (e.g., "put down his money and went over"), relative clauses (e.g., "Once there was this coyote who always like [sic] to play tricks"), dependent clauses (e.g., "When Coyote approached Fox, Coyote asked . . ."), and complement clauses (e.g., "Coyote trusted Fox and told him to take all his money") (Westby et al., 1989, p. 64). Peterson and McCabe (1983) identified a variety of linguistic forms in the oral narratives of children between 3 and 6 years of age that were used to orient the listener to events in their narrative and to evaluate the events. They found that, during orientation clauses, speakers used past progressive tense (e.g., "it was raining"). Speakers also used causal statements to explain ongoing events in their narratives (e.g., "because"). Evaluative utterances were marked by gratuitous terms (e.g., "very," "just," "really"), adjectives ("fun," "ugly," "exciting"), and adverbs ("we finally got him to do it"). Negatives to describe events that did not occur were also evaluative in that they informed the listener of expectations that were not met (e.g., "He didn't cook the frog").

Some oral linguistic devices include parallelism, prosody, and thematic contrasts (Gee, 1989a). Parallelism occurs when a series of utterances have "similar structure and match each other in content and topic" (Gee, 1989a, p. 79). In addition to matching content and topic, these lines may also match in terms of rate of speech and of the location of stressed words. Parallelism is illustrated in an excerpt presented by Gee (1986):

1. an' my mother's bakin' a cake
2. an' I went up my grandmother's house while my mother's bakin' a cake
3. an' my mother was bakin' a cheese cake
4. my grandmother was bakin' a whipped cream cup cakes (p. 397)

Each of these lines (except line 4) are similar in structure: X bakin' a Y cake, where X is the agent and Y is an optional adjective. Likewise, lines 1 through 3 are similar in content in that they end in the word "cake." In addition, lines 1 and 3 are about "mother," and lines 2 and 4 are about "grandmother."

Prosodic cues such as speech rate, stress, duration of vowel (or syllables), and intonation contours are used by some speakers who are closer to the oral end of the oral–literate continuum. Elongation of vowels is used by some speakers to indicate emphasis (e.g., "that was a lo:ng trip") (Peterson & McCabe, 1983) and to mark shifts in characters (Hyter, 1994; Michaels & Collins, 1984). Research on narratives produced by African American speakers indicates that certain intonation contours are used to mark the structural aspects of discourse (Gee, 1989c). For example, falling contours are used to mark the end of an episode rather than the end of an utterance, whereas a nonfalling contour occurs at the end of an utterance.

Part of what makes a narrative understandable, interesting, reportable, and worth telling is determined by the various perspectives that are portrayed (Astington, 1994; Hewitt, 1994; Labov, 1972). Diverse perspectives from multiple speakers (e.g., narrator, listener, character) contribute to the complexity of the narrative. The word "then" was found to be used by some adult speakers in an oral narrative to indicate shifts between objective and subjective perspectives; that is, a shift to "a new scene in the objective world of the story, or to a subjective perspective of a viewer regarding events in the story" (Duchan, Meth, & Waltzman, 1992, p. 1374). For example, the objective perspective may be descriptions of what is happening in the film without being attributed to the speaker's or to a character's voice such as simply relaying the events in the story. This perspective would be equivalent to what Labov categorizes as a narrative clause fulfilling the referential function of the narrative.

Subjective perspectives, however, are attributed to various voices produced by speakers. For example, speakers may use their own voice to make an evaluative statement ("I thought that part [of the movie] was funny"). Speakers may also use the voice of a film viewer, which usually includes some references to how the events are portrayed in the film itself ("Then the scene changes and the frog is in the kitchen"). Furthermore, speakers may use the voice of a character in the narrative ("The boy yelled, 'no'") (Duchan et al., 1992). The following example illustrates "then" being used to shift from an objective perspective to a subjective perspective (i.e., film viewer):

> the frog came near his feet
> and he picked it up
> then the scene changes and it showed the boy going to the kitchen

MULTIPLE PERSPECTIVE NARRATIVE ANALYSIS

The narrative analyses discussed focus on narrative structure as documented through a "unichannel" or "bichannel" framework. It takes more than a sequential description of events, however, to construct an effective, understandable, and interesting story. Beyond narrative structure it is important to consider the narrator's ability to tell why the narrative was told in the first place (i.e., the point of the story). To be a mature and successful narrator, one needs to be able to see events from multiple perspectives exhibited through various linguistic (lexical and prosodic) and kinesic markers. Also important for making the narrative understandable is the narrator's ability to maintain cohesion in the narrative, which may be done through multiple channels—lexical, prosodic, and kinesic. We use a narrative transcript to illustrate a multiple perspective narrative analysis to identify the various perspectives (voices) that exist in the narrative, how those voices are encoded across linguistic (lexical and prosodic) and kinesic channels, and how cohesion is maintained across multiple channels.

The following text was one of 30 narratives elicited as part of a study on referential strategies used by preadolescent African American speakers (Hyter, 1994). A textless film called *Frog Goes to Dinner* (Osborn & Templeton, 1985), based on the book by Mercer Mayer (1975) of the same title, was used as stimulus for the narratives because it contains several characters (21) that the narrators needed to be able to refer to throughout their narration. This type of film made it possible to assess the speakers' ability to maintain referential cohesion and demonstrate various perspectives in their narratives.

The subjects first viewed the film without the examiner (Hyter) being present. To promote clear, detailed retellings (narratives), subjects were told that the examiner had not previously viewed the film. After they watched the movie, they were individually asked to tell the examiner about the film. Each narrative was elicited with the prompt, "So, what was happenin' in the movie?" Many descriptions of action sequences were provided by the speakers. Subjects were familiar with this telling activity, as they used it daily to tell friends about movies or television shows that they had seen.

The following text is from a speaker, referred to as Kenya, a typically functioning 13-year-old African American who is performing at grade level in her seventh-grade classroom. The narrative is separated into scenes that correspond to the scenes that are depicted in the film (see Appendix B for a full description of the film). Utterances within each scene were segmented into clauses, which may be independent or may contain subordinate or relative clauses (Berman & Slobin, 1994). The transcript is presented in standard orthography with pronunciation modifications (see Appendix A for transcription codes).

Narrative Text (Kenya)

Home Scene

1. It was a little boy
2. 'n (h)e was goin' to dinner with (h)is mother and [2,1]father #
3. a:nd (h)e took (h)is pet frog
4. an' (h)e put it in (h)is [3,2]pocket #
5. so dey got in da car
6. and dey was goin' to dinner

Menu Scene

7. and (h)e was sittin' (th)ere rea'in da menu
8. and da frog (h)e jumped out a (h)is [2,1]pocket
9. and (h)e di' n't know

Music Scene

10. and the frog got into a [2,1]tu:ba
11. and the man started playin'it
12. and den the frog flew right out the tu:ba into um # where the crabs and the lobsters stay in the tank
13. and the lobsters saw (h)im
14. an' (h)e was 'bout tə um snap at (h)is foot
15. but (h)e jumped in a bowl of salad ##

Soup and Salad Scene

16. an' da ma:n (h)e was goin' to da table where da people order salad
17. and (h)e was mixin' it for 'em
18. and the frog was in (th)ere
19. (h)e put e:ggs and peppe:rs and **yucky** stuff in'ere
20. and the frog was in'ere
21. and # he mixed it up
22. and (h)e gave it to da um ## the la:dy # and the ma:n
23. and she was eatin' it #
24. it was nasty
25. and she was eatin' it
26. and den she moved da um pieces of salad
27. and she saw the fro:g
28. and she did she did like dis [audible breath]
29. and den she said + . . .
30. and den she looked back
31. and the frog wa'n't dere
32. and den she looked on her husband hea:d
33. and it was on the man hea:d
34. and he had a toupee
35. and h(e) did like **dat** # [right hand lifted over the speaker's head and then moves backward as if brushing something off of her head]
36. and the toupee flew in dis lady soup

37. and the fro:g wen' somewhere else#
38. so # da lady was like "e:w" [*high writhing pitch on "ew"*]
39. an' so den dey start gettin' up an' lea:vi:n' and e'rythæ:ng

Water Scene
40. den da frog was in da water in a jar of water
41. and da ma:n went to go pour da wate:r in dis uh man cup
42. and da frog was in the cup
43. and (h)e went to go drink it
44. and (h)e looked at it
45. and he said # [*facial grimace*]
46. and de:n him and his wife got up
47. and dey started leavin' #

Kitchen Scene
48. den da fro:g he got in to the kitchen #
49. I don't know how (h)e got into the kitchen #
50. (h)e was on the tray
51. and den da ma:n was tryin' to get (h)im wit(h) a pot and kept on doin' like dis
     [*action imitating man's movement accompanied by verbal sound effects—"sha
     bam"*] #
52. cou' n't get (h)im
53. and um ## (h)e (h)is # da frog kept on jumpin' up and do:wn
54. den dat ma:n # (h)e had a cake in (h)is ha:nd
55. and the other man still tryin' to catch (h)im
56. den (h)e trip
57. and da other man with the cake in (h)is ha:nd fell
58. an' the cake went in o:n (h)is face
59. **dat** wasn't funny [*laughter*]

Head Chef Scene
60. and um # den da um da ma:n
61. you know dose men da have a beards and dey all be in the kitche:n and they
     alway be cookin' #
62. da chefs yeah
63. da chef # he came out
64. and (h)e was lookin' at da frog
65. and (h)e got ma:d
66. he picked up the frog
67. and den he put some e:ggs and some um
68. what is it
69. some green stuff in da pa:n
70. and (h)e was (a)bout to chop da um frog legs off and make frog le:gs

Boy Peeking Scene
71. and den the bo:y # (h)e was searchin' arou:nd #
72. and (h)e was looking
73. and (h)e was um under da
74. (h)e wen' under da table: #
75. he went # through da um # plants
76. and den dats when he figured out
77. and (h)e went in the kitchen

Home Again Scene
78. and da man wa(s) 'bout to cut (h)im
79. and (h)e screamed ##
80. and den dey just showed him and his mom and his dad come in the house
81. and (h)e was walkin' up da steps
82. and (h)is mom and (h)is dad start laughi:n'
83. and den when (h)e got in the room (h)e s- uh frog uh burped
84. and den (h)e started laughi:n'
85. and den it went off

Kenya provided an informative and entertaining narrative; however, when scrutinizing this transcript, one may identify what may be categorized as "problems." For example, on two occasions Kenya did not clearly introduce a character that was new to a scene. In Clause 16, Kenya introduces the first character in that scene with, "an' da ma:n (h)e was goin' to da table where da people order salad" (a similar character introduction also takes place in Clause 41). It is not clear who the man is because of the absence of a relative clause (e.g., "the man *who had the salad*"). It can, however, be inferred from the context that "da ma:n" is a waiter about to serve salad to some restaurant patrons. The character introduced in Clause 41 is even more difficult to define from the context. One could ask whether in Clause 41 the man who poured the water ("da ma:n went to go pour da wate:r") is the same man who "had a toupee" (Clause 34).

One thing that Kenya does do, however, is to use subject apposition and vowel prolongation during references to new characters. Let's revisit Clause 16: "an' da ma:n (h)e was goin' to da table where da people order salad." Kenya produces nominal apposition ("the man he") and also prolongs the vowel in man ("ma:n"). Both of those characteristics are oral communicative strategies commonly used by individuals operating more closely to oral end of the oral–literate continuum to indicate that temporarily a new topic is being introduced. Nominal apposition and vowel elongations occur several times in Kenya's transcript when new characters are being introduced.

Kenya also omits some background information that would inform the listener about the parents' activities while in the restaurant. For instance, the listener is not informed that the parents were waiting for the little boy in the car while he ran back upstairs to his room to pick up his frog. Similarly, Kenya did not make clear that, while the frog was making its rounds to the patrons' tables, the little boy had snuck away from his parents at the dinner table to look for his frog. Kenya's description makes it sound as if the little boy started looking for his frog after the frog found its way into the kitchen area (see Clauses 71–77).

Kenya's narrative presents some minor problems, but they do not hinder the listener's ability to follow the narrative; besides, her story is entertaining. Kenya demonstrated her narrative strengths by using a variety of linguistic and cognitive perspective-taking strategies. The following section includes illustrations of perspective taking to show the type of voices that occurred in Kenya's narrative and how those voices were coded linguistically (lexically and prosodically) and/or kinesically. Illustrations of narrative cohesion are also provided to show how Kenya maintained cohesion in her narrative by using lexical, prosodic, and kinesic cues.

Kenya's Voices

Illustrations of Perspective Taking   Kenya's use of different voices or perspectives in her narrative contributed to its effectiveness. First, she presents narrative events from an objective perspective (descriptions of events occurring in the film that are not attributed to the speaker's or to a character's voice) (Duchan et al., 1992). A total of 19 (22%) of the 85 clauses in Kenya's narrative contained an objective perspective. This objective perspective is illustrated in the following examples.

3. (h)e took (h)is pet frog
5. so dey got in da car

Clauses conveying a subjective perspective (perspectives attributed to a particular voice) make up 78% of the narrative (66 clauses). Therefore, most of Kenya's narrative contained clauses that demonstrated her ability to speak from multiple perspectives. These various voices include the narrator in dialogue with herself and with the listener, the narrator as film viewer, the narrator as characters in the narrative, and the narrator making evaluative statements about the characters or events in the narrative.

Kenya's narrative exhibits one instance of the narrator in dialogue with herself when she expressed doubt about an event that occurred in the film. This perspective is illustrated in Clause 68:

66. lie picked up the frog
67. and den he put some e:ggs and some um + . . .
68. **what is it** [*lowered pitch*]

Clause 68 is marked by a pitch that is lower than Kenya's habitual pitch and by decreased intensity and rate, suggesting that she is speaking to herself and trying to remember the name of the ingredient used by the chef while he was preparing to cook the frog. Kenya's dialogue (as narrator) with the listener is also characterized by prosodic variations, particularly changes in pitch and rate of speech. Note that each clause was also accompanied by a direct look at the listener:

24. it was nasty [*faster rate, pitch lower than usual*]
49. I don't know how (h)e got into the kitchen # [*rate faster than usual*]
59. dat wasn't funny [*stress put on that (dat), pitch lower than usual*]
61. you know dose men da' have a beards and dey all be in the kitche:n [*faster rate, pitch lower than usual*]

The clauses were made "off line"; that is, they are representative of free clauses (Labov, 1972) that contain comments about the events taking place in the narrative as opposed to actually describing the events taking place in the narrative.

The narrator's dialogues with herself and with the listener were primarily marked with a lower pitch level and a faster rate of speech. Clause 61, however, was not marked with a lower pitch level, but one that was higher than Kenya's habitual pitch. This shift suggested that Kenya was posing a question to the listener as opposed to making a statement.

One can identify the film viewer's perspective when a narrator describes events while referring to the film itself. Kenya's use of a film viewer's perspective (as described by Duchan et al., 1992) is illustrated when she stated the following:

80.   and den *dey just showed* him and his mom and his dad come in the house
85.   and den *it* went off

In the previous text, *"they"* refers to the people who produced the film, and *"it"* refers to the film itself. The shift to a film viewer's perspective was marked by the word *"then"* as described by Duchan et al. (1992).

Character voices were represented in several ways: by the narrator expressing what the character understood (knew) about the events occurring in the narrative; by quotes representing the narrator's interpretation of the character's voice, which were accompanied by prosodic variations, as well as manual and facial gestures; and by the narrator's presupposition about a character's intent. Kenya used prosodic and kinesic markers to enact (or perform) the characters' attitudes, feelings, and actions. In Clauses 9, 13, and 76, Kenya describes what some characters did or did not know and see:

9.   and (h)e di'n't *know [referring to the boy who the narrator claims did not know the frog had jumped out of his coat pocket]*
13.   and the lobster *saw* (h)im *[referring to the lobsters in the tank, where the frog landed after jumping out of the saxophone]*
76.   he went # through da um # plants and den dats when *he figured out [referring to the boy "realizing" that the frog was in the kitchen; accompanied by diectic and action gestures, produced by a hand moving from the narrator's torso forward and back again during the word "through"]*

The gesture accompanying Clause 76 represents the perspective of the character (agent, as in McNeill & Levy, 1982): it demonstrates the character's movement through the plant. Clauses 28, 38, and 45 illustrate the narrator's interpretation of character voices:

28.   and she did she did like dis {audible inspiration} *[referring to the lady who found the frog sitting in her salad]*
38.   so # da lady was like "e:w" {high writhing pitch accompanied "e:w"} *[referring to the lady in whose soup a toupee landed]*

In Clause 38, Kenya uses a lexical quote (quote of the woman's word), as well as a high writhing pitch suggestive of displeasure. In Clause 45, Kenya actually makes the facial expression that is made by a character in the film when the frog is discovered in the glass of water:

45.   and (h)e looked at it and he said # {facial grimace} *[referring to the man who found the frog in his glass of water]*

Kenya presupposed character intentions quite often during her narrative by using what Todorov (1977) refers to as aspectual transformations, auxiliary verbs used to indicate the beginning, duration, or end of an action:

14. an' (h)e *was 'bout tǝ* um snap at (h)is foot but . . . *[referring to the lobster in the tank in which the frog landed after jumping out of the saxophone; accompanied by action gesture depicting the snapping movement of the lobster's claw produced during the word "snap"]*

41. and da ma:n *went to go pour* da wate:r in dis uh man cup

When speaking from the characters' perspectives, Kenya embodied the characters' vocal pitch, style, facial expressions, and movements. Gee (1989b) refers to this aspect of narrativizing as being "performative or enactive in that it utilizes various dramatic and expressive devices to create a dramatic performance that the listener is enactively caught up in" (pp. 292–293).

Kenya also provided explicit evaluative statements by using adjectives, adverbs, gratuitous terms, and negative forms. In Clauses 19 and 24, Kenya uses an adjective to describe the ingredients the waiter was putting into the salad and her perception of how the salad tasted, respectively:

19. (h)e put e:ggs and peppe:rs and *yucky* stuff in'ere *[adjective]*
24. it was *nasty [adjective]*

The words "yucky" and "nasty," although colloquial, are used as adjectives in this narrative. Kenya also emphasized "yucky" and "nasty" with increased stress. Therefore, the evaluative statements were provided lexically (i.e., word choice indicating something distasteful or unpleasant) and prosodically (i.e., increased stress). Kenya also used adverbs to evaluate a character's action:

55. and the other man *still* tryin' to catch (h)im *[adverb]*

Finally, Kenya marked evaluative statements with the use of negative terms. Negative statements used to describe events that did not occur mark the expectations of the narrator (or of a character being described by the narrator) that were not met (Labov, 1972; Todorov, 1977):

8. and da frog (h)e jumped out a (h)is pocket
9. and (h)e *di'n't know*
30. and den she looked back
31. and the frog *wa'n't dere*

Illustrations of Cohesion   Kenya used nominals and pronominals to refer to characters in her narrative. Of the 30 references to characters she made, only two instances (6%) of lexical forms can be confusing. Therefore, the majority (94%) of Kenya's references to characters were unambiguous. This finding also was consistent within the larger corpus. Specifically, of 618 references to characters found in the larger dataset, 94% were clearly marked (unambiguous). This finding is contrary to what has typically been reported for African American speakers. The literature suggests that the frequent use of anaphoric pronouns by African American speakers makes their narratives difficult to follow (Michaels & Collins, 1984).

Kenya's narrative displayed several cohesive characteristics that typically fall on the oral end of the oral–literate continuum, such as using nominal apposition and falling intonation contours to mark narrative structure. Kenya also prolonged vowels to indicate shift in referents and as an emphatic device. Some of those instances are presented in the following excerpt. Kenya uses similar stress and vowel elongation in "tuba" in Clauses 10 and 12. In Clause 19 vowel elongation is used to emphasize the ingredients of the salad. Vowel elongation seems to be used by Kenya to emphasize new and unusual or unexpected information:

10. and the frog got into a *tu:ba*
11. and the man started playin' it
12. and den the frog flew right out the *tu:ba* into um # . . .

This excerpt also demonstrates syntactic and prosodic parallelism. Clauses 10 and 11 have parallel syntactic structures: *X did Y,* where *X* refers to a character and *Y* refers to the character's action. Clauses 10 and 12 also have parallel prosodic structures: the same prosodic cues are produced on each production of "tuba."

19. (h)e put *e:ggs* and *peppe:rs* and yucky stuff in'ere . . .
32. and den she looked on her husband *hea:d* and it was on the man *hea:d*

In addition to vowel elongations, Kenya uses "semantically empty expressions" (Gee, 1989a, p. 297), such as "and everything," which causes listeners to determine for themselves what "and everything" includes.

39. an' so den dey start gettin' up an' lea:vi:n' and e'rythæ:ng

Vowel elongations are also used to emphasize the introduction of new characters. The introduction of new characters also is marked with nominal apposition (e.g., "the lady, she . . . "), a device used to indicate a change in topics:

16. an' *da ma:n (h)e* was goin'. . .
41. and *da ma:n* went to go pour da wate:r . . .
48. den *da fro:g he* got into . . .

The literature on character reference suggests that speakers tend to nominalize characters with changing scenes or episodes (Clancy, 1980; Hyter, 1994; Levy & McNeill, 1992). The new scene appears to make the narrator feel as if the character being referred to in the upcoming scene is also new, even if it is not (Levy & McNeill, 1992). Kenya seems to be following this rule by treating the frog as a new character and marking it with vowel prolongation and nominal apposition.

Speakers adept at oral communication strategies use prosodic cues to mark narrative structure (Gee, 1989b; Gee & Grosjean, 1984). Specifically, falling intonation contours (e.g., ^{2,1}) are used to mark the end of an episode rather than the end of an utterance:

1. ^{2}it was a ^{2}little ^{2}boy
2. 'n (h)e was goin' to dinner with (h)is mother and ^{2,1}father *[introductions]*
3. a:nd (h)e took (h)is ^{2}pet ^{2}frog
4. an' (h)e put it in (h)is ^{3,2}pocket # *[orientation]*

8. ^{2}and ^{2}da ^{3,2}fro:g ^{2}(h)e ^{2}jumped ^{2}out a (h)is ^{2,1}pocket *[initiating event]*

14. an' (h)e was 'bout tə um snap at ^{2}(h)is ^{2}foot
15. ^{2}but ^{2}(h)e ^{3}jumped ^{2}in a ^{2}bowl of ^{2,1}salad ## *[end of a scene]*

36. and the toupee flew in dis ^{2}lady ^{2}soup
37. ^{1}and ^{2}the ^{3}fro:g ^{2}wen' ^{2}somewhere ^{2,1}else # *[end of a scene]*

Kenya seems to be using falling contours to differentiate scenes. Note that the falling contours occurred at a transitional part of the narrative.

Kenya's narrative illustrates the various perspectives and cohesive devices that can occur in an oral narrative. Kenya demonstrates that she is beginning to use various voices (perspectives) and cohesive devices across communicative channels. Besides being able to order past events sequentially, narrators also must be able to take multiple perspectives and to use evaluative statements. Those additional elements, which have not traditionally been the focus of narrative assessment, increase the complexity of the narrative and enhance the speaker's ability to produce a "good" narrative. Another aspect of making the narrative understandable is the use of various lexical or prosodic markers to maintain cohesion. In the following section, a systematic method to document the speaker's use of perspective taking and narrative cohesion is provided.

Using the Multiple Perspective Narrative Analysis

A Multiple Perspective Analysis Element Checklist and Student Profile (Appendix C) were used to document specific instances of multiple perspective taking and narrative cohesion exhibited in Kenya's transcript. This checklist allows the calculation of the number of clauses in the narrative that contain elements (multiple perspectives and narrative cohesion) essential for effective narrativization. The student profile summarizes the student's narrative strengths in using various perspectives, evaluative statements, and cohesive devices. The Multiple Perspective Narrative Analysis framework can be used to determine whether the essential elements for effective narrativization are present in an oral narrative.

As illustrated in Appendix C, the majority of Kenya's narrative contained clauses that demonstrated her ability to speak from multiple perspectives. That is, of the 85 clauses in Kenya's narrative, 78% were from a subjective perspective (attributed to voice). Kenya also used nonlexical and communicative strategies that typically are not from a literate tradition. For example, when Kenya portrays a character (through the use of a quote or a performance), she relies more on the prosodic and kinesic channels than on the lexical channels. In addition, evaluative statements frequently were made prosodically and kinesically, rather than with explicit lexical statements. This finding further emphasizes the importance of venturing beyond a structural framework and a unichannel (lexical only) framework when assessing communicative skills with discourse. The Multiple Perspective Analysis Element Checklist and Student Profile would be beneficial for intervention purposes. These tools provide information on the elements that are present (or absent) from the speakers' narrative, thus providing a starting point for intervention (blank checklists are provided in Appendix D).

CONCLUSION

The social and cognitive skills of preadolescents and adolescents grow in numerous ways. Increased working memory enables youth to interrelate several pieces of information simultaneously. This ability, combined with increased social awareness and perspective taking, allows them to comprehend complex plots that involve multiple characters and to produce narratives in which they incorporate the perspectives of multiple characters. Students' cultural experiences influence the ways in which they structure their narratives and the style they use in telling their stories. Language assessment and intervention with older students must consider these developmental changes in narrative abilities. All too often, language assessment has relied on a highly literate analysis approach that has considered the lexical/syntactic components of narratives exclusively. Such an approach has often resulted in the failure to recognize the narrative abilities of students who use prosodic and kinesic channels to convey information. The assessment procedures proposed in this chapter provide a means of documenting narrative competence, that is, what the student both does and does not do. Such an approach can reduce the overidentification of culturally diverse students as language delayed or disordered.

In addition, this approach provides a framework for understanding what kinds of information can be taught to facilitate students' narrative development or acquisition of literate style narratives. Two components are essential for the literate style narratives that schools expect from preadolescent and adolescent students: 1) the information in narratives must be conveyed through lexical and syntactic coding rather than through only kinesic or prosodic cues, and 2) narratives should include a landscape of consciousness as well as a landscape of action.

The educator can assist students who tell more oral style narratives (using prosodic and kinesic channels) by providing strategies for coding kinesic and prosodic information lexically and syntactically. Strategies for developing literate style narratives follow.

1. Teach lexical and syntactic cohesion principles.
   a. Teach strategies for unambiguous use of pronominal reference. This can be accomplished by showing wordless picture books or textless videos with multiple characters (including both males and females) and having students tell or write the story for other students who have not seen the book or video. The story should be told or written clearly enough so that students who have not seen the book or video can answer questions about what the various characters did. The teacher or speech-language pathologist also can produce a story from a video or wordless picture book with numerous ambiguous references and have students work in groups to identify and correct the ambiguities.
   b. Teach a variety of conjunctions. The conjunctions *"and," "so,"* and *"then,"* are the primary conjunctions used in oral narratives. Literate narratives make use of a wider variety of conjunctions, including, for example, *"but," "because," "before," "after," "when," "if," "therefore,"* and *"while."* The teacher or speech-language pathologist can find short articles or stories that use a variety of conjunctions. The paragraphs and sentences can be cut apart and students can be asked to reassemble the stories, using the conjunctions as cues to the sequence of the sentences or paragraphs.
   c. Teach colorful adjectives, adverbs, and descriptive verbs. Have students work in groups to generate multiple ways of describing a setting, event, or person. Have them "rewrite" dull stories to make them more exciting. Instead of writing "It was a nice day," brainstorm alternative words such as "sunny, hot, humid day," "a sultry day," or "an ominous, cloudy day." Instead of saying "the boy walked from rock to rock," try "the agile young man leaped (sprung, vaulted) from rock to rock."
   d. Facilitate students' development of more complex syntactic structures. Sentences combining activities have shown to be effective in increasing syntactic complexity (Strong, 1985). Groups of students can work together to determine how many ways they might combine sentences such as:

> Tyrone was working on his test.
> Jamal slipped Tyrone a note.
> Tyrone unfolded the note carefully.
> He didn't want his teacher to see.

Some possible ways to combine these sentences are:

> Tyrone was hard at work on his test when Jamal slipped a note to him. Not wanting his teacher to see, Tyrone unfolded it carefully.

> Tyrone was working hard on his test when Jamal slipped him a note, which he carefully unfolded because he didn't want his teacher to see.

2. Facilitate students' abilities to translate between written and oral discourses.
   a. Provide students with stories in which the characters' voices reflect the voices of the students. This provides students with a format for how the sounds of their voices can be conveyed in a literate mode. Books by the African American author Walter Dean Myers give voice to urban youth. In *The Mouse Rap* (1990) each chapter begins with a "rap" created by the main character; *Scorpions* (1988) and *Fallen Angels* (1988) offer a depth in the landscape of consciousness as they explore friendships and bonding among young African American males. Have students rewrite familiar stories into stories told through their voices.
   b. Read literature and have students convert stories into plays, complete with dialogue and stage directions that describe the gestures, body movements, and voice or dialect the characters should use. Then have the students produce the plays. The play director can use words to describe how the characters should act and talk and how the characters should translate the words into behaviors.

For students who exhibit little or no landscape of consciousness in their narratives, the educator will want to develop students' social-cognitive abilities so that they can engage in the multiple perspective taking essential for a landscape of consciousness in stories. This can be done in several ways:

1. Teach vocabulary necessary for coding the landscape of consciousness. The landscape of consciousness includes two types of words reflecting a mental state:
   a. Teach words that refer to mental cognitive states (e.g., "think," "guess," "forget," "remember," "hypothesize," "determine," "imagine," "speculate," "analyze"). Educators can model these words, saying, for example, "I'm *wondering* how your story will end. I *imagine* that the monster will *scheme* to get away." They can also provide students with activities in which they are asked to engage in metacognitive tasks and talk aloud as they are completing the tasks. Talking aloud while planning activities such as field trips, a science project, or a video production is a particularly good way to encourage the use of metacognitive terms.
   b. Teach words that refer to emotional states beyond the usual "happy," "sad," "mad" (e.g., "jealous," "ashamed," "embarrassed," "relieved," "frustrated," "terrified," "enamored"). Provide opportunities for students to tell or write about events in which they felt these various emotions. When reading stories, engage students in discussions of characters' feelings, what caused the feelings, and what the characters did as a result of the feelings.
2. Develop social pragmatic skills by:
   a. Role-playing social events, discussing what would be said and how it would be said, including what different people having different roles

would say in a situation (e.g., the principal catches a student coming into school late. What would the principal say, what would the student say? Another student sees the student coming in late. What do the students say to one another; how is that different from what the student would say to the principal?).

b. Discuss how different types of people might say something. For example, what might the following people say if they were hungry: a truck driver, a 5-year-old child, a business woman, a space alien, and so on.

3. Use books to develop multiple perspective taking.

a. Read and discuss books that present stories through the eyes of multiple characters. Books such as *The True Story of the Three Little Pigs* by A. Wolf (which tells the story from the perspective of the wolf) (Scieszka, 1989), *The Untold Story of Cinderella* (Shorto, 1990) (which tells the story from the perspective of the three stepsisters), can be one way to introduce character perspective taking. Compare books with similar themes or stories across cultures. For mid-elementary school children one could compare versions of *The Three Little Pigs* such as Paul Galdone's (1970) traditional version, *The Three Little Hawaiian Pigs and the Magic Shark* (Hawaiian version; Laird, 1981), and *The Three Little Javelinas* (a Southwest version; Lowell, 1992). Educators can have older elementary or middle school students compare versions of Cinderella: *Mufaro's Beautiful Daughters* (African; Steptoe, 1987), *The Talking Eggs* (Southern African American; San Souci, 1989), "Turkey Girl" (Native American; in Velarde, 1989), and *Yeh-Shen* (Chinese; Louie, 1982). Educators can guide students in considering how experiences, environments, values, and beliefs contribute to the similarities and differences among these stories.

b. Discuss controversial topics that involve differences in perspectives. Talking about beliefs, values, biases, and prejudices provides an opportunity to use one's own voice and realize how the perspectives and voices of others differ. Mildred D. Taylor's novels (*Roll of Thunder, Hear My Cry* [1975], *Let the Circle Be Unbroken* [1981], and *The Road to Memphis* [1990]) about the Logan family bring alive fragments of the history of African American life in the Deep South before the civil rights movement. *Maniac Magee* (Spinelli, 1990), a popular chapter book for preadolescents, addresses racial conflict in an urban community through the voices of the children and adults in the community. The story has a parablelike quality. Maniac is able to hear the voices of the community and is successful in enabling the East End and West End children and their families to rise above their racism and ignorance.

c. Read books that tell the story in the first person, such as *Hatchet* (Paulsen, 1987), which relates the thoughts and feelings of a boy who is the lone survivor of a plane crash in the Canadian wilderness or *Toning the Sweep* (Johnson, 1993), which relates the stories of three generations of African American women through the eyes of the adolescent granddaughter.

d. Teach the concept of trickery, a concept that depends on the landscape of consciousness. Trickery involves a disjunction between what is thought and what is said. It requires an awareness that the purveyor of the trick and the character being tricked have different perspectives on the events and different interpretations of what is being said. Use trickery tales from different cultures: Brer Rabbit (Southern) (Lester, 1990), Anansi the Spider (African) (McDermott, 1972), Raven (Northwest Indian) (McDermott, 1993), Iktomi (Plains Indian) (Goble, 1990), or Coyote (Southwest Indian) (McDermott, 1994). Have students role-play the stories, with one student taking the external voice of a character and another student taking the internal voice of the character.

In summary, assessments of the narratives of preadolescent and adolescent students should consider the students' use of the landscape of consciousness and the variety of channels through which students may code it. The goals of narrative intervention with older students are threefold: 1) to develop the social-cognitive knowledge essential for perspective taking that underlies the landscape of consciousness; 2) to develop an appreciation of the stylistic variations necessary to convey the landscape of consciousness, and 3) ability to translate between the oral style and the literate style approaches to presenting the landscape of consciousness in narratives. Students from culturally or linguistically diverse backgrounds may have the ability to use a landscape of consciousness in their narratives, but they may lack the literate style linguistic strategies and experiences required for producing a literate style narrative.

REFERENCES

Astington, J.W. (1994). Children's developing notions of others' minds. In J.F. Duchan, L.E. Hewitt, & R.M. Sonnenmeier (Eds.), *Pragmatics: From theory to practice* (pp. 72–87). Englewood Cliffs, NJ: Prentice Hall.

Bamberg, M. (1986). A functional approach to the acquisition of anaphoric relationships. *Linguistics, 24*, 227–284.

Berman, R.A., & Slobin, D. (1994). *Relating events in narrative: A crosslinguistic developmental study*. Hillsdale, NJ: Lawrence Erlbaum Associates.

Bruner, J. (1986). *Actual minds, possible worlds*. Cambridge, MA: Harvard University Press.

Chatman, S. (1978). *Story and discourse: Narrative structure in fiction and film*. Ithaca, NY: Cornell University Press.

Clancy, P. (1980). Referential choice in English and Japanese narrative discourse. In W. Chafe (Ed.), *The pear stories: Cognitive, cultural and linguistic aspects of narrative productions* (pp. 127–199). Norwood, NJ: Ablex.

Damico, J. (1993). Language assessment in adolescents: Addressing critical issues. *Language, Speech, and Hearing Services in the Schools, 24*, 29–35.

Duchan, J., Meth, M., & Waltzman, D. (1992). Then as an indicator of deictic discontinuity in adults' oral descriptions of a film. *Journal of Speech and Hearing Research, 35*(6), 1367–1375.

Engle, S. (1995). *The stories children tell: Making sense of the narratives of childhood.* New York: Freeman.

Galdone, P.C. (1970). *The three little pigs.* New York: Houghton-Mifflin.

Gee, J. (1986). Units in the production of narrative discourse. *Discourse Processes, 9,* 391–422.

Gee, J. (1989a). The narrativization of experience. *Journal of Education, 17*(1), 75–96.

Gee, J. (1989b). Two styles of narrative construction and their linguistic and educational implications. *Discourse Processes, 12,* 287–307.

Gee, J. (1989c). Two styles of narrative construction and their linguistic and educational implications. *Journal of Education, 17*(1), 97–115.

Gee, J. (1990). *Sociolinguistics and literacies: Ideology in discourses.* New York: Falmer Press.

Gee, J., & Grosjean, F. (1984). Empirical evidence for narrative structure. *Cognitive Science, 8,* 59–85.

Goble, P. (1990). *Iktomi and the ducks: A Plains Indian story.* New York: Orchard Books.

Goodwin, M.H. (1990). *He-said-she-said: Talk as social organization among black children.* Bloomington: Indiana University Press.

Gumperz, J. (1982). *Discourse strategies.* Cambridge: Cambridge University Press.

Gutierrez-Clellen, V., & Quinn, R. (1993). Assessing narratives of children from diverse cultural linguistic groups. *Language, Speech, and Hearing Services in the Schools, 24,* 2–9.

Heath, S.B. (1983). *Ways with words: Language, life, and work in communities and classrooms.* Cambridge: Cambridge University Press.

Hewitt, L.E. (1994). Narrative comprehension: The importance of subjectivity. In J.F. Duchan, L.E. Hewitt, & R.M. Sonnenmeier (Eds.), *Pragmatics: From theory to practice* (pp. 88–103). Englewood Cliffs, NJ: Prentice Hall.

Hyter, Y.D. (1994). *A cross-channel description of reference in the narratives of African-American children: English speakers.* Unpublished doctoral dissertation, Temple University, Philadelphia.

Johnson, A. (1993). *Toning the sweep.* New York: Scholastic.

Karmiloff-Smith, A. (1979). *A functional approach to child language: A study of determiners and reference.* Cambridge: Cambridge University Press.

Labov, W. (1972). The transformation of experience in narrative syntax. In W. Labov (Ed.), *Language in the inner city* (pp. 354–396). Philadelphia: University of Pennsylvania Press.

Labov, W., & Waletsky, J. (1967). Narrative analysis: Oral versions of personal experience. In J. Helm (Ed.), *Essays on the verbal and visual arts.* Seattle: University of Washington Press.

Laird, D.M. (1981). *The three little Hawaiian pigs and the magic shark.* Honolulu: Barnaby Books.

Larson, V., McKinley, N., & Boley, D. (1993). Service delivery models for adolescents with language disorders. *Language, Speech, and Hearing Services in the Schools, 24,* 36–42.

Lester, J. (1990). *Further tales of Uncle Remus: The misadventures of Brer Rabbit, Brer Fox, Brer Wolf, the doodang, and other creatures.* New York: Dial Books.

Levy, E., & McNeill, D. (1992). Speech, gesture, and discourse. *Discourse Processes, 15,* 277–301.

Loban, W.D. (1976). *Language development: Kindergarten through grade twelve.* Urbana, IL: National Council of Teachers of English.

Louie, A.L. (1982). *Yeh-Shen: A Cinderella story from China.* New York: Philomel Books.

Lowell, S. (1992). *The three little javelinas.* Flagstaff, AZ: Northland Publishing.

Mandler, J.M., & Johnson, N.S. (1977). Remembrance of things parsed: Story, structure, and recall. *Cognitive Psychology, 9,* 111–151.

Mayer, M. (1975). *Frog goes to dinner.* New York: A Puffin Pied Pipe.

McDermott, G. (1972). *Anansi the spider: A tale from the Ashanti.* New York: Holt, Rinehart & Winston.

McDermott, G. (1993). *Raven: A trickster tale from the Pacific Northwest.* San Diego: Harcourt Brace Jovanovich.

McDermott, G. (1994). *Coyote: A trickster tale from the American Southwest.* San Diego: Harcourt Brace Jovanovich.

McKeough, A.M. (1987, July). *Stages in storytelling: A neo-Piagetian analysis.* Paper presented at the IX Biennial meetings of the ISSBD, Tokyo, Japan.

McNeill, D. & Levy, E.(1982). Conceptual representations in language activity and gesture. In R.J. Jarvella & W. Klein (Eds.), *Speech, place, and action.* Chichester, England: John Wiley & Sons.

Michaels, S. (1981). "Sharing time": Children's narrative styles and differential access to literacy. *Language in Society, 10,* 423–442.

Michaels, S., & Collins, J. (1984). Oral discourse styles: Classroom interaction and the acquisition of literacy. In D. Tannen (Ed.), *Coherence in spoken and written discourse.* (pp. 231–240). Norwood, NJ: Ablex.

Myers, W. (1988). *Fallen angels.* New York: Scholastic.

Myers, W. (1988). *Scorpions.* New York: Harper & Row.

Myers, W. (1990). *The mouse rap.* New York: Harper Collins.

Nippold, M.A. (1988). Introduction. In M.A. Nippold (Ed.), *Later language development: Ages nine through nineteen* (pp. 1–10). Austin, TX: PRO-ED.

Nippold, M.A. (1993). Developmental markers in adolescent language: Syntax, semantics, and pragmatics. *Language, Speech, and Hearing Services in the Schools, 24,* 21–28.

Osborn, S. (Producer) & Templeton, G. (Director). (1985). *Frog goes to dinner* [Film]. Rochester, NY: Phoenix Films.

Paulsen, G. (1987). *Hatchet.* New York: Bradbury Press.

Peterson, C., & McCabe, A. (1983). *Developmental psycholinguistics: Three ways of looking at a child's narrative.* New York: Plenum.

Piaget, J., & Inhelder, B. (1969). *The psychology of the child.* New York: Basic Books.

Poyatos, F. (1983). *New perspectives in nonverbal communication.* New York: Pergamon Press.

Quintana, S.M. (1994). A model of ethnic perspective-taking ability applied to Mexican-American children and youth. *International Journal of Intercultural Relations, 18*(4), 419–448.

Rumelhart, D.E. (1977). Understanding and summarizing brief stories. In S. LaBerge & S. Samuels (Eds.), *Basic processes in reading: Perception and comprehension* (pp. 21–38). Hillsdale, NJ: Lawrence Erlbaum Associates.

San Souci, R. (1989). *The talking eggs.* New York: Dial.

Schuler, A.L. (1989). Preface. In A.L. Schuler (Ed.), *Seminars in Speech and Language, 10*(1), v–viii.

Scieszka, J. (1989). *The true story of the three little pigs.* New York: Viking.

Scollon, R., & Scollon, S. (1981). *Narrative, literacy and face in interethnic communication.* Norwood, NJ: Ablex.

Scott, C.M. (1988). Spoken and written syntax. In M.A. Nippold (Ed.), *Later language development: Ages nine through nineteen* (pp. 49–95). Austin, TX: PRO-ED.

Selman, R.L. (1979). *Assessing interpersonal understanding: An interview and scoring manual in five parts constructed by the Harvard-Judge Baker Social Reasoning Project.* Boston: Harvard-Judge Baker Social Reasoning Project.

Shorto, R. (1990). *The untold story of Cinderella.* New York: Citadel.

Shuman, A. (1986). *Storytelling rights: The uses of oral and written texts by urban adolescents.* Cambridge: Cambridge University Press.

Spinelli, J. (1990). *Maniac Magee.* New York: Scholastic.

Stein, N.L., & Glenn, C.G. (1979). An analysis of story comprehension in elementary school children. In R.O. Freedle (Ed.), *New directions in discourse processing* (pp. 53–120). Norwood, NJ: Ablex.

Steptoe, J. (1987). *Mufaro's beautiful daughters.* New York: Lothrop Lee & Shepard.

Strong, W. (1985). *Creative approaches to sentence combining.* Urbana, IL: National Association of Teachers of English.

Tannen, D. (1982). The oral/literate continuum in discourse. In D. Tannen (Ed.), *Spoken and written language: Exploring orality and literacy* (pp. 1–16). Norwood, NJ: Ablex.

Taylor, M. (1975). *Roll of thunder, hear my cry.* New York: Dial.

Taylor, M. (1981). *Let the circle be unbroken.* New York: Dial.

Taylor, M. (1990). *The road to Memphis.* New York: Dial.

Todorov, T. (1977). *The poetics of prose.* Ithaca, NY: Cornell University Press.

van Dijk, R., & Kintsch, W. (1983). *Strategies of discourse comprehension.* New York: Academic Press.

Velarde, P. (1989). *Old grandfather storyteller.* Santa Fe, NM: Clear Light Publishers.

Wertsch, J.V. (1991). *Voices of the mind: A sociocultural approach to mediated action.* Cambridge, MA: Harvard University Press.

Westby, C.E. (1994). The effects of genre, structure, and style of oral and written texts. In G. Wallach & K. Butler (Eds.), *Language learning disabilities in schoolage children and adolescents.* Columbus, OH: Charles E. Merrill.

Westby, C.E., VanDongen, R., & Maggart, Z. (1989). Assessing narrative competence. *Seminars in Speech and Language, 10,* 63–76.

Wolf, D., & Hicks, D. (1989). The voices within narratives: The development of intertextuality in young children's stories. *Discourse Processes, 12,* 329–351.

APPENDIX A

Transcription Symbols

Lexical Transcription

The following lexical notations are included in the example texts:

#	Pause
( )	Parenthesis surrounds the phoneme(s) that were omitted by the speaker: an(d)
um, er, eh, uh	Filled pauses
[:]	Standard English spelling of words provided before brackets: dey [: they]
( )	Occurs at the end of the example text and references the subject from Hyter's (1994) data. For example, (23m12:1–3) represents the subject number (23), gender (m = male), age (12), and utterances (utterances 1 through 3).

Prosodic Transcription

Bold	Increased stress and intensity
2	Level contour
1,2 or 2,3	Rise contour
2,1 or 3,2	Fall contour
1,2,1 or 2,3,2	Rise–fall contour
:	Vowel elongation: ma:n

Kinesic Transcription

Gestures are described in italics following the clause that the gesture accompanied.

APPENDIX B

Detailed Description of "The Frog Goes to Dinner"

Scene 1. The movie begins with a young boy running up the stairs to his bedroom. He retrieves a frog from a bowl on his dresser and then runs downstairs while putting the frog in his pocket. He gets into a car, where his parents are waiting and they drive off to a restaurant.

Scene 2. The family arrives at the restaurant. The valet opens the car doors, and as the family is getting out of the car the frog croaks. The valet gives the young boy an inquisitive look to which the boy looks surprised. He then runs into the restaurant behind his parents.

Scene 3. Once seated, the family receives menus and napkins from a waiter. While the family is looking at their menus, the frog jumps from the boy's pocket, without his knowledge, on to the floor underneath the table.

Scene 4. In another sequence, a quartet is shown playing a song. The frog hops from under the table into a saxophone. The saxophonist picks up the saxophone and attempts to blow it, but it is difficult because the frog is inside. The saxophonist blows really hard and the frog is blown from the saxophone into a lobster tank.

Scene 5. The boy feels his pocket for his frog and realizes that his frog is gone. The parents look at the boy and then resume reading their menus. While they are reading menus, the boy sneaks away from the table.

Scene 6. The waiter pushes a salad tray near the lobster tank. When the waiter is getting some items from the cabinet below the salad tray, the lobster tries to snap the frog's foot. Consequently, the frog jumps out of the lobster tank, into the salad below.

Scene 7. The waiter pushes the salad to a table where a couple is seated. The waiter prepares a caesar salad and then serves the salad. The lady eats part of the salad and then sees the frog. She begins to scream, but when she looks back down at her plate, the frog is no longer there. She then looks at the man who is with her and sees the frog on his head. She then screams and points. The man feels his head, realizes something is on it, and then throws the frog and his toupee off of his head. The toupee lands in an older lady's bowl of soup and the frog lands in a pitcher of water. This couple then leaves the restaurant in a huff. The lady with the soup pulls the toupee out of her soup and looks at it disgustingly.

Scene 8.   The waiter serves water from a pitcher that now contains the frog to a couple holding hands. The frog is poured into the man's glass with the water. The man lifts his glass to drink his water, while looking at the woman. The frog croaks and then the man realizes that a frog is in his water. This couple leaves the restaurant in a huff.

Scene 9.   The parents notice that their son is missing from the table. At the same time, the boy is crawling through the restaurant on the floor in search of his frog.

Scene 10.   A soufflé, is served to an older couple and their daughter. The frog jumps upon the soufflé and the soufflé falls. This couple and their daughter leave the restaurant.

Scene 11.   A dishwasher is shown washing dishes. The frog is brought into the kitchen on a tray with dirty dishes. The frog croaks and the dishwasher looks at the frog. It jumps on the kitchen counter and the dishwasher tries to catch the frog by covering it with bowls, but it keeps jumping away. The dishwasher thinks he has caught the frog under one of the bowls, so he looks under each bowl. At that time, one of the bowls moves toward the edge of the counter. The dishwasher tries to catch the bowl but the moving bowl falls to the floor and the frog jumps out. The dishwasher tries to catch the frog to no avail. A cake maker, who is in the kitchen, turns to look at the commotion behind him. The dishwasher lunges at the frog and knocks the cake maker over. The cake maker falls to the floor with a cake in his hands and his face lands in the cake. The frog continues to jump around the kitchen floor while the dishwasher and the cake maker try to catch it. A waiter brings in a tray of dirty dishes and, after seeing all the commotion in the kitchen, leaves looking exasperated.

Scene 12.   While the events were taking place in the kitchen, the boy peaked around the corner and through some plants. The parents, on the other hand, are near the lobster tank looking for their son.

Scene 13.   The head chef comes out of the freezer and looks angrily at the mess on the floor. He sees the frog and reaches down to pick it up while laughing. He then holds the frog while preparing a skillet with parsley and oil to cook the frog. He then lifts the frog by its legs while holding a knife; however, the boy runs into the kitchen and yells "stop."

Scene 14.   The family enters the door of their home, and the boy has the frog in his hands. The parents look disgusted and the boy looks at the parents and smirks. The father nods his head toward the top of the stairs and then the boy goes upstairs with his frog. The parents look at each other and laugh. When the boy gets to the top of the stairs, he turns and smiles, goes into his room, closes the door, and laughs while the frog croaks.

Appendix C

Checklists

**Essential Elements for Effective Narrativization:
Dialogues and Character Perspectives**

Subjective perspectives	Clause Number								Total number of clauses
	0-10	20	30	40	50	60	70	80	
Self-dialogue						68			1
Dialogue w/listener		24	34	49	58	60			5
Film viewer perspective							79		1
Character aspects									
Character portrayal									
Quote (lexical)									0
Prosodic		28							1
Kinesic			35	45	51				3
Character perspective									
Beliefs									0
Desires									0
Feelings						65			1
Intentions (aspect)	1, 6, 11, 14, 15		39	41, 43, 46			70, 78		11
Knowledge							74		3
Referential cohesion (lexical, prosodic, & kinesic)									
Nominal apposition	2, 8, 15			48	54	63	71		7
Vowel elongations	15			41, 48	51, 54				6
Deictic gestures									0
Total # of clauses									39

Essential Elements for Effective Narrativization:
Evaluating Events

Event aspects (evaluations)	Clause Number								Total number of clauses
	0-10	20	30	40	50	60	70	80	
Lexical									
Adjectives	19	24							2
Adverbs					54			80	2
Gratuitous terms									0
Negatives	9, 15		31		52				4
Prosodic/kinesic									
Vowel elongation	10, 19		32, 38, 39	41, 46	54, 57	61, 67, 69	70	81, 84	15
Facial expressions				44					1
Total # of clauses									24

Lexically Noncohesive Devices
(adapted from Cox, 1986/1987)

I. **Potentially ambiguous references:**   1[a]

Devices that are potentially ambiguous occur when their presuppositions cannot be retrieved from the text:
   1. Jim and Jack went to a party.
   2. **He** met a girl **he** liked. Devices may be referenced exophorically

   1. Beth came into the room.
   2. She put her books over **there**.

or to the narrator's personal knowledge:
   1. **We** wanted to build something.
   2. **We** built **it** outside.

II. **Potentially poor references:**   1

Devices that are potentially poor occur when their presupposition is present in the text but is hard to retrieve. Poor referencing occurs when the presupposition is in a preceding clause that is some distance from the cohesive device or the device is related cataphorically to the presupposition (in a subsequent clause). In addition, the incorrect marking of number, gender, person, or case causes poor referencing.

III. **Inappropriate voice:**   0

Inappropriate voice occurs when the author abruptly shifts role in the story.
   1. **I** was driving along the road.
   2. Then **we** stopped for lunch.

Total number of clauses that contain noncohesive devices: **2**

Total number of clauses: **85**

Percentage of clauses that contain noncohesive devices: **6%**

[a]Number of occurrences.

Profile of essential elements for effective narrativization.

Name: Kenya   Birthdate: 7/81   Age: 13   Grade: 7
Examiner: Hyter   School: PA

Frequency of Use

	0	10	20	30	40	50	60	70	80	90	100

	Frequency of Use
Total Number of Clauses	85
Total Number of Clauses Containing an Objective Perspective	19
Total Number of Clauses Containing a Subjective Perspective	66
Subjective Perspectives	
Dialogues (self and listener)	5
Film viewer's perspective	1
Character Aspects	
Character portrayal	
Lexical	1
Prosodic/kinesic	4
Character perspectives	
Total	15
Referential Cohesion	
Nominal apposition	7
Vowel elongations and deictic gestures	0
Event Evaluations	
Lexical evaluative statements	9
Prosodic and kinesic evaluative indications	16

281

Appendix D

Blank Checklists

**Essential Elements for Effective Narrativization:
Dialogues and Character Perspectives**

Subjective perspectives	Clause Number								Total number of clauses
	0-10	20	30	40	50	60	70	80	
Self-dialogue									
Dialogue w/listener									
Film viewer perspective									
Character aspects									
Character portrayal									
Quote (lexical)									
Prosodic									
Kinesic									
Character perspective									
Beliefs									
Desires									
Feelings									
Intentions (aspect)									
Knowledge									
Referential cohesion (lexical, prosodic, & kinesic)									
Nominal apposition									
Vowel elongations									
Deictic gestures									
Total # of clauses									

Essential Elements for Effective Narrativization:
Evaluating Events

Event aspects (evaluations)	Clause Number								Total number of clauses
	0-10	20	30	40	50	60	70	80	
Lexical									
Adjectives									
Adverbs									
Gratuitous terms									
Negatives									
Prosodic/kinesic									
Vowel elongation									
Facial expressions									
Total # of clauses									

Lexically Noncohesive Devices

(adapted from Cox, 1986/1987)

I. Potentially ambiguous references:

Devices that are potentially ambiguous occur when their presuppositions cannot be retrieved from the text:

1. Jim and Jack went to a party.
2. **He** met a girl **he** liked. Devices may be referenced exophorically

1. Beth came into the room.
2. She put her books over **there**.

or to the narrator's personal knowledge:

1. **We** wanted to build something.
2. **We** built **it** outside.

II. Potentially poor references:

Devices that are potentially poor occur when their presupposition is present in the text but is hard to retrieve. Poor referencing occurs when the presupposition is in a preceding clause that is some distance from the cohesive device or the device is related cataphorically to the presupposition (in a subsequent clause). In addition, the incorrect marking of number, gender, person, or case causes poor referencing.

III. Inappropriate voice:

Inappropriate voice occurs when the author abruptly shifts role in the story.

1. **I** was driving along the road.
2. Then **we** stopped for lunch.

Total number of clauses that contain noncohesive devices:

Total number of clauses:

Percentage of clauses that contain noncohesive devices:

[a]Number of occurrences.

Profile of essential elements for effective narrativization.

Name: _____ Birthdate: _____
Examiner: _____ School: _____

Age: _____ Grade: _____

Frequency of Use

	0	10	20	30	40	50	60	70	80	90	100

Total Number of Clauses
Total Number of Clauses Containing an Objective Perspective
Total Number of Clauses Containing a Subjective Perspective
Subjective Perspectives
  Dialogues (self and listener)
  Film viewer's perspective
Character Aspects
  Character portrayal
    Lexical
    Prosodic/kinesic
  Character perspectives
  Total
Referential Cohesion
  Nominal apposition
  Vowel elongations and deictic gestures
Event Evaluations
  Lexical evaluative statements
  Prosodic and kinesic evaluative indications

12

Cultural Influences on Language

Implications for Assessing African American Children

April Massey

Child language investigation and remediation are arduous tasks that have perhaps been approached too specifically. As Wolfram (1983) states, "the use of formal testing instruments in speech and language pathology derives from a simple concern within the profession—to provide an orderly, systematic, and convenient basis for tapping the language capabilities of a population of speakers" (p. 21). He further remarks, "objectifiable, formal measurement is a token of definitiveness that is difficult to resist" (p. 21). In our attempts to streamline intervention protocols, pertinent aspects of the dynamics that shape individuals' language practices and preferences and that help us determine their language needs and ability to meet those needs have been obscured. As Rees and Gerber (1992) state, "for practitioners whose fascination with language has led them to language disorders as a field of study and a professional commitment, language in use has turned out to be of bottomless complexity and, yet, of central importance" (p. 15). Several questions frame the intervention process. For example, what triggers language development? What social and cultural variables initiate and propel the process of language acquisition? What defines normal language development and use? How do we know if a child's language development is on target? That is to say, what variables frame the ideal interaction for gathering and assessing language development data? This list of questions speaks to the depth of the task of language investigation. As important, our clinical accuracy is predicated on the accuracy of our answers to these questions. Responding to these questions has been a driving force behind child language research. Language researchers have long undertaken the task of gathering normative data to improve assessment of the quantity and quality of children's linguistic growth. Studies of language development abound, predating the 1940s (Leopold, 1939; McCarthy, 1930; Piaget, 1926). The adequacy of the existing database given the task of language intervention in a culturally and linguistically diverse society is increasingly questioned.

This chapter examines the extent of our knowledge (theoretical and applied) on cultural influences on language development and use. It explores the implications of research for clinical practice generally and for African American children more specifically. Given the mandates of evolving special education law, recommended practice standards guiding speech-language pathology assessment and intervention, and the rapidly changing cultural/ethnic dynamic of the United States, the potential impact of this evolving body of information is far-reaching.

LANGUAGE IN CONTEXT: OUTLINING THE PROBLEM

The ultimate goal of child language research continues to be efficacy—accurate diagnoses and identification of best fit academic and therapeutic programs—in a nutshell, ensuring the realization of potential. The appropriateness of our clinical programs is necessarily tied to the extent to which a database can represent the sociocultural dynamic of a population. The degree of representation defines the limits of the generalizability of results to other members of that population, and our assumptions about "normality" are embedded in the data that we compile. Wolfram (1983) suggests that a number of questions have been raised regarding the validity of standardized measures. He remarks that "one of the most persistent issues concerns their application across cultural groups" (p. 22).

It is unfortunate that the bulk of the contributions to the child language research base prior to the 1980s flowed largely from monolithic investigations of language acquisition that practically ignored social dynamics and their impact on language. These early psycholinguistic studies investigated child–caregiver interaction, primarily mother–child interaction, and focused almost exclusively on interactional patterns across mothers and children in mainstream, middle-class, North American settings. Results supported a parent–child interaction characterized by a child-centered communicative style and modified adult input. These studies underscored the importance of the insights derived from ethnographic approaches (Rees & Gerber, 1992), but they violated basic ethnographic principles by allowing the results of this research to be promoted as standard of parent–child interaction across the United States. Ochs and Schieffelin (1984) suggest that the modified caregiver register documented in those studies is a culturally related phenomenon, reflecting the values and beliefs of that particular sociocultural group. Van Kleeck(1994) reports that this fact is little referenced with regard to the aforementioned works. Ochs and Schieffelin (1984) refer to this phenomenon as the "invisible" culture of child language studies. It is more likely that there is a continuum of communicative accommodation along which cultures vary with regard to their child–caregiver interaction (Crago, 1992). This body of research is investigated further in a later section of the chapter.

Notwithstanding their limitations, these data have been used extensively to structure language intervention. Considerable interest has been shown in clinician and caregiver input in the clinical process, and much of the training of parents to intervene with young children has been based in large part on the results of these early, methodologically limited psycholinguistic investigations. More recently, however, this practice has come under attack. Van Kleeck(1994) addresses the potential cultural biases in language intervention approaches that borrow from available research on child–caregiver interaction. She concludes that, reflective of this database, the goals of many such plans and programs are entrenched in middle-class, white family values and in no way acknowledge the culture-bound nature of child–caregiver interaction and the likelihood of variance inter- and intraculturally.

As we set forth to train parents to intervene with their children and as we as clinicians adopt intervention strategies, we must be mindful of the appropriateness of the strategies we promote. Advances in our understanding of language cross-culturally are challenging these practices. The educational and clinical application of findings drawn from this very homogeneous subject set have been questioned as researchers look to answer the question of whether there is a definition of normal language acquisition determined by who is being tested, where they live, who they live with, how they live, how they are viewed in the scheme of life, what they expect from life—in short who they are.

In the 1970s and 1980s, language scientists and clinicians witnessed very fundamental changes in the priorities of language research and clinical intervention. As ethnographers, sociolinguists, psycholinguists, and anthropologists unearthed the impact of culture on communication, the need to study language in use inter- and intraculturally within primary, natural, and routine social contexts became clear. In the 1990s there has been an increased understanding of the interdependent relationship of language and culture. Moreover, understanding of the impact of this relationship on language development and use in a heterogeneous society and the implications of this marriage for language research, clinical evaluation, and intervention have broadened.

LANGUAGE AND CULTURE

The Need for a New Paradigm

As Heath (1983) states, "language learning is cultural learning. . . . Language socialization is, in the broadest sense, the means by which individuals become members of their primary speech community and, later, the secondary speech communities beyond the family" (p. 85). An exploration of cultural influences on language warrants examining language "in use" in primary cultural environments. It would follow that studies of early developmental patterns be studies of children interacting with primary caregivers in naturally occurring circumstances. Studying cultural influences on developing communicative patterns is founded in analysis of socializing rituals and routines—the who, why, where, how, when, and what of behavior in context. What culturally relevant beliefs, values, and practices underlie child–caregiver interaction, and how are these relationships realized in language interaction?

Variance in socialization patterns that exists not only cross-culturally but also within seemingly homogeneous cultural groups must be acknowledged (Feldstein & Welkowitz, 1978). Differences across and within cultures regarding what is believed about and expected of children are considerable (Romaine, 1984). The conventions that dictate child-rearing style and have a significant impact on child–caregiver language interaction are not universal but have been shown to reflect cultural orientation (Garvey, 1984; Ochs & Schieffelin, 1983). More information is needed.

Van Kleeck(1994) suggests that there are five areas of culture that underlie or dictate child–caregiver interaction, including aspects of social organization related to interaction, the value of talk, how status is handled in interaction, and beliefs about intentionality and teaching language to children. These areas are addressed in more detail in a later section. The primary factors of interest are 1) primary partners/allowable partners, 2) allowable settings, 3) allowable topics, 4) allowable interactant styles, and 5) expectations for interaction. Across cultures different communication skills are considered important, different approaches to teaching are valued, and different situations and people are available to teach them (Crago, 1994). Furthermore, it must be acknowledged that cultures are not static and that inter- and intracultural variation in language socialization across sociohistorical time needs to be documented (Crago, 1994).

Language, then, serves as a primary vehicle for transmitting socializing rituals and routines. Its primary role is the transmission of culture. Within the American mainstream, conversation emerges as a principal language environment for giving and receiving information (Owens, 1995). Conversational exchanges, those basic give-and-take language encounters that most people find themselves engaged in several times daily as they negotiate their environments (husband to wife, father to son, boss to subordinate, clerk to customer), are a primary language resource for preserving and extending culture or patterns of socialization and the principal context for child–caregiver interaction identified in the American mainstream.

Mainstream findings support that the maintenance of cultural traditions and patterns of being begins in the child–caregiver symbiotic. The simple, nurturing child–caregiver exchanges that may start simply as caregiver-directed sound play quickly become full-blown language exchanges with the rules for participation so ingrained that the interactions proceed generally with no conscious thought. This relationship takes flight in the immediate neonatal period (mother talks, baby quiets; mother sings, baby smiles; mother tells a silly story and laughs, baby smiles and gurgles; baby burps, mother remarks that the baby must feel better) and continues to develop over the lifetimes of the partners. It is guided by cultural rules for child–caregiver interaction that are shared and enforced by the partners' cultural community. This relationship is dynamic, with shifts in partner roles predicated on the expectations and allowances of their cultural system. As much as this relationship serves to indoctrinate the child in the cultural system of his or her community, the dynamics of this association are bound to cultural dictates for caregiver–child interaction shared by that community. Terrell (1985) describes this "first relationship" and suggests that the quality of the interactions between infant and caregiver have important implications for the development of sociocommunicative and other skills.

Again, conversation—that is, language across partners—is well recognized as the primary communication context of young children and their caregivers in the mainstream. It is within the supportive and nurturing environment of the home that children are pulled into the language game. Interacting with people and contexts provides the young child with "on-the-job training" (Bernstein, 1993). Children acquire the knowledge to achieve different purposes through their communication. They learn about effects and contingencies of different communication partners and the differences in communication within different situations (Bernstein, 1993). Children learn to monitor their communicative behavior and modify it relative to their relationship with their co-interactant.

Language, then, must be examined from the perspective of its role in the human experience, the transmission of culture. Language is both a tool for transmitting culture and a tool whose use is intimately guided by the culture it serves to extend. Schieffelin (1990) suggests two major areas of socialization: 1) socialization through the use of language and 2) socialization to the use of language. The study of cultural influences on language development and use in simplest terms is the study of how young children learn to use language to manipulate their environments within the guidelines of their cultural group. Sometimes the socializing routines are explicitly taught (e.g., a parent preparing a child to meet an elder). On other occasions, one may be forced to deduce acceptable or expected behavior empirically (e.g., a mother's finger to her lips when her youngster begins talking during church service). Inter- and intracultural variations are in operation.

Nonetheless, researchers wishing to understand language development must not separate observations of linguistic performance from the contexts (persons, situations, and rules governing the interaction of those persons in that environment) that facilitate or even permit the linguistic performance being observed.

It has long been thought that language was not overtly taught to children, and emerging cross-cultural data are challenging descriptions of just how language development is facilitated (Crago, 1994; van Kleeck, 1994). Notwithstanding, it is hard to deny that cultural expectations for language interaction (whom we talk to and how we talk to them) and language content (what we can talk about given who we are, where we are, and whom we are talking to) are clearly enforced and often overtly enforced. Parents may regard this as teaching their children to be polite or socially appropriate. Language researchers refer to this aspect of language as language use or pragmatics, rules that govern language use in social contexts (Bernstein, 1993). Ochs and Schieffelin (1983) view the pragmatic or use aspect of language development as concerned with the child's ability to use language to meet specific communicative needs within the dictates of a cultural frame. Hymes (1974) called this development the development of communicative competence.

Clearly, the study of language development cannot be separated from the study of the cultural dictates of the community that the language user is a part of. As important, the relation between primary language, the cultural experiences that shape the use of that language, and success with later societal demands (e.g., school) cannot be ignored. Given the heterogeneity of American society and the continued expectation of a standard performance in mainstream interactions, the importance of the relation of primary language to mainstream language cannot be denied. Early "conversational" ability appears to have significant impact on later language learning and success. The degree of match between primary cultural-linguistic experiences (largely played out in conversational exchange) and the language expectations of mainstream institutions (e.g., school) has significant implications for success (Michaels, 1985; Roth, 1988; Tannen, 1982) and clinical intervention when warranted. The similarity or dissimilarity between primary language experiences and secondary or academic modes of language use appears to have tremendous influence over the ease or difficulty with which facility in the academic and more literate mode is acquired. This relationship refuels the difference versus disorder dilemma. The implications for clinical practice are tremendous. The acquisition of competence in standard discourse seems to hinge on the degree of match between primary language learning and use contexts and more standard use contexts. Standard practices that are discontinuous with home socialization practices, and consequently language use, present formidable challenges to the acquisition of mainstream modes of information transmission. The expanse of diversity found in and across communities precludes drawing any conclusions about cultural-linguistic groups and suggests that opportunities for mismatch between the primary and standard languages are high. The pressure to acknowledge this natural diversity in language-related behaviors is ever increasing, and descriptions of that diversity are being sought in different populations of children (Blake, 1984).

Given the argument for the need to examine language development in use in culturally relevant contexts and the relation of early acquired language skills to later life success, a summation and analysis of research addressing language development in the contexts of primary partners and primary environments follows. The discussion begins with an overview of the vast body of psycholinguistic investigations of mother–child interaction conducted primarily during the 1970s and concludes with a summary of more recent works that have targeted culturally and/or linguistically diverse groups for study. The final section of the chapter considers the impact of more recent developments in child language research on clinical practice with African American children.

Observations in Context: A Review

Naturally occurring language interactions have been studied since the 1960s (Butler, 1985; van Dijk & Kintsch, 1983; van Kleeck, 1994). A large body of mother–child studies was generated by psycholinguists during the 1960s, 1970s, and 1980s. Bloom (1970), Bates (1976), Bruner (1975, 1983), Snow (1975), Garvey (1977), Blount (1984), Corsaro (1979), and Berko-Gleason (1973), among others, systematically investigated child–caregiver interaction and patterns of accommodation and negotiation across partners during language use. This seminal research effort was motivated by interest in children's development of the ability to signal communicative intent and parents' interpretation of the children's behavior or assignment of intent. These researchers were also interested in how parents assisted the children's efforts to be communicative and, thus, shaped the children's development of language. The research presupposes that a specific parent–child interactive style and a well-tuned caregiver register exist.

Blount (1984) states that mother–infant interaction studies completed during the 1970s and 1980s are characterized by three features. The first feature described is interest in the process. Blount asserts that the coordinated interaction of mother and child has sparked a number of research questions. The second feature is the role of the infant in this process. Blount asserts that infants are viewed not merely as passive respondents to maternal initiatives, but rather as contributing in a variety of ways to the ongoing flow of interactions. The third feature is methodological. Blount asserts that this concern is necessitated by the complexity of the subject matter. The concern is how to preserve observations of mother–infant behavior for later analysis.

Several characteristics of this early interaction for both child and caregiver are described, and much of the attention of researchers compiling these data is directed at establishing the impact of the linguistic environment provided by caregivers on children's language acquisition and the universal nature of these early child–caregiver exchanges. Aspects of these interactions that were targeted include parent linguistic characteristics, the relation between child linguistic development and parent linguistic input, the context-bound nature of the exchanges, and the roles of parent and child. A brief summary of the research involving each of these aspects follows.

In 1964, Ferguson summarized research on the structural characteristics of adult speech to babies. In an article titled "Baby talk in six languages," Ferguson reports several identified cross-cultural features of "baby talk." He indicates a predominance of consonant-vocal-consonant-vocal (CVCV) and consonant-vocal-consonant (CVC) canonical structure and stop and nasal consonants. He notes that phonological reduplication is common; that inflectional affixes are generally absent, except for a special baby talk affix; and that lexical domains are mostly kin terms, body parts, and animals. Ratner and Pye (1984) indicate elevated pitch as a prominent expressive feature in mothers addressing their infants. Further "motherese" characteristics detailed include redundancy, repetitiveness, semantic relatedness, and reduced syntactic complexity, that is, shorter utterances.

The language development studies of the 1970s pursued linguistic environment issues not only to isolate the characteristics exhibited by parents but also to examine what parental input factors show adjustment and which factors influence children's development of language. Sigel and McGillicuddy-Delisi (1984) profess that numerous studies indicate that parents' speech is a critical factor in influencing children's language acquisition. They posit the belief that children's level of language ability appears to affect the way parents talk to their children. The work of Snow (1972, 1975) and others (e.g., Holzman, 1974) suggests a "syntactic fine-tuning" or "simplicity" hypothesis. This theory proposes that maternal language to young children is simplified and redundant and that the length of utterances and the syntactic complexity of maternal speech increased with the age of the child (Ringler, 1973, 1978).

The impact and extent of the so-called modified caregiver register have been questioned. Nelson, Denninger, Bonvillian, Kaplan, and Baker (1984) state that

> a debate has raged between advocates of the position that adults provide few useful language adjustments to young language-learners and advocates of the position that adults, and particularly mothers, provide fine-tailored, well-adjusted input that is maximally designed to facilitate the progress in language of children. (p. 31)

To examine this debate, Nelson et al. cited empirical illustrations that support both positions. They examined 25 mother–child pairs using an interactional model to investigate syntactic development. The pairs were followed for approximately 5 months (between 22 and 27 months of age for the children). They found that the mothers sampled did not adjust their utterances in any sensitive way to the children's utterance length. Further investigation by Nelson and colleagues revealed auxiliary use by the mothers sampled to correlate directly with the auxiliary use of their children. Examination of the children's syntactic growth relative to the contingent replies given by their mothers revealed that high maternal use of simple recasts and continuations were positively correlated with facilitating children's language growth. The role of recasts in language facilitation has also been looked at by Newport (1976) in a sample of 12- to 33-month-olds and by Wells (1980) in a sample of 18- to 42-month-olds, and it was found to be positively associated with language growth in children. The Nelson et al. study concludes that syntactic development in children 22–27 months is facilitated by maternal contingent input that is closely aligned semantically to the child's prior utterances but that shows simple structural alterations.

Newport, Gleitman, and Gleitman (1977) reported that few measures of the syntactic complexity or well-formedness of mothers' speech predicted children's language growth. Cross (1977), for example, provided evidence that suggests that syntactic aspects of speech are not the primary source of variation in adults' speech to the child. She studied mothers' speech and its association with rate of linguistic development in young children. Cross was interested in determining the relevance of 60 features of mothers' speech to their children's rates of linguistic acquisition. By process of elimination, she constructed a short list of the features that play a major role in facilitating the acquisition process. Cross wanted to isolate a small set of features that would differentiate the primary inputs to children who learn language rapidly from those children who were slower. Her findings are not conclusive, but they suggest that acceleration in linguistic acquisition is associated with an input that is substantially matched to the child's own intentions. She found that mothers of accelerated children provided an input that contained more expansions, expansionlike utterances, and semantic extensions than did mothers of children who developed more slowly. Based on the study's outcome, Cross hypothesized that it is the extent to which the mother's discourse adjustments permit the child to guess her meaning accurately that is important to acquisition. Cross further suggested that by matching the child's semantic intentions and ongoing cognitions, the mother's speech may free the child to concentrate on the formal aspects of her expression and thus enable the child to acquire syntax efficiently.

Another prominent feature detailed during these early investigations of child–caregiver interactions was the context-bound nature of the interchanges. This body of works has well established that young children and caregivers talk about the present. Children often center their interaction on objects and activities in the immediate environment. Sometimes they physically bring the objects into the environment to talk about them. Brown (1973) examined the contextualized nature of young children's speech in his longitudinal study of linguistic development in three children. He asserted that an indicator and goal of linguistic maturity is the ability to use decontextualized language. Bloom (1970), Bates (1976), and Bloom and Lahey (1978), among others, also illustrated the dependence of young children on the situational context to support or facilitate communicative interchange. These researchers also examined how parents or caregivers use the situational context to initiate and sustain interaction with young children and rely on it to comprehend the children's utterances. The classic example offered to illustrate the dependence of young children on the sociocultural context in their expression of meaning and the ambiguity that is created when adults attempt to assign meaning to young children's utterances taken out of context is the utterance "Mommy sock" of Bloom's (1970) subject Allison. In isolation this utterance can be assigned several meanings (e.g., possession, "Mommy's sock"; existence, "Mommy there's a sock"). The intent of the utterance, as determined by Bloom upon review of the physical context surrounding the child's production of the utterance, was existence. This example illustrates well the necessity of context in deciphering meaning from young children's utterances and the context-bound nature of young children's speech.

Blount (1984) asserted that infants are viewed not merely as passive respondents to maternal initiatives, but rather as contributing in a variety of ways to the ongoing flow of interactions. Gustafson, Green, and West (1974) suggest that infants help to define, sometimes extensively, the patterning of interaction. The works of Brazelton (1982), Eilers (1980), and Freedle and Lewis (1977) indicate that infants are preadapted in various ways for social interaction and their social participation reflects a natural phenomenon. Bruner (1975, 1983) described the roles of both child and parents in the language acquisition process as active. The parent serves in a facilitative role that allows or ensures the child's participation in communicative interchange (Lieven, 1978). Bruner used several terms, including *scaffolding,* as constructs to characterize the parents' framing of interaction to draw the child in.

Earlier research completed by Snow (1972) corroborates Bruner's work. The results of her research indicate that parents assign intent to behaviors of children that often are not intentional on the part of the children and build communicative interchanges around these behaviors. These dyadic interchanges are often associated with specific activities that become routinized. The research suggests that participating in these routinized interactions allows the child to develop the schemata or cognitive sets that may undergird all future language development. Dore (1986) stated that the infant's random behavior is gradually interpreted as more and more purposeful in his or her interactions with mother. MacMurray (1961) proposed that the infant's only adaptive behavior is the ability to express needs to those who think of him or her. Dore (1986) stated that, by living this way, the infant immediately partakes of both a loving and rational environment in the form of a caring, thoughtful mother. He suggested that the infant's existence requires an informed cooperation and a bonding with the mother. This union requires the unique ability to communicate. Dore purported that it is the infant's mother who gives his or her behavior meaning. The theorist alleged that even though the infant may be genetically capable of symbolic behavior, prior to this awareness he receives inputs, and after it he receives confirmation of his symbol-making attempts. Dore further said that, in this scheme, speech is a complex skill that provides the necessary means of reciprocal communication with others. MacMurray (1961) stated that long before the child learns to speak, he or she is able to communicate, meaningfully and intentionally, with his or her mother (p. 60).

This body of psycholinguistic studies initiated the "motherese" hypothesis, proposing that special properties of adult speech have an important role in language acquisition. This literature promotes parents, more specifically mothers, as children's primary communicative partner and recognizes conversation as the primary language tool employed during these child-centered exchanges. This body of work is generally inconclusive on the specific behaviors or communicative environment that facilitates language development, but it does establish that language development is aided by external input (specifically communicative interaction) and that the home environment serves as the primary environment for this interaction for the child–caregiver dyads sampled. Acknowledging this connection further underscores the relation of culture to language development and the need to investigate language in a cultural framework.

Whereas the psycholinguistic investigations of the 1960s, 1970s, and 1980s purport a general "motherese" profile, many of the sociolinguistic studies that followed investigated characteristics of this profile to demonstrate the diversity in child–caregiver interactions. The basic tenets of the "motherese hypothesis"— parent as primary language partner and the home as the primary language learning environment—have been shown to be at variance with mainstream American findings. Ratner and Pye (1984) suggest that characteristics of motherese probably differ from class to class and across sociolinguistic cultures. Bernstein (1993) indicates that aspects of maternal input and regulation may include universal characteristics as well as culturally specific aspects. She further states that the maternal linguistic differences indicate that language is ultimately the result of social interaction in specific speech communities. The next section of the chapter reviews investigations of early parent–child language interaction across various cultures.

The cry for data on the extent of cultural influence on language use continues to be echoed, but the database remains small. Crago (1994) summarized studies of language socialization across a variety of cultures. She noted 15 studies, including the works of Boggs (1985), Clancy (1986), Crago (1988), Demuth (1986), Heath (1983, 1986, 1989, 1990), and Schieffelin (1990). Van Kleeck(1994) referenced a similar body of works. Citing 23 studies, she referred to this set of work as frequently cited studies of non-American and American nondominant cultures and social groups. An expansion of the lists of Crago and Van Kleeck is presented in Table 1.

As noted, specific research on African American children has included the work of Ringler (1978), Heath (1982, 1983, 1989), Blake (1984), Vaughn-Cooke and Stockman (1986), and Massey (1992). Although the studies of Blake (1984) and Vaughn-Cooke and Stockman (1986) examined African American children's developing language systems in an interactional frame (mother–child), these researchers were interested primarily in the children's acquisition of specific lin-

Table 1 Summary of cross-cultural studies of language socialization

Reference	Research subjects or locale
Blount (1972)	Luo in Kenya
Ward (1971)	Lower SES AA
Freedman (1979)	Navajo
Schieffelin (1979), Schieffelin & Eisenberg (1984)	Kaluli of Papua New Guinea
Scollon & Scollon (1981)	Athabaskans of Alaska and Canada
Saville-Troike (1982)	Native American (Navajo)
Eisenberg (1982)	Mexican American
Ochs (1982, 1984, 1988)	Western Samoans
Heath (1982, 1983, 1989)	Lower SES AA and White
Phillips (1983)	Native American (Warm Springs Indians)
Romaine (1984)	Mohave, Tlingit
Blake (1984)	Working-class AA
Boggs (1985)	Hawaiian
Demuth (1986)	Basotho in Lesotho
Clancy (1986)	Tokyo suburbs
Waston-Gegeo & Gegeo (1986)	Kawara'ae
Miller (1982)	Lower SES White
Bridgeforth (1986)	Working-class AA
Seymour & Wyatt (1988)	Working-class AA
Vaughn-Cooke & Stockman (1986)	Working-class AA
Crago (1990)	Inuit of Arctic Quebec
Massey (1992)	Middle-class AA

Adapted from Crago (1994) and Van Kleeck (1994).

guistic behavior and did not focus on mother language input or its impact on the child's linguistic performance. Blake (1984) studied the language of three working-class children longitudinally. She examined the dimensions of form, content, and use in the children's developing language systems via interactions of the children and their mothers. Vaughn-Cooke and Stockman (1986) examined the acquisitional order and age at which working-class African American children acquire 1) categories of meaning and 2) the syntactic, morphological, and phonological forms for coding those semantic categories. Their study involved a longitudinal design, and caregiver–child interaction served as the context for data collection. Ringler (1978), Heath (1983), and Massey (1992) were specifically interested in the relation between child and mother language behavior. Brief summaries of these works follow.

Ringler (1978) completed a longitudinal study of 10 African American mothers of lower socioeconomic status (SES) and their first-born, full-term babies. The research questions addressed changes in the mother's language to the children over time and the relation between maternal input and language development. Ringler made adult-to-child and adult-to-adult comparisons. She found that the mothers' rate of speech to their children was significantly slower and that it increased as the children grew older. Shorter utterances were addressed to the children, and utterance length increased as the children grew older. In addition, she discovered that speech to the children was grammatically simpler and contained more single-clause sentences, more content words, and fewer function words. Complexity was observed to increase over time. Specific characteristics of maternal language input were correlated with the children's rate and breadth of language development at age 5.

Heath (1983) studied language use in two working-class communities (one white, Roadville; and one black, Trackton) in the Carolina Piedmonts. Heath examined the oral-literate traditions of the two communities and how those traditions are made available, taught, or shared with the children of those communities. She tracked the children's language development longitudinally and was particularly interested in their acquisition of literate forms. She describes Trackton as a rural community. She further indicates that the Trackton children's early prelinguistic vocalizations were not perceived as communicative. Heath suggests that the Trackton children were not made a part of the adult talk around them until they had mastered adult conversational skill. She concluded that the Trackton children were members of a largely oral community with strong adult-directed interaction practices for language use.

Massey (1992) used a descriptive design to examine normal variance in topic introduction (TI) behavior within a sample of seven 4-year-old, middle-class African American boys residing in the Midwest. She also investigated patterns of accommodation across child and mother communicative partners. The child–mother dyads were recorded as they interacted in their homes around routine, naturally occurring circumstances. Cohesiveness of the discourse, linguistic and nonlinguistic forms of TI utterances, frequency of occurrence of TI utterances in the discourse structure, and level of accommodation in language use across dyad partners were observed. Results support a range of normal variability for the children and mothers regarding the frequency, type, and form characteristics of TI utterances analyzed. Generally, mothers produced more language than their sons, suggesting that mothers bore the burden for keeping the interaction going. In addition, within dyads, son TI language tended to mirror the language of his mother. Facilitation of cohesion and disruption of the discourse also tended to be similar across mothers and sons within dyads. Even though mothers appeared to take responsibility for maintaining the interaction (e.g., greater number of utterances produced, greater number of TI utterances produced, greater number of TI utterances that presented as clarifiers, reprimands, and refocusers interjected seemingly to facilitate on-task behavior), the pattern of communicative accommodation across partners appeared child centered.

An analysis of the studies cited in Table 1 reveals some broad categorizations across this work along an etic/emic distinction. Some were interested in determining how data on other cultural groups compared with existing data regarding the socialization and language patterns provided their young (Heath, 1982; Massey, 1992; Miller, 1982). Others were interested in detailing the cultural and language practices of groups with no a priori assumptions about outcomes (Crago, 1990;

Ochs, 1982). Also, while all of these studies employed an interactional model and a primary environment of language use for data collection, not all of the above-mentioned studies were examining the dynamics of this interaction and the impact of these dynamics on the children's present and future language practices (Blake, 1984; Vaughn-Cooke & Stockman, 1986).

Further analysis of existing cross-cultural language socialization studies was provided by Van Kleeck(1994). She framed her discussion with five areas of culture underlying caregiver–child interaction:

1. Social organization—Who cares for children?
2. Value of talk—How is verbosity regarded, how is language taught, who teaches language, how is linguistic competence demonstrated?
3. Handling of status in social interactions—Who initiates adult–child interaction, who directs it, who adapts to whom, who carries the burden for keeping it going?
4. Beliefs regarding intentionality—Can we interpret others' intentions, and when does intentionality begin?
5. Language teaching beliefs—Is language development facilitated by conversational participation, direct teaching, observation, multiple methods?

A diversity of findings on each of these areas flows from the cited research. Some of the studies report findings that mirror outcomes of mainstream studies (for example, Massey (1992) reported a child-centered, child-directed style of child–caregiver interaction for the middle-class African American families she investigated). Ringler (1978) reported a pattern of adaptation by mothers in the sample of lower-SES African American families she studied. Other studies contrast sharply with the bulk of the mainstream research base. Miller's (1982) investigation of lower-income white families in Baltimore shows reliance on direct teaching prompts; Ward's (1971) study of rural, southern African American families reveals that children are not allowed to participate in direct discourse; and Heath (1982) reported similar findings for the Trackton community she studied. Still other studies show similarity and difference with available mainstream research. For instance, Watson-Gegeo and Gegeo (1986) studied language socialization patterns in Inuit culture and found child-centered and situation-centered communicative accommodations. For each of the five areas outlined by Van Kleeck (1994), considerable variability exists across the groups examined. For example, regarding who cares for children, parent, sibling, paid provider, and extended family schemes are revealed in the research. Relative to how talk is valued, a number of continua and expectations operate for children and include verbosity/linguistic reticence, direct teaching/no teaching, and linguistic performer/observer. Furthermore, the literature reveals a number of differences about the development of intentionality. Romaine (1984) reported that the Mohave and Tlingit also consider young infants to be capable of understanding speech. She reported that, by contrast, in some Japanese cultures the parent does not believe the baby understands anything and tends not to encourage sound play. In contrast to mainstream findings, Ochs (1982) reported that Samoan caregivers do not interpret child utterances as imperfect adult forms and generally do not expand them.

Although the number of studies is limited, the findings flowing from this body of cross-cultural language socialization research demonstrate the tremendous diversity of language socialization patterns across groups in and outside of the United States. Variability within these groups should also be expected. These data are more than sufficient to unseat any notion of a universal motherese theory. More important, they poignantly speak to the danger of applying our knowledge of mainstream language socialization patterns in clinical practice in a blanket manner. Given this diversity, no assumptions can be made about the communication practices of children and their primary providers|Familiarity with the findings of cross-cultural research and the implications of this research should be prerequisite to any clinical encounter—not to memorize these findings and catalogue them neatly into cognitive schemata for African American language practices or Inuit language practices, but to broaden our sociocultural views and understanding of individual differences and the impact of that understanding on our clinical interactions. The desired outcome is clinical encounters that are ethnographic, individualized examinations that allow for the development of best fit clinical programs. The importance of this research to clinical intervention further highlights the need to expand this data base and embed it in clinical science. It must be expected that, as this database grows, the diversity of its findings is sure to grow exponentially. The last section of the chapter examines what this growing body of sociolinguistic data implies for clinical intervention, with particular emphasis on its impact on service delivery to African American children.

Revising Clinical Science and Applying New Paradigms

To generate a profile of the ideal clinical encounter between a speech-language clinician and a language-disordered child and his or her family, one would borrow heavily from language socialization research on primary child–caregiver interactions. As the foregoing discussion illustrates, these data underscore the importance of early language experiences in primary sociocultural contexts to the development of primary and secondary language systems (e.g., school). Although the diversity of findings in this area seems endless, and the more we know the more it seems that we need to know, there are definitive clinical guidelines embedded in this research. Minimally, the following sociocultural guidelines should frame every clinical encounter.

The foundational clinical guideline that has emerged from these studies is to not generalize. Approach each client as a cultural and linguistic individual. Within seemingly homogeneous cultural or linguistic groups, even within the family unit, significant differences in communication patterns and preferences may hold. Existing data should not be used to stereotype the cultural or linguistic behaviors of a group of people. Clinicians should approach each encounter with a "clean slate" mind-set. We clearly remember the dangers of the lists of cultural behaviors (family composition or family dynamics, language(s), education, income, interests, understanding of time, expectations, likes or dislikes, etc.) generated during the 1970s and 1980s for African Americans, Asians, Hispanics, and Native Americans. Rather than demystify cultural difference, these broad generalizations further perpetuated stereotypes and led to the misidentification of difference as disorder. Make no assumptions.

The second guideline is to accept that language is a culture-governed activity and that it cannot be observed, evaluated, or remediated outside of the cultural contexts that maintain it. Decontextualized clinical encounters should be avoided and replaced with formats that regard what children routinely do, where, and with whom as they give and get information in the process of satisfying daily living needs. Though not void of bias, sociocultural assessment formats have been shown to provide much more comprehensive pictures of children's language abilities. Sociocultural methods allow children to demonstrate the expanse of their linguistic competence and its socially appropriate application in ongoing dyadic or multi-partner interactions, in other words, their communicative competence. Our understanding of these early culture-based language exchanges has important implications for predicting later life success. Preschool language competence and the cultural similarity of the home have been identified as predictable determinants of successful mastery of academic language.

The third guideline is to subordinate clinician expectations and desired outcomes to culturally relevant, contextually necessary, client-directed expectations and desired outcomes. Intervention plans should be dynamic and flexible and show considerable consistency with the daily language needs and uses of the client. This type of plan will have a considerably greater impact on the quality of the client's communicative functioning because it will be better suited to establishing usable, "generalizable" change.

The fourth guideline is to be familiar with your own preferences and biases about communication patterns and understand how those preferences may potentially affect clinical interaction. If you do not believe that a particular social dialect has linguistic legitimacy, how might your judgments of a client's communication functioning be affected? Can you provide fair, unbiased services to the client? Is your awareness of your potential biases sufficient to override them in the clinical setting? If not, do you or the client have other options? These questions need to be addressed long before the client is standing at your office door.

Should There Be Special Considerations for African American Children?

Seemingly, the findings of cross-cultural language socialization studies hold the same benefits clinically for African American children as they do for any other potential client base. Nonetheless, special concern for how African American children may or may not benefit from the outcomes of sociocultural language investigations is not unfounded. Social scientific investigations of African American children's language development and patterns of use have historically been shrouded in bias. The research and clinical evaluation of African American children's language has an offensive history and an uncertain future. African American children have been and continue to have their communication needs disproportionately underserved or inappropriately served. African American male children are misdiagnosed at significantly higher rates than children in other groups (Boykins & Toms, 1985; Cole, 1986; Mercer, 1983). No assumptions can be made about the impact of recent sociolinguistic developments on service delivery to this population.

Since the early 1980s, Stockman and Vaughn-Cooke, among many others, have lauded the benefits of using sociocultural language intervention methods with African American children (e.g., Stockman & Vaughn-Cooke, 1981). Stockman (1986) eloquently, but fiercely, describes the benefits of naturalistic methods and the inappropriateness of applying mainstream standards in assessment and remediation for African American children. Yet it is still not uncommon to see clinicians continuing to expend energy arguing the legitimacy of African American children's language systems relative to a mainstream standard while ignoring the benefits of our sociocultural language knowledge and the demonstrated appropriateness of the use of this framework with such children. Furthermore, available sociocultural data on African American families have been consistently relegated to creating new stereotypes and perpetuating equally damaging difference versus disorder debates.

What Should Happen?   Truly there is no magic, no special formula. When interfacing with African American children clinically, each of the four guidelines outlined applies. The geographic proximity of African Americans to mainstream groups in no way in gains the sociocultural complexity or diversity of this population. Neither can a degree of assimilation be assumed nor can we assume or estimate any impact of exposure to mainstream media such as television. As important, cultural group assignment should not be made synonomous with race or skin color, and even within groups identified as a cultural community, cultural variation exists. Clinicians who desire to sidestep the clinical traps imposed by decades of damaging research on African American children should 1) make no assumptions, 2) formulate clinical judgments in appropriate sociocultural contexts, 3) allow the client's functional daily communication needs to dictate the intervention plan, and 4) be familiar with his or her own biases and what potential impact they may have on the clinical encounter. In other words, provide African American clients the same culturally relevant and culturally sensitive practices that all clients should be afforded.

CONCLUSIONS

The breadth of cultural influence on language use and development has yet to be characterized, is theoretically as broad as the world census, and is in no way as limited as investigations of one group. Cross-linguistic data continue to underscore the cultural specificity of language interaction, particularly the early child–caregiver interaction that frames important stages of language development and use. The connections between the interactive aspects of primary language both developed and used in the home and secondary language requirements continue to be interpreted.

As unbiased, nondistorting paradigms for studying language development that consider cultural dictates on language development and use across contexts continue to be uncovered, it is imperative that minority groups, particularly African American children, be represented in the research and that the outcomes of the research be applied in appropriate ways clinically and educationally. The ways and means of supporting and promoting the linguistic growth of students, particularly minority students, in primary and secondary language environments depend on accurate, culturally relevant pictures of their language abilities—their ability to participate in the exchange of information and the construction of infrastructures that minimize the potential mismatch between their primary language facility and the expectation for language use in secondary environments. The more accurate the profile of functioning, the more appropriate the "bridges" constructed and the higher the quality of the educational and clinical services afforded children, particularly minority children, will be.

REFERENCES

Bates, E. (1976). *Language and context: The acquisition of pragmatics.* New York: Academic Press.

Berko-Gleason, J. (1973). Code switching in children's language. In T.E. Moore (Ed.), *Cognitive development and the acquisition of language* (pp. 159–167). New York: Academic Press.

Bernstein, D.K. (1993). The nature of language and its disorders. In D.K. Bernstein & E. Tiegerman (Eds.), *Language and communication disorders in children* (3rd ed., pp. 1–23). New York: Charles E. Merrill.

Blake, I. (1984). *Language development in working-class black children: An examination of form, content, and use.* Unpublished doctoral dissertation, Columbia University, New York.

Bloom, L. (1970). *Language development: Form and function in emerging grammars.* Cambridge, MA: MIT Research Monograph 59.

Bloom, L., & Lahey, M. (1978). *Language development and language disorders.* New York: John Wiley & Sons.

Blount, B.G. (1972). Aspects of Luo socialization. *Language in Society, I,* 235–248.

Blount, B.G. (1984). Mother-infant interaction features and functions of parental speech in English and Spanish. In A. Pellegrini & T. Yawkey (Eds.), *The development of oral and written language in social contexts* (pp. 3–29). Norwood, NJ: Ablex.

Boggs, S.T. (1985). *Speaking, relating, and learning: A study of Hawaiian children at home and at school.* Norwood, NJ: Ablex.

Boykin, A.W., & Toms, F.D. (1985). Black child socialization: A conceptual framework. In H.P. McAdoo & J.L. McAdoo (Eds.), *Black children: Social, educational, and parental environments* (pp. 35–51). Beverly Hills, CA: Sage.

Brazelton, T.B. (1982). Joint regulation of neonate-parent behavior. In E.Z. Tronick (Ed.),

Social interchange in infancy: Affect, cognition, and communication (pp. 7–22). Baltimore: University Park Press.

Bridgeforth, S. (1986). *The language functions of three- and four-year-old black children from working-class families.* Unpublished doctoral dissertation, Georgetown University, Washington, DC.

Brown, R. (1973). *A first language: The early stages.* Cambridge, MA: Harvard University Press.

Bruner, J. (1975). The ontogenesis of speech acts. *Journal of Child Language, 2,* 1–19.

Bruner, J. (1983). *Child's talk: Learning to use language.* New York: Norton.

Butler, K. (1985). From the editor. *Topics in Language Disorders, 5*(2), iv–v.

Clancy, P.M. (1986). The acquisition of communicative style in Japanese. In B. Schieffelin & E. Ochs (Eds.), *Language socialization across cultures* (pp. 213–250) New York: Cambridge University Press.

Cole, L. (1986). The social responsibility of the researcher. In F. Bess, B. Clark, & H. Mitchell (Eds.), *Concerns for minority groups in communication disorders.* ASHA Report 16. Rockville, MD: American Speech-Language-Hearing Association.

Corsaro, W. (1979). Young children's conception of status and role. *Sociology of Education, 56,* 46–59.

Crago, M.B. (1988). *Cultural context in communicative interaction of young Inuit children.* Unpublished doctoral dissertation, McGill University, Montreal.

Crago, M.B. (1990). The development of communicative competence in Inuit children of northern Quebec: Implications for speech-language pathology. *Journal of Childhood Communication Disorders, 13*(1), 54–76.

Crago, M.B. (1992). Ethnography and language socialization: A cross-cultural perspective. *Topics in Language Disorders, 12*(3), 28–39.

Crago, M.B. (1994). Ethnography and language socialization: A cross-cultural perspective. In K. Butler (Ed.), *Cross-cultural perspectives in language assessment and intervention* (pp. 3–12). Gaithersburg, MD: Aspen.

Cross, T. (1977). Mothers' speech adjustments: The contribution of child listener variables. In C. Snow & C. Ferguson (Eds.), *Talking to children: Language input and acquisition* (pp. 151 100). Cambridge: Cambridge University Press.

Demuth, K. (1986). Prompting routines in the language socialization of Basotho children. In B. Schieffelin & E. Ochs (Eds.), *Language socialization across cultures* (pp. 51–79). New York: Cambridge University Press.

Dore, J. (1986). The development of conversational competence. In R. Schiefelbusch (Ed.), *Language competence: Assessment and intervention* (pp. 3–60). San Diego, CA: College-Hill Press.

Eilers, R.E. (1980). Infant speech perception: History and mystery. In G.H. Yeni-Kamshian, J.F. Kavanaugh, & C.A. Ferguson (Eds.), *Child phonology: Vol. 2. Perception* (pp. 23–39). New York: Academic.

Eisenberg, A. (1982). *Language acquisition in cultural perspective: Talk in three Mexican homes.* Unpublished doctoral dissertation, University of California, Berkeley.

Feldstein, S., & Welkowitz, J. (1978). A chronography of conversation: In defense of an objective approach. In A. Siegman & S. Feldstein (Eds.), *Nonverbal behavior and communication* (pp. 327–378). Hillsdale, NJ: Lawrence Erlbaum Associates.

Ferguson, C.A. (1964). Baby talk in six languages. *American Anthropologist, 66,* 103–114.

Freedle, R., & Lewis, M. (1977). Prelinguistic conversations. In M. Lewis & L.A. Rosenblum (Eds.), *Interaction, conversation, and the development of language* (pp. 157–185). New York: John Wiley & Sons.

Freedman, D. (1979, January). Ethnic differences in babies. *Human Nature Magazine,* pp. 36–43.

Garvey, C. (1977). The contingent query. In M. Lewis & L.A. Rosenblum (Eds.), *Interac-*

tion, conversation, and the development of language (pp. 63–93). New York: John Wiley & Sons.

Garvey, C. (1984). *Children's talk*. Cambridge, MA: Harvard University Press.

Gustafson, G.E., Green, J.A., & West, M.J. (1979). The infant's changing role in mother-infant games. The growth of social skills. *Infant Behavior and Development, 2*, 301–308.

Heath, S.B. (1982). What no bedtime story means: Narrative skills at home and at school. *Language in Society, 11*(1), 49–76.

Heath, S.B. (1983). *Ways with words: Language, life, and work in communities and classrooms*. New York: Cambridge University Press.

Heath, S.B. (1986). Sociocultural contexts of language development. In *Beyond language: Social and cultural factors in schooling language minority children* (pp. 143–186). Developed by the Bilingual Education Office, California State Department, Sacramento. Los Angeles: Evaluation, Dissemination, and Assessment Centre.

Heath, S.B. (1989). The learner as cultural member. In M. Rice & R.L. Schiefelbusch (Eds.), *The teachability of language* (pp. 333–350). Baltimore: Paul H. Brookes Publishing Co.

Heath, S.B. (1990). The children of Trackton's children: Spoken and written language in social change. In J.W. Stigler, R.A. Shweder, & G. Herdt (Eds.), *Cultural psychology* (pp. 496–519). New York: Cambridge University Press.

Holzman, M. (1974). The verbal environment provided by mothers for their very young children. *Merrill-Palmer Quarterly, 20*, 31–42.

Hymes, D. (1974). The ethnography of speaking. In B.G. Blount (Ed.), *Language, culture, and society: A book of readings* (pp. 189–223). Cambridge: Winthrop.

Leopold, W. (1939). *Speech development of a bilingual child* (4 vols.). Evanston, IL: Northwestern University Press.

Lieven, E. (1978). Conversations between mothers and young children: Individual differences and their possible implications for the study of language learning. In N. Watson & C. Snow (Eds.), *The development of communication* (pp. 173–187). New York: John Wiley & Sons.

MacMurray, J. (1961). *Persons in relation*. London: Faber.

Massey, A. (1992). *Topic initiation in a sample of four year old males*. Unpublished doctoral dissertation, Howard University, Washington, DC.

McCarthy, M. (1930). *The language development of the preschool child*. Institute of Child Welfare Monograph Series No. 4. Minneapolis: University of Minnesota Press.

Mercer, J.R. (1983). Issues in the diagnosis of language disorders in students whose primary language is not English. *Topics in Language Disorders, 3*, 46–56.

Michaels, S. (1985). Hearing the connections in children's oral and written discourse *Journal of Education, 167*(1), 36–56.

Miller, P. (1982). *Amy, Wendy, and Beth: Learning language in South Baltimore*. Austin: University of Texas Press.

Nelson, K., Denninger, M., Bonvillian, J., Kaplan, B., & Baker, N. (1984). Maternal input adjustments and nonadjustments as related to children's linguistic advances and to language acquisition theories. In A. Pellegrini & T. Yawkey (Eds.), *The development of oral and written language in social contexts* (pp. 31–56). Norwood, NJ: Ablex Publishing.

Newport, E. (1976). At morning it's lunchtime: A scriptal view of children's dialogues. *Discourse Processes, 2*, 73–94.

Newport, E., Gleitman, H., & Gleitman, L. (1977). Mother I'd rather do it myself: Some effects and non-effects of maternal speech style. In C. Snow & C. Ferguson (Eds.), *Talking to children: Language input and acquisition* (pp. 109–150). Cambridge, MA: Cambridge University Press.

Ochs, E. (1982). Talking to children in Western Samoa. *Language in Society, 11*, 77–104.

Ochs, E. (1988). *Culture and language development: Language acquisition and language socialization in a Samoan village.* New York: Cambridge University Press.

Ochs, E., & Schieffelin, B. (1983). *Acquiring conversational competence.* Boston: Routledge & Kegan Paul.

Ochs, E., & Schieffelin, B. (1984). Language acquisition and socialization: Three developmental stories and their implications. In R.A. Shweder & R.A. LeVine (Eds.), *Culture theory: Essays on mind, self, and emotion* (pp. 276–322). New York: Cambridge University Press.

Owens, R. (1995). *Language disorders: A functional approach to assessment and intervention* (2nd ed.). New York: Merrill.

Piaget, J. (1926). *The language and thought of the child.* London: Routledge & Kegan Paul.

Philips, S.U. (1983). *The invisible culture.* New York: Longman.

Ratner, N., & Pye, C. (1984). Higher pitch in BT is not universal: Acoustic evidence from Quiche Mayan. *Journal of Child Language, 11,* 515–522.

Rees, N., & Gerber, S. (1992). Ethnography and communication: Social-role relations. *Topics in Language Disorders, 12*(3), 15–27.

Ringler, N. (1973). *Mothers' language to their children and adults over time.* Unpublished doctoral dissertation, Case Western Reserve University, Cleveland, OH.

Ringler, N. (1978). A longitudinal study of mothers' language. In N. Waterson & C. Snow (Eds.), *The development of communication* (pp. 151–158). New York: John Wiley & Sons.

Romaine, S. (1984). *The language of children and adolescents: The acquisition of communicative competence.* Oxford: Basil Blackwell.

Roth, F. (1988, April). *Discourse patterns of learning disabled students: A view toward assessment and intervention.* Paper presented at the Howard University Mini-Conference Series in Communication Disorders, Washington, DC.

Saville-Troike, M. (1982). *The ethnography of communication: An introduction.* Oxford: Basil Blackwell.

Schieffelin, B. (1979). Getting it together: An ethnographic approach to the study of the development of communicative competence. In E. Ochs & B.B. Schieffelin (Eds.), *Developmental pragmatics* (pp. 93–108). New York: Academic Press.

Schieffelin, B. (1990). *The give and take of everyday life.* New York: Cambridge University Press.

Schieffelin, B., & Eisenberg, A. (1984). Cultural variation in children's conversations. In R. Schiefelbusch & J. Pickar (Eds.), *The acquisition of communicative competence* (pp. 377–422). Baltimore: University Park Press.

Scollon, R., & Scollon, S. (1981). *Narrative, literacy, and face in interethnic communication.* Norwood, NJ: Ablex.

Seymour, H., & Wyatt, T. (1988). *Code switching behavior in African-American children.* Paper presented at the annual meeting of the National Black Association for Speech, Language, and Hearing, Washington, DC.

Sigel, I., & McGillicuddy-Delisi, A. (1984). Parents as teachers of their children: A distancing behavior model. In A. Pellegrini & T. Yawkey (Eds.), *The development of oral and written language in social contexts* (pp. 71–92). Norwood, NJ: Ablex.

Snow, C. (1972). Mothers' speech to children learning language. *Child Development, 43,* 549–565.

Snow, C. (1975). The development of conversation between mothers and babies. *Pragmatics Microfiche.* 1.6 AZ.

Stockman, I. (1986). Language acquisition in culturally diverse populations: The black child as a case study. In O. Taylor (Ed.), *Nature of communication disorders in cultur-*

ally and linguistically diverse populations (pp. 117–155). San Diego, CA: College-Hill Press.

Tannen, D. (1982). The oral/literate continuum in discourse. In D. Tannen (Ed.), *Spoken and written language: Exploring orality and literacy* (pp. 1–16). Norwood, NJ: Ablex.

Terrell, B. (1985). Learning the rules of the game: Discourse skills in early childhood. In D. Ripich & F. M. Spinelli (Eds.), *School discourse problems* (pp. 13–28). San Diego: College-Hill Press.

vanDijk, T.A., & Kintsch, W. (1983). *Strategies of discourse comprehension.* New York: Academic Press.

van Kleeck, A. (1994, January). Potential cultural bias in training parents as conversational partners with their children who have delays in language development. *Journal of Speech-Language Pathology,* 67–78.

Vaughn-Cooke, A.F., & Stockman, I. (1986). Implications of a semantic category research for language assessment of nonstandard speakers. *Topics in Language Disorders, 6,* 15–26.

Ward, M. (1971). *Them children: A study in language learning.* Prospect Heights, IL: Waveland Press.

Watson-Gegeo, K., & Gegeo, D. (1986). Calling-out and repeating routines in kwara'ae children's language socialization. In B.B. Schieffelin & E. Ochs (Eds.), *Language socialization across cultures* (pp. 17–50). New York: Cambridge University Press.

Wells, G. (1981). *Language through interaction.* New York: Cambridge University Press.

Wolfram, W. (1983). Test interpretation and sociolinguistic differences. *Topics in Language Disorders, 3*(3), 21–34.

13

Written Language Abilities of African American Children and Youth

Cheryl M. Scott and Lisa M. Rogers

In a book about language development and disorders of African American children, a chapter about writing may seem unusual. Speech-language pathologists have not always considered the assessment and remediation of children's writing to be within their scope of practice. The history of research in African American children's language has been one of inquiry into spoken language (phonological and syntactic development), the use of African American English (AAE), and narrative discourse. Writing has received much less attention. However, there are several important reasons for language clinicians to concern themselves with writing. This chapter begins with a discussion of the place of writing in early language and literacy development and the importance of writing throughout schooling. The following section provides a summary and critical analysis of the existing research on the writing of African American children and adolescents. The final section discusses possible implications of this material for

This work is supported in part by grant #H029B20224 from the U.S. Department of Education, Office of Special Education and Rehabilitative Services.

the assessment and teaching of writing to African American children in clinical and education settings.

THE PLACE OF WRITING IN
LANGUAGE DEVELOPMENT AND SCHOOLING

Writing in Early Literacy

One reason for addressing writing as central in the discussion of African American children's language has to do with the place of writing in early literacy development. To many, the term *literacy* is synonymous with reading. This is understandable because most people spend considerably more time reading than writing. Even so, writing is of crucial importance in both the early stages and the long-term development of literacy.

As one of several possible modalities of language expression, writing begins to develop long before the writing "lessons" of school and can therefore be viewed as a naturally unfolding cognitive and linguistic activity worthy of study in its own right (Scott, 1989). Between the ages of 3 and 5, children produce lines of scribble, strings of forms (e.g., lines, half-circles), letterlike forms, and even real letters and words. Such writing is produced both spontaneously during drawing and "reading" activities and in response to specific requests to "write something" by an adult (Ferreiro, 1984; Sinclair, 1984). Eventually, children become spelling "inventors" who follow underlying principles as they write (e.g., one letter equals one syllable). Students of children's early writing stress the constructive aspects of the process and emphasize the logical problems that must be solved (Clay, 1991; Himley, 1986; Scinto, 1983).

Writing develops hand in hand with reading from the child's earliest literacy socialization experiences through adult levels of literacy. Examples of reading and writing interactions have been documented by Dobson (1988), who observed young children during naturalistic reading and writing activities over 2 years. She identified five levels of advancing print awareness and showed how particular levels of awareness developed first in either reading or in writing. To illustrate, the awareness that spoken text should match written text developed first when children "read" their own "writing" (i.e., not when they "read" real books). Children demonstrated such awareness by making a unit-to-unit match between words in a message and printed letters or by tracking a line of print several times until the spoken message was finished. The same strategies developed at a later time when children "read" others' writing (e.g., storybooks).

Further support for early connections between reading and writing comes from investigations into invented spelling. Sulzby, Branz, and Buhle (1993) emphasized the role of invented spelling, a writing activity, as an indicator of children's phonemic awareness, a skill thought to be crucial in early reading (Blachman, 1994). These researchers, in a longitudinal study of emergent literacy, concluded that invented spelling was a more sensitive indicator of phonemic awareness than more widely used tasks such as segmentation and blending. It was also an activity that could be relatively easily elicited by teachers.

These and other studies underscore the fact that children learn things about reading through the act of writing and vice versa. Throughout schooling, reading and writing are so intertwined that it is difficult to think of children doing one without the other (e.g., writing answers to comprehension questions, reading to gain more information for writing). Reading and writing are also interconnected from the perspective of the "true" purpose of school writing. With some reluctance, Moffett (1988) concluded that the major purpose of writing in school is "to test reading—either reading comprehension, or the comprehensiveness of one's reading" (p. 73).

Cultural and Individual Factors in Early Literacy   Culture and ethnicity, as well as individual differences, can be expected to influence literacy development. The vast majority of projects on early literacy have studied white children, many of them growing up in "high-print" homes where parents provide particular kinds of scaffolding for early reading and writing (Westby, 1994). The often-cited work of Heath (1983) in the Piedmont Carolinas underscores differences among townspeople, working-class African American, and working-class white families in the literacy contexts provided for children. Specific to writing, Heath (1983) found that different types and amounts of writing characterized adults in the three groups. In the homes of townspeople, children observed adults writing lists and recipes (i.e., the use of writing as a memory aid), messages, and social and business letters. Adults in town homes also wrote the occasional longer informational text (e.g., reports brought home from work, church meeting summaries). Children in working-class families observed adults writing messages and lists, but there were even fewer occasions to observe writing of more extended texts such as letters or reports. Although there were few occasions for observing longer texts, Heath (1989) was impressed with the value the community placed on written texts and the group oral negotiation that surrounded writing events. She hypothesized that these "community" contexts for writing were, perhaps, a better match for the realities of the workplace where collaboration over written texts is common. Such contexts contrasted, however, with the "solo" nature of academic writing, resulting in wider gaps between home and school literacy experiences for children from working-class families (Heath, 1983, 1989).

Individual as well as cultural differences can also be expected in early writing. Walter (1994) observed a group of Native American children in a Head Start program weekly over the course of a school year. The program provided an environment where literacy activities could be self-chosen (e.g., a reading corner, a writing table). Walter found three levels of literacy engagement (both reading and writing) among the children. Twenty-two percent of the children displayed *high literacy engagement*. These were children who attempted to "read," who could retell stories using story language, and who recognized words and others' names.

The children also liked to write and wrote their first name as well as others' names. Thirty-nine percent of the children showed *little literacy engagement.* They could not retell stories, were not aware that print "said" something, scribbled for their name, and were generally uninterested in writing. An equal number of the children, a *mid-literacy engagement* group, fell somewhere between the high and low groups. Walter (1994) did not observe the children at home and therefore was unable to associate home literacy experiences with preschool engagement levels. The children's backgrounds were thought to be relatively homogeneous, however, as they were members of one tribe and most lived on the tribal reservation. Although there is no comparable study of African American children, similar individual differences in early literacy engagement among children from otherwise comparable homes could be expected.

Writing as a Special Form of Language

A second reason for the importance of writing as a topic in language learning stems from its uniqueness both as a linguistic process (cognitive activity) and a linguistic product (form). The writing process allows time for contemplation. As such, it differs from speaking, an on-line language production activity with more demanding time constraints. A writer might conceivably spend several minutes producing just one sentence. The writer needs to think about the audience, how the content of the sentence fits within the broader text, and the most effective lexical and syntactic forms to convey the content. Several revisions of the sentence are likely. A speaker who takes a minute to produce each sentence would soon be without listeners. This major difference in process contributes to form differences between written and spoken language. Even very young writers show that they know (albeit unconsciously) about writing and speaking differences because they write sentences that they would be unlikely to say (Perera, 1986; Scott, 1989, 1995). As a result of its unique form, writing can be difficult to process by ear when speakers read from a written text. Writing is better read than heard, but speaking is better heard.

Differences between spoken and written language at the sentence level have been studied extensively by Halliday (1985, 1987) and Biber (1986, 1988, 1992). One of the major differences is the emphasis on nominal embedding in writing. Written sentences more frequently contain long subject and object noun phrases (NP) with considerable degrees of premodification and postmodification of head nouns. Information coded in such nominal constructions in written language tends to be coded in spoken language in subject–predicate (clause) form (e.g., "Yanis followed a wandering goat" in writing, but "a goat went up a mountain off too far away from the herd and Yanis followed it" when spoken).

Scott (1994, 1995) has reviewed how such sentential differences in written and spoken form develop in children and the potential implications for academic performance. By the age of 10, children's writing begins to take on this more "written" form (Perera, 1986). Of particular interest for the present chapter, a similar distinction between nominal expansion (or complementation as it is sometimes called) and verbal complementation is also said to characterize topic-centered versus topic-associating narrative organization (Gee, 1986; Westby, 1994). Whether the topic-associating spoken narrative style of some African American children is as transferable to written form as the topic-centered style of mainstream children is a question examined further in the following section.

Once a child becomes a fluent writer, the relationship between written and spoken language is, in all probability, a reciprocal one. Thus, forms learned in a written context (both read and written by the child) may transfer to spoken language for use in academic contexts, such as oral argumentation and reporting.

Writing and Success in School and Work

A third rationale for including the topic of writing concerns the crucial gatekeeping role played by writing in academic and work life (Gee, 1986). Regardless of their speaking skills, children and adolescents who have difficulty spelling, forming grammatical sentences, and organizing texts for particular audiences will be at a serious disadvantage in academic settings (Gee, 1986). Popular and professional literature on American education abounds with references to the importance of writing in the curriculum. Students who are unable to spell and write at acceptable levels are at a much greater risk for dropping out. If they manage to graduate from high school, poor writers face continuous risk whether they pursue more education or enter the work force.

It should be acknowledged also that academic and occupational standards for written form permit little, if any, variation. Whereas standards of spelling in earlier centuries were more flexible when fewer people were literate (Corbett, 1981), the printing press and the spread of literacy have led to narrowed choices for modern writers, so that almost all words have one and only one sanctioned spelling. There is little tolerance for spelling errors. One misspelling in a text of 1,000 or more words is unacceptable in most academic and occupational contexts. Grammatical forms characteristic of Standard American English (SAE) are more likely to be required by teachers and work supervisors in written language. Thus, a teacher might find "they was all there for the funeral" acceptable as a spoken utterance from a dialect speaker but unacceptable when written by the same person. Whereas a student might be able to conceal certain reading difficulties or inaccuracies, writing is there for all to see.

In summary, writing plays a central role in literacy development. In addition, writing has unique structural properties that must be learned and contributes to academic and occupational success. It is important, then, to ask about the writing development of African American children and youth. The next section takes a broad view of the topic of writing development, reviewing studies from kindergarten through college levels.

THE DEVELOPMENT OF WRITING
IN AFRICAN AMERICAN CHILDREN AND YOUTH

A myriad of topics are of interest on the general subject of writing development. For the very young writer, topics include emergent writing and invented spelling in the early school years, as well as the literacy environment of the home. Conventional writing could be studied with an emphasis on sentence grammar or spelling (i.e., a form emphasis) or text-level concerns (e.g., text organization, coherence). Writing researchers have turned their attention to writing processes in addition to products. When processes are the focus of attention, questions about how children actually plan, generate, and revise their writing come to the fore (Bereiter & Scardamalia, 1987; Hayes & Flower, 1980, 1987). Because writing develops over a long time, the writing products and processes characteristic of adolescents and even young adults are also of interest.

Data-based research on writing development in African American children and youth is sparse, with wide gaps in coverage. A major focus of investigators in the 1970s and early 1980s was the use of AAE forms in writing. The extent to which speakers of AAE use the same forms when they write has been studied across the elementary and secondary grades. Unfortunately, the use of different protocols for collecting writing samples and calculating occurrences of AAE forms complicates comparisons among studies. To the authors' knowledge, the longitudinal data that would be necessary for a complete developmental picture on the use of AAE in writing are not available.

In addition to a relatively large body of work on AAE forms in writing, a few investigators have looked into other topics. The work of Heath (1983) remains one of the few ethnographic studies of early literacy socialization in African American working-class families. A 5-year longitudinal investigation of emergent writing and reading in low-socioeconomic status (SES) children is in progress (Olson & Sulzby, 1991; Sulzby et al., 1993). Secondary writing by African American students on the National Assessment of Educational Progress assessments has been analyzed by Smitherman (1992). Additional information on writing as it develops in African American children can be found in the occasional case study and anecdotal account. Several articles suggest causes for the failure of many African American children to develop sufficient levels of literacy, including writing. And, of course, authors have been willing to suggest potential remedies specific to particular writing difficulties or concerned more broadly with literacy and academic success.

Emergent Writing

It is well known that many children engage in reading- and writing-like behaviors (emergent reading and writing) before they become more or less accurate readers of unfamiliar texts and writers at the text level (conventional reading and writing). Examples of emergent writing include the use of scribbling, letter-like forms, and invented spelling with real letters to "write" words, sentences, and entire stories or other texts (Ferreiro, 1984; Sinclair, 1984). Such writing has been shown to occur at home and in preschool, kindergarten, and early elementary classrooms both spontaneously and in response to teacher (or researcher) requests to "write a story your own way." Studies of emergent literacy with mainstream children reveal an abundant inventory of behaviors and concepts about reading and writing that are presumed to be significant for later conventional literacy (Bissex, 1980; Dyson, 1986; Sulzby, 1985).

Sulzby and colleagues recently reported on emergent writing (and reading) of children in eight low-SES urban kindergarten and first-grade classrooms (Olson & Sulzby, 1991; Sulzby et al., 1993). A majority of the children were African American. These reports summarize results from the first 2 years of a 5-year longitudinal project (Computers in Early Literacy; Sulzby et al., 1993). The researchers are analyzing the results of classroom observations and interviews and elicited samples of the children's writing and reading with and without computers. Children participated in one-on-one interactions with the researchers during which they were asked to tell a story and then to "write" a story and "reread" it. The children were told that their written story did not have to be like "grown-up writing" and that they could do it "their own way" (Sulzby et al., 1993, p. 191). The children were also asked to "read" a story that had been read repeatedly by their teacher. The children's letter-sound-word knowledge was also probed.

The major finding was that the African American children engaged in emergent reading and writing in developmental patterns similar to those of other groups studied by Sulzby (1985). The low-SES children were described as more adamant in their initial refusals to "read" and write than middle SES children, making statements such as "I cannot do that" (Sulzby et al., 1993, p. 193). Once reassured that they could do it their own way, however, they were willing to participate. Sulzby et al. (1993) provided no descriptions or examples of the children's writing. However, they reported that the low-SES children did not perform as well as middle-SES children in phonemic awareness as indicated by invented spelling, but were responsive to modeling and supportive elicitation of invented spelling. An important finding was that emergent writing was rarely encouraged by teachers of the low-SES classrooms. Rather, writing activities were restricted to isolated phonics lessons and copying model stories from the chalkboard.

To evaluate the effect of computers on emergent literacy, the same low-SES classrooms and several middle-SES classrooms in another community were supplied with Macintosh SE computers, along with MacPaint, Playroom, and StoryWriter software (Olson & Sulzby, 1991). The children were shown in small groups how the programs worked. This was followed by sessions when they could use the software with the help of the researchers. Afterward, they were free to choose the programs they wished to use either independently or with classmates. Computer writing was observed in naturalistic contexts and in response to researchers' requests to compose and "read" the resulting text. In naturalistic contexts, the children chose to work at the computer, either independently or collaboratively, and the researchers were passive observers.

Results indicated that kindergarten children rarely advanced to the stage of composing actual stories, even though many of them were able to compose with paper and pencil. Rather, they used the computer to scribble and draw, made random and patterned letter strings, and practiced invented spelling. They also made lists of conventionally spelled words. In the first grade, unelicited story composition increased steadily, with a mixture of invented spelling and conventionally spelled words. Low-SES children traversed the same stages and showed the same patterns as middle-SES children, but at a slower rate. Olson and Sulzby (1991) cautioned that differences in the two groups' performance may be attributed to several factors. One was that computers had been in place in the middle-SES classroom longer. Another was the teachers' familiarity with emergent literacy facilitation techniques and computers as writing tools. Teachers of the low-SES children did not have as much experience and training as the teachers of middle-SES children. Thus, it appears that the rate differences in groups could be explained by extrinsic factors.

Olson and Sulzby (1991) elaborated on ways in which paper-and-pencil and computer writing differed for these young children. The nature of electronic text, keyboard entry, and interactions necessitates different writing strategies but did not seem to discourage the children. An initial obstacle might become a facilitator later on. For example, automatic reformatting caused the children to lose their place in the text, but later they used this to advantage "in deliberate ways as they arranged and edited text" (p. 116). Researchers observed relatively more collaborative computer writing than paper-and-pencil writing.

The researchers concluded that computers were a useful tool in the total emergent literacy scheme. More important, the common observations across two sites (low-SES classrooms in Pontiac, Michigan, and middle-SES classrooms in Ann Arbor) strengthen the interpretation of emergent writing as a developmental phenomenon. As shown elsewhere in this book, poor urban African American children have other linguistic skills that support emergent literacy (e.g., complex syntax, as studied by Craig & Washington, 1994).

Writing at the Elementary Level

In the early elementary years, children move from emergent to conventional writing. Whereas writing in any form (e.g., letter-like forms, invented spelling) may have been encouraged and rewarded in kindergarten and first grade, standard spelling and grammar are soon expected. The young elementary child faces the simultaneous requirements of legible printing, conventional spelling, punctuation, capitalization, formulation at the sentence and text levels, and audience presupposition (i.e., what the absent reader knows and doesn't know about the topic). In comparison to speaking, texts of beginning conventional writers are frequently less complex at the level of sentence grammar (Kroll, 1981), a finding that some attribute to the competing simultaneous requirements of early writing when the mechanics of writing and spelling are not yet automatic. Very soon, however, between the ages of 8 and 10, writing begins to diverge in form from speaking (Kroll, 1981; Perera, 1986), indicating that children have begun to learn about the uniqueness of the written form, as discussed.

The transition from emergent to conventional writing may be more difficult for AAE-speaking children, particularly because the beginning stages of spelling are more closely tied to speech. As Cronnell (1981) pointed out, all children must learn to represent the "b" in the spelling of *climb* even though they don't pronounce it, but AAE-speaking children have additional dialect-related spelling and pronunciation differences to learn. Research into African American children's writing has been concerned almost exclusively with dialect features. The following section reviews results from several studies concerned with phonological and grammatical dialect features in children's writing. The 1970s and early 1980s were periods of active research on this topic.

AAE Forms and Spelling   Typically AAE forms are categorized according to whether they represent a phonological or a grammatical contrast with SAE. (The distinction between phonological and grammatical features is not unambiguous, however, for features such as final cluster reduction [e.g., "moved," /muv/; "kissed," /kɪs/; "drives," /draɪv/ or /draɪz/].) Research on developmental spelling demonstrates that initially children attempt to represent the sounds of words rather than a memorized letter sequence (Read, 1986; Treiman, 1993). This being the case, AAE-speaking children's early spelling should reflect the phonological features of AAE.

Sullivan (1971) studied spelling patterns of 69 African American and 72 white second-grade children in Texas. The children were asked to repeat 40 sentences and spell 15 words. The spelling list was constructed after analyzing the repeated sentences for words that differed from standard pronunciation or were expected to differ based on previous dialect research. Each spelling word was paired and dictated with a sentence that provided a context for its use. Spelling that differed from the target was classified as irrational or rational. An irrational spelling was one in which the phoneme–grapheme relationship was not represented in English (e.g., in "geny" for the target "gets," the -ny is not a possible representation of /ts/). A rational spelling error was closer to the target (e.g., "muther" for "mother").

African American children had significantly more omissions (i.e., no attempt to spell the word), irrational words (no grapheme was correct by position—e.g., "rgat" for "helps"), and irrational substitutions than white children. Half of the white children's spelling errors were irrational, but the African American children made three times as many irrational errors. It should be noted, however, that in 65% of the phoneme–grapheme comparisons, African American and white children did not differ significantly in spelling accuracy. Of particular interest, for both groups, written spelling differences exceeded spoken pronunciation differences from SAE, a pattern that does not hold for grammatical AAE forms in speaking and writing comparisons, as will be shown later. Also of interest was the finding that the relationship between pronunciation and spelling was feature specific. Although certain features were prominent in both modalities (e.g., omission of final sibilants and omission of /l/ before /r/), others were not (e.g., /t/ omission in /st/ clusters, final /f/ for /θ/, and medial /d/ for/ð/).

Kligman, Cronnell, and Verna (1972) also compared African American and white second-graders on a spelling task. A recognition (multiple-choice) spelling task was developed to test 43 AAE phonological features. To illustrate the task, for the word "mouth," the examiner read the word in isolation and in a sentence context. The child's choices included potential AAE varieties ("mauf") as well as non-AAE varieties (e.g., "moath"). African American children made significantly more total errors (44% errors, compared with 36% for the white students). Furthermore, they chose AAE-related responses significantly more often (25% compared with 16%). The groups did not differ on non-AAE–related errors. In spite of the statistically significant finding for AAE–related choices, however, there was substantial similarity between groups in the way in which AAE features affected spelling choices. Those features that were most and least error prone were the same for both groups (80% of the time). No comparable similarity was found for non-AAE–related incorrect choices. The fact that spelling choice patterns thought to reflect AAE were not unique to African American children could be due to several factors or combination of factors, including overlap in spoken dialect among the groups and levels of morphological development. (The finding of nonuniqueness of AAE-related patterns for other groups of speakers will appear in additional studies reviewed in this chapter.) A final result was that the 43 AAE features were not equal sources of AAE-related spelling choices.

Both the Sullivan (1971) and Kligman et al. (1972) investigations had serious flaws. Sullivan's groups were not matched according to SES criteria, a factor known to affect school performance. In the Kligman et al. work, no measures of spoken dialect status were taken; the authors report only "visiting" the classroom and determining that the African American children "appeared" to be AAE speakers and white children SAE speakers.

In a follow-up study with 50 African American and 50 white second-grade children, Kligman and Cronnell (1974) looked at the relationship between six AAE spoken features and spelling in a more direct manner by more carefully determining spoken dialect characteristics and using a spelling-generation (rather than recognition) task. To determine spoken dialect, the researchers asked children to repeat 60 sentences, 30 of which contained target words assumed to be pronounced differently in the two dialects. The same target words (dialect and control) were elicited in a spelling task where the children filled in a blank representing a dictated spelling word embedded in a sentence. An example of a dialect target word was "bleed" where the final /d/ was subject to devoicing, omission, or glottal stopping; the corresponding control word for /d/ was "body."

Results showed an effect of the child's dialect status on total spelling errors, with AAE speakers making three times as many errors. There was a significant interaction between speaker group and word type, with dialect words representing a much greater margin of difference for the two groups. African American children misspelled dialect words almost five times more frequently than the white children; control words were misspelled twice as often. As expected, the African American children's spelling errors were more often dialect-related errors.

Kligman and Cronnell (1974) were also interested in the fact that some AAE features affect spelling more significantly than others. The rank order of difficulty for the six features in their study (from easiest to most difficult) was: d# ("proud"), -s ("goats"), 's ("Sam's"), th# ("north"), -l- ("bald"), and -ed ("spelled"). The effect of the grammatical status of the dialect feature was also investigated. Although targets that had grammatical significance were harder to spell for both groups, the effect was not as great as expected for African American children. The errors of African American children on grammatical targets were more frequently dialect-related errors (e.g., omitting the *d* in "climbed").

The frequency of spoken dialect features was found to predict the overall spelling accuracy. Feature-specific predictions between speaking frequency and spelling difficulty were not obtained, however, with the exception of the plural and possessive *s* for African American children. In general, the strongest statement that can be made is that children who are AAE speakers will be more likely to make dialect-related spelling errors than children who speak SAE.

Kligman and Cronnell (1974) designed a final study in this series to answer specific questions about final clusters. The grammatical status of the final cluster (e.g., comparisons of nonaffixed "guest" with suffixed "missed") as well as phonetic environment (e.g., consonant versus vowel context immediately following the cluster as in "A dog chased my cat yesterday" vs. "A dog chased a cat yesterday") were variables of interest. The same second-grade children as in the previous study served as subjects. Overall, when speaking, African American children reduced almost half of all clusters, whereas white children reduced only one seventh of them. A following consonant increased the occurrence of spoken cluster reduction for both groups. Speakers of AAE reduced nonaffixed /st/ clusters three times as often as suffixed -s clusters (third-person singular present tense and plural forms) and also more often than past-tense cluster forms, although by not as great a margin. They reduced third-person singular -s clusters more often than plural -s clusters. It should be noted that African American girls made fewer errors than boys.

Speakers of AAE misspelled over 40% of the cluster words, and 61% of their errors were dialect related. Speakers of SAE erred on less than 10%, with only 21% of their errors classified as dialect related. Results on the spelling task for clusters were quite different than oral repetition (speaking) results. African American children were less accurate spellers of past-tense cluster /st/ forms than nonaffixed /st/ words. Neither context (a following vowel or consonant) nor suffix meaning (plurals or third-person singular) affected spelling.

The findings from the three studies by Kligman and colleagues shed light on the dialect relationships between spoken and written language of young African American children. Children can be expected to spell words in ways influenced by their spoken dialect, but the relationship is not a simple one. Spoken AAE forms do not affect spelling equally, and the degree to which they do affect spelling is not necessarily predicted by speech data. Those AAE forms that affect grammatical markers cause more spelling errors than those that have no grammatical effects.

AAE Forms and Sentence Structure   Other investigations have concentrated on grammatical dialect features and have asked whether children use the same set of grammatical AAE features in their speech and writing. DeStefano (1972) studied 21 low-SES African American children between the ages of 9 and 10 enrolled in an urban summer remedial language arts program. Although all the children were entering the fifth grade, not all were reading at grade level. The children wrote compositions describing a walk through the neighborhood surrounding the school. Features examined included nonstandard verb forms (e.g., forms of "to be," third-person singular -s, past tense -ed, progressive and perfect forms, irregular verb forms), noun forms (possessives, article–noun agreement, count or mass nouns, possessive pronoun forms), and sentence patterns (negative statements, noun and pronoun doubling, embedded yes/no questions, prepositional phrases, and relative clause markers).

A comparison of speech and writing revealed differences in the distribution of AAE features. Whereas AAE verb features accounted for 72% of all dialect forms in speaking, they represented only 58% of nonstandard forms in writing. There were dramatic differences for particular features. For example, the only consistent written "to be" feature was noun–verb agreement ("the rivers was deep"), but this feature never occurred in speaking. Conversely, although absence of "to be" ("they nice to know") accounted for 13% of all nonstandard forms in speaking, only one child used the same feature in writing. DeStefano (1972) concluded that dialect speakers are more aware of certain whole-word features (e.g., "be" in the preceding example) and thus more successful at avoiding their use in writing. Absence of the third-person singular -s accounted for 45% of all nonstandard spoken features but never occurred in writing. Sentence pattern features were proportionally less frequent in writing (4% compared with 25% in speaking). By way of contrast, noun features were relatively more prevalent in writing (26%) than in speaking (2%); most of the difference was attributable to difficulty with count–mass noun properties ("I saw some wrecked car"). A caveat when interpreting the different distributions of features across speaking and writing is the different types of written and spoken samples examined by DeStefano (1972).

Cronnell (1984) analyzed writing samples of 99 third-grade and 68 sixth-grade African American children who attended a low-income Los Angeles school. The third-graders wrote a story in response to a picture (a monkey and elephant on roller skates at a starting line), and the sixth-graders wrote a persuasive piece convincing a friend to watch a television show. One third of the errors of both groups of children were thought to be related to dialect (although no spoken samples were analyzed). The largest category of errors for both grades related to verbs (50% and 41% of all errors for third- and sixth-graders, respectively). Third-person singular -s and past tense/past participle -ed accounted for most of the verb errors for both groups. Noun–verb agreement errors on forms of "be" decreased substantially across the two grades. There was only one instance of invariant "be" ("Mork be talking") in the entire corpus. Plural -s omission and dialect-related misspellings were relatively frequent feature types at each grade. The most frequent spelling feature was the omission of final consonants in words ending in clusters (e.g., "pon" for "pond"). The word "and" was frequently spelled "an" or even "in." Cronnell also discussed the occurrence of hypercorrections— those instances when a child adds a morpheme or letter (e.g., spells "fine" as "find"), although he did not report frequency data. Cronnell stated that the overall AAE feature usage for any one child was not necessarily related to the quality of writing, but he provided no independent verification. In other words, an essay might be relatively error free, but "short, simple, and dull" or filled with errors and "lengthy, complex, and interesting" (Cronnell, 1984, p. 135).

Findings of Cronnell (1984) compared with those of DeStefano (1972) underscore the importance of considering the type of writing represented in the research samples. Whereas DeStefano (1972) found that 9- and 10-year-olds did not omit the third-person singular -s in descriptive writing (a walk through their neighborhood), the same error was frequent in the narrative writing of Cronnell's third-grade subjects.

Whether the investigators' focus was spelling, grammar, or some combination, the implications of research thus far summarized seem clear. Language clinicians should not expect to find, a priori, the same set and distribution of nonstandard features across spoken and written language of African American children.

Knowledge about the relationship of AAE forms in the writing and speaking of elementary children has suffered from a lack of information about speaking. In the writing literature, one senses an implicit assumption that children's spoken use of AAE forms is a settled issue—a well-known database to which writing can be compared. But this is not the case. Washington and Craig (1994) demonstrated considerable AAE variability in both frequency and variety of 17 AAE forms in a group of 45 poor, urban African American preschool children. Two children used no AAE forms and 14 children used AAE infrequently (2%–14% of all utterances). The three most frequent AAE users produced forms in 30%, 33%, and 39% of all utterances. Whereas two forms, zero copula and subject–verb agreement, were used by almost all the children, nine others were used by less than a quarter of the children. These results underscore the difficulty of predicting written use from spoken use of AAE.

Sentence Complexity Few studies have used more global measures of syntactic complexity in the writing of African American elementary school-age children. Raybern (1975) compared oral and written narrative summaries produced by 80 randomly selected third- and fifth-grade low-SES children (Raybern did not establish AAE speaker status for the children). The children watched two silent films; half the subjects gave oral summaries of the films, and half wrote their summaries. Measures included total words, words per T-unit, number of T-units, and clauses per T-unit. As a measure of vocabulary diversity, type–token ratios were computed. Raybern also tallied occurrences of six AAE features: omission of third-person singular -s, plural -s, and copula; multiple negation; use of "been" in active voice; and invariant "be."

The four measures that showed significant increases across grades were total words, total number of T-units, number of words per T-unit, and vocabulary diversity. Subordination, as measured by the number of clauses per T-unit, did not increase across grades, but showed a significant modality difference in favor of writing. Even though written T-units were more highly subordinated, they were not significantly longer, as measured by number of words per T-unit. Spoken narratives contained overall more words. Raybern reported that fewer AAE features occurred in writing, but features were infrequent generally. She concluded that many of the children were not dialect speakers.

Raybern's findings (1975) are very similar to other studies of syntax with children (Loban, 1976; O'Donnell, Griffin, & Norris, 1967). Global quantitative measures of syntactic complexity increase with age slowly (Scott, 1988). Compared with T-unit length, subordination measures (clauses per T-unit) increase less monotonically, with several plateaus (Loban, 1976). Consequently, Raybern's lack of developmental change for clauses per T-unit is not surprising. Like Raybern, researchers who have compared children's oral and written productions *on the same discourse genre* have found that spoken samples are substantially longer (Scott & Klutsenbaker, 1989).

Text Structure and Meaning Very few studies have looked beyond the question of dialect in writing. McClure and Stefensen (1985), however, thought it unlikely that dialect was the major cause of literacy difficulties in children from underrepresented groups. They studied the use of conjunctions in third-, sixth-, and ninth-grade children of white, African American, and Hispanic ethnicity. Children were asked to write conclusions to sentences in which the first clause ended with "and," "because," "but," or "even though" (e.g., "He bought a new TV screen even though . . . "). The same order of difficulty across the conjunctions was found for all three groups: "because" < "and" < "but" < "even though." The grade of mastery differed, however. White subjects exhibited earliest mastery, followed by African Americans. Hispanic children were the last group to master the conjunctions. The authors concluded that children from underrepresented groups may need extra instruction in the use of connectives in writing. Problems with this study include the small number of subjects (e.g., seven African American ninth graders) and few stimuli (only six) per conjunction. Whether children's conjunction use in self-generated writing tasks would be predicted from the completion task used here is also unknown.

One significant gap in the literature on African American children's writing is the study of narrative form. This is somewhat surprising in light of the current interest in cultural differences in spoken narrative form, specifically the topic-associated oral narrative style said to be characteristic of African American children and youth (Campbell, 1994; Collins, 1985; Westby, 1994; see also Chapters 10 and 11). One of the differences between topic-associated and topic-centered oral narrative form centers on verb versus noun complementation. Topic-associated narratives elaborate on actions with verb complement structures, whereas topic-centered narratives elaborate more on characters with nominal complements (e.g., premodification and postmodification of head nouns). In the first section of this chapter, the same structural distinction (i.e., verb vs. noun complementation) was emphasized as characteristic of spoken versus written language. Other structural differences between topic-associated and topic-centered oral narratives have also been uncovered in comparisons between spoken and written language, such as prosodic versus structural marking of character reference with relative clauses.

The implications seem obvious. If the topic-associated narrative style is a less literate style *to begin with,* then AAE-speaking children have a more difficult task in learning that written code. Children from mainstream backgrounds also have to learn the more tightly structured, explicit forms of written language, but presumably many have a "practice" advantage because of the closer match between literate spoken and written form. Evidence already suggests that the spoken narratives of African American children who do not use a "proto-literate" style (Collins, 1985, p. 61) fare poorly in classrooms where teachers expect a more topic-centered style (Meier & Cazden, 1982; Michaels, 1981). We could expect similar and perhaps even more unfavorable evaluations of these children's written narratives. Both Collins (1985) and Gee (1986) have commented on the association of narrative style and spoken versus written style and the potential implications for language learners.

Writing at the Secondary Level and Beyond

AAE Forms and Sentence Structure   Smitherman and Wright (1984) and Smitherman (1992) analyzed the writing of a large sample of essays (2,764) written by 17-year-old African American high school students in the 1969, 1979, 1983, and 1988–1989 National Assessment of Educational Progress (NAEP) datasets. Smitherman became interested in these datasets when the 1979 NAEP results showed substantial gains in the narrative scores of African American students since 1969, an improvement rate actually twice that of white students. (Neither group improved on descriptive writing, and white student essays continued to receive higher scores, overall.) Specifically, she wondered whether the higher scores were related to a decreased usage of AAE (decreolization). Examples of a low-rated and a high-rated descriptive (informative) essay written by 17-year-old African American students follow. The task was to describe something the writer knew about (a place or thing) so that the reader could recognize it:

1969 Descriptive High Female. On a college campus near my home there is a large streach of land that many of the students like to visit. There also is a large hill that is covered with flowers and beautiful grass in the spring, which makes it one of the most beautiful sights of the city during this season. To the left of the large hill is the college chapel, looking very serene while being nestled by the surrounding trees. To the right of the hill is green grass, grass as far as you can see, grass that reminds you of a green ocean when the wind blows. The hill itself has yellow and red flowers coming down one side and yellow, orange and violet coming down the other. It definitely stand out among its surroundings When you first see the hill from a distance you think that the blue of the sky has come down and settled around it because the contrast of the blue & green is so bright and beautiful.

1969 Descriptive Low Female. It is very large. People go there to have fun. It's about 59 blocks long. There is a long walk a very long walk You can walk on it the day And in the night it is very romantic. Right near this walk there is a large body of water If I tell you the name you would what I was talking about. There are lots of things you can get on to ride And there are lots of places to buy food. And at some of the thing you can get on they play music. And everytime you go there it is all ways crowd. And the most important thing you can win presents, prizes, grifts etc. Everything thing you want to do you do there, You can swim, eat, dance, ride, win prizes. It is only open in the summer or it open right before easter every year. (Smitherman & Wright, 1984, pp. 31–32)

Smitherman and Wright (1984) searched the essays for examples of 19 AAE features. They found that the majority of AAE features decreased in narrative writing over the 10-year span. The decrease was noted to be particularly significant for five AAE features: passives, -s morpheme (plural, possessive, and third-person singular), subject–verb agreement, past, composite regular verbs, and irregular verbs. The use of AAE predicted narrative scores assigned by raters (even though the primary trait scoring does not ostensibly evaluate grammar, punctuation, spelling, and usage). In contrast to the findings for narrative essays, AAE usage in descriptive essays increased for several features, including irregular verbs, composite regular verbs, and subject–verb agreement for past tense (note that these are three of the five AAE features that decreased in narrative writing).

The genre-specific nature of these changes was of particular interest from an educational standpoint. Because a set of features is found in one type of writing may or may not predict its occurrence in other types of writing. Another finding of educational interest was the relationship between AAE usage and the overall length of essays, as measured by the total number of words. Although the 1979 narrative essays contained fewer instances of AAE, they were also shorter. Smitherman and Wright raised the possibility that the students may have learned to control AAE features *at the expense of* self-expression, an effort that was rewarded when such essays scored higher.

Smitherman (1992) expanded the tracking of NAEP scores by 10 years with the analysis of the 1984 and 1988–1989 results. One reason for continuing to track AAE usage at this national level was Labov's contention that AAE and SAE were diverging in form (Labov & Harris, 1986). As discussed, Smitherman and Wright's previous comparison (1984) provided contradictory support for convergence. Because the NAEP elicitation stimuli and the scoring methods changed after 1979 (e.g., the holistic rating scale increased from a four-point to a six-point scale), Smitherman compared the 1984 and 1988 essays, and differences were then juxtaposed with the 1969–1979 differences. The results showed that the 1969–1979 convergence trends were continuing. The sum of all AAE features showed a clear decline from 1984 to 1988, with significant results for copula, -ed morpheme (past, perfect, adjective, and passive), -s morpheme, and "it" expletive features. Thus, at least for written language, the divergence hypothesis was not supported (although no such claim was made by Smitherman for the African American oral repertoire). Smitherman (1992) attributed the writing convergence to educational successes in helping students become better editors and more aware of standard written form.

Unlike the 1969–1979 analysis where AAE usage showed a significant inverse relationship with both primary trait and holistic scores, in the 1984–1988 analysis AAE usage was associated only with holistic scoring. Holistic scoring takes mechanics, grammar, and spelling into account, whereas primary trait scoring, at least theoretically, considers only how well the writer executes the discourse-level features of the specific genre. The ability of raters to dissociate primary traits from AAE usage was an encouraging finding that Smitherman attributed to efforts to educate teachers and the public about social dialects. Finally, and also contrary to the 1969–1979 comparison, there were no dramatic improvements in ratings for African American students, although there were improvement trends.

Smitherman's work (Smitherman, 1992; Smitherman & Wright, 1984) also provides important documentation on the frequency of usage of AAE forms in writing. Across the 20-year span of data, reported frequencies range from a high of 32% (composite regular verbs[1] in 1969 on low-scoring narrative essays) to a low of 0% ("it" expletive, e.g., "it is a lot different things that would brighten up our community," on 1988 informative essays). Of the 57 reported AAE frequency rates in the two publications, 25 (52%) occurred less than 10% of the time, 16 (33%) occurred between 10% and 20% of the time, and 7 (15% of all features) occurred more than 20% of the time. The frequency of occurrence was computed by dividing the number of instances of a nonstandard form by the total number of potential occurrences (i.e., nonstandard and standard). For any one genre, the highest overall AAE frequency rate was 14% for 1979 informative writing compared with a lowest overall rate of 5% for 1988 persuasive writing. Although these data represent group means, we can assume that, for the vast majority of African American elementary- and secondary-age children and youth, standard and AAE forms of grammatical rules co-occur, with standard usage the far more common occurrence.

A study of Sternglass (1974) provides additional data on frequency of occurrence for AAE forms in the writing of African American college freshmen.

---

[1]The term *composite regular verb* is not defined in either Smitherman and Wright (1984) or Smitherman (1992). The authors assume it represents rates of occurrence summed across several different features that occur with regular, lexical verbs, such as past-tense -ed omission and perfect -ed omission.

Sternglass was also interested in comparing nonstandard features used by African American and white students. She examined essays written by 223 white and 81 African American students enrolled in freshman college-level remedial composition classes for 17 nonstandard grammatical forms. The major finding of the study was the low frequency of occurrence of nonstandard features for both groups. The African American writers used only two features (out of 17) at a rate exceeding 5%. Omission of third-person singulars occurred 5.53% of the time, and nonstandard pronoun use occurred at a 16.39% rate. Nonstandard pronoun use included faulty pronoun reference (gender or number), pronouns without antecedents, pronoun case, and indefinite pronoun agreement. Pronouns were also problematic for the white writers, but their rate of error frequency was lower (8.82%). All other features were produced less than 5% of the time by both groups. Spoken language was not studied, so comparisons with writing were not available. Sternglass (1974) interpreted the low rate of nonstandard usage to mean that these young writers were aware of the stigma attached to nonstandard features in a college writing class and were successfully able to suppress them. She attributed the singular difficulty with pronouns to the students' nonrecognition that pronoun features were stigmatized in a formal writing register.

Like Sternglass (1974), Kirschner and Poteet (1973) studied the use of nonstandard features in the writing of several groups of writers, including African Americans. Specifically, they tallied occurrences of 14 features in essays written by African American, Hispanic, and white students. The students were enrolled in a remedial English class in an urban community college. Significant rank-order correlations were found among the groups, indicating similar relative frequencies of nonstandard features. Spelling features ranked high for all groups, occurring in one fourth to one third of all sentences. Fragments and punctuation and capitalization features were also frequent.

Writing at the Text Level   By the time a student has spent many years in the educational system, it is more difficult to isolate factors that account for writing difficulties and then determine cause-and-effect relationships. As an example, Garcia and Pearson (1991) cite the successive revisions of an African American woman on a college entrance examination. According to Garcia and Pearson, as the woman attended to dialect features in the first version, she also lost some of the fluidity and clarity of her ideas as well as her "voice." Her final version, while dialect-free, was choppy and voiceless:

First attempt: When I am alone, I dream about the man I want to be with. He a man that every woman wants, and every woman needs.

Second attempt: I daydream alot about what my knight in shining armor will be like. He has to be everything rolled all in one and nothing suppose to be wrong with him.

Third attempt and the beginning of the essay she ultimately turned in: My make-believe man is everything. He is perfect from his head down to this toes. He's handsome, romantic and intelligent. (Garcia & Pearson, 1991, pp. 9-10)

A similar conclusion was reached by Farr and Janda (1985) following an extensive comparison of extensive oral and written discourse samples in an 18-year-old African American male (Joseph) enrolled in a college basic writing class. The researchers found ample evidence of forms seen more frequently in written discourse, including passive voice, nominalization, and series constructions. Although their subject used several phonological and syntactic features of AAE when he spoke (and at high frequencies), the same forms were not present in his writing. Furthermore, he used explicit text structure organization (e.g., he stated his main point clearly, used connectives as signal words):

> People should not smoke for three reasons, and in this passage I will focus on all three. First of all people should not smoke because it is fatal. The reason for this statement is because smoking is the main cause of lung cancer. many people die from lung cancer every year. One good example that supports my factual statement is Peter Scott. The Drummer for the Allman Brothers Band, who died of lung cancer was 37. Secondly people shouldn't smoke because it is destructive. Smoking destroys all kind of Marriages don't work. Families cannot function. Friends lose all respect for the person who smokes. Finally, people shouldn't smoke because it smells bad. Smoking makes your breath stink. It ruins the fresh air. It makes public places smell bad like restaurants, washrooms, airplanes, movie theaters, etc. It ruins the smell of your cologne. It also gets into the lining of your clothes and makes them smell bad. In conclusion, I have given you 3 sound reasons why people shouldn't smoke. The are Death, Destruction and Odor now you know. and Furthermore, I think people who smoke are total losers. (Farr & Janda, 1985, p. 66)

The analysis of this passage by Farr and Janda (1985) is instructive and is therefore quoted in full:

> This passage demonstrates that although Joseph seems eager to fulfill the form he has been taught, he does not emphasize the communicative function of writing. Joseph seems to be writing not to convey information to, or convince, a reader but to satisfy certain structural criteria. Knowing that a writer is supposed to focus, he announces that he intends to do so; knowing that a statement should be supported by three reasons, he marshalls three ideas. When he has three ideas down on the page, he announces that he has reached a conclusion. That the three ideas are not explicitly connected and that they are out of proportion to one another does not seem to matter. Logical relationships are truncated (Smoking is fatal), generalizations are unelaborated (Families cannot function), and examples are left dangling (The drummer for the Allman Brothers Band, who died of lung cancer was 37. Secondly . . .). As a result, the paragraph does not illustrate the power of language to convince. The problem is not that Joseph's meaning is obscured by grammatical errors or nonstandard usage; the problem is that Joseph has not created a coherent, elaborated text which provides a convincing vehicle for his meaning (pp. 66-67).

Joseph, like many other writers his age, may have learned the lessons of form *at the expense of meaning and voice*. We might speculate that some African American writers, by virtue of dialectal and cultural differences, have had to devote proportionally more of their writing energies to form. Such writers may then be at greater risk for developing the unconvincing, truncated patterns featured in the example shown here. Motivation may also play a major role. Mahiri (1991) contrasted the frequently passive literacy events found in school settings with non-school literacy events centered around neighborhood basketball associations. Specifically, he detailed sophisticated newspaper or sports section reading behaviors among preadolescent African American males when the purpose was gaining enough information to make bets on the NCAA Final Four. It is difficult to imagine the same amount of enthusiasm for writing an essay on the evils of smoking (Joseph's task). Similarly, Heath (1989) drew a contrast between the orally negotiated written texts in families and peer groups of African American children with the first-draft-only, solo writing tasks in classrooms.

Writing as Process In studies reviewed thus far, researchers have described *writing products,* the actual texts produced by writers. In the early and mid-1980s, investigators of children's writing turned their attention to *writing processes,* the actual behaviors of children and youth in the act of writing (Bereiter & Scardamalia, 1987; Graves, 1983; Hayes & Flower, 1980). Because writing processes are silent cognitive activities and hence not readily observable, process researchers have used methods such as think-alouds (verbalizing thoughts while writing), videotaping, and measuring temporal events (e.g., pauses).

A small number of researchers observed the writing behaviors of African American and other dialect speakers as they plan, generate, and revise texts. Fowler (1985) was interested in the effect of dialect on the writing process in African American adolescents. Three subjects who were low, moderate, and high users of nonstandard features in writing were observed as they wrote six compositions. The extent of dialect use in writing was found to affect how long it took to write a given number of words, the types of thoughts verbalized while writing, and the number of translations (i.e., converting a spoken dialect feature to SAE before writing it down). The high-dialect writer took the most time (both prewriting and actual writing) to complete the assignment, paused more frequently, but nevertheless wrote fewer words. This same writer voiced more concern about "writing the right way," whereas moderate- and low-dialect writers talked more about mental outlines for the content of their texts. The high-dialect writer made the greatest number of translations. Fowler (1985) emphasized the need for free writing to help writers gain more fluency.

Cleary (1988) observed 13 high school students who were all nonstandard dialect speakers in basic writing classes (African American, Hispanic, and white working-class students). She illustrated the frustration these students experienced while writing by describing Carlos, an Hispanic student who spoke a "street talk" dialect influenced by Spanish and AAE. During composing-aloud sessions,

> Carlos would sit at a desk with books and papers spread around him and on his lap. He groaned, swore under his breath, and in moments of greater frustration, pounded his forehead with his palm, as if to force the clogged words and ideas onto the page. [p. 59]. . . . He planned sentences and parts of sentences that he didn't write. He said things in standard English and then wrote them in his dialect, and he wrote things in standard English that he had said in dialect. He spelled the same words correctly and

incorrectly even within the same sentence. He often practiced a sentence before actually writing it but then was interrupted during transcription by one of his many concerns and forgot what he was going to write. He made reading mistakes in the constant rereading of his text which were necessary for going on, causing further mistakes. All this made for a stop-and-go process. (p. 62)

Cleary (1988) described the writing process faced by Carlos as one of "cognitive overload" (p. 61). He was worried about so many things simultaneously that he had little room left for keeping an overall message in mind. Several of Cleary's suggestions for helping Carlos and others like him are discussed in the next section.

CONCLUSIONS

Literacy is woven into the fabric of home and community culture so intricately that it is sometimes difficult to stand back and dissect the events that transmit skills and attitudes toward reading and writing. We do know that the literacy experiences of children from underrepresented groups, from an early age, can be different from those of children from mainstream groups and from those experiences reinforced in most schools (Gee, 1986; Heath, 1983, 1989; Yellin & Koetting, 1990). When kindergarten and first-grade teachers receive training in techniques that foster emergent literacy, however, African American children from low-SES homes "read and write" in ways very similar to children from middle-SES homes, although they may need extra encouragement on initial attempts (Sulzby et al., 1993) and may take longer to develop a particular behavior (Olson & Sulzby, 1991).

Language clinicians and teachers of young African American children should be encouraged to use the full range of emergent literacy and writing-as-process approaches available, for these approaches emphasize meaning and voice, love of language, and a constructivist approach to meaning making (whether reading or writing). When African American children use AAE forms in writing, editing for SAE can begin early. Gillet and Gentry (1983) outlined a four-step editing procedure in a language experience paradigm, a common emergent literacy approach. The first story is a verbatim transcription of what the child says in order not to interfere with the speaking or writing connections facilitated by dictation. Recording exactly what the child says also avoids sending unspoken but negative messages about the child's language. Gillet and Gentry then begin a series of bridging steps between dialect and SAE version. Stories are transformed not only at the level of sentences where most dialect features are found, but also at the text level. Dialect features are maintained for quoted material, however.

Young African American writers who are dialect speakers can be expected to make spelling and grammatical errors related to AAE features. Developmental decreases occur with certain features over the elementary school years, but others (e.g., third-person singular -s past-tense -ed omissions) remain at relatively high rates. Even high rates of occurrence, however, are under 50%. To date, researchers have not delved into possible linguistic or situational context explanations for the alternations between AAE and SAE forms. Whether context or processing explanations (i.e., an "editor" is more active under certain conditions) underlie the observed variation is unknown. There is preliminary evidence that the type of text the child writes may play some role (Cronnell, 1984; DeStefano, 1972).

AAE usage in writing continues to decline in secondary school years. Smitherman's (1992) analysis of NAEP data showed that most features occurred less than 20% of the time. Over a 20-year period of NAEP results, Smitherman found evidence of a decrease in AAE usage in narrative, but not informational writing. This finding again points to the possibility of genre-specific effects on AAE versus SAE form.

The relationship between spoken and written language is not a direct one. Certain spoken features are rarely seen in spelling, for example, and occasionally a feature occurs at a higher rate in spelling than speaking (Kligman & Cronnell, 1974; Kligman et al., 1972; Sullivan, 1971). Several grammatical features are extremely rare in writing (e.g., invariant "be"). The language professional can expect idiosyncratic AAE phonological and grammatical features in writing, from the standpoint of both presence or absence and frequency of occurrence. The writing of any one child or adolescent should be analyzed as a potentially unique system.

Researchers of African American children's writing agree that children are harmed when form, specifically the elimination of AAE features, receives the sole or major emphasis in writing programs. Cronnell (1984) stated that "although BE influences may be found in the writing of Black students, this is not to say that any writing problems are due only—or even primarily—to dialect" (p. 233). Nevertheless, no one advocates ignoring AAE forms in writing. In fact, Morrow (1985) warned that sentence-level problems that writers have rarely "go away" on their own just by increased exposure to print. Suggestions for helping African American students develop fluency and SAE form in their writing follow.

1. Because of the highly individualized nonstandard usage in African American writers, no single program will work with all writers (Sternglass, 1974). Prepackaged language arts programs designed for wide distribution should be used with discretion (Sullivan, 1971). Individualize editing or proofreading for AAE features (DeNight, 1992).
2. Free writing (nonstop writing) may be useful in developing fluency (Fowler, 1985).
3. Editing for AAE should concentrate on one feature at a time (Markham, 1984).
4. Writers may be inaccurate when reading out loud as an editing or proofreading activity. They read AAE forms that are not in the text and change AAE forms in the text to SAE. Oral proofreading has not been found to be more effective than silent proofreading (DeNight, 1992).
5. Peer editing (reading others' papers) may increase critical editing (Fowler, 1985).

6. Several AAE features are "resistant" to editing (they are routinely missed by older students). These include subject–verb agreement, plural -s omission, and past-tense and past participle -ed omission (DeNight, 1992). Special training with these features may be necessary.

7. Teach students to identify SAE and well as AAE versions of features. The number of times an SAE form is used may provide encouragement.

8. Repeated editing or proofreading scans are recommended. Students find more features on second and third readings (DeNight, 1992).

Work on dialect-related and nondialect features (e.g., sentence fragments) at the sentence level can be viewed as a form-directed activity. A host of other form-directed activities in a discourse could be adapted for use. Scott (1995) has recommended that specifically "written" forms can be taught directly if embedded in academic types of discourse contexts. Cleary (1988) remarked that conscious understanding of the differences between personal and formal language would help nonstandard dialect students understand their differences as ones of form rather than ability.

Form is merely the carrier of meaning. From the earliest signs of emergent writing throughout formal schooling, all writers need readers who are interested in the thoughts conveyed through their writing. The emphasis on form rather than meaning in this chapter reflects the literature base presently available on the writing of African American children and adolescents. We hope that the next generation of research on this topic will have more to say about meaning and text.

REFERENCES

Bereiter, C., & Scardamalia, M. (1987). *The psychology of written composition.* Hillsdale, NJ: Lawrence Erlbaum Associates.

Biber, D. (1986). Spoken and written textual dimensions in English: Resolving the contradictory findings. *Language, 62,* 384–418.

Biber, D. (1988). *Variation across speech and writing.* New York: Cambridge University Press.

Biber, D. (1992). On the complexity of discourse complexity: A multidimensional analysis. *Discourse Processes, 15,* 133–163.

Bissex, G. (1980). *GYNS AT WRK: A child learns to write and read.* Cambridge, MA: Harvard University Press.

Blachman, B. (1994). Early literacy acquisition: The role of phonological awareness. In G. Wallach & K. Butler (Eds.), *Language learning disabilities in school-age children and adolescents* (pp. 253–274). New York: Macmillan.

Campbell, L. (1994). Discourse diversity in Black English Vernacular. In D. Ripich & N. Creaghead (Eds.), *School discourse problems* (2nd ed., pp. 93–131). San Diego, CA: Singular.

Clay, M. (1991). *Becoming literate.* Portsmouth, NH: Heinemann.

Cleary, L. (1988). A profile of Carlos: Strengths of a nonstandard dialect writer. *English Journal, 77,* 59–64.

Collins, J. (1985). Some problems and purposes of narrative analysis in educational research. *Journal of Education, 167,* 57–70.

Corbett, E. (1981). The status of writing in our society. In M. Whiteman (Ed.), *Writing: The nature, development, and teaching of written communication: Vol. 1. Variation in writing: Functional and linguistic-cultural differences* (pp. 47–52). Hillsdale, NJ: Lawrence Erlbaum Associates.

Craig, H., & Washington, J. (1994). The complex syntax of poor, urban, African-American preschoolers at school entry. *Language, Speech, and Hearing Services in Schools, 25,* 181–190.

Cronnell, B. (1981). *Dialect and writing: A review.* Southwest Regional Laboratory Educational Research and Development Technical Report No. 2–81/17. Washington, DC: National Institute of Education. (ERIC Document Reproduction Service ED 211 997)

Cronnell, B. (1984). Black-English influences in the writing of third- and sixth-grade black students. *Journal of Educational Research, 77,* 233–236.

DeNight, S. (1992, August). *Detecting and correcting BEV features in writing through silent and oral proofreading.* Paper presented at the International Conference on Critical Thinking and Educational Reform, Rohnert Park, CA.

DeStefano, J. (1972). Productive language differences in fifth-grade black students' syntactic forms. *Elementary English, 47,* 552–558.

Dobson, L. (1988). *Connections in learning to write and read: A study of children's development through kindergarten and grade one.* Technical Report No. 418. Champaign, University of Illinois at Urbana-Champaign, Center for the Study of Reading.

Dyson, A. (1986). Children's early interpretations of writing: Expanding research perspectives. In D. Yaden & S. Templeton (Eds.), *Metalinguistic awareness and beginning literacy* (pp. 201–218). Portsmouth, NH: Heinemann.

Farr, M., & Janda, M. (1985). Basic writing students: Investigating oral and written language. *Research in the Teaching of English, 19,* 62–83.

Ferreiro, E. (1984). The underlying logic of literacy development. In H. Goelman, A. Oberg, & F. Smith (Eds.), *Awakening to literacy* (pp. 154–173). London: Heinemann.

Fowler, R. (1985). The composing process of black student writers. In C.K. Brooks (Ed.), *Tapping potential: English and language arts for the black learner* (pp. 182–186). Urbana, IL: Black Caucus of the National Council of Teachers of English.

Garcia, G., & Pearson, P.D. (1991). *Literacy assessment in a diverse society.* Technical Report no. 525. Champaign, IL: University of Illinois at Urbana-Champaign, Center for the Study of Reading.

Gee, J.P. (1986). Orality and literacy: From the savage mind to ways with words. *TESOL Quarterly, 20,* 719–746.

Gillet, J., & Gentry, J.R. (1983). Bridges between Nonstandard and Standard English with extensions of dictated stories. *The Reading Teacher, 36,* 360–364.

Graves, D. (1983). *Writing: Teachers and children at work.* London: Heinemann.

Halliday, M.A.K. (1985). *Spoken and written language.* Oxford: Oxford University Press.

Halliday, M.A.K. (1987). Spoken and written modes of meaning. In R. Horowitz & S.J. Samuels (Eds.), *Comprehending oral and written language* (pp. 55–82). New York: Academic Press.

Hayes, J., & Flower, L. (1980). Identifying the organization of writing processes. In L. Gregg & E. Stenberg (Eds.), *Cognitive processes in writing: An interdisciplinary approach* (pp. 3–30). Hillsdale, NJ: Lawrence Erlbaum Associates.

Hayes, J., & Flower, L. (1987). On the structure of the writing process. *Topics in Language Disorders, 7,* 19–33.

Heath, S.B. (1983). *Ways with words.* Cambridge: Cambridge University Press.

Heath, S.B. (1989). Oral and literate traditions among black Americans living in poverty. *American Psychologist, 44,* 367–373.

Himley, M. (1986). Genre as generative: One perspective on one child's early writing growth. In M. Nystrand (Ed.), *The structure of written communication* (pp. 137–157). New York: Academic Press.

Kirschner, S., & Poteet, G.H. (1973). Non-standard English usage in the writing of black, white, and hispanic remedial English students in an urban community college. *Research in the Teaching of English, 7,* 351–355.

Kligman, D., & Cronnell, B. (1974). *Black English and spelling.* Southwest Regional Laboratory for Educational Research and Development Technical Report No. 50. Washington, DC: U.S. Department of Health, Education and Welfare. (ERIC Document Reproduction Service ED 108 234)

Kligman, D., Cronnell, B., & Verna, G. (1972). Black English pronunciation and spelling performance. *Elementary English, 49,* 1247–1253.

Kroll, B. (1981). Developmental relationships between speaking and writing. In B. Kroll & R. Vann (Eds.), *Exploring speaking-writing relationships: Correctional contrasts,* (pp. 32–54). Champaign, IL: National Council of Teachers of English.

Labov, W., & Harris, W.A. (1986). De facto segregation of black and white vernaculars. In D. Sankoff (Ed.), *Diversity and diachrony* (pp. 1–24). Amsterdam: John Benjamins.

Loban, W. (1976). *Language development: Kindergarten through grade twelve.* Research Report No. 18. Champaign, IL: National Council of Teachers of English.

Mahiri, J. (1991). Discourse in sports: Language and literacy features of preadolescent African-American males in a youth basketball program. *Journal of Negro Education, 60,* 305–313.

Markham, L. (1984). "De dog and de cat": Assisting speakers of Black English as they begin to write. *Young Children, 39,* 15–24.

McClure, E., & Steffensen, M. (1985). A study of the use of conjunctions across grades and ethnic groups. *Research on the Teaching of English, 19,* 217–237.

Meier, T., & Cazden, C. (1982). Research update: A focus on oral language and writing from a multicultural perspective. *Language Arts, 59,* 504–512.

Michaels, S. (1981). "Sharing time": An oral preparation for literacy. *Language in Society, 10,* 423–442.

Moffett, J. (1988). *Coming on center: Essays in English education* (2nd ed.). Portsmouth, NH: Heinemann.

Morrow, D. (1985). Dialect interference in writing: Another critical review. *Research in the Teaching of English, 19,* 154–180.

O'Donnell, R., Griffin, W., & Norris, R. (1967). *Syntax of kindergarten and elementary school children: A transformational analysis.* Research Report No. 8. Champaign, IL: National Council of Teachers of English.

Olson, K., & Sulzby, E. (1991). The computer as a social/physical environment in emergent literacy. *National Reading Conference Yearbook, 40,* 11–118.

Perera, K. (1986). Language acquisition and writing. In P. Fletcher & M. Garman (Eds.), *Language acquisition* (2nd ed., pp. 494–533). Cambridge: Cambridge University Press.

Raybern, J. (1975). An investigation of selected syntactic differences present in the oral and written language of lower socioeconomic status black third and fifth grade students. *Dissertation Abstracts International, 35,* 6122–A.

Read, C. (1986). *Children's creative spelling.* London: Routledge & Kegan Paul.

Scinto, L. (1983). The development of text production. In J. Fine & R. Freedle (Eds.), *Developmental issues in discourse* (pp. 225–268). Norwood, NJ: Ablex.

Scott, C. (1988). Spoken and written syntax. In M. Nippold (Ed.), *Later language development: Ages nine through nineteen* (pp. 49–95). San Diego, CA: College-Hill Press.

Scott, C. (1989). Learning to write: Context, form, and process. In A. Kamhi & H. Catts (Eds.), *Reading disabilities: A developmental language perspective* (pp. 261–302). San Diego, CA: College-Hill Press.

Scott, C. (1994). A discourse continuum for school-age students: Impact of modality and genre. In G. Wallach & K. Butler (Eds.), *Language learning disabilities in school-age children and adolescents* (pp. 219–252). New York: Macmillan.

Scott, C. (1995). Syntax for school-age children: A discourse perspective. In M. Fey, J. Windsor, & S. Warren (Eds.), *Language intervention: Preschool through the elementary years* (pp. 107–144). Baltimore: Paul H. Brookes Publishing Co.

Scott, C., & Klutsenbaker, K. (1989, November). *Comparing spoken and written summaries: Text structure and surface form.* Paper presented at the Annual Convention of the American Speech-Language-Hearing Association, St. Louis, MO.

Sinclair, A. (1984, July). *Three-year-olds' "writing" behavior.* Paper presented at the Third International Congress for the Study of Child Language, Austin, TX.

Smitherman, G. (1992). Black English, diverging or converging? The view from the national assessment of educational process. *Language and Education, 6,* 47–64.

Smitherman, G., & Wright, S. (1984). *Black student writers, storks, and familiar places: What can we learn from the National Assessment of Educational Progress?* Urbana, IL: National Council of Teachers of English. (ERIC Document Reproduction Service No. ED 259 328)

Sternglass, M. (1974). Dialect features in the compositions of black and white college students in remedial composition classes: The same or different? *College Composition and Communication, 25,* 259–263.

Sullivan, R. (1971). *A comparison of certain relationships among selected phonological differences and spelling deviations for a group of Negro and a group of white second grade children.* Final Report, Project No. 1F038. Washington, DC: U.S. Department of Health, Education, and Welfare. (ERIC Document Reproduction Service No. ED 057 021)

Sulzby, E. (1985). Children's emergent reading of favorite storybooks: A developmental study. *Reading Research Quarterly, 20,* 458–481.

Sulzby, E., Branz, C.M., & Buhle, R. (1993). Repeated readings of literature and low socioeconomic status black kindergartners and first graders. *Reading and Writing Quarterly, 9,* 183–196.

Treiman, R. (1993). *Beginning to spell: A study of first-grade children.* New York: Oxford University Press.

Walter, E. (1994). *A longitudinal study of literacy acquisition in a Native American community: Observation of the 4-year-old classes at Lummi Headstart.* Report submitted to the Lummi Tribal Council, EDRS #RC 019 460. WA: Lummi Tribal Council. (ERIC Document Reproduction Service ED 366 479)

Washington, J., & Craig, H. (1994). Dialectal forms during discourse of poor, urban, African American preschoolers. *Journal of Speech and Hearing Research, 37,* 816–823.

Westby, C. (1994). The effects of culture on genre, structure, and style of oral and written texts. In G. Wallach & K. Butler (Eds.), *Language learning disabilities in school-age children and adolescents* (pp. 180–218). New York: Macmillan.

Yellin, D., & Koetting, R. (1990). Literacy instruction and children raised in poverty: A theoretical discussion. *Journal of Curriculum Theorizing, 8,* 101–114.

14

Assessment, Intervention, and Pedagogical Issues with Older African American Children and Youth

Wanda K. Mitchener-Colston

This chapter discusses several issues related to adolescent and young adult language in general and elaborates on language and communication within this age group in the African American speech community. The chapter focuses on a review of research on adolescent language and the benefits of using a holistic approach to assessment and intervention with adolescents and young adults. An analysis of young adult speaker perceptions of dialect use and its impact on speaking and writing in postsecondary education is highlighted.

The first section of this chapter discusses advances in understanding general assessment trends and issues. The second section explores intervention issues and strategies. The final section focuses on adolescent and young adult communication goals for education and in the work force. Throughout, cultural considerations unique to the African American adolescent and young adult speech community are highlighted. The chapter concludes with a discussion of three pedagogical issues related to teaching and understanding dialect, bidialectalism, and communication alternatives in this age group.

LANGUAGE DEVELOPMENT AND ADOLESCENCE

Research on language development during preadolescence, adolescence, and young adulthood has increased since the 1980s (Nelson, 1993; Nippold, 1988; Rowe, 1992). A comprehensive literature review of adolescent language development conducted by Rowe (1992) reveals a research trend toward the understanding of developmental paradigms that guide adolescent and young adult communication across cultures. Rowe's review of relevant research on language development in adolescence confirms the tenet that oral and written language continue to develop through adulthood and across the life span.

The literature offers minimal discussion of the special concerns of adolescents and young adults in the African American speech community. Increased investigation would improve the present paucity of information in this area, and research efforts should be dual focused. First, research should explore the developmental patterns unique to this age group. Second, the social, cultural, and environmental influences that affect language in the African American speech community should guide service delivery and recommended practice.

Research has documented the intricacies of language growth during adolescence. Adolescent and young adult language growth is marked by gradual and often subtle improvements in syntax, semantics, and pragmatics (Nippold, 1993). Early research and clinical observations of language development in children made vague references to specific skill growth beyond early childhood. There is increasing information (Nelson, 1993; Nippold, 1988) about adolescent and young adult language growth expectations and communication transitions. Nippold (1988, 1993) has discussed the contrast between early and late stages of language development in children. In summarizing these contrasts in development, Nelson noted the following features of adolescent language: the gradual incline of the language learning curve, magnified individual variability, and increasing contributions of formal education and sociocultural and sociolinguistic variation.

Research confirms the impact of environmental and social variables on oral and written communication skills in this age group. Adolescents and adults use language that solidifies them with the peer group. Adolescents use emotive, connotative, and socially coded language (Rowe, 1992).

Nelson (1993) discusses a broader view of language learning systems from infancy through adolescence. This broader view establishes the link between the skills and knowledge that adolescents possess and the equally important impact of context and communicative environment on the language learning process. Nelson introduces in her work the importance of considering social and naturalistic context when assessing this age group.

APPROACHES TO ASSESSMENT

Assessment Issues

Assessment is best viewed as a cyclical process where identification, evaluation, interpretation, and recommendation for intervention are all equally relevant. If assessment does not ultimately move beyond a "filed report" and result in client progression toward change, the assessment goal has not been accomplished. The identification of language disorders in adolescence and young adulthood must be approached comprehensively. The increase since the 1980s of research that identifies adolescent language developmental stages (e.g., Adler, 1993; Larson & McKinley, 1987; Rowe, 1992) will require practitioners to become familiar with this growing body of knowledge.

The assessment process for adolescents and young adults begins with an appropriate response to the following questions:

1. What is the historical influence of experiential and environmental exposure for these youths?
2. What does analysis of the primary through secondary academic background reveal?
3. What formal and informal measures of development best measure communication behavior?
4. What does the medical and health history reveal?
5. What psychological and sociological factors may have an impact on current communication behavior?

Multifaceted and comprehensive analysis of communication behavior assumes variability within this age group. A variety of factors influence youths' communicative behavior, including social, cognitive, motivational, physical, and emotional functioning. In order to empirically investigate and understand the nature of language disorders or differences in this age group, all of the extraneous variables that may have a direct or indirect impact on language behavior must be identified and controlled.

The comprehensive process for analyzing and understanding language skill and communicative intent in adolescents and young adults should proceed in the following multifaceted sequence: identification and referral, assessment, interpretation and explanation, and recommendations and intervention. Each level of this four-tiered process will reassure clients, families, and agencies that assessment will be comprehensive in scope.

Identification and Referral   Observations of adolescent language and communication needs are frequently made in the educational setting, but may also be made in vocational training environments, community outreach programs housed in churches and recreational centers, and public health or medical centers. Although the identification and referral process for adolescents and young adults may best rest with the educational agency, other public and private agencies are also in positions to observe and refer "at-risk" and otherwise communicatively challenged youths for assessment. Bashir (1989) and Maxwell and Wallach (1984) have noted that the expression of language disorders may change over time. As a result, adolescents and young adults may need different services at different stages of development (Nelson, 1993).

The identification and referral process recognizes that early intervention and preventive strategies are relevant to the later language developmental stages of adolescence and young adulthood. Intervening with a preadolescent to improve or enhance communication skills will ensure better secondary, postsecondary, and job-related outcomes for his or her future.

Assessment   Early attempts to fully assess this age group were hampered by the paucity of information on adolescent language development. Nippold (1988) suggests that many of these tests reflected the "cart before the horse" syndrome. In the absence of a solid frame of reference for later language development, such tests lacked psychometric properties appropriate for older children (Stephens & Montgomery, 1985).

The assessment of adolescents and young adults must include a comprehensive multimeasure battery that measures both oral and written language development. The assessment of language development should be supplemented by the knowledge gained through interdisciplinary collaboration. Although a single discipline or agency may serve to coordinate the assessment and evaluation process for adolescents, input from all disciplines and agencies that have formal and informal assessment information is vital. When "single-assessment-only" approaches to language development are used with adolescents and young adults, academic, social, medical, and vocational assessments help answer the important questions that remain.

Formal and Informal Assessment   Norm-referenced (formal) and descriptive (informal) methods are considered "best practice" for all language assessments regardless of age or suspected disorder. This approach is especially important in meeting the holistic needs of adolescents and young adults. Few formal assessment instruments are capable of reflecting the subtle, abstract, and discourse-related nature of adolescent and young adult language acquisition (Nelson, 1993; Nippold, 1988; Stephens & Montgomery, 1985).

Observations made of preadolescent and adolescent youth for a period of 17 years at an urban developmental diagnostic center confirmed the importance of assessing the speech and language skills of older children in a context that was more relevant to their interests (Transgenerational Project; Mitchener-Colston, 1990b). The clinical observations and research data collected confirmed that informal assessment strategies provided information that was important in confirming, clarifying, or disqualifying information gained from formal batteries. During the period of observation, standardized tests were supplemented by assessment of the same skill using familiar contexts. For example, a clinician might initiate formal test procedures using a standardized instrument, Test X, that requires the reading of a 100-word passage and evaluation of the adolescent's response to several questions as a measure of language comprehension. With the formal–informal paired strategy, a supplemental test protocol of an informal, 100-word passage that corresponded to the youth's interest in computer games would also be used to solicit answers to questions in the same way. Paired formal and informal responses to tasks that measure similar skill in language knowledge can reveal the extent to which adolescents may not be conveying optimal performance. If optimal performance does not exist, the information gained regarding communication needs is invalid.

Interpretation and Explanation   Adolescents and young adults should become involved in the team process by receiving information provided by the interpretation and explanation of test data. The opportunity for questions will contribute to the adolescents' willingness to participate and take ownership of language needs. Nelson (1993) asserts that

> because in many adolescents, metacognitive and metalinguistic awareness increase and they can focus more consciously on their own abilities, adolescents may also be able to more actively plan their own programs. They may exhibit a new readiness to respond to reeducation intervention techniques that take advantage of their increased capabilities to reflect on their own behavior and to adopt conscious strategies to reduce impairment or compensate for disabilities. (p. 396)

Recommendations and Interventions   The recommendation process is representative of the final phase of assessment. This phase may begin a new cycle through referral (identification) to a new agency or the use of an interventionist. It is not until this process is complete that the goal of assessment is realized. The assessment goal is realized through the thorough evaluation of adolescent and young adult language performance and the delineation of realistic language performance goals for optimal educational and employment success.

Intervention planning and intervention techniques for adolescents should emphasize the use of relevant materials and opportunities to practice in naturalistic environments. It is important to ascertain information about the adolescent's personal goals for communication. Prevocational and academic interests can be used to ensure intervention relevance. Networking between agencies can result in "intervention practicums" for adolescents, allowing them to practice new communication goals and strategies in real-life settings.

Cultural Considerations

Assessment in the adolescent African American speech community should be guided by an understanding of the relevant cultural uniquenesses of this group. African American adolescents and young adults function essentially as a culture within a culture. As with other ethnic groups, unique life ways guide communication form, content, and use. Our understanding of their communication behavior and its impact on social, academic, and vocational success is essential.

Approaches to assessment of the adolescent and young adult must begin with an understanding of the dual challenge of using 1) strategies appropriate for the age or stage of adolescent development and 2) strategies appropriate for unique cultural and linguistic differences in communication.

Bilingualism and Dialect Difference   Research on dialect and code switching in African American adolescents and young adults has increased since the 1980s (Adler, 1993; Baruth & Manning, 1992; Taylor, 1986a). Arguments continue between those who propose assimilation versus pluralism and mandatory versus elective bidialectalism. Research about the impact of dialect on written communication skills in youth has been sporadic (Mitchener-Colston, 1994), but it is clear that as African American youth mature, the number of variables that affect their communication use increases. The assessment of language within this speech community should consider the impact of academic, social, and political factors on evaluative outcomes.

Much more significant than with younger children, assessment strategies must motivate, stimulate, and induce participation in a process that must be shown to be relevant. Barriers to rapport in this population are deeply rooted in clinician–client congruity. Linguistic differences and preferences may play a pivotal role in how communication is used by African American youth. Issues related to bilingualism and dialect difference cannot be isolated from broader issues of language learning (Nelson, 1993), socialization, and employability.

Assessment must be guided by the question posed in the mid-1980s by speech-language pathologists, linguists, and sociolinguists of whether the adolescent or young adult African American evidences behavior that is "deficient" or "different." Taylor (1986b) proposes an approach to understanding and assessing culturally and linguistically diverse populations. Table 1 proposes a comprehensive listing of safeguards for assessing adolescent and young adult African Americans. A holistic approach combined with culturally valid procedures should successfully control the high level of academic, social, medical, and environmental variability within this group.

Speakers from nontraditional speech communities have been penalized traditionally by an overreliance on standardized tests normed on cultures unlike their own. Social skills, richly related to cultural life ways, may alter a speaker's expression and comprehension in ways that may be misinterpreted and misunderstood by traditional tests and methods.

Since the mid-1980s several speech, language, and communication tests have been revised. Some revisions have been an attempt to decrease test bias and increase the reliability and validity of these measures and their use with African American adolescents and young adults. A report of the National Alliance of Black School Educators (1984) stated that "testing . . . African American children with alien cultural content is a scientific error and is, in [their] opinion, profes-

Table 1. Comprehensive safeguards for assessment of older adolescent and young adult African American youth

Comprehensive scope		Procedural safeguards[a]
Psychological evaluation:	To assess cognitive and learning style functions, social and emotional functions	Culturally valid assessment procedures should 1. Recognize that clients may perform differently under differing clinical conditions because of their cultural and language backgrounds
Educational evaluation:	To assess academic achievement levels, learning style preferences	
Medical evaluation:	To assess current health status, historical health issues	2. Recognize that different modes, channels, and functions of communication events in which individuals are expected to participate in a clinical setting may result in differing levels of linguistic or communicative performance
Social/ environmental evaluation:	To assess familial and peer relationships, community relationships, self-help skills, etc.	
Nutritional evaluation:	To assess knowledge of nutrition, independent food preparation skill, dietary habits, etc.	3. Use ethnographic techniques for evaluating communicative behavior and establishing cultural norms to determine the presence or absence of communication disorders
Communication evaluation:	To assess linguistic and metalinguistic skill; expressive, receptive, and integrative language skill	

[a]Adapted from Taylor (1986a).

sional malpractice" (p. 28). The selection of tests and procedures for both oral and written communication assessment should be coupled with a willingness to conduct a multidisciplinary assessment in multienvironmental contexts as necessary.

Long-range effects plague the successful enrollment, matriculation, and job prospects for this population when assessment and evaluation errors are made. Valid and reliable procedures used to assess communicative competence in adolescent and young adult African Americans diagnosed with a language delay showed a widening discrepancy between age and performance on standardized measures of language as children progressed in age from 6 to 13 years (Mitchener-Colston, 1990a).

A similar pattern of increased deficit can be seen in the use of educational tests. The lack of academic progression as monitored by these tests can mark the continual decline in the African American child's chances for graduation from the secondary education system and entrance into postsecondary education. According to Gollnick and Chinn (1990), standardized tests have limited the access of minority group members to more rigorous study at all educational levels.

Procedural Safeguards: Interdisciplinary Teaming

The approach to assessing older adolescent and young adult language skills should be viewed holistically. A multifaceted, ethnographic analysis and interdisciplinary teaming strategy should be used to address the tremendous amount of environmental and experiential variability within this age category. Mecham and Willbrand (1985) and Nelson (1993) point out the importance of gathering multidisciplinary background information. Single disciplines rarely have the capacity to deal with complex differences in this age group. According to Nelson (1993),

> The specialist should gather a variety of background information when assessing problems of later stage language acquisition. As in early and middle stages, assessment question, related to impairment, disability, and handicap can be answered only if multiple sources of information are considered. (pp. 53–54)

The **teaming** concept is based on a philosophy that interdisciplinary collaboration produces optimal outcomes for persons served. This concept also embraces the need to involve the youth, family, interventionists, teachers, and community in the assessment and evaluation process. A comprehensive and holistic model of diagnosis and assessment should involve all of the disciplines relevant to the evaluation of the adolescent and young adult experience. Sociocultural, psychological, medical, educational, environmental, and communication factors need to be investigated, and the investigation must be done with the full cooperation of the adolescent or young adult. Table 1 summarizes the comprehensive model for the assessment of adolescent and young adult communication behavior. This model has been overlaid with culturally valid assessment procedures proposed by Taylor (1986a).

Every attempt should be made to solicit as much information as possible from all disciplines. Although some overlapping and possibly contradictory findings may be revealed by this process, the interdisciplinary interchange provides useful and insightful information.

The interdisciplinary teaming approach to evaluation summarized in Table 1 helps ensure that the adolescent or young adult communicator benefits from a full and comprehensive assessment of language and communicative behavior. This approach offers additional information, such as that provided by the following parameters that further clarify adolescent and young adult language development and communication performance: environmental limitations and distractions; sociopolitical misinterpretations in the schools; transgenerational parental/caregiver influences; and cultural traditions and expectations for behavior.

APPROACHES TO INTERVENTION

Intervention Issues

Speech and language interventionists working with adolescents and young adults should be sensitive to the age- and stage-related communication needs of this population. Mitchell (1979) divides adolescence into three stages: early adolescence, middle adolescence, and late adolescence. Language and communication needs within each stage may be uniquely different (Larson & McKinley, 1993). Therefore, it is important to parallel intervention goals with the age- or stage-related needs of older children.

Long-range outcomes for this age group require a larger variety of next-step environments to be considered. For example, whereas the younger or primary-level child with a language delay may need goal planning related to academic success, the adolescent's goal planning may need to include social and vocational considerations. Larson and McKinley (1993) propose a three-phase focus of service delivery for adolescents. They suggest that during the early stages, intervention should stress the achievement of communication competency necessary for academic success and personal-social interaction. During middle adolescence, communication behaviors needed to reach vocational potential should be added. Intervention in late adolescence should emphasize the communication skills needed to enhance personal-social interactions and the fulfillment of vocational potential.

A Holistic Intervention Approach

The Adolescent as Partner   Intervention should occur in a context that values input from the adolescent or young adult communicator. As discussed during the assessment process, adolescents and young adults are uniquely suited to help articulate their language needs and participate in the goal-planning process. Motivated by personal vocational and career goals, these youth will demonstrate more enthusiasm for interventions that they perceive as having an inherent relevance to their lives.

Traditional approaches to intervention with adolescents, especially within the school environment, have been challenged by the need to institute new or modified programs to meet the needs of adolescent learners (Work, Cline, Ehren, Keiser, & Wujek, 1993). Program options are now available in several public school settings around the United States. Work et al. argue that the treatment approach must be based on the individual adolescent's unique needs.

Multidisciplinary and Multiagency Partnerships   Intervention partnerships grow from interdisciplinary teaming during the assessment phase. The partnership suggests that collaboration among specialists and agencies may be necessary to gain optimal outcomes for older children. To accomplish interventions uniquely suited to the adolescents' vocational and career goals, a partnership between interventionist, vocational training agency, and other specialists offers the most potential for successful intervention.

Intervention partnerships in the adolescent or young adult learning environment ensure that the view of the youth's total needs will be considered. Partnerships that grow directly from interdisciplinary teaming are most effective (Figure 1).

Cultural Considerations

Several intervention strategies have been postulated to obtain optimal outcomes for 1) adolescents and young adults and 2) culturally diverse groups in this age category (Adler, 1993; Baruth & Manning, 1992; Taylor, 1986b). Such intervention strategies include, but are not limited to, instructional conversations (ICs),

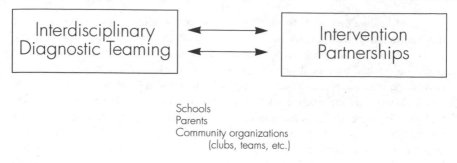

Figure 1. Assessment and intervention model for older adolescents and young adults.

cooperative learning, integration of language and communication, and a focus on metacognitive learning strategies (Dianda, 1993). Taylor's culturally based conceptual model advises that "when it has been validly determined that an individual from a given culture has a communication disorder, culturally and linguistically valid therapy may ensue" (1986b, p. 17). The author goes on to suggest that treatment must occur in the context of the values, attitudes, and wishes of the indigenous culture relative to communication disorders and what to do about them. Treatment should also take into account the preferred learning style of the adolescent or young adult and the rules of social and communicative interaction as defined by the client's indigenous cultural or linguistic group (Taylor, 1986b).

The basic tenet of culturally sensitive intervention has been well summarized by Nelson (1993):

> To exhibit multicultural sensitivity, language specialists must
> • appreciate the richness of cultural variation;
> • be familiar with language systems other than standard English;
> • recognize the need for modified language assessment and intervention strategies for children from varied language-learning communities. (pp. 53–54)

Procedural Safeguards: Naturalistic and Relevant Contexts

A naturalistic approach to exposing youth to new language patterns and concepts best serves the psychosocial and linguistic needs of the adolescent and young adult. Rowe (1992) points out that student-centered, concept-based transactional learning fosters learning in the adolescent. The author further suggests that adolescent language development can be achieved by 1) student initiative, 2) incorporation of prior knowledge, 3) inclusion of the learner's cultural context, and 4) interaction between school and society.

Milieu teaching, a naturalistic strategy for teaching functional language skills, is a class of language interventions that provide specific teaching techniques such as incidental teaching (Hart & Risley, 1968) and mand-model (Warren, McQuarter, & Rogers-Warren, 1984). Milieu teaching was originally designed to give children opportunities to practice a communication skill during the normal adult–child interactions that naturally arise in an unstructured situation such as free play (Hart & Risley, 1975).

In addition, milieu teaching uses a basic antecedent-response-consequence paradigm rooted in applied behavioral interventions (Hart & Rogers-Warren, 1978). Milieu procedures differ from more traditional direct instruction in the types of antecedents (child interest vs. teacher prompt) and consequences (functionally related to the response vs. consistent across trials) associated with the child's response. Both the environmental arrangement to provide a context for teaching and the use of a responsive interactive style in conversation with the child are often described as auxiliaries to the instructional procedures. Using experience gained from what we know about context-relevant intervention, clinical practices with older youth can be structured to be more environmentally and experientially relevant.

The implications of research on adolescent language needs and the specific needs of culturally and linguistically diverse youth are clear. Clinical management of the communication needs of older adolescents and young adults must not be severed from the context of relevance in their lives. The intervention partnerships concept of therapeutic intervention for adolescents and young adults (Mitchener-Colston, 1994) targets the modeling of new approaches to communication in naturalistic settings that are relevant to the client. This concept meets both the short-term and long-term needs of older youth who are progressing toward the job market.

COMMUNICATION GOALS FOR EDUCATION AND THE WORK FORCE

Written Communication:
Dialect and Code Switching in Adolescents and Young Adults

African American English (AAE) has been the subject of much research and discussion since the late 1960s. Early studies have defined AAE as a rule-governed language system (Baratz, 1969; Labov, 1966, 1969; Taylor, Stroud, Moore, Hurst, & Williams, 1969). Since that discussion, research has sought to investigate the impact of dialect on communication processes and learning. Although academic correlates between dialect use and school success are well documented (Adler, 1993; Cleary, 1988; Smitherman, 1985), research on dialect and written language expression has received little focus.

Academic Considerations Expectations for written language expression increase as children age and the curriculum shifts to include more writing concepts. In addition, teaching concepts have been in a constant state of transition since the mid-1980s in an attempt to reach consensus on a common goal for multicultural education. Much research and published discussion has dealt with the development of multicultural curricula and teaching strategies (Adler, 1993; Gollnick & Chinn, 1990; Menkart, 1993); Three major questions guide the discussion of "academic success and dialect":

1. Do African American college youth have accurate self-perception of dialect use in oral and written communication? Do these youth perceive the need for communication adequacy for specific career fields?
2. Does dialect have an impact on oral and written communication skills in the older adolescent and young adult African American?
3. Should older adolescents and young adult African Americans be taught code-switching behavior and techniques?

Self-Perception of Dialect Use   First, speaker understanding and self-perception of dialect use and its relevance to academic and employment settings varies. A 1994 survey (Mitchener-Colston, 1994) of African American young adults enrolled in an urban, postsecondary institution revealed the extent to which these youth perceived themselves to be African American dialect speakers. The majority of respondents ($n = 25$) perceived themselves to be dialect speakers, but several respondents indicated some uncertainty about the nature of dialect and the accuracy of their perceptions. African American college youth vary in their exposure to and understanding of dialect research. Many were not aware of the specific characteristics or features that serve as descriptors of AAE phonology and grammar (Taylor, 1986a; Wolfram, 1970). This uncertainty is heightened by the change in the referent since the 1980s from Black English to Ebonics (Owens, 1992) or AAE (Adger 1993) and Black Vernacular English (Smitherman, 1992).

The knowledge base of today's youth causes some concern for their ability to understand the impact of dialect on speaking and writing in the academic and in the employment arenas. The question remains of whether speaker self-perceptions of adequacy and communication needs should be routinely assessed in each speech community.

Dialect Use and Academic Achievement and Employability   Second, dialect does continue to be a relevant issue pertaining to the oral and written language skills of African American youth, their academic achievement, and employability. Although controversy exists, much has been written about dialect and possible correlates with academic difficulties (Adler, 1993; Owens, 1992; Smitherman, 1992). Likewise, some data confirm possible correlates between dialect and employment success for African Americans (Terrell & Terrell, 1983). Owens (1992) discussed the difficulties speakers of AAE have interpreting Standard American English (SAE). According to Owens, speakers of other dialects may have difficulty with reading and spelling. In general, he notes, children read orally in accordance with their dialects. The resultant differences are not errors in word recognition. Phonemic differences may make it difficult for the teacher to interpret the child's oral reading. Surface phonemic differences may also account for the child's spelling errors. Researchers have pointed out the dilemma: If speakers of AAE do not recognize the significance of the grammatical markers that they omit, those differences will not exist for them.

Adler (1993) asserts that the "pivotal problem facing the teachers of culturally diverse children is that they are confronted with dialects that differ from their own and they . . . fail to perceive them as different dialects" (p. 29). Similarly, postsecondary educators grapple with these difficulties in an environment that is more "graphic," or writing-intensive. Smitherman (1992) and Mitchener-Colston (1994) have collected data that evaluate the impact of dialect on written language. More research is necessary to study how oral and written language correlates for secondary and postsecondary students. Smitherman analyzed the frequency and distribution of AAE and the covariance of AAE with rater scores in the essays of 17-year-old African American students. Results suggest that AAE has converged with edited SAE and that students were not penalized for using AAE in primary trait scoring.

In a sample of 17- to 21-year-old freshmen college students, Adler (1993) discussed the damaging relationship between nonstandard speech and reading and writing problems. Although research documents the impact of dialect on written language, there have been few attempts to study written language to determine similarities in differences or deficits that correspond with verbal differences. For example, a phonological rule used by some speakers of AAE results in the deletion of the noun plural markers ("-s" and "-es"). To what extent are these markers also absent in the writings of African American speakers?

Cleary (1988), in a case study of a student with a native dialect difference, points out that, although students spend hours of classroom time doing grammar exercises, they do not always call up those lessons when they write. Sometimes the lessons can cause more confusion because they use a strategy of editing that attempts to correct on the basis of whether it "sounds right" to an already confused ear. Cleary further articulated the impact of dialect on writing as "cognitive overload." In her case study, the writing process was more difficult for the dialect speaker because of too much to attend to during the writing process. The following account of her observations is graphic in its detailing of the struggle and overload process in the subject:

> When. . . he said aloud what he was thinking while he was writing, I better understood his frustration. He planned sentences and parts of sentences that he didn't write. He said things in standard English and then wrote them in his dialect, and he wrote things in standard English that he had said in dialect. . . . He made reading mistakes in the constant re-readings of his text which were necessary for going on, causing further writing mistakes, all of this made for a stop-and-go process. (p. 61)

Mitchener-Colston (1994) also examined how frequently AAE forms occurred in oral and written samples produced in the speechmaking process of African American college students. Results revealed minimal dual occurrence of dialect forms when the oral message was compared with the unedited written messages of 21 of 25 speakers. However, occurrences of dialect in both speaking and writing for four African American youth were evident. An analysis of their full-text, unedited writing revealed the same AAE forms as were observed in the spoken presentation.

These findings warrant further research to improve teaching and intervention strategies for written communication in African American youth. Among others, the following questions remain: 1) Should there be unique strategies for "dialect writers" within the area of written language intervention? 2) Do secondary and postsecondary language and English teaching faculty fully understand the impact of dialect differences on oral and written communication?

Awareness of Code Switching and Bidialectism   Third, pedagogy should incorporate the teaching of concepts about dialect and research related to academic achievement and employment. The arguments for and against the teaching of code-switching behavior and bidialectism in African American youth are compelling and will probably not be resolved. Research continues to substantiate the need to know speaker goals and personal preference (Taylor, 1986b). It is important to understand that, in matters of behavioral change, older adolescent and young adult African American youth must be given 1) information about the nature of the bidialectalism and code-switching arguments and 2) the opportunity to make choices related to personal goals and communication strategies.

The interrelationship among talking, reading, and writing has been well documented (Adler, 1987; Bergin, 1982; Taylor et al., 1969). Standard American English is the assumed foundation upon which all teaching and learning is based. When there is a mismatch between the language of the speaker and language of the school, academic achievement may be jeopardized. This is well documented by volumes of research on poverty and language (Hechinger, 1985) and on dialect and language (Taylor, 1986a; Webb, Humber, & Taylor, 1991; Williams, 1975; Wolfram & Fasold, 1974).

Adler (1993) discusses the importance of bidialectism, code switching, and bidialectal pedagogy. Secondary and postsecondary educators are addressing a crisis in general classrooms all over this country in the area of written language (Adler, 1993). Many students are reporting to campuses with both documented and undocumented learning differences. In addition, universities are challenged by an increasingly diverse student population. Frequently, students from diverse cultures and ethnic/minority groups are enrolled in special educational programs and compensatory courses designed to enhance basic skills.

Vocational Considerations   Frequently, older adolescents who have been identified as having communication and language difficulties are placed in the prevocational and vocational tracks in their schools. According to the National Center for Research in Vocational Education (1978/1985), the goal of vocational education is to provide students with the knowledge, skills, and attitudes they need to become competent in their chosen occupations. Laboratory instruction helps students develop the needed competencies.

In addition, African American youth without communication disorders may need to consider the impact of dialect on career choices. A lack of familiarity with code switching may hamper entrance into and progress through the chosen career path. The following list shows the kinds of communication skills that correlate with career planning in vocational education:

1. Words: plurals; prefixes, suffixes, and root words; contractions and abbreviations; dictionary; synonyms, antonyms, and homonyms; meaning and context; books
2. Listen: literal comprehension; interpretive comprehension; evaluative comprehension
3. Talk: pronunciation; diction and word choice; fluency; organization of ideas; ask 6W questions; give information and directions; use telephone
4. Read I: literal comprehension; interpretive comprehension; evaluative comprehension
5. Read II: forms; notes; letters or memos; charts and tables; manuals; roman numeral X; roman numerals XXX; roman numeral M
6. Write I: phrases on forms; sentences on forms; paragraphs on forms; sentences; paragraphs; short notes; take notes
7. Write II: forms letters; single paragraph letters; internal memos; business letters; information reports; recommendation reports; technical reports (National Center for Research in Vocational Education, 1978, pp. 59–60).

Language proficiency requirements delineated by Workforce 2000 (Hudson Institute, 1987) can be compared with targeted careers within vocational education programs:

The fastest growing jobs require much higher math, language, and reasoning capabilities than current jobs.
Example of rankings in the area of language development:
Job Rated (6) might require an individual to read literature or scientific and technical publications, and to write journals or speeches
Job Rated (?) might require only the ability to read stories and simple instructions, write compound and complex sentences, and speak using all tenses. (p. 98)

The matching of identified communication competency levels for specific career paths will become language/communication intervention goals. If this matching of communication needs and career interests occurs as early as middle school, the probability of increased communication success on the job is good.

Optimal teaching and learning in secondary and postsecondary educational environments must require 1) increased knowledge and understanding of sociocultural correlates that have an impact on development and learning; 2) improved diagnostic and testing services and procedures for African American youth with oral and written communication deficits and differences; and 3) innovation in intervention programming for youth with oral and written communication deficits and differences (i.e., speaking and writing across the curriculum).

CONCLUSIONS

The diversity in primary, secondary, and postsecondary institutions of education presents an opportunity to conduct applied research. Knowledge gained from such research will greatly enhance the capability for providing the most relevant and necessary communication goals for adolescents, young adults, and African American youth.

Several researchers have made contributions to what we know about dialect, culture, diversity, and social impact on language and learning in this century. This information is the catalyst by which we attempt to understand the special language needs of the older adolescent and young adult African Americans. Assessment, intervention, and pedagogy within the multicultural milieu challenge all behavioral scientists to visit and revisit the discussion of valid, reliable, ethical, and human service delivery approaches.

REFERENCES

Adler, S. (1987). Bidialectalism? Mandatory or elective? *Asha*, 29(1), 41–44.

Adler, S. (1993). *Multicultural communication skills in the classroom.* Needham, MA: Allyn & Bacon.

Baratz, J.C. (1969). Language and cognitive assessment of negro children: Assumptions and research needs. *Asha, 10,* 87–91.

Baruth, L.G., & Manning, M.L. (1992). *Multicultural education in children and adolescents.* Needham, MA: Allyn & Bacon.

Bashir, A.S. (1989). Language intervention and the curriculum. *Seminars in Speech and Language, 10*(3), 181–191.

Bergin, K. (1982). *The relationship of English composition grades to oral (social) dialect: An analysis of dialectal and nondialectal writing errors.* Master's thesis, The University of Tennessee, Knoxville.

Cleary, L. (1988). A profile of Carlos: Strengths of a nonstandard dialect writer. *English Journal, 77*(5), 59–64.

Gollnick, D.M., & Chinn, P. (1990). *Multicultural education in a pluralistic society* (3rd ed.). New York: Macmillan.

Hart, B., & Risley, T.R. (1968). Establishing the use of descriptive adjectives in the spontaneous speech of disadvantaged preschool children. *Journal of Applied Behavior Analysis, 1,* 109–120.

Hart, B., & Risley, T.R. (1975). Incidental teaching of language in the preschool. *Journal of Applied Behavioral Analysis, 8,* 411–420.

Hart, B., & Rogers-Warren, A. (1978). Milieu approach to teaching language. In R.L. Schiefelbusch (Ed.), *Language intervention strategies* (pp. 193–235). Baltimore: University Park Press.

Hechinger, F. (1985, October 29). "Warning over people ignoring pupils living in poverty." *The New York Times,* p. C11.

Hudson Institute. (1987). *Workforce 2000: Work and workers for the twenty-first century* (pp. 98–101). Indianapolis, IN: Author.

Labov, W. (1966). *The social stratification of English in New York City.* Washington, DC: Center for Applied Linguistics.

Labov, W. (1969). The logic of nonstandard English. In J.E. Alatis (Ed.), *Report of the twentieth annual roundtable meeting on linguistics and language studies* (pp. 1–43). Washington, DC: Georgetown University Press.

Larson, V.L., & McKinley, N.L. (1993). Clinical forum: Adolescent language. *Language, Speech and Hearing Services in Schools, 24,* 19–20.

Maxwell, S.E., & Wallach, G.P. (1984). The language-learning disabilities connection: Symptoms of early language disability change over time. In G.P. Wallach & K.G. Butler (Eds.), *Language learning disabilities in school age children.* Baltimore: Williams & Wilkins.

Mecham, M., & Willbrand, M. (1985). *Treatment approaches to language disorders in children.* Springfield, IL: Charles C Thomas.

Menkart, D. (Fall, 1993). *Multicultural education: Strategies for linguistically diverse schools and classrooms.* NCBE Program Information Guide Series, No. 16. Washington, DC: George Washington University.

Mitchell, J. (1979). *Adolescent psychology.* Toronto: Holt, Rinehart, & Winston.

Mitchener-Colston, W.K. (1990a). *An investigation of visual and auditory processing deficits and language conceptualization of temporal and spatial concepts in learning disabled children.* Unpublished doctoral dissertation, Howard University, Washington, DC.

Mitchener-Colston, W.K. (1990b). *Transgenerational project manual.* Rockville, MD: Maternal and Child Health, Department of Health and Human Services.

Mitchener-Colston, W.K. (1994, June). *Speaker self-perceptions and dialect occurence in verbal and written expression.* Paper presented at University of Memphis Postdoctoral symposium, Memphis, TN.

National Alliance of Black School Educators. (1984). *Saving the African American child.* Washington, DC: Author.

National Center for Research in Vocational Education. (1978). *Minimum competencies and transferable skills: What can be learned from two movements.* Columbus: The Ohio State University (Information Series No. 142).

National Center for Research in Vocational Education. (1978/1985). *Toward excellence in secondary vocational education.* Columbus: Ohio State University Press.

Nelson, N.W. (1993). *Childhood language disorders in context: Infancy through adolescence.* New York: Merrill.

Nippold, M.A. (Ed.). (1988). *Later language development (ages nine through nineteen).* Boston: College-Hill Press.

Nippold, M. (1993). Developmental markers in adolescent language: Syntax, semantics, and pragmatics (Clinical Forum: Adolescent language) *Language, Speech and Hearing Services in Schools, 24,* 21–28.

Owens, R.E. (1992). *Language development: An introduction* (3rd ed.). Columbus, OH: Merrill.

Rowe, V. (1992). *Language development in adolescence and beyond.* (Position Paper). Washington, DC: Department of Education.

Smitherman, G. (1992). Black English, diverging or converging?: The view from the national assessment of educational progress. *Language and Education, 6*(1), 47–61.

Stephens, M.I., & Montgomery, A.A. (1985). A critique of recent relevant standardized tests. *Topics in Language Disorders, 5*(3), 21–45.

Taylor, O.L. (Ed.). (1986a). *Nature of communication disorders in culturally and linguistically diverse populations.* Boston: College-Hill Press.

Taylor, O.L. (Ed.). (1986b). *Treatment of communication disorders in culturally and linguistically diverse populations.* Boston: College-Hill Press.

Taylor, O.T., Stroud, V., Moore, E., Hurst, C., & Williams, R. (1969). Philosophies and goals of ASHA black caucus. *Asha, 11,* 216–218.

Terrell, S., & Terrell, F. (1983). Effects of speaking Black English upon employment opportunities. *Asha, 26,* 27–29.

Warren, S.F., McQuarter, R.J., & Rogers-Warren, A.K. (1984). The effects of mands and model on the speech of unresponsive language-delayed preschool children. *Journal of Speech and Hearing Disorders, 49,* 43–52.

Williams, R. (1975). *Ebonics: The true language of black folks.* St. Louis, MO: Institute of Black Studies.

Work, R.S., Cline, J.A., Ehren, B.J., Keiser, D.L., & Wujek, C. (1993). Adolescent language program. (Clinical forum: Adolescent language). *Language, Speech and Hearing Services in Schools, 24,* 43–53.

Wolfram, W. (1970). *A sociolinguistic description of Detroit Negro speech.* Washington, DC: Center for Applied Linguistics.

Wolfram, W., & Fasold, R.W. (1974). *The study of social dialects in American English.* Englewood Cliffs, NJ: Prentice Hall.

Afterword

Anna F. Vaughn-Cooke

This book should be applauded. Its chapters contribute to a much-needed and long-awaited expansion of language development research on children and youth who speak African American English (AAE). The chapters, particularly those focusing on methodology, grammar, phonology, vocabulary, narratives, and communicative competence, represent an important step toward the creation of a more comprehensive body of knowledge on how African American children learn language. Why has it taken so long to conduct and publish the kind of research represented in this volume? There have been a number of barriers.

The first and most serious barrier was the deficit theory, first proposed in the 1960s. Its principal claim was that the language of working-class African American children is deficient both grammatically and conceptually (Bereiter & Englemann, 1966; Deutsch, 1967). Proponents of this view ignored the groundbreaking descriptions and insightful explanations of phonological, syntactic, and semantic development that were so abundant in the literature on mainstream children (e.g., Brown, 1973). The studies by Bereiter, Englemann, and Deutsch that supported the deficit theory promulgated a set of erroneous claims about the language of African American children and affected the research conducted with these children for many years to come.

Finding evidence to refute the deficit theory became the primary goal of researchers interested in the language of African American children.

This goal was much more important than describing the developing language systems of African American children. Researchers were interested in either documenting the similarities of the language spoken by AAE speakers and speakers of Standard American English (SAE) or showing that the differences that existed were rule governed. If the children were young enough, differences were rarely found.

In a representative study, Steffensen (1974) examined the acquisition of grammatical features in two young boys who were exposed to AAE. One child was 17 months old at the beginning of the study, and the other was 20 months old. Samples of language were taken until both children were 26 months old. The samples were analyzed for the emergence of the plural and possessive inflections, pronominal case, copula and auxiliary verbs, third-person singular, and past-tense inflections. The language of the child exposed to AAE was virtually the same as that of the child exposed to SAE. This finding was not surprising given the age of Steffensen's subjects. During the very early stages of development, it is often difficult to identify dialectal features in children's language.

In contrast, studies that compared older children usually found rule-based differences in the use of grammatical features that distinguish AAE from SAE (e.g., Cole, 1979; Kovac, 1980; Reveron, 1978; Stokes, 1976). Even though these researchers did not set out to document how African American children acquired the phonological, syntactic, semantic, or pragmatic systems of their language, this research laid the foundation for future studies that addressed this question. Once the deficit view of AAE was refuted, researchers could focus their research efforts on describing the development of AAE. The chapters in this book that focus on the development of different aspects of language development in AAE-speaking children and youth are a logical extension of this early work. Although the information presented in these chapters significantly advances our understanding of the language systems of AAE-speaking children and youth, it is only a beginning. There are many other aspects of the language and communication of AAE-speaking children and youth that need to be investigated with the same scholarly rigor evident in the present volume.

A second important barrier to the expansion of the knowledge base on language development in African American children has been the limited resources to support such research. The limited support from external funding agencies has significantly restricted the type and scope of studies that can be initiated. Large-scale cross-sectional and longitudinal studies are difficult to conduct without funding resources. Only a handful of researchers with interest in studying language development and disorders in AAE-speaking children and youth have been able to obtain external funding from the major funding agencies. Researchers with such support include Craig and Washington (1994), Seymour (1994), Stockman and Vaughn-Cooke (1980, 1985), and Vaughn-Cooke and Wright-Harp (1984, 1988, 1992). Major funding agencies have recognized the need for research on minority populations. Researchers need to take advantage of this recognition because the level of funding may diminish in future years.

In addition to the barriers that affected the kind and scope of research conducted on African American children, a large number of research studies that have been conducted have never been published. One reason for this is that the studies have never been written for publication. Another reason involves the perception among some researchers that journals are not interested in research about language development or disorders in African American children. The failure to publish the results of completed investigations has impeded the development of an accessible knowledge base because the results of these studies have not been widely disseminated. A number of these studies have been dissertations, including those by Steffensen (1974), Stokes (1976), Reveron (1978), Cole (1979), Kovac (1980), Peters (1983), Blake (1984), Bridgeforth (1987), Wyatt (1991), Massey (1992), Hyter (1994), and Champion (1995).

The research reflected in the more recent dissertations was concerned primarily with describing the language development of AAE-speaking children rather than documenting differences between AAE and SAE. For example, Peters (1983) and Bridgeforth (1987) studied aspects of pragmatic development in young African American children. These pioneering works on the acquisition of conversational discourse skills remain unpublished. The studies conducted by Massey, Wyatt, and Hyter are represented in this volume. These researchers have presented their research at conferences throughout the country, but this is still not enough, because the studies have not yet been published in scholarly journals. Journals have a much broader audience and are more accessible than books and conferences. Journals published by the American Speech-Language-Hearing Association, for example, are received by more than 50,000 speech-language pathologists. The *American Journal of Speech-Language Pathology* has a circulation over 60,000.

Presenting research at conferences and publishing the research in books is thus only a beginning. This research needs to be published in the scholarly journals in our field so that it is accessible to all individuals interested in language development and disorders in African American children and youth. All of the contributors to this volume recognize this need, and I know that many of them are working very hard to publish their research in scholarly journals. Although these researchers may still encounter barriers in achieving this goal, these barriers seem a little less formidable than they did in the 1960s and should continue to fall.

REFERENCES

Bereiter, C., & Englemann, S. (1966). *Teaching disadvantaged children in the preschool.* Englewood Cliffs, NJ: Prentice Hall.

Blake, I. (1984). *Language development in working-class black children: An examination of form, content, and use.* Unpublished doctoral dissertation, Columbia University, New York.

Bridgeforth, C. (1987). *The development of language functions among black children from working-class families.* Unpublished doctoral dissertation, Georgetown University, Washington, DC.

Brown, R. (1973). *A first language: The early stages.* Cambridge, MA: Harvard University Press.

Champion, T. (1995). *A description of narrative production and development in child speakers of African American English.* Unpublished doctoral dissertation, University of Massachusetts, Amherst.

Cole, L. (1979). *A developmental analysis of social dialect features in the spontaneous language of preschool black children.* Unpublished doctoral dissertation, Northwestern University, Evanston, IL.

Craig, H., & Washington, J. (1994). *Oral language profiles of African American children.* National Institutes of Health, grant #NIH1R01DC02313-01A1.

Deutsch, M. (1967). The role of social class in language development and cognition. In M. Deutsch & Associates (Eds.), *The disadvantaged child.* New York: Basic Books.

Hyter, Y. (1994). *A cross-channel description of reference in the narratives of African American vernacular English speakers.* Unpublished doctoral dissertation, Temple University, Philadelphia.

Kovac, C. (1980). *Children's acquisition of variable features.* Unpublished doctoral dissertation, Georgetown University, Washington, DC.

Massey, A. (1992). *Topic introduction behavior in a sample of four year old males.* Unpublished doctoral dissertation, Howard University, Washington, DC.

Peters, C. (1983). *A pragmatic investigation of the speech of selected black children.* Unpublished doctoral dissertation, Howard University, Washington, DC.

Reveron, W. (1978). *The acquisition of four Black English morphological rules by black preschool children.* Unpublished doctoral dissertation, Ohio State University, Columbus.

Seymour, H. (1994). *Language disorders in African American children.* National Institutes of Health, grant #1R01DC02172-02.

Steffensen, M. (1974). *The acquisition of Black English.* Unpublished doctoral dissertation, University of Illinois, Champaign-Urbana.

Stokes, N. (1976). *A cross-sectional study of the acquisition of negation structures in black children.* Unpublished doctoral dissertation, Georgetown University, Washington, DC.

Stockman, I., & Vaughn-Cooke, F. (1980). *A developmental study of Black English: Semantic, grammatical, and phonological features.* National Institute of Education, grant #NIE-G-80-0135.

Stockman, I., & Vaughn-Cooke, F. (1985). *The development of dynamic and stative locative knowledge.* National Science Foundation, grant #BNS8418587.

Vaughn-Cooke, F., & Wright-Harp, W. (1984). *The emergence of semantic categories in the language of black children.* National Institutes of Health, grant #RR08005-21.

Vaughn-Cooke, F., & Wright-Harp, W. (1988). *The coordination of semantic categories in the language of black children.* National Institutes of Health, grant #RR08005-22.

Vaughn-Cooke, F., & Wright-Harp, W. (1992). *Lexical development in working-class black children.* National Institutes of Health, grant #RR08005-23.

Wyatt, T. (1991). *Linguistic constraints on copula production in Black English child speech.* Unpublished doctoral dissertation, University of Massachusetts, Amherst.

Index

Page numbers followed by "f" or "t" indicate figures or tables, respectively.